Elizabethan Love Tragedy

1587-1625

Elizabethan Love Tragedy

1587-1625

by

Leonora Leet Brodwin

"Pride, greatness, honours, beauty, youth, ambition,
You must all down together, there's no help for't:
Yet this my gladness is, that I remove
Tasting the same death in a cup of love."

Middleton

New York
London

New York University Press
University of London Press Ltd
1971

To my husband
Stanley Brodwin
And to my father
Cecil Robert Leet
In loving tribute

Copyright © 1971 by New York University
Library of Congress Catalog Card No. 71-124519
ISBN-0-8147-0955-9
Manufactured in the United States of America

Preface

If a study of the genre of love tragedy in the Elizabethan drama has never before been undertaken it may be because the subject matter seemed obvious and such tragdies few and relatively unimportant. It was, at any rate, under such a misapprehension that this study was begun, the initial plan being to trace the decline of purity and faith which is generally recognized to be the history of the Elizabethan drama as it manifested itself within this special aspect of the drama.

The serious study of any body of new material, however, soon reveals the inadequacy of the researcher's initial premises and demands that it be taken on its own terms and followed through many false turns to an obscure destination. Plays whose meaning seemed quite clear developed new dimensions and implications when studied as members of a genre of love tragedy. They formed a body of new material which could be charted only by the inner relationships that the plays assumed when viewed from this perspective.

The first thing that became clear was that in the Elizabethan drama there was not, as I had originally thought, a single type of love tragedy and standard of "true love." It therefore became necessary to create a definition which would delimit the genre without the prejudice of a preconceived standard of love tragedy while including what seemed to be its significant manifestations.

I thus defined love tragedy simply as the tragedy resulting from the protagonist's involvement in what he at least and at the start of his tragic involvement considered to be love. With such a definition, the genre grew from its formerly minor proportions to include approximately half the total number of Elizabethan tragedies. It then became clear that the type of love tragedy represented by *Romeo and Juliet* had only a minor importance in the Elizabethan tragic drama and, what was more important, that the major segment of the genre seemed to reflect another and antithetical standard of "true love," a norm which only the plays themselves could help to define. Having become satisfied that there was not one but two categories of Elizabethan love tragedy, I was faced with a group of leftover plays which conformed to neither. In the process of contemplating these plays as a group, I became aware that they formed a separate and distinct category, one that treated a form of love that proved in the course of its development to be "untrue" and yet could not be identified with lust.

The present organization of this work divides the genre into the three categories which have emerged from its study and traces the development of each of the three categories historically. Such a tripartite historical treatment accomplishes in more complex terms the original intention with which the study was begun, to show the way in which the changing sensibility of the age manifested itself within a specific genre of the Elizabethan drama.

But as the historical treatment of the drama became more complex, so, too, did the study of the historical background of the love that appears in the Elizabethan drama. It was no longer sufficient to suggest that romantic love had its origin in eleventh century Provence because the love that dominated the Elizabethan drama, that which I have named "Worldly Love," was essentially opposed to that which had derived from Courtly Love. Having isolated the existence of this love in the Elizabethan drama, I now had to determine its possible historical origin. Once the question was posed, answers suggested themselves, both in terms of cultural and philosophic history. These suggestions, as well as those for the Courtly Love background to the Elizabethan tragic drama, form the primary subjects of the Introduction and serve to explain the paradoxical appearances of love in the Elizabethan tragic drama.

In the course of analyzing the individual plays, distinct and developing patterns of dramatic action emerged for each of the three modes of love tragedy. The Conclusion provides a summary of these dramatic patterns and reveals deeper relationships between them than was apparent in the separate consideration of these patterns necessitated by the divided structure of this study. It also considers the historical relationships between the three modes of love tragedy in terms of their relative strengths throughout the period 1587–1625 and demonstrates that both the genre and the drama as a whole was moving toward the final tragic ideal of Worldly Love. The chart of the plays that appears on p. 359 of the Conclusion serves to define the extant corpus of love tragedies in the Elizabethan drama.

The final justification of this study is, however, not historical but critical, and again this value of the study only emerged after it was begun. Although I had intended simply to trace the way in which certain romantic themes were modified in accordance with a changing sensibility, the study of this group of plays specifically as love tragedies served to illuminate the tragic meaning of the individual plays in a way that, in most cases, had never before been seen and which appears to be necessary for an adequate appreciation of these plays. Since my critical aim became an attempt to illuminate the tragic meaning of the plays by focusing upon their love action, my dramatic analyses necessarily assumed both an extended and limited form; I was forced to curtail my exploration of other aspects of the plays while expanding upon the implications of this love action. I feel, however, that this reduction in the scope of the analyses should be justified not only by the specific concern of this study but by the fact that these other aspects have already been dealt with widely. This study seeks to redress the critical imbalance that has resulted from the almost complete disregard of the love theme in most of these plays. It is hoped, therefore, that what might seem to be a critical reduction of the total meaning of the plays may provide a greater illumination of their primary meaning. My practice in two regards might also be noted here: the dating of the plays, except where noted, is based on the Alfred Harbage *Annals of English Drama,* rev. S. Schoenbaum (Philadelphia, 1964); and there has been no attempt to normalize quotations from original spelling dramatic texts other than to eliminate the italicization of proper nouns; all stage directions, conversely, have been uniformly italicized.

I wish, finally, to acknowledge my great indebtedness to those who have helped and counseled me in the long preparation of this work. Foremost of these has been Eugene M. Waith of Yale University, whose untiring and thoughtful aid, rendered over a period of more than five years with unfailing personal sensitivity and concern, enabled me to carry this work from initial idea to its first complete version. I am also grateful for the encouragement and counsel of the late Una Ellis-Fermor, of Bedford College at the University of London, under whom I began the actual writing of this first version while on a Fulbright Fellowship to England. To Louis L. Martz, also of Yale University, I owe a special debt of gratitude for the strength, understanding, and fine sense of discrimination with which he guided me through the difficult task of reducing the size of the study without sacrifice of its essential scope. In this form, it was accepted as a dissertation by the Faculty of the Graduate School of Yale University in candidacy for the degree of Doctor of Philosophy. Although it is difficult to enumerate all the friends and acquaintances who in many different ways have helped the progress of this work, I should like to give special thanks to those whose influence and suggestions, perhaps forgotten by them, have germinated fruitfully in its intellectual structure, in particular: Milton Gold of Rutgers University (Newark), Herbert Weiss of Brooklyn College, Miss Jackie Pritzen of Hampshire College, Mrs. Sydney Jacobs Harth of Edgewood College of the Sacred Heart (Madison), and Mrs. Joann Ryan Morse of Barnard College. In the final, extensive revision of this work from dissertation to book form, I am particularly grateful to John Collins Pope of Yale University and to Robert H. Ball of Queens College for their considerate and helpful suggestions, and last as first to Mr. Waith for his continuing advice and support. I should also like to express my appreciation to the trustees of Juniper Lodge in

New Hampshire for having made it possible for me to spend six weeks at this beautiful retreat while writing a few chapters of this work and to Mrs. Charles McClumpha for the consideration she showed me while there. Parts of Chapters III, VI, and VII originally appeared in *Studies in Philology, Studies in English Literature,* and the *Journal of English Literary History,* and I am grateful to the editors of these journals for permission to reprint this material. My final gratitude is reserved for the incalculable support given me by my husband in the last effort of revision.

Contents

Elizabethan Love Tragedy

1587-1625

1

Introduction to the Study of Elizabethan Love Tragedy

The theatre today seems to have outgrown love tragedy. Sexual obsession, to be sure, ravages or redeems those wanderers in the world of Williams, Miller, Osborne, and the more recent *avant guarde* theatre; but they, and we, are never to mistake it for love. For love tragedy we must turn today either to the nineteenth-century realm of opera and ballet or to the popular tear-jerkers of Hollywood. Though even Hollywood has tried to "grow up," in its Grade-B features we may still meet an irresistible, self-destructive but exalting passion, defeated by the obstacles that society, chance, or innocence has strewn in its path but rising above them in a final, moving love-death. We know what to expect, for the stereotypes have been a part of our cultural heritage since those days of yore when knights suffered for their lady fair, and we yield to the tugging of our heartstrings despite the good-humored chagrin with which we later shrug it off. It is the same realm of feeling in which we are enthralled by Verdi, Wagner, and "Swan Lake," though the glories of art transport our sentimental responses into an emotion of which we feel more proud.

If none of this seems to apply very well to our sceptical, post-Freudian world, if a genuine love tragedy like Lorca's *Blood Wedding* seems to us oddly obsolete as well as being virtually isolated in the contemporary theatre, we still enjoy an occasional emotional vacation into this nostalgic realm of heroic make-believe and feel very well satisfied with what our stock responses have told us about the nature of love tragedy. If asked to name the greatest English love tragedy, *Romeo and Juliet* comes immediately to mind. But after it, what? Nothing, most probably, or suggestions offered with hesitation and uncomfortable qualification. For, in truth, among prominent English tragedies, and for these we can look only to the Elizabethan and modern drama, *Romeo and Juliet* is the only one that conforms to our unarticulated ideas of what a love tragedy should be.

Nor does the modern English and American drama give us any cause for discomfort. Love is the emotion that ingenues and some married couples feel in comedy, a not very thrilling preoccupation, but pleasant, sometimes touching, and always serviceable. Consider, for instance, *Candida, Ah! Wilderness,* and *The Matchmaker.* Serious drama is another story, however. There such naive pleasantries are cast aside and we watch the human animal writhing in the soul-destroying, sexual intanglements that were supposed to redeem him from his inhibitions. Here we can easily number *A Streetcar Named Desire, The Crucible,* and *Epitaph for George Dillon.* Although such modern tragedians as Miller and Eliot can still treat spiritual integrity as a tragic ideal (*The Crucible* again and *Murder in the Cathedral,* yet even here it must be displaced to more heroic times), no significant modern dramatist has built a tragedy about a love even remotely idealized by its protagonist. What emotion is felt is carefully and appropriately named a sexual urge.

With such exposure to nineteenth-century concepts of romantic love and twentieth-century concepts of sexual obsession, the contemporary attitude toward love in the Elizabethan[1] drama is not surprising. *Romeo and Juliet* is naturally enough considered exclusively as a love tragedy, while *Antony and Cleopatra, The White Devil,* and *The Changeling* are variously treated as tragedies of sexual obsession, that is, when the "romantic" element in such plays is considered at all. The proliferating studies of Courtly Love and of its influence in Elizabethan love poetry have reinforced the critical attitude that this is the concept of love that we may expect to find in the Elizabethan drama. Since tragic manifestations of such love in this drama are rare, and since tragedies concerned with any other mode of romantic or sexual involvement cannot be considered to be tragedies of "true love," consideration of Elizabethan love tragedy has always stopped before it could properly be said to have begun. The unspoken conclusion has been that there is no such significant body of drama with which to be concerned. While love is conceded to be the mainstay of French classical tragedy, it is generally thought that the Elizabethan tragic drama is as "tough" as the modern in largely eschewing such romanticism—hence its modernity— that it concerns itself either with such "masculine" redemptive values as aspiration, honor, and revenge or with the opposite deterioration of personality effected by sexual obsession.

From this it would almost seem as though the old national stereotypes are valid: that the Continent is the true home of love, while England is the preserve of the manly virtues. But if, among the great tragedies, *Romeo and Juliet* alone conforms to the notion of exalted love bred and nourished by Europe, it does not necessarily follow that the remainder of English—and particularly Elizabethan— tragedy is unconcerned with love, sim- ply that it is unconcerned with this traditional European form of passion. The very inability of critics to recognize and cope with the declared love manifested in the majority of Elizabethan tragedies indicates in itself that we may well be faced with a form of romantic idealization that has somehow escaped the notice of scholarship. The major finding of this study is, in fact, that the Elizabethan drama has something different to show us in the way of romantic idealization which, precisely because of this, has either been ignored or misunderstood. More particularly, it is a main contention of this book that such Elizabethan tragedians as Marlowe, the later Shakespeare, Webster, and Middleton were virtually unique in the history of Western culture in exalting a non-courtly mode of love into a tragic ideal. That a historical body of literature can shed new light on the development of Western sentiment should be reason enough for its study. But the very jangling of new and traditional concepts of love in the Elizabethan tragic drama makes for a variety in the treatment of love tragedy whose richness is perhaps unsurpassed in any similar body of literature and which makes its study all the more rewarding. Flowering at that juncture between the Medieval and modern worlds, Elizabethan love tragedy reflected the past and future crosscurrents of a culture at its crisis to reveal as nowhere else the full variety and confusion of love attitudes to which the modern world is heir.

First though not foremost in Elizabethan dramatic production was that survival of Medieval love theory which is today known by the name of Courtly Love. To understand not only the love tragedies that conform to this category but the other modes of love which may be isolated in the Elizabethan tragic drama, it is first necessary to define those features of the Courtly Love tradition which are pertinent to the study of this drama. Perhaps the most distinctive feature is the undeniably religious framework of its rhetoric. Most students of the subject agree that the earliest troubadours, if not believers in a heretical religion,[2] did not imagine their "Religion of Love"[3] but were seriously influenced by one or more of the current streams of religious and quasi-religious mysticism. Whether Bernadine or Hispano-Arabic mysticism is the more decisive influence, the essential factor in either case is Neo-Platonism,[4] "the *unio mystica* which," as Peter Dronke has noted, "both in Islam and in Christendom has always belonged to a minority."[5]

Following from this broad Platonic derivation, the definition of Courtly Love adopted in this study is one that sees the lover as ultimately desiring union with the Absolute, achieving this union through a purifying service to a lady who represents this Absolute in apprehensible form. Since the function of this service is the lover's ennoblement, this cannot be achieved through an easy success but must be the product of an arduous testing. And since what is being tested is the constancy of his desire for such ultimate union, this desire must never be allowed to relapse. For both these reasons the mechanics of Courtly Love cannot operate without obstruction.

This is clearly seen in a definition of Courtly Love provided by Andreas: "For what is love but an inordinate desire to receive

passionately a furtive and hidden embrace." [6] The importance
of obstruction is further underscored in Andreas' consideration
of the means by which this love may be increased after consummation: "it is said to increase if the lovers see each other rarely
and with difficulty." [7] Alexander J. Denomy discusses such obstructed desire as the prerequisite for the lover's ennoblement:
"Since complacency in the attainment of the beloved may lead
to quiescence in the beloved object and so to satiety, troubadour
love must remain desire, a yearning that is unappeased. . . .
because it is desire which is the means to the end and purpose
of Courtly Love: the ennobling of the lover." [8] The factor of
obstruction is important to this inquiry because in the Elizabethan drama it is one of the distinguishing marks of Courtly
Love tragedy. What Denis de Rougemont has noted in relation
to *Tristan and Iseult* is also true of the courtly lovers in Elizabethan love tragedy: "Objectively, not one of the barriers to
the fulfillment of their love is insuperable, and yet each time
they give up." [9] If De Rougemont's conclusions are perhaps extreme, the fact remains that the courtly lovers in Elizabethan
tragedy not only pursue an obstructed love but passively accept
the validity of the obstruction.

In the circle for whom Andreas addressed his compendium,
the fundamental obstruction was provided by marriage. True
love is adulterous, as was established in the decision of the Countess of Champagne, handed down in a Court of Love on May
1, 1174: "We declare and we hold as firmly established that
Love cannot exert its powers between two people who are married to each other. . . . since the worth of character of neither
can be increased thereby . . ." [10] C. S. Lewis has shown that
Courtly Love existed side by side with a different conception of
marital affection accepted by the Church and that these were
mutually exclusive.[11] Even more explicit was the decision of
Lady Ermengarde of Narbonne in the question of whether there
was greater affection between lovers or married persons: "We
consider that marital affection and the true love of lovers are
wholly different and arise from entirely different sources." [12] If
Andreas betrays no conscious awareness of an anterior spiritual
discipline behind that "inborn suffering" [13] which defines his

concept of "true love," in his focus upon the requirement of adultery he does reveal the essentially obstructed quality of the Courtly Love relationship.

From this very quality Maurice Valency was "tempted to conclude that the concept of true love was not framed to include success." [14] But the difficulty of Courtly Love serves a higher mystic purpose, however obscured this purpose may become in the social manifestations of this love. As Dronke has indicated: "The *value* of the way is intimately related to its difficulty; therefore the lady should not take pity too easily. In any case the lover must orient himself to an absolute love, if necessary a love unto death." [15] This last point is particularly important for the tragic manifestations of Courtly Love with which this study is concerned. De Rougemont argues that the courtly lover "triumphs in a transfiguring Death." [16] This is, indeed, what most distinguishes the tragic courtly lover from other tragic lovers in the Elizabethan drama, his rapturous embrace of death in the name of love. But De Rougemont is, I believe, wrong in the conclusion he draws from this: "Unawares and in spite of themselves, the lovers have never had but one desire—the desire for death!" [17] The courtly lover does not have a "love of Death" [18] but of the Absolute, the Infinite, all that is beyond the sphere of mortal contingency. Rather, he despises death because it is the final proof of the hated contingency and limitations of human life from which he wishes to disassociate himself. But the tragic paradox of his love of the Absolute is that it can only be truly realized in that utter transcendence of mortality which involves his death. If he "triumphs in a transfiguring Death," it is because his fearless embrace of death in the name of an infinite love raises him above its power and unites him to the Absolute. His transfiguration in death is the sign of his triumph over death.

My conclusions, in brief, are that Courtly Love is a peculiar outgrowth of a broad Platonic tradition, that it is directed to union with the Absolute, that it adores and desires the beloved as a manifestation of the Absolute, that such a desire is defeated by temporal possession as an end in itself but is purified and ennobled through the intensification of obstruction, and that, in its tragic form, it achieves its true end, union with the Absolute, through a paradoxical embrace of death.

Since Courtly Love is a much disputed subject in literary history, the above interpretation is hardly proof against all objections, but, as Theodore Silverstein amusingly notes: "The trouble with Courtly Love is that it gives its lovers no rest, and the modern critical devotee is hardly less jealous for his favorite theory of its nature and source than was the troubadour." [19] The interpretation here adopted, however, attempts to explain the most characteristic qualities of this love as it appears in the Elizabethan tragic drama, in particular: such early efforts as Wilmot's *Tancred and Gismund* and Kyd's (?) *Soliman and Perseda,* the later Stoic reformulations of the courtly ideal in Marston's *Sophonisba* and Chapman's [20] *The Second Maiden's Tragedy,* and Shakespeare's transcendent *Romeo and Juliet.*

In one respect, the absence of adultery, all the plays just listed depart from the outline of Courtly Love given above. The veneration of *Romeo and Juliet* is partly due to the belief that in it the evil of adultery has been purged from Courtly Love and that we have instead the true basis of the modern concept of married love. The theory that married love is an outgrowth of Courtly Love and was, moreover, an exclusive product of English literature was first presented by Vernon Lee[21] and developed by C. S. Lewis in his influential work *The Allegory of Love.*

Whether or not the essential form of Courtly Love is, as the Countess of Champagne insisted, adulterous, the fact remains that there was a long tradition of nonadulterous Courtly Love which actually began in the Countess' own court. Those critics like Gaston Paris,[22] De Rougemont, and, in his earlier discussion, Lewis himself, who stress the adulterous nature of Courtly Love have naturally devoted their attention to Chrétien exclusively upon his adulterous romance of *Lancelot.* This romance conforms to the Countess of Champagne's insistence upon adultery, however, because she furnished him with both "the material and the treatment." [23] In the romances he wrote without such express command, he completely rejects adultery. While *Erec* apparently predates his knowledge or interest in Courtly Love, both *Cliges* and *Yvain* are concerned with a Courtly Love resulting in marriage. It was, moreover, in these rather than in *Lancelot* that Chrétien most influenced the subsequent development of romance.[24] Following Chrétien's lead, Arthurian romance is, for the most part, nonadulterous. When the Amadis de Gaul cycle supersedes the Arthurian at the end of the fourteenth century, this lack of adultery becomes universal, as it is also in the Renaissance romantic epics of Boiardo, Ariosto, and Tasso.

The nonadulterous tradition of Courtly Love has a history, then, almost as old as the adulterous form, surely dating back to the time of the Countess of Champagne. In the majority of Medieval and Renaissance romances the major concern is with "courtship," as we now understand the word. The romance of "courtship" begins with the lady in either an imperiled or hopelessly obstructed position; the struggle against this obstruction ennobles the lover at the same time as it intensifies his love; and, when the obstruction is finally overcome and the knight's prowess is rewarded with the hard-won hand of his lady, the romance is at an end. It is said that they live happily ever after, but rarely is this marriage of courtly lovers portrayed. The most notable instance of conjugal Courtly Love is Chrétien's *Yvain,* and it is here that the essentially obstructed quality of courtly marriage is most clearly revealed.

Yvain falls irrevocably in love with Landine under the most impossible circumstances as, imprisoned for having killed Landine's husband, Yvain observes her immoderate grief at the bier. But however hopelessly obstructed the situation had appeared, he soon wins the lady and they are married. Shortly thereafter Gawain arrives and upbraids Yvain for begining to act like a married man:

> "What? will you be one of those . . . who degenerate after marriage? . . . Slip off the bridle and halter and come to the tournament with me, that no one may say that you are jealous. . . . Pleasures grow sweeter through postpone-

ment; and a little pleasure, when delayed, is much sweeter to the taste than a great pleasure enjoyed at once." [25]

Gawain appeals to Yvain not only to continue his bachelor knight-errantry but to comport himself toward his wife as though he were not married to her, intensifying his desire through delay. Landine grants him leave to go away for one year, after which her "love will change to hate." [26] This, of course, happens when Yvain simply forgets and stays away an extra year. Now that he finds himself once again in a hopeless position, the suffering "he has brought upon himself" [27] proves so great that he becomes temporarily insane. Cured of his madness but wounded, he is brought to Landine in disguise. She wishes him to remain with her, but he considers this impossible "until I knew certainly that I had regained my lady's goodwill." [28] And to her prayer that he may have such joy, he merely mutters that "though you know it not, you hold the casket in which my happiness is kept under lock." [29] Rather than try to unlock his happiness, however, Yvain hurries to leave Landine's presence before even his wounds have been cured. After many more adventures and continuing torments, he finally realizes that "he was dying for love of her" [30] and allows himself to be reconciled to her through a ruse that might have been employed at their earlier meeting. The romance ends on a note of mythic bliss: "All has turned out well at last; for he is beloved and treasured by his lady, and she by him." [31]

Although Yvain cannot be said to be psychologically motivated in the same sense in which modern literary characters are, the romance conventions which Chrétien has his characters follow so unquestioningly depict the course of "true love" as perpetually obstructed, the conventions of Courtly Love making no distinction in this between its adulterous and conjugal forms. If the plot has revealed anything, it is that the bliss of courtly marriage is only the myth with which the romancer closes his long tale of suffering. The sufferings of courtly marriage are not, however, germane to the married state; they are not the sufferings caused by living together, but by obstruction. Though the history of courtly marriage is as old as that of courtly adultery, it has never succeeded in portraying its mythical wedded bliss. In attempting to direct such an obstructed love toward marriage, the initial confusion between mystical and romantic love has only been more seriously compounded.

Despite the important phenomenon, later to be discussed, that in the sixteenth century some members of the highest aristocracy suddenly embraced the ideal of married love, this concept is at bottom a product of the *bourgeoisie*. Shakespeare was not an aristocrat—and neither was Chrétien. As Cross and Nitze show: "Chrétien, poet of the *courtoeis* world, remains at heart a *bon bourgeois*." [32] The *bourgeois* tendency to reconcile Courtly Love with marriage began almost as soon as the adulterous ideal was first proclaimed by the troubadours. But these opposites have been reconciled only by portraying marriage in a way that approximates the state of adultery. Though marriage be the realized or unfulfilled desire of all of the courtly lovers in Elizabethan love tragedy, their love is defined by a condition of obstruction similar to that depicted by Chrétien.

From its very inception, however, the voices of resistance to the code of Courtly Love were never wholly silenced. Andreas, in the seventh dialogue, presents such a case of wrongheaded resistance:

I have a husband who is greatly distinguished by his nobility, his good breeding, and his good character, and it would be wicked for me to violate his bed or submit to the embraces of any other man, since I know that he loves me with his whole heart and I am bound to him with all the devotion of mine. The laws themselves bid me refrain from loving another man when I am blessed with such a reward for my love.[33]

Though the man replies with "surprise" that she wishes "to misapply the term 'love' to that marital affection which husband and wife are expected to feel for each other," [34] she not only insists on so doing but it is clear that in Andreas' work such "marital affection" is not a conversion of Courtly Love to the ends of marriage but that the two are "wholly different and arise from entirely different sources." Her refusal to accept his definition of love as "an inordinate desire to receive passionatetly a furtive and hidden embrace" is doubly significant since it was by just such an argument that Gawain convinced the married Yvain to absent himself from his wife.

In the objections of Castiglione's Lord Gaspar to the un-natural conventions of feminine behavior at the court of Urbino a more serious strain against this code can be detected:

> And though they love withal, yet rejoice they at the torment of lovers, because they suppose that grief, afflictions and the calling every hour for death, is a true witness that they are beloved. . . . rages into which unhappy lovers are led by these wild beasts, that have greater thirst of blood than the very tigers.[35]

Andreas' woman was objecting with the righteous indignation of centuries behind her; Lord Gaspar objects to the unnatural-ness of what has since become the established code, and is far less able to articulate what a truer love should be. But what was mere straining on his part becomes open revolt elsewhere in Italy. The historic originals of Webster's characters—the Duchess of Amalfi and the Duke of Bracciano—bear witness to the des-perate lengths that lovers were beginning to go to realize an entirely different romantic concept, not a conversion of Courtly Love to marriage, but a truly conjugal love.

Dronke has shown that the romantic assumptions of what he calls "the courtly experience" [36] have appeared in many ages and places, from the Egypt of 1300 B.C. to tenth-century Ice-land.[37] But as this love has always reflected an esoteric cult, so there has always been a more popular type of love defined not by obstruction but by the habitual quality of its relationship. I have chosen to call this antithetical mode of love, Worldly Love. Although such a love has always existed, in the Renaissance

it became a general mode of love, exalted by the lovers themselves and by the Elizabethan dramatists of this love. It is
true, however, that apart from these Elizabethan tragedies and
the Italian *novellas,* which were their primary literary source,
Worldly Love received little literary attention. But while poets
and philosophers continued to write of a Platonized courtly ideal,
a new transformation in the mode of love was nonetheless taking
place in actuality, one that was as important to the later development of European culture as the earlier emergence of Courtly
Love in eleventh century Provence.

Though lovers like the Duchess of Amalfi and the Duke
of Bracciano do not seem to have taken the Church too seriously—as both feigned pilgrimages to religious shrines to cover
love journeys—it was the long-standing position of the Church
on love and marriage that, unawares to them, provided the mori-
bund form they were to imbue with new vitality. The theoretical
basis of Worldly Love was as much a part of the unconscious
assumptions of the Renaissance as the obscured mystical source
of the code of Courtly Love, but it awaited the right historical
conditions to emerge into active life.

As C. S. Lewis has noted, the position of the Church as
defined by Aquinas was based on Aristotle's analysis of friendship.[38] Though the influence of Artistotle's theory in the Renaissance was primarily in reference to masculine friendship proper,
Aquinas discerned its broader implications to embrace the whole
subject of love. Aristotle also recognized that his theory of friendship actually provides the basis for an understanding of love:
"love is ideally a sort of excess of friendship." [39] In this special
perspective as a study of love, Aristotle's theory of friendship is
not only of historic importance in relation to Aquinas, but is
perhaps the most comprehensive analysis of the love dominating
Elizabethan love tragedy. With Aquinas' important extensions,
it provides a thus-far unrecognized theoretical basis not only for
an important phenomenon of the sixteenth century but for the
Elizabethan drama which resulted from and immortalized it. For
these reasons, I will center my discussion of Worldly Love on
a careful study of Aristotle and Aquinas.

For Aristotle, the ability to love is rooted in a man's attitude towards himself:

> For (1) we define a friend as one who wishes and does what is good, or seems so, for the sake of his friend, or (2) as one who wishes his friend to exist and live, for his sake. . . . And (3) . . . as one who lives with and (4) has the same tastes as another, or (5) one who grieves and rejoices with his friend. . . . Now each of these is true of the good man's relation to himself. . . . he wishes himself to live and be preserved, and especially the element by virtue of which he thinks. For existence is good to the virtuous man, and each man wishes himself what is good, while no one chooses to possess the whole world if he has first to become some one else. . . . Therefore, since each of these characteristics belongs to the good man in relation to himself, and he is related to his friend as to himself (for his friend is another self). . . . the extreme of friendship is likened to one's love for oneself.[40]

Before a person can love another (and this, for Aristotle, means the wish to live with him, to share his grief and pleasure, to desire what is good for him, especially the preservation of his life and individuality) he must first cherish his own existence. The person who, not loving his true self, wishes to transcend his individual existence cannot love in this way, which for Aristotle is the only true way:

> . . . when one party is removed to a great distance, as God is, the possibility of friendship ceases. This is in fact the origin of the question whether friends really wish for their friends the greatest goods, e.g. that of being gods. . . . The answer is that if we were right in saying that friend wishes good to friend for his sake, his friend must remain the sort of being he is, whatever that may be; therefore it is for him only so long as he remains a man that he will wish the greatest goods. But perhaps not *all* the greatest goods; for it is for himself most of all that each man wishes what is good.[41]

For Aristotle, the truly lovable is the finite man in all his particularity. The true lover does not raise his beloved to the status of a god, or desire that they may both become gods through love, for what he loves in himself and the beloved is the individuality that makes them human. In loving, he embraces "another self" and would preserve his own individuality to the same extent that he respects the individuality of the other.

Here Aristotle explicitly rejects the Platonic theory of love in which the mysticism of Courtly Love is rooted:

> And the true order of going, or being led by another, to the things of love, is to begin from the beauties of earth and mount upwards for the sake of that other beauty, using these as steps only. . . . if man had eyes to see the true beauty—not clogged with the pollutions of mortality and all the colors and vanities of human life—thither looking, and holding converse with the true beauty simple and divine. . . . in that communion only, beholding beauty with the eyes of the mind, he will . . . become the friend of God and be immortal, if mortal man may.[42]

While Plato regards man's finite existence as the great evil he must endeavor to transcend through an immortalizing communion with the divine, for Aristotle "existence is good to the virtuous man." If for Plato the supremely good man detaches himself from existence and is "ever pursuing death and dying," [43] for Aristotle he justly glories in the very consciousness of his own existence. Since it is in this consciousness that existence is made valuable, the lover desires not only the existence of the beloved but that consciousness of his existence that can only be truly gained if "they do and share in those things which give them the sense of living together." [44] Where Plato's lover desires to "become the friend of God," Aristotle recognizes that in such a desire the "possibility of friendship ceases" since "friendship is said to be equality." [45]

The prime impulse of this love is "goodwill," [46] and in the generosity that springs from this the lover realizes his highest good. Though the true lover is conscious only of the desire to give, this desire rebounds in good for himself since it is answered with a like return: "each gets from each in all respects the same as, or something like what, he gives." [47] In this exchange the lover's own goodness is increased: "the friendship of good men is good, being augmented by companionship; and they are thought to become better too by their activities and by improving each other." [48] For Aristotle, the companionate love of equals is also ennobling.

Worldly Love, then, is "worldly" insofar as it is directed toward reaping the goods of this world: it is in diametric opposition to the otherworldly orientation of Courtly Love. If Courtly Love is otherwordly in its pursuit of purity, Worldly Love is "worldly" in the usual meaning of the term as well in that it accepts the "impurity" of the world as the necessary basis of its existence. The individuality which the courtly lover would lose through love is prized by the worldly lover both as a good in itself and as a basis for achieving the true relatedness without which his sovereign preservation would be meaningless: "For without friends no one would choose to live, though he had all other goods." [49] The ultimate value of his individuality lies, then, in its power to achieve relations with other finite beings, relations that would cease upon his loss of individuality. In the very name of love, therefore, he must preserve his sovereignty even within the love relationship. And what is true of relatedness is also true of benevolence. Only because he reserves the final gift of self is he capable of the benevolence that is the true activity of loving, for the man who loses himself is incapable of either giving or receiving. Both relatedness and compassion, then, are seen to be functions of a preserved individuality.

Although Aristotle does not so indicate, it is from this ultimate preservation of sovereignty that the seeds of tragedy are sown in even the finest Worldly Love relationships. The preserved individuality which makes Worldly Love possible and enables it to find fulfillment in life is also the means by which it can be corrupted and ultimately defeated. If the tragedy of Courtly Love arises from its desire to transcend finite individuality, the tragedy of Worldly Love arises from the desire for its preservation: "for it is for himself most of all that each man wishes what is good." The danger of Courtly Love is its denial of self, which renders the lover incapable of fighting for life. The danger of Worldly Love is that it can place the preservation of personal sovereignty and of life above the good of the relationship that gives this preservation its highest meaning, thus weakening the power of this love to withstand both internal and external attack. Their final difference lies in their relation to death. When the worldly lover's attempt to achieve love makes death unavoidable, he does not, like the courtly lover, eagerly embrace death in the name of his love and for its eternal fulfillment. Though fully committed to his love, it is a love for life and not for death. When he finally does accept the inevitability of death, it is his personal dignity rather than his love that impels him to it. Aristotle and the modern expounders of Worldly Love [50] are alike innocent of the tragic potential of the ideal they set up in conscious opposition to Courtly Love. But the Elizabethan tragedies of Worldly Love enable us to learn this final implication of a love bound not to death but to life.

The Elizabethan tragedies of what I have named Worldly Love may be numbered as follows: such early coterie[51] and closet dramas as Marlowe's *Dido,* Daniel's *Cleopatra,* and Lady Carey's *Mariam;* the anonymous domestic tragedies *Arden of Feversham* and *A Warning for Fair Women;* Shakespeare's *Othello* and *Antony and Cleopatra,* Webster's *The White Devil* and *The Duchess of Malfi,* Massinger's *The Duke of Milan,* and Middleton's *Women Beware Women.*

The tragic liability of preserved sovereignty within a love relationship is perfectly symbolized by casting the lover in the role of a king. It is, in fact, because of the double meaning of "sovereignty" that I have stressed this term in considering the worldly lover's attitude towards his individuality, that inviolable identity which sets him apart as a being of unique significance. Because most of the worldly lovers in Elizabethan tragedy are also "sovereign" in the second sense of the word, which means the supreme authority in a state, critics have felt indisposed to treat these tragedies as preeminently tragedies of love. It is, however, precisely this circumstance that clarifies the nature and implications of this love. It is significant that in the other categories of tragic love no lover is cast as a ruler, while almost all of the worldly lovers are sovereign in their own domain: Dido, Othello (in Cyprus), Antony (as Triumvir in control of the Eastern Mediterranean) and Cleopatra, the Duke of Brachiano in *The White Devil*, the Duchess of Malfi, the Duke of Milan, and the Duke of Florence in *Women Beware Women*. In almost every case the lover's undeniable sense of sovereignty, both as ruler and significant individual, comes into conflict with his love; but however poorly he may fulfill the sovereign side of his nature and even wish to relinquish it, he is never able to free himself from its demands and ends by affirming it.

The preoccupation of critics with Courtly Love has blinded them to the very different truth of Worldly Love, and so made a proper evaluation of the great tragedies of Worldly Love impossible. *The White Devil*, for instance, has been analyzed by Clifford Leech[52] without a single reference to love and considered by Madeleine Doran to be representative of a genre which she calls "the tragedy of sex." [53] If we expect worldly lovers to act like courtly lovers they cannot fail to fall short of our expectations. But it is these expectations, rather than the behavior of the worldly lovers, that have fallen short of the ideal. We cannot properly appreciate the tragedy of Worldly Love until we understand the very different ideal it sets for itself and to which it is "true" even in its defeat.

Although Aritotle did not recognize the tragic potential of his ideal, he alone recognized that there were less ideal forms of Worldly Love in which serious difficulty could develop. For the initial condition of self-love, out of which Worldly Love arises, has a higher and a lesser form: that based upon genuine self-esteem, and that which we would now call "narcissism."[54] Included in this lower type are those "who assign to themselves the greater share of wealth, honours, and bodily pleasures . . . who are grasping with regard to these things." [55] Aristotle argues that such a man "does not seem to be amicably disposed even to himself, because there is nothing in him to love." [56] The narcissist, according himself all worth precisely because he does not truly love himself, is incapable of the higher form of Worldly Love. In the form of Worldly Love based upon narcissistic rather than genuine self-love, that which Aristotle terms "the friendship of utility," [57] the beloved never becomes, for the lover, a person in his own right, but is simply a means of selfish gratification. Since the beloved is a person, resentments arise which eventually destroy the relationship. When the beloved is not content to be used as an instrument, the narcissist feels abused: such lovers "think they have got less than they should, and blame their partners because they do not get all they 'want and deserve.' " [58] The narcissist is conscious, only "that his excess of love is not met by love in return." [59] But it is not returned precisely because his love was not directed toward "the other person himself" [60] but toward an image of the other which was only a projection of his own self-love.

The two forms of Worldly Love must always be carefully distinguished. There is a noble form, to which our age would apply the ultimate value term of "healthy," and the unhealthy or narcissistic form. Both healthy and narcissistic Worldly Love are products of expansive personalities; but the expansiveness of the former may be compared to that of a flower, of the latter to that of a balloon. The Elizabethan tragedies of this narcissistic Worldly Love are *Dido, Othello,* and the two tragedies based on Josephus' record of Herod and Mariamne, *Mariam* and *The Duke of Milan.* But whether narcissistic or noble, the worldly lover always preserves his own sovereignty. He is an individual straining at the same time both for greater relatedness and greater personal power, and although these two primary factors are complementary necessities for the richest human life, they are opposite in nature and can come into conflict. The healthier the Worldly Love is, however, the closer do these conflicting drives come into harmony. At its best, as in *The Duchess of Malfi,* the worldly lover desires self-realization through a compassionate relationship with another sovereign being, equal in goodness, in which personal sovereignty is mutually preserved and respected. Although Worldly Love does not always result in compassion, in its highest form it is indistinguishable from it. This affinity is understandable, for both compassion and Worldly Love are alike in being directed towards the living and accepting its corruption. The worldly lover is at home in this world and embraces life with all its corruption and limitations as the proper habitat of his spirit.

The essential affinity between the ethics of Aristotle and the Judaic-Christian tradition was most profoundly recognized by Aquinas. As opposed to the Platonic tradition as his "Philosopher," he used Aristotle to combat its then all-pervasive influence. In his special emphasis on the "love of concupiscience," however, Aquinas extended and completed the theory of Worldly Love.

Aquinas directs his argument against the kind of love extolled by the troubadours when he says: "love is not a wounding passion, but rather one that preserves and perfects." [61] He argues that love "belongs to the concupiscible power, because it regards good absolutely, and not under the aspect of difficulty." [62] In his discussion of absence, the distinction he is drawing between desire and love becomes apparent: "desire implies the real absence of the beloved: whereas love remains whether the beloved is absent or present." [63] When he does treat the element of desire in love, its nature appears in a very different light from the desire of courtly passion. "Passion . . . properly so called" [64] is, for Aquinas, not the pangs of ceaseless desire: "*love* . . . is nothing else than complacency in that object; and from this complacency results a movement towards that same object, and this movement is *desire;* and lastly, there is rest which is *joy.*" [65] While courtly desire does not wish to be alleviated by consummation, worldly desire is a movement from "complacency" to the "rest which is *joy.*" Unlike Courtly Love, which needs the obstruction of infrequent meetings, "in love of concupiscience he who desires something intensely, is moved against all that hinders his gaining or quietly enjoying the object of his love." [66] The worldly lover overcomes the obstructions to his love so that he can quietly enjoy it. He desires the sustained presence of the beloved because "Good is loved inasmuch as it can be communicated to the lover. Consequently whatever hinders the perfection of this communication, becomes hateful." [67] This desire for communication underlies Aquinas' analysis of the ecstasy proper to this love:

> . . . the lover is taken out from himself, in a certain sense;
> in so far, namely, as not being satisfied with enjoying the
> good that he has, he seeks to enjoy something outside him-
> self. But since he seeks to have this extrinsic good for him-
> self, he does not go out from himself simply, and this move-
> ment remains finally within him.[68]

Although the worldly lover finds his existence "good," he also
finds it unsatisfactory to the extent that he cannot relate it to
"something outside himself." In the relatedness of Worldly Love,
however, individuality is not annihilated but preserved and en-
riched. Worldly Love preserves individuality and perfects it in
charity: "Charity denotes, in addition to love a certain perfection
of love, in so far as that which is loved is held to be of great
price, as the word itself implies." [69] For Aquinas, the perfection
of love in charity results from the lover's high valuation of the
beloved, and this not only in herself but also for his own existence: "when we love a thing by desiring it, we apprehend it
as belonging to our well-being." [70] Though he is "moved against
all that hinders his gaining or quietly enjoying the object of his
love," his feeling of gratefulness for possessing such a precious
companion results in an overflowing of generosity to the beloved.
While the Elizabethan tragedies of Worldly Love do show instances of perfect charity both within and without the love relationship—such as the Duchess of Malfi—we more often find
this seeming paradox between hostility to all who oppose the
love and an overflowing generosity within the love relationship,
as in the case of Brachiano. Aquinas helps us to understand how
a love both devoted to charity and perfected by it can be moved
to appear as its opposite in relation to the outside world.

Aquinas completes Aristotle's analysis of Worldly Love by
revealing not only the sources of its goodness but of its power.
This difference in emphasis may, however, be due to what they
were combating. As Aristotle was arguing against Plato's theories,
he was concerned to show that the aim of love was not to become
a god by transcending the individuality of the self and the beloved
but to enjoy the "sense of living together" through recognizing
the true lovableness of their finite individualities. Aquinas, how-

ever, was combating the influence of Courtly Love, and this differed from Platonic love in its emphasis on suffering and obstruction. But in arguing against such desire, he was led to recognize that Worldly Love is also a powerful passion.

Although this abstract discussion of the love of concupiscence is not related to the questions of marriage and adultery, Aquinas applies it to these questions at a later point in the *Summa Theologica.* In accepting the argument of Sixtus the Pythagorean that "He that is insatiable of his wife is an adulterer,"[71] he is arguing that the marriage of courtly lovers is still adultery since their love is an "insatiable" desire rather than a movement from complacency to joyful rest. On the other hand, "the marriage goods, in so far as they consist in a habit, make the marriage honest and holy." [72] Marriage, in fact, perfects the love of concupiscence "by depriving the act to which concupiscence inclines of its outward shamefulness." [73] Such a marriage is a sacrament which confers "grace." [74]

The concept of conjugal love exemplified in the writings of Aquinas continued to play a powerful role in Renaissance theory; not in Italy, where Ficino's Platonic theories held sway, but in the North. In the sixteenth century, the Northern Renaissance or Reformation resulted in an act of the most far-reaching importance, the Lutheran acceptance of sacerdotal marriage. Not only did the Protestant clergy demand for themselves the right to marry but they wrote numerous tracts and sermons in which the ideal of married love was vigorously set forth. The Elizabethan writings of this nature have been ably discussed by William and Malleville Haller, with the following conclusions:

This dedication of the Puritan clerical caste to conjugal life was hardly less important in its effects than that of courtly poets to the worship of feminine beauty. . . . from magnifying the religious significance of marriage Puritan thought easily proceeded to magnify the emotional, romantic, and idealistic aspects of the marriage relation. . . . The one imperative need was for solace of that loneliness of the spirit from which man even in paradise was not exempt . . .[75]

Although it is only Heywood who affirmed this view of married love in its precise formulation, the other Elizabethan tragic dramatists must have been equally aware of that love, glorified by Puritan theory, which did not exalt suffering and death but the solace of spiritual loneliness.

This discussion has led to the conclusions that Courtly Love seeks an obstructed relationship which, at the very least, approximates the conditions of adultery, while Worldly Love is naturally fulfilled by marriage. As has been seen, however, the literary manifestations of Courtly Love, particularly in England, tended more and more to become identified with the desire for marriage. In considering the historical appearance of Worldly Love, this paradoxical inversion of theory and practice becomes even more startling. If we were to judge its historical form primarily on the evidence of the Elizabethan tragedies of Worldly Love, we would have to conclude that Worldly Love manifested itself largely in terms of adultery. In the Elizabeth tragic drama, there is a nearly complete reversal of the essential nature of these two opposing loves. While Courtly Love almost entirely appears in the form of innocent young lovers who wish to marry, Worldly Love most often appears in the form of seemingly more experienced lovers who commit adultery. Before attempting to explain the second half of this reversal of theory and practice, the essential difference between courtly and worldly adultery should be noted.

True courtly adultery, such as that of Lancelot or Tristan, never looks forward to marriage as the fulfillment of its desire. Indeed, this concept of a love relationship seems framed to include the husband in order to provide the intensifying obstruction necessary for the perpetuation of desire. Worldly lovers, however, enter into adultery because they want to live together and for them the husband is an undesirable obstruction which they would overcome in order that they might marry. They illustrate Aquinas' observation that "he who desires something intensely, is moved against all that hinders his gaining or quietly enjoying the object of his love." While courtly lovers respect the husband's rights to such an extent that they may be driven in desperation to suicide, when worldly lovers become desperate enough they will rather murder the husband. This is the case in four of the Elizabethan tragedies of Worldly Love, all based on actual sixteenth-century occurrences in England and in Italy: the anonymous *Arden of Feversham* and *A Warning for Fair Women,* which deal with the notorious criminal cases of Alice Arden and Anne Sanders (sentenced with their lovers in 1552 and 1573, respectively, for the murder of their husbands); Webster's *The White Devil,* the story of the Duke of Bracciano and Vittoria Accoromboni; and Middleton's *Women Beware Women,* the story of the Duke of Florence and Bianca Capello. Even where adultery is not the prelude to legal marriage, as in Shakespeare's *Antony and Cleopatra,* the sustained and open quality of its fulfillment more closely approximates the condition of marriage than of a furtive and hidden adultery. Just as courtly marriage approximates the condition of adultery, so worldly adultery either approximates the condition of marriage or wishes to be fulfilled by marriage. This is different from either form of Courtly Love, since the courtly lovers who wish to marry are not adulterous and the adulterous courtly lovers only desire to perpetuate the state of adultery. Even where Worldly Love assumes the form of adultery, then, its essential affinity to marriage is still clear. Why Worldly Love should have made its historical appearance in terms of adultery remains to be answered.

Although there was a substantial and honored theory of Worldly Love available to such Renaissance lovers as became the subjects of Webster's and Middleton's tragedies, they appear nonetheless to be acting without any sense of theoretical sanction. To explain how these Renaissance lovers could have developed their concept of love is a far greater problem than that of tracing the historical rise of Courtly Love. For Courtly Love has not only been extensively explored by modern scholars but extensively theorized by its historical proponents. In the case of Worldly Love, however, the historians and critics who have indicated the existence of such a love and suggested an historical origin for some of its distinctive features were not aware of the necessity for distinguishing it from Courtly Love.[76]

One thing alone seems to be clear, that as Courtly Love was

the product of various forces which converged in the eleventh century in Provence, so Worldly Love seems to have been a peculiar product of the Italian Renaissance and to have been disseminated to the North by it. This is not to say that Worldly Love did not exist before the Renaissance. The theories of Aristotle and Aquinas, as also the character of Andreas' woman, seem to reflect a more popular view of love, which has required articulation largely to counter the influence of esoteric cults of love, and must have had some basis in fact. Furthermore, Plutarch's account of the love of Antony and Cleopatra would seem to indicate its essentially worldly character, and this very fact might account for its popularity in Renaissance tragedy from Garnier through the Countess of Pembroke's coterie to Shakespeare and his followers. It is still possible to say, however, that in the Renaissance Worldly Love became a general mode of love which not only inspired lovers but, for the only time in dramatic history, tragic dramatists. The rise of this mode of love in the Italian Renaissance would seem to be, quite simply, the product of the development of personality that took place in both men and women during this period. The humanistic education of women resulted in their development of new characteristics which, in turn, made possible the development of a new mode of love based upon a respect for individuality. As Jacob Burckhardt has shown, the highly individualized man turns for love "to another individuality equally developed, namely, to his neighbour's wife."[77]

With this last point before us, we can see why Worldly Love should have made its first historical appearance in terms of adultery. This reason appears to be identical with the social explanation for courtly adultery; simply that in sixteenth century Italy, as well as in eleventh century Provence, the young girls were secluded from society and the only upper-class women with whom men could have contact were married women. Since marriages were still arranged with no thought to love, but only to dynastic and material considerations, the development of a true Worldly Love in terms of marriage could only have occurred in the rarest of circumstances. The conditions of marriage during these centuries being generally inimicable to love, the result was that any form of true love, whether courtly or worldly, was bound to make its initial appearance in terms of adultery. As Lewis has also suggested: "Any idealization of sexual love, in a society where marriage is purely utilitarian, must begin by being an idealization of adultery." [78]

It would thus appear that the source of the love that predominates in the Elizabethan tragic drama was not primarily literary but actual, originating in the new realities of Renaissance personality and education. Alfred Harbage has shown that one of the dominating ideals of what he considers the popular tradition in the Elizabethan theatre was a new concept of wedded love, whose development was influenced by the Puritan preachers advocacy of married love, by the humanistic education of women, and, perhaps, by the example of Henry VIII.[79] In tracing this background, he has arrived at conclusions almost identical to mine:

> That Spenser, Shakespeare, and Milton all sprang from the same broad sector of society in the same age suggests that the ideal we are treating is not essentially a literary product. . . . we can be certain that the conception of a certain type of woman and a certain type of marriage was not newborn in the sixteenth century. We can be equally certain that the conception had never before been so widely disseminated or so articulate.[80]

David Lloyd Stevenson has also focused upon a distinctive form of love relationship, traceable to the influence of the Italian Renaissance and the humanistic education of women,[81] which characterizes what he has called Shakespeare's "love-game comedy." He notes that in *Othello* and *Antony and Cleopatra*, "Shakespeare treats the same conflict as that presented in *Much Ado*," [82] and that this portrayal of love reflects "the sixteenth-century effort to discover a psychology and theory of love more practicable than that presented by courtly or Petrarchan ideals." [83] For Stevenson, this love had its "first public triumph" [84] in the marriage of Henry VIII to Anne Boleyn.

Though Stevenson views Anne Boleyn as "the coming to life of courtly love,[85] while Harbage cannot recognize his popular ideal of love apart from its strictly conjugal form, I submit that we have all isolated, as a distinctive feature of the Elizabethan drama, what is essentially the same mode of love. I share Harbage's amusement with C. S. Lewis for "plucking the flower 'monogamic idealism' out of the nettle 'courtly adultery.' " [86] I would also point out, however, that the "Puritan art of love" [87] which helped to shape his new ideal of wedded love was the product of a broader Renaissance movement toward a new type of idealized love relationship between companionate equals. A moral distinction may exist between those lovers who were true to the marriage bond as envisioned by the Puritan preachers and those, like Vittoria Accoromboni and Bianca Capello, who betrayed their vows for an adulterous love. But they were alike in espousing a love directed toward a shared existence and in opposing the sufferings of an obstructed relationship which characterize Courtly Love. It was, in fact, to include both of these types of lovers that I have devised the more generic term of Worldly Love.

As Courtly Love, soon after its initial adulterous appearance, was converted to the ends of marriage, at least in theory, so too was Worldly Love. As has already been indicated by Stevenson and Harbage, the most outstanding example of this historical phenomenon was the marriage of Henry VIII to Anne Boleyn, a marriage that signified an extraordinary change in human sentiment. This change was reflected not only in Anne Boleyn's insistence upon marriage, but in her energy and ability to effect her will.[88] Needless to say, Anne Boleyn was herself the most prominent Renaissance martyr to the ideal of Worldly Love. And if the impermanence of Henry's affection led to her tragic death, it was, while it lasted, strong enough to cause Henry to accept excommunication and the severance of the English Church from Rome in order to achieve its fulfillment in marriage.

Burckhardt shows that in the sixteenth century there "began those morganatic marriages of affection which in the fifteenth century, on grounds either of policy or morality, would have had no meaning at all." [89] This natural development of Worldly Love toward its essential conjugal nature was not only true in Italy, and for those sixteenth-century Italian lovers who became the subject of Elizabethan Worldly Love tragedy, but, even more significantly, in the North. For the most spectacular Northern example of this general sixteenth-century trend was the Lutheran acceptance of sacerdotal marriage. The heroic desire of the early Protestant clergy for marriage also led, however, to martyrdom at the hands of a Church and society not yet ready to accept its truth.[90] The desire of the Lutheran clergy and of Henry VIII for marriage were but equal manifestations of the Northern Renaissance spirit, alike in this to the Italian Renaissance in espousing the new ideal of Worldly Love.

The love of Anne Boleyn for Henry VIII is only the most prominent example of a veritable wave of love tragedy which swept over the aristocracy of at least Italy and England in the sixteenth and early seventeenth centuries. The most notable later instance in England is that of the pretender to the throne of James I, Lady Arabella Stuart, whose tragic love, as F. L. Lucas has shown,[91] paralleled that of the actual Duchess of Amalfi, and who has imprisoned in the Tower at the time that Webster's *The Duchess of Malfi* was produced in London. Lucas suggests that this connection may have been in Webster's mind and would certainly have occurred to some members of his audience. And what was true of the aristocracy was also true of the provincial lower classes, as indicated by the Elizabethan domestic tragedies of Worldly Love and by the tragic instances among the early Protestant clergy. Though courtly sonneteers were content to write to their mistress "Idea," the tragedians of Worldly Love were writing of the actual tragedies that surrounded them.

The final paradox in this study of the paradoxical appearances of love in the Elizabethan tragic drama now emerges. While all of the Elizabethan tragedies of Courtly Love were fictitious, all but *Dido* and *Othello* among the Elizabethan tragedies of Worldly Love were based upon actual history, and not only on contemporary but on ancient history as well. Beyond showing that the sources of Courtly Love were literary while the sources of Worldly Love were historical, such a circumstance might lead one to question whether a tragic Courtly Love was ever more than a fiction and whether it was not rather Worldly Love that has always inspired actual lovers to risk all for love. If such a statement is not a historical distortion, the strange paradox which must then be faced is that the love that has exalted suffering and death has actually produced no historic martryrs to its truth while the love that has exalted happiness and life has inspired that true dedication to love which could meet the tragic test of history. The startling fact seems to be that, despite the honor in which courtly lovers hold a death for love, it is the worldly lovers who have actually died for love.

The present confusion in dealing with Elizabethan love tragedy is the inevitable result of the various historical confusions of theory and practice that I have been tracing. The most important of these is that concerning marriage and adultery. We have seen how it came about that in the Elizabethan period the essentially adulterous Courtly Love should have manifested itself in the form of apparent innocents who wished to marry, while the essentially conjugal Worldly Love should have appeared in terms of seemingly experienced adulterers. These confused appearances had an inevitable effect, however, upon the development of love and of attitudes toward it, an effect that is the result of taking these appearances at their face value. Not recognizing the *mystique* that gives to each of these loves its true meaning, Courtly Love is regarded simply as the model marriage and Worldly Love as base promiscuity. The perfect example of this critical error is provided by Harbage who, despite his firm handling of the historical background, can consider Juliet as "instinctively monandrous" [92] and Antony as a case of "moral debility." [93]

If there have always been esoteric cults of love, which in the eleventh century assumed the form known as Courtly Love, and also a more popular type of love that in the sixteenth century assumed the form I have named Worldly Love, so there has probably always been a form of shallow sentiment masquerading to itself as love but incapable of that depth of commitment which true love can inspire. By the Elizabethan period, however, the profanation of Courtly Love and popularization of wedded love had progressed to such a state that the joys of romantic love must have seemed the birthright of every freeborn Englishman, an expectation that has only grown with the ensuing centuries. That the rich strands of romanticism which had entwined themselves during the Renaissance were ill understood by the ordinary lover made little difference since most were fortunate to escape any undue testing of their romantic assumptions. But they did not wholly escape the tragic testing of the Elizabethan dramatists. Tragedies of such "love," in fact, form an important and distinct category of the genre of Elizabethan love tragedy which I have been defining. Opposed to the true romanticism of both Courtly and Worldly Love, I have named this form of sentiment False Romantic Love.

The false romantic lover does not make a deep spiritual investment in love because he is conscious of no real spiritual needs. Looking upon his life with a complacent self-confidence, he also looks upon love as a desirable but not very serious matter. The result is that he responds to a "style" of love rather than being committed to its essence. Marriage for the true courtly lover and adultery for the true worldly lover may be perversions of the essential directions these loves should take, but they are not "styles" since, for the initiate, courtly marriage proves to be obstructed while worldly adultery achieves an open, habitual quality.

How these two primary forms of love became debased into styles may be more readily understood by reverting to an earlier suggestion that the Elizabethan form of the courtly lover *seems* more innocent than his worldly counterpart. The purity of Courtly Love is not innocent because it is true to an infinite ideal which lifts it above the corruptions of love. What is innocent is the attempt at purity without reference to an infinite ideal, since life is not and cannot be pure in its own terms. Without this reference, the meaning of obstruction as both an intensifier of passion and purifying agent is lost. This is why the innocent who follows the code of Courtly Love without an understanding of its *mystique* will not be able to withstand obstruction and why the initiate of Courtly Love cannot be seduced from his love by it. So the style of Courtly Love comes to mean a first love, a love whose purity can never be returned to, but which must be outgrown. Worldly Love, on the other hand, *seems* more experienced than Courtly Love in that it accepts natural corruption as a necessary constituent of life. In the style of Worldly Love, however, the corrupt is embraced for its own sake and without reference to the spirit it makes flesh. Satisfaction is then desired not to realize something finer through it but in its basest terms and, since it is only spirit that can be committed, the satisfaction becomes completely casual. In their loss of *mystique,* then, the styles of Courtly and Worldly Love not only accept the reversed directions of the true loves they would imitate but actually come together, the model marriage resulting in promiscuous adultery, and this because that marriage which would be modeled on a misunderstanding of purity is insecure and can easily be tempted into adultery.

The false romantic lover becomes easily involved in a love relationship but, not understanding either his own emotion or the nature of intimate relationships, he takes love to be a much simpler thing than it is. He is not committed, therefore, for better or worse, but only for better. Since he has not invested his love with the deep spiritual import that can strengthen it to meet adversity, he is not able to withstand either the obstructions to his love or the temptation of some new love which seems to be still "better." Not being able to appreciate the good that he does have, he breaks his engagement easily and, indeed, thoughtlessly, however much he may try to rationalize it, at the first sign of serious temptation. But in embracing this temptation, he learns to his horror that he has embraced something vicious and exposed himself to a world of evil which bars the return to his former good. He had earlier accepted this good with a complacent assurance of his own worth. Now he realizes that through his own unworthiness he has lost the good he has come to appreciate too late. He may now rise, however, to a final true love for his lost beloved which enables him to accept the justice of his defeat and redeems him in his fall. The Elizabethan tragedies that follow this pattern of False Romantic Love are *A Woman Killed With Kindness* and *The English Traveller* by Heywood, *The Insatiate Countess* by Marston, *Cupid's Revenge* and *The Maid's Tragedy* by Beaumont and Fletcher and *The Double Marriage* by Fletcher and Massinger, *The Witch of Edmonton* by Dekker, Ford and Rowley, and *The Changeling* by Middleton and Rowley.

The tragedies of False Romantic Love reveal the complete profanation of the language of Courtly Love. When the Elizabethan tragedians turned to the portrayal of Worldly Love, they had to deal with a love that had not been extolled by centuries of poets and, therefore, had developed no language of its own. Although Shakespeare may try to indicate the distinctive nature of Worldly Love when he writes, "The nobleness of life/ Is to do thus; when such a mutual pair/ And such a twain can't do't," he is writing without the support of a traditional body of amorous language. While it is remarkable to what an extent the tragedians of Worldly Love have eschewed the language of Courtly Love and tried to develop more appropriate expression for this different love, inevitably some courtly language did creep in. In the tragedies of False Romantic Love, however, the converse is true. There, even more than in the true tragedies of Courtly Love, extensive use is made of the language of Courtly Love. The original engagement is subjected to all the eulogy derived from the romances of "courtship" while the subsequent infidelity is excused by the language of irresistible passion. The "passion" of the false romantic lover is, of course, not irresistible but simply irresponsible. But, as might be expected, in the tragedy of irresponsibility the characters make a totally irresponsible use of language. Their irresponsibility is partially due to their naive use of this language, for it has instilled in them certain expectations that remain unsatisfied either by their own emotions or the relationships into which they enter. They are intoxicated by a language that does not actually transport them to perfect bliss but leaves them empty. Their marriages prove infirm; their grand passions sordid little affairs. This is the final devolution of Courtly Love from a mystic passion to a conventional language capable of inciting irresponsibility.

The result of such a mistaken application of romantic conventions to the ordinary and uninspired circumstances of life was apparent to Chaucer. His Criseyde was probably the first full-length portrait of a false romantic lover. And this form of love continued to be embodied in the frail flesh of the fair Criseyde through the successive versions of Henryson and of playwrights now lost, finally to achieve another masterful expression in Shakespeare's bitter comedy. Chaucer, too, begins the convention of treating False Romantic Love with a disapproving Christian morality. For him, however, this involved an ultimate rejection of the false romanticism of life with the final commendation of the young to the love of God, "For he nyl falsen no wight, dar I seye." [94] With Henryson, this censure comes from Criseyde herself, as she recognizes and sorrows for her sin. This moral formulation enters into the dramatic treatment of False Romantic Love. To this poetic tradition was probably added another contributing strain from the drama, specifically from the long tradition of the Medieval Morality play,[95] which applied to the pattern of romantic irresponsibility the simple Christian morality of the recognition and repentance of sin leading to ultimate grace. Henry H. Adams' study of domestic tragedy shows that "The reliance on the principle of easily achieved divine mercy in the domestic tragedies is the result of their subordination to popular theology." [96] But it was Heywood alone of the early domestic tragedians who applied this popular theology and the dramaturgy of the Moralities to the treatment of False Romantic Love. Heywood's synthesis of these two factors was successively elaborated in the more sophisticated treatments of Beaumont and Feltcher and of Middleton.

This general introduction has attempted to define the three modes of love that may be isolated in the Elizabethan tragic drama and to indicate the possible historic origin of the specific forms they take in this drama. To allow the Elizabethan drama to reveal the nature and relative importance of its love tragedies, however, it was necessary to approach its study without the prejudice of a preconceived standard of love tragedy. The following simple definition was adopted, therefore, as the basis of this study. *Love tragedy is that tragedy resulting from the protagonist's involvement in what he at least and at the start of his involve-*

ment considered to be love. In terms of this definition approximately half of the total number of Elizabethan tragedies are love tragedies. The primary aim of this book is to establish this group of tragedies as a special genre in the Elizabethan drama, isolating for purposes of organizational clarity the modes of love and of dramatic patterning which may be exhibited and tracing their historical development. To do this, of course, is to assume a perspective outside of the living reality of this theatre. What appear from this perspective to be clearly distinguishable modes of love and of developing patterns of dramatic action may not have seemed so clear to the dramatists trying to forge new concepts and patterns for their plays out of the dishevelled mass of literary conventions, new and old learning, and their own instinctual responses. But since we are here and not there, perhaps the best one can do is to try to see what patterns and distinctions do finally emerge from their work, to illuminate what they were, perhaps more darkly, striving to accomplish. The final value of these categories is the new understanding they can provide for the individual plays thus studied. The critical method adopted is to focus primary attention upon the love element in the most significant plays coming under the definition of love tragedy, thus redressing the critical imbalance that has developed in their regard.

While critics have been almost unanimous in disregarding the romantic content of most of these tragedies in their search for major significance, the present study starts from the premise that only by taking seriously the value of the love they affirm can an adequate understanding of these plays' tragic meaning be attained. In the tragedy of aspiration, prime Elizabethan examples being *Tamburlaine, Bussy D'Ambois,* and *Macbeth,* the defeat of aspiration is redeemed by the hero's continuing refusal to cry "Hold, enough!" The tragedy of aspiration affirms the value of extending individual power even to the point at which it comes into mortal conflict with earthly limitation. It affirms man's individual grandeur in the face of an oppressive universe. In non-romantic tragedy, whether the inspirational idea be ambition, honor, or revenge, salvation results from man's positive relations to his inner gods. Non-romantic tragedy is concerned with the redeeming value of the isolated individual. Love tragedy differs in being concerned with the individual's striving for relatedness. It sees man not simply as an isolated individual with the power to assert personal values in the face of a hostile universe, but as a related individual with power to create a redemptive sphere of love in that hostile universe. In love tragedy man is redeemed by his ability to love in an otherwise unbenevolent world and to affirm the saving value of this love in the face of the overwhelming hostility that has defeated it. Critics who treat the love manifested in a love tragedy as an incidental feature of its tragic vision, one that must be looked through to find the essentials of this vision, necessarily miss what is truly essential to its tragic affirmation, that through love alone individual man can be redeemed in a world otherwise lacking in benevolence.

Section I

Tragedies of Courtly Love

2

The Classic Pattern
of Courtly Love Tragedy

Tancred and Gismund

The ideal of Courtly Love received its most radiant dramatic manifestations through two stories which were first dramatized at the beginning of Elizabeth's long reign and then reworked at its end. Bandello's story of Romeo and Giulietta inspired what was probably the first English attempt at love tragedy. At least Arthur Brooke, in the 1562 preface to his poem *Romeus and Juliet*—which was to become the source of the greatest tragedy of Courtly Love in the English language—mentions having seen such a lost play. The first love tragedy to have survived, however, is the work of five students at the Inner Temple who, in 1566, "framed" *The Tragedie of Gismund of Salerne* from Boccaccio's *Decameron* tale for performance before Queen Elizabeth. This tragedy, having much to commend it, was revised by Robert Wilmot, the author of the original fifth act and epilogue, and given to the press in 1591 as *The Tragedy of Tancred and Gismund.*[1] The late Elizabethan love tragedies of Wilmot and Shakespeare, which represented Courtly Love in its purest form, were, then, based upon plots that had inspired the only vernacular love tragedies in the early English drama.

The classic pattern and meaning of Courtly Love tragedy

can be seen most clearly in *Tancred and Gismund*. Originally written to be performed before the Queen and then published as closet drama intended for the aristocracy, this play demonstrates the literary results of the tradition of Courtly Love before it had to accommodate itself to the groundlings.

As with most Elizabethan mistresses of Courtly Love tragedy, Gismund's first thought upon falling in love is of marriage. But whatever her father may decree, she is prepared to accept "the fortune of my starres" (1. 359) with a total commitment to her fated love. Tancred's refusal to permit his daughter's marriage provides the lovers with the obstruction necessary for the peculiar trials of the Courtly Love relationship, as is early indicated by the loved Guiszhard:

> What greeuous pain they dure which neither may
> Forget their Loues, ne yet enioy their loue.
> I know by proofe, and daily make assay,
> Though Loue hath brought my Ladies hart to loue
> My faithfull loue with like loue to requite:
> This doeth not quench, but rather cause to flame
> The creeping fire, which spreading in my brest
> With raging heat, graunts me no time of rest. (11. 699–706)

In the obstructed state of their love, the fact that his lady returns his love only intensifies the pain of ceaseless desire. Nor does he give any thought to overcoming either the obstruction to his love or the futile love which has been its result, contenting himself with the daily proofs of his grievous situation. Gismund, however, manages to send him a message that informs him of a vault opening into her chamber, which may provide "recure of both our pain" (1. 766). When Guiszhard reads the letter, his grief turns to an unbounded joy which rises to the following heroic close:

> Not onely through a darke and dreadfull vaut,
> But fire and sword, and through what euer be,
> Mistres of my desires, I come to thee. (11. 799–801)

In the joy which succeeds his grief, however, the primary inspiration is not the "recure" of pain but the more dangerous test to which his formerly passive love will now be put. To the former proofs of suffering, he now longs to add the final proof of his love's ability to withstand "fire and sword." His joy comes from this imaginative leap to the thought of possible death for love. From what has passed it would appear that the aim of his love is not satisfaction but a purgative ordeal which proceeds through suffering to joyful death.

Guiszhard has not long to wait for this satisfaction of his infinite desire, for Tancred, coming upon their fatal union[2] by accident, sentences him to death. Brought before Tancred, Guiszhard joyfully accepts his fate:

> Then this hath been my fault, for which I ioy
> That in the greatest lust of all my life,
> I shall submitte for her sake to endure
> The pangues of death. Oh mighty Lord of loue
> Strengthen thy vassall, boldlie to receaue
> Large wounds into this body for her sake. (11. 1252–1257)

This is the only place in the Elizabethan tragic drama in which the historical connection between Courtly Love and a "Religion of Love" has been clearly retained. Guizhard is not so much the vassal of his lady as of the "mighty Lord of loue," and he joys that in the religious service of this love he may prove worthy to endure the final test of purgative suffering.

At his execution, Guiszhard is forced to explain to the non-initiates who wrongly bemoan his fate that he is "far more glad apaide/ Death to imbrace thus for his Ladies sake,/ Than life, or all the ioyes of life" (11. 1467–9), which presumably include the earthly satisfaction of his love. Such a death he sees to be the highest reward for the purity of his love. Gismund had earlier accepted "the fortune of my starres" and now Guiszhard embraces this fortune joyfully:

> This was to him of all the ioyes that might
> Reuiue his heart, the chiefest ioy of al,
> That, to declare the faithfull heart which he
> Did beare to her, fortune so wel did fall,
> That in her loue he should both liue and die. (11. 1481-5)

Purified by suffering, ennobled by faith, he goes eagerly to meet the true fulfillment of his ceaseless desire in a transfigured love-death.

Gismund approaches her own death by poison with no less eagerness:

> So now is come the long expected houre,
> The fatall hower I haue so looked for. . . .
> Lo here, this harty draught . . .
> Dreadlesse of death (mine Earle) I drink to thee.
> So now worke on, now doth my soul begin
> To hate this light, wherein there is no loue. . . .
> Now passe I to the pleasant land of loue,
> Where heauenly loue immortall flourisheth: . . . (11. 1605-6,
>   1717, 1719-20, 1725-6)

Here is made explicit the mystic's hatred of the material and evil world and the longing for union with the source of "heauenly loue." Both have longed for a love which could only be fulfilled in death. This death has not, however, been desired as an end in itself but as the ultimate witness to the triumph of their spiritual purity over that hated "light, wherein there is no loue." Gismund dies to prove herself worthy of Guiszhard's "pure loue" (1. 1732) just as his "chiefest ioy" was that "fortune so wel did fall" that he was enabled to give her this ultimate proof of his "faithfull heart."

Though love has transfigured death, they do not die in order to achieve a personal reunion. Gismund was, of course, alive when Guiszhard joyfully embraced his death. He joyed simply "that in her loue he should both liue and die," that his truth to love had been consistently proven in all his actions up to the last. Love had been a spiritual discipline that had taught him how to face the sufferings of life and death with joy. Gismund, too, though she calls heaven and hell to "Witnesse with me I die for his pure loue/ That liued mine" (11.1732–33), does not die to be personally reunited with Guiszhard but, rather, to pass "to the pleasant land of loue,/ Where heauenly loue immortall flourisheth." Though she dies to affirm the truth of her love, the reward of her truth in the afterlife will be her admittance to "heauenly loue." Both have been the humble vassals of the "mighty Lord of loue" and if death seems to promise them the true joy for which they have suffered, this joy transcends the earthly instruments that brought them thither. The true mistress of Guiszhard's desires is not Gismund but "heauenly loue immortall."

In the very sufferings which enable them to achieve a transfigured death, moreover, there was no element of that personal melancholia which is to dominate the behavior of courtly lovers in later Elizabethan tragedy. If Guiszhard equated the loss of life with that which he "esteemed least," it was in virtue of the higher value of a deathless love which he reverenced with a religious faith. When Gismund's soul begins "to hate this light," it is with a divine hatred which places her in the company of "the Gods" who equally "abhorre the company of men" (1. 1727). The personal element is almost entirely absent not only from their relationship but from the very quality of their love. They move unquestioningly through a quasi-religious ritual which purifies their souls to the point where they can convert the terrors of death into joy. Guiszhard had earlier identified the "darke and dreadfull vaut," leading to union with his mistress, with death, but, in dying for a transcendent love, he as well as she becomes "dreadlesse of death." Their love has not only robbed death of its proper dread but converted this dread into a promise of joy. In the sufferings which prefigure the final "pangues of death," Guiszhard had also experienced a kind of joyful wonder. If their love impels them towards suffering and death, it also transmutes not only their own characters but the quality of their torments.

They achieve a victory in defeat, and this in the largest

sense. Gismund appeals to the "sterne Goddesse of reuenging wrongs" (1. 1731) to witness her pure sacrifice for love, thus converting her very sacrifice into an instrument of revenge against the hated light. By such a death, the power of his daughter's love converts Tancred's blind opposition to its truth, and he enacts upon himself the penance of blindness and death. Though the chorus had counseled Gismund against love and against her suicide for it,[3] though Tancred's opposition had driven love to death, love triumphs over all caution and opposition as it meets death in pure radiance. In *Romeo and Juliet* the explicit mysticism of *Tancred and Gismund* is given immortal form.

Romeo and Juliet

Shakespeare's tragic masterpiece of Courtly Love was written in 1595,[4] when the vogue of courtly sonneteering was at its height. In considering "the fearful passage of their death-mark'd love,"[5] critics like E. E. Stoll have been at considerable pains to show that the love of Romeo and Juliet was the normal product of youthful innocence, that "not because there is anything wrong with them do the youth and maiden perish but only because 'love is strong as death,' and fate unfriendly."[6] Granville-Barker has written with greater insight into the specific characteristics of the youth and maiden which have made their love "strong as death," but he, too, misses the fuller implications of this love.[7] At the opposite extreme is Franklin Dickey who argues, from the vantage point of the Renaissance moralists, that Romeo and Juliet are afflicted with a love disease the evil consequence of which is death: "fortune has operated here to punish sin and . . . this avenging fortune is the work of heaven."[8] While Dickey performs a service in stripping the play of its romanticism and showing that the quality of its love leads inevitably to death, he is untrue to the tone of the play. *Romeo and Juliet* is not a tract against Courtly Love, but a supreme expression of its spiritual *mystique*. Of this Paul N. Siegel is clearly aware for, in relating the play to the conventions of a courtly "Religion of Love,"[9]

he has indicated the literary tradition through which this extraordinary work must be approached and so come closest to an
understanding of the precise nature of this love.

The love of Romeo and Juliet, while ever in fatal interaction
with the feuding world of Verona, yet exists on a plane of experience totally divorced from its normal expectations. The capsular
quality of this love, which can run its complete course without
betraying its secret existence, is, in fact, the subject of much
of the play's dramatic irony, Romeo's confidants patronizing his
love for Rosaline while his true love for Juliet is flowering and
Juliet's father bustling about her marriage while still believing
that it is an honor that she dreams not of. While this counter-
pointing of the brawling, bawdy, festive, and practical world
with the lovers' poetic night world is meaningful, the vitality
of the naturalistic presentation tends to obscure the poetic symbolism. The quasi-comic treatment of much of the play puts
readers on their guard against taking the lovers' utterances with
too much seriousness, and the lovers' occasional playfulness seems
to confirm the impression of youthful impetuousness, singing
bird-like of its joy.

But if Shakespeare has endowed romance convention with
an unusual naturalism, he, no less than the romancers, is vitally
concerned with "the allegory of love." Though his lovers react
with greater psychological realism to their dilemmas than do the
cardboard lovers of romance, they follow as unquestioningly an
implicit code of love and, in their poetic utterances, point to its
symbolic implications. Although the psychological and symbolic
levels are often interpenetrating, there are moments when the
symbolism becomes completely divorced from naturalistic presentation. When, for instance, Romeo refers to Juliet as his
"conceal'd lady" (III, iii, 98), the rhetoric of human love has
been completely displaced by one appropriate to a mystical religion of love.

The tragedy which is to so transcend the ordinary conventions of romance begins with a caricature of them. Romeo's
love for Rosaline has been "rais'd with the fume of sighs" (I, i,
197) and "nourish'd with lovers' tears" (I, i, 199). He has carefully conformed to all the prescribed rules of Courtly Love,

spending the night with tears and making "himself an artificial night" (I, i, 147) with the coming of day. But this stylized behavior is not so different from the convention which allows Romeo and Juliet to fall irrevocably in love at first sight and for Juliet quite naturally to say: "Go ask his name.—If he be married,/ My grave is like to be my wedding bed" (I, v, 136–7). These two loves are not different, then, in kind but in the quality of the poetry in which they are expressed, the earlier a patchwork of conventional Petrarchanisms, the later a profoundly mystical exploration.

Through this conventional behavior, however, suggestions of character do emerge. Romeo is a youth in search of an infinitely thrilling love, a love for which he is prepared to face suffering and even death. Though the indulgence of his feelings for Rosaline causes him to feel slightly ridiculous—"Dost thou not laugh?" (I, i, 190)—he cherishes "the devout religion of mine eye" (I, ii, 92) and longs to put it to the test. Hitherto sinking passively "under love's heavy burthen" (I, iv, 22), he is suddenly jarred from a purely imaginative to an active role by the suggestion that he compare his beloved's beauty with that of others at the Capulet feast.

Although he had only wished to view his love and prove the constancy of his heart, a sudden premonition of the danger of thus venturing into the enemy's camp elicits from him his first profoundly personal utterance:

> . . . my mind misgives
> Some consequence, yet hanging in the stars,
> Shall bitterly begin his fearful date
> With this night's revels and expire the term
> Of a despised life, clos'd in my breast,
> By some vile forfeit of untimely death.
> But he that hath the steerage of my course
> Direct my sail! On, lusty gentlemen! (I, iv, 106–13)

In this speech the character of Romeo emerges from the role of conventional courtly lover to reveal a deeper quality of doom.[10]

In terms of the action Romeo rightly fears that in so venturing to see Rosaline he may be forfeiting his life to fate, for it is from Tybalt's recognition of him at the feast that the fatal consequences of his exile are to issue. But however eager he was to nourish his "lover's tears," the prospect of possible death for the love of Rosaline is another thing. Suddenly faced with this prospect, he recognizes that such death would be a "vile forfeit." If he nonetheless continues his fatal voyage, it is no longer the desired sight of Rosaline but the challenge of fate which spurs him on. If fate has marked him out, he will not be "fearful" but hold his "despised life" in as much contempt.

Although it was earlier acknowledged that his immediate love for Juliet was a stock romance convention, this crucial speech, which just precedes his first sight of Juliet, may suggest a motivation for the fatal urgency with which he approaches his love. As he is risking his life in the name of a love which has not inspired him to the point where he can consider his life's loss as more than a "vile forfeit," his need for a truly inspirational love becomes urgent. Having accepted fate's challenge, he is now concerned to transmute this "vile forfeit" into a glorious surrender.

And this inspiration comes to him at the radiant sight of Juliet:

> O, she doth teach the torches to burn bright!
> It seems she hangs upon the cheek of night
> Like a rich jewel in an Ethiop's ear—
> Beauty too rich for use, for earth too dear! (I, v, 46–9)

Where Rosaline's beauty had left him in the utter darkness of an unhappy human love, Juliet's beauty, because it seems to him too precious for the usages of life, can truly illuminate the night. From this first encounter, however, Romeo conceives of his lady not as an ordinary mortal but as a symbol of divine beauty, which, in the "touching," can make him "blessed" (I, v, 53). His earlier premonition of death has been displaced by this intimation of heavenly blessing; but the close association of these two in "this night's revels" is significant.

From what has just been shown, we can see the way in which Shakespeare invests a stock convention of romance, that of love at first sight, with suggestions of both human motivation and symbolic implication. And what he has done for Romeo he does in lesser measure for Juliet: if Romeo meets Juliet at a fateful moment in his life, the same is true for her. She had just been informed by her mother that she must "think of marriage now" (I, iii, 69). And, although she had said that "it is an honour that I dream not of" (I, iii, 66), she is forced for the first time to consider marriage as a real and imminent possibility. In doing so, her maiden heart gains a new susceptibility which will cause her to look at men differently this night: "I'll look to like" (I, iii, 97).

As Romeo had come to the feast to behold Rosaline, feeling that in venturing thus into the enemy's camp he was forfeiting his life to fate, so does Juliet come to inspect the man to whom her parents would likewise have her dedicate her fate. Both, however, instead of looking where they had intended, seem compelled to make a last desperate comparison before their fate is irrevocably sealed. Under a similarly fatal urgency, Romeo finds in Juliet's radiant beauty the inspiration he had been seeking; and Juliet suddenly finds herself inspired by Romeo's passionate prayers. This love at first sight, then, is not simply a submission to fate but a choosing of their fate. When Romeo learns that "my life is my foe's debt" (I, v, 120) and Juliet the same, they can therefore accept their fate with a commitment that redeems it from being a "vile forfeit."

Their love has been born in the heart of obstruction, and if their knowledge of this crucial fact was "muffled still," the passionate need by which they found each other out could "without eyes see pathways to his will" (I, i, 178–9). For this central obstruction to their love, rather than deterring their passion serves only to intensify it: "Temp'ring extremities with extreme sweet" (II, Pro., 14). Romeo had chanced such an extremity in coming to the feast and Juliet in choosing another than the one her parents had appointed before they were aware of the true extremity they had embraced, and, when they do become aware of the obstruction to their love, they accept its necessity without question. Though Romeo and Juliet marry, their marriage so approximates the adulterous union of night that it even borrows from the troubadours the traditional verse form of the *aubade* or dawn song, which celebrates the adulterous lovers' hour of parting. "More light and light—more dark and dark our woes" (III, v, 36) is not the language of marriage but of lovers who "steal love's sweet bait from fearful hooks." (II, Pro. 8). The marriage of Romeo and Juliet, while it legitimizes that union which Gismund and Guiszhard stole without such sanction, in no way changes the obstructed situation which makes the necessity of their partings "such sweet sorrow" (II, ii, 186).

If their meetings can only take place in the night, night has for the lovers a special significance. They do not covet night for itself but because it is only then that the power of love can be truly illuminating. As has been seen, it is Juliet's radiance which first strikes Romeo.[11] Again, as he stands beneath the balcony, she appears to irradiate the night:

> But soft! What light through yonder window breaks?
> It is the East, and Juliet is the sun!
> . . . her eyes in heaven
> Would through the airy region stream so bright
> That birds would sing and think it were not night. . . .
> O, speak again, bright angel! for thou art
> As glorious to this night, being o'er my head,
> As is a winged messenger of heaven . . . (II, ii, 2–3, 20–2,
>   26–8)

Juliet converts the terrors of night to glory. It is for this reason that Romeo can say:

> I have night's cloak to hide me from their sight;
> And but thou love me, let them find me here.
> My life were better ended by their hate
> Than death prorogued, wanting of thy love. (II, ii, 75–8)

In a night containing Juliet's love, death need not be dreaded and is far preferable to his otherwise uninspired life. He eagerly

ventures into the night since it is only in "the dark night" that
Juliet's "true-love passion" (II, ii, 104–6) can be revealed. But
if Juliet's love robs death of its terror, it nonetheless is in intimate association with death. As Juliet informs Romeo, in a statement loaded with symbolic as well as practical meaning, the
place where she abides is "death, considering who thou art" (II,
ii, 64). Though Romeo faces a practical danger in approaching
thus close to her feuding kinsmen, it is also true on the symbolic
level that the approach to a Juliet who is heavenly "light" and
"bright angel"—that is, to a love object beyond the mortal condition—must ultimately be made by way of death.

Realizing that the way to his "bright angel" is barred by
his name, Romeo exclaims:

> Call me but love, and I'll be new baptiz'd;
> Henceforth I never will be Romeo. . . .
> Had I it written, I would tear the word. (II, ii, 50–1, 57)

Though Romeo feels that the receipt of Juliet's love would be
a rebirth for him, the rebirth in the heavenly love which Juliet
represents requires not simply the tearing of his name but of
the mortal self which that name identifies. Yet however much
it may be symbolic of death, he embraces the night in which
the infinitude of Juliet's love has been disclosed as a "blessed,
blessed night!" (II, ii, 139).

As Juliet symbolizes a divine love to Romeo, even answering
him with a celestial accent, so he assumes a similar role to her.
In Juliet's invocation to night, the full implications of this worship of night are revealed:

> Come night; come, Romeo; come, thou day in night;
> For thou wilt lie upon the wings of night
> Whiter than new snow upon a raven's back.
> Come, gentle night; come, loving, black-brow'd night;
> Give me my Romeo; and when he shall die,
> Take him and cut him out in little stars,
> And he will make the face of heaven so fine

> That all the world will be in love with night
> And pay no worship to the garish sun. (III, ii, 17–25)

Romeo is a creature of night, and, as such, Juliet coaxes night to loan her Romeo until such time as he shall die and be returned to night, arguing that when such a true lover should be returned by death he would impart a special glory to the love of night. Though night and death are here seen to be interrelated and Romeo in their power, it is yet his special virtue to irradiate their darkness. As Juliet had emblazoned the night for Romeo, so he to her is "day in night." While disdaining "the garish sun," that which exhibits all the concreteness and limitations of terrestrial life, it is not the annihilating darkness of night in itself which they worship but the special radiance of the limitless which shines for them in the heart of darkness. If night is symbolic of death, death itself is but the other face of the Infinite.

Romeo's catechism of love concludes on such a note of infinite aspiration:

> I am no pilot; yet, wert thou as far
> As that vast shore wash'd with the farthest sea,
> I would adventure for such merchandise. (II, ii, 82–4)

He had earlier accepted fate's steerage of his sail to whatever death might chance; now that his fate is revealed to him in the person of Juliet he eagerly embarks on the fearful passage to that "farthest sea." In Juliet's pledge of infinite love, her love becomes one with that same sea:

> My bounty is as boundless as the sea,
> My love as deep; the more I give to thee,
> The more I have, for both are infinite. (II, ii, 133–5)

And Romeo will prove a "desperate pilot" (V, iii, 117) as he navigates his "seasick weary bark" (V, iii, 118) to the port of his infinite desire. The "vast shore wash'd with the farthest sea" where the symbolic Juliet abides is, as she had told him, death to him; but he sees it only under the aspect of eternity. It is, however, the eternity enclosed in the instant of love's fulfillment, an instant for which death is a small price:

> But come what sorrow can,
> It cannot countervail the exchange of joy
> That one short minute gives me in her sight.
> Do thou but close our hands with holy words,
> Then love-devouring death do what he dare—
> It is enough I may but call her mine. (II, vi, 3–8)

Using conventional love rhetoric, Romeo rightly describes their meeting as one of enemies: "I have been feasting with mine enemy,/ Where on a sudden one hath wounded me/ That's by me wounded" (II, iii, 49–51). From the perspective of life, they are each other's true enemies, for their love's fulfillment means their death. If the love of Romeo and Juliet aspires to the Infinite and tends to clothe the other in symbolic garments, they remain for all this convincingly real characterizations and, on their non-allegorical dimension, undergo the natural conflicts that such a "death-mark'd love" must occasion.

Juliet had reminded Romeo of the danger in pursuing her love, but she soon begins to perceive that her acceptance of his love is likewise dangerous to her. And with this recognition, reason arises to stop the headlong plunge:

> Although I joy in thee,
> I have no joy of this contract to-night.
> It is too rash, too unadvis'd, too sudden;
> Too like the lightning, which doth cease to be
> Ere one can say 'It lightens.' (II, ii, 116–20)

It is not this contract, however, but her own "true-love passion" which has, with such sudden rashness, left the shore of enduring content. The need to overcome the internal resistance to her love causes it to develop into an even more reckless passion than Romeo's. Whereas he was content with the mere exchange of lover's vows, she insists upon a binding consummation of their love from which there can be no release but death.

No such doubts arise to divide Romeo's spirit. It is the Friar who must reply to his "sudden haste" (II, iii, 93), "Wisely, and slow. They stumble that run fast" (II, iii, 94). But even the Friar is caught up by the impetuousity of the lovers' infinite longings to "make short work" (II, vi, 35). While Romeo has shown no hesitation in pursuing his love, he soon finds it not such a simple matter to tear his name. However fully his spirit may assent to the aims of his love, his human situation does cause some resistance to it.

This is fully brought out in the duel between Romeo and Tybalt. Romeo first counters Tybalt's overtures in the conviction that he is "new baptiz'd" by love. With Mercutio's death on his hands, however, Romeo realizes that he is a Montague still and that, in wishing to deny this fact, he had proved false to himself: "O sweet Juliet,/ Thy beauty hath made me effeminate/ And in my temper soft'ned valour's steel!" (III, i, 118–20). Juliet had called her place "death, considering who thou art," and now Romeo once again has a premonition that, being Romeo, his pursuit of love into the enemy's camp will prove fatal: "This day's black fate on moe days doth depend;/ This but begins the woe others must end" (III, i, 124–5). And again he accepts his fate and challenges Tybalt. Having killed him and understood that the consequences will be disastrous, however, his old fear arises once more and causes him to cry out: "O, I am fortune's fool!" (III, i, 141). As before he had feared, when accepting fate's challenge, that his "untimely death" would be a "vile forfeit," so, now that fate lowers once again, the prospect of his death seems inglorious. The Prince will immediately ask: "Where are the vile beginners of this fray?" (III, i, 146). And this is Romeo's fear, that his death will not be a glorious martyrdom for love but the vile execution of a street brawler. Even so, he would prefer vile execution to banishment: "Ha, banishment? Be merciful, say 'death';/ For exile hath more terror in his look,/ Much more than death" (III, iii, 12–4).

In his discussion of the implications of banishment, the essential quality of his love is again revealed:

'Tis torture, and not mercy. Heaven is here,
Where Juliet lives. . . . More validity,
More honourable state, more courtship lives
In carrion flies than Romeo. They may seize
On the white wonder of dear Juliet's hand
And steal immortal blessing from her lips . . . (III, iii, 29–
    30, 33–7)

Although viewed from one aspect, the place where Juliet lives is death, from another it is "Heaven," the source of purity and "immortal blessing." In the "courtship" of this "immortal blessing" Romeo sees the only basis for "validity" and "honourable state." "Death, though ne'er so mean" (III, iii, 45), would be preferable to the continuance of a meaningless life, exiled from even the possibility of "immortal blessing," this indeed a fit symbol of hell: " 'banished'?/ O friar, the damned use that word in hell;/ Howling attends it:" (III, iii, 46–8).

The Frair had said: "Affliction is enamour'd of thy parts,/ And thou art wedded to calamity" (III, iii, 2–3). The Friar's philosophy is always directed toward worldly well-being, and, from this perspective, in marrying Juliet Romeo has become "wedded to calamity." But to the Friar's advice, Romeo replies: "Hang up philosophy!/ Unless philosophy can make a Juliet" (III, iii, 57–8). Romeo sees "more validity" in "courtship" than in worldly philosophy.

Exiled from his love, he sees no alternative but to "fall upon the ground, as I do now,/ Taking the measure of an unmade grave" (III, iii, 69–70). Juliet, likewise, does not distinguish between his exile and his death. Thinking he is dead, she says: "Vile earth, to earth resign; end motion here,/ And thou and Romeo press one heavy bier!" (III, ii, 59–60) Learning he is exiled, she nonetheless exclaims: "I'll to my wedding bed;/ And death, not Romeo, take my maidenhead!" (III, ii, 136–7). Rejecting her life as "vile earth," she immediately leaps to the though of lying with Romeo in death. Like Romeo, she is "wedded to calamity," and in her decision to fulfill her wedding not with Romeo but with death, the meaning of this wedding becomes clear. It becomes yet clearer after the wedding's earthly consummation. Romeo's alternatives, "I must be gone and live, or stay and die" (III, v, 11) exist not only for this dawn but for as long as their love shall last. A premonition of this causes Juliet to see even the departing Romeo "as one dead in the bottom of a tomb" (III, v, 56).

If they are "wedded to calamity," however, it is partly because Juliet accepted his love so absolutely in the face of extreme obstruction. It is, in fact, the extreme passion generated by the impossible position she has created for herself that proves to be fatal. As Lady Capulet informs Juliet: "thou hast a careful father, child;/ One who, to put thee from thy heaviness,/ Hath sorted out a sudden day of joy" (III, v, 108–10). It is also Paris' understanding that "his wisdom hastes our marriage/ To stop the inundation of her tears" (IV, i, 11–12). Without knowing its true origin, Capulet recognizes her passion as a danger to her well-being, one which, he tells her, "without a sudden calm will overset/ Thy tempest-tossed body" (III, v, 137–8). In Capulet's figure, Juliet's passion is once again compared to the sea, but here the voyage on its waves is shown to be as dangerous for the "bark" (III, v, 134) of Juliet's mortal body as it is for Romeo's "seasick weary bark." But Juliet is now "past hope, past cure, past help!" (IV, i, 45)

Though Juliet hopes for a more positive solution to her plight, she herself can think of none other than death: "I'll to the friar to know his remedy./ If all else fail, myself have power to die" (III, v, 243–4). If this is not as immediate an impulse to death as she experienced upon thinking that the unknown Romeo might be married, or that he be dead, or upon learning that he was exiled, she does accept it as a final means by which to preserve the deathless integrity of her love. Though Juliet does not desire death, she does befriend death at every opportunity in which the imperfections of life would cause her to be untrue to the infinite purity of her love. And so, given the flawed nature of life, her absolute commitment does make her "star-cross'd" (I, Pro. 6). Having placed her "faith in heaven" (III, v, 207), above the contingencies of her mortal existence, it is no wonder that "heaven should practice stratagems/ Upon so soft a subject" (III, v, 211–2). The Friar is shortly to tell her grieving parents: "Heaven and yourself/ Had part in this fair maid; now heaven hath all,/ And all the better is it for the maid" (IV, v, 66–8). As long as both heaven and earth have part in Juliet, both will continue to practice stratagems against the other to her greater distress.

The Friar's strategem to preserve life with honor through a counterfeit death is, however, most interesting. Here, as always when we encounter a long-standing romance convention accepted without question, we may expect to find allegorical meaning. Although Juliet earnestly hopes that through this device she will be able "to live an unstain'd wife to my sweet love" (IV, i, 88), its allegorical suggestion is that the only remedy by which she can preserve her faith is death itself. And, indeed, it is this device which proves fatal. It is, moreover, symbolically accurate that the Friar's stratagem should be doomed to failure since it is not a remedy native to life but "A thing like death to chide away this shame,/ That cop'st with death himself to scape from it" (IV, i, 74–5). Since the battle is to be fought on death's home ground, it will hardly be able to cope with heaven's stratagems. The counterfeit death, not being a real alternative, can only delay this eventuality. It is a dramatic forestalling device which symbolically illustrates the "death-mark'd" quality of this love.

It does, however, permit a more telling view of Juliet's feelings toward death than does her actual death scene. If in her earlier poetry she had conceived of death as something "so fine/ That all the world will be in love with night," she now reveals a profound "terror of the place" (IV, iii, 39). No matter how amorous death may have been in her imagination—"I'll to my wedding bed;/ And death, not Romeo, take my maidenhead!"— when the reality presents itself, she shows no love but rather a "horrible conceit of death and night" (IV, iii, 38). The exuberant vitality of life is still strong within her and struggles to the end. Perceiving that the Friar's potion, whether through malice or mischance, might lead to her death, she hesitates in accepting the now apparent horrors of "death and night" until a hallucination depicting Romeo's mortal danger speeds her act. Then only does her love's truth surmount her terror of death to seek a deathless union: "Romeo, I come! this do I drink to thee."

(IV, iii, 59) Although Romeo's feelings concerning death will prove even more complex than Juliet's, he, too, will amorously embrace a death for which he feels not love but profound abhorrence. But if the lovers are not in love with death, they are so in love with their passion's power to transcend death that they rush to its embrace. Though Juliet had hoped that she would find Romeo with her upon awakening from "this borrowed likeness of shrunk death" (IV, i, 104), in her hallucinated state she drinks what she believes to be poison to join him in death.

The Friar's original plan for her is, however, matched by Romeo's dream:

> If I may trust the flattering truth of sleep,
> My dreams presage some joyful news at hand. . . .
> I dreamt my lady came and found me dead
> (Strange dream that gives a dead man leave to think!)
> And breath'd such life with kisses in my lips
> That I reviv'd and was an emperor. (V, i, 1–2, 6–9)

Beginning with the fact of his death, his joyful dream pictures him being revived to richer life by Juliet's kisses. Once again he experiences that infinite rebirth in love by which he feels "new baptiz'd." But well may he "trust the flattering truth of sleep" which tells him that he can only experience this joyous reunion with Juliet through death. The "joyful news" presaged by this dream is the apparent fact of Juliet's death, claimed by Balthasar as well as the Friar to be the state of highest felicity: "she is well, and nothing can be ill./ Her body sleeps in Capel's monument,/ And her immortal part with angels lives" (V, i, 17–9). While seemingly an ironic conclusion to his expectations, the news proves to be fully consistent with the thematic development of ideas in the dream as well as in the whole preceding play. The "joy past joy" (III, iii, 173) that Romeo has always anticipated in the company of Juliet is a joy beyond the compass of his mortal state.

Upon learning of Juliet's supposed death, Romeo resolves with conventional promptitude upon his own. But it is in his treatment of Romeo's confrontation with death that Shakespeare most fully illuminates the accepted conventions of Courtly Love. Though Romeo is dying in order to be united with Juliet, it is with a Juliet who has at last discarded all earthly vestiges to become pure symbol. And now the supreme symbolic function of Juliet becomes clear; she is the means which permits Romeo to confront his fate as a man with joy. If he has made "a dateless bargain to engrossing death" (V, iii, 115), this steadfast commitment to something beyond all mortal contingency raises him above the normal human condition. Juliet had earlier said of him:

> He was not born to shame.
> Upon his brow shame is asham'd to sit;
> For 'tis a throne where honour may be crown'd
> Sole monarch of the universal earth. (III, ii, 91–4)

As in his dream love made him an "emperor," so does the honor of his love make him the universal monarch, raise him to godhead. It is through love of a Juliet symbolically raised to divine status that he redeems his own divine birthright from the "shame" of mortality's yoke.

But the paradox of this desire for the Infinite is that it can only be fully embraced in death. It is important to note that nowhere does Romeo conceive of death as but a gateway to, in the words of Gismund, "the pleasant land of loue." Death for him is "love-devouring," "engrossing"; it is a final fact, but a finality irradiated by joy. It is the infinite freedom experienced in the ecstatic instant of self-annihilation. But to this note of ecstasy, Romeo now adds a deeper note of defiance: "Is it e'en so? Then I defy you, stars! . . . Well, Juliet, I will lie with thee to-night" (V, i, 24, 34). Romeo defies the stars and all mortal contingency by accepting the worst they have to offer, thereby transmuting it into a spiritual triumph.

The love-death as a defiance of fate becomes the dominant note as he approaches the tomb:

Thou detestable maw, thou womb of death,
Gorg'd with the dearest morsel of the earth,
Thus I enforce thy rotten jaws to open,
And in despite I'll cram thee with more food. (V, iii, 45-8)

Romeo here reveals what is probably his truest attitude toward death. Whereas before he had interpreted every symbolic identification of his love with death as a sign of its infinite glory, betraying no anxiety toward the actual fact of death, he now reveals a deep revulsion toward death. Far from glorious, death here is profoundly felt to be "detestable" and "rotten," and this not in reference to a death vilely brought about through insufficient inspiration or irrelevant accident but chosen by himself under the greatest of inspirations.

Why then, we may well ask, has he been so fatally hasty in choosing his present death? Paradoxical as it may seem, the source of his headlong rush toward death appears to lie not in a love of death but a horror of death so extreme that it has poisoned his life. Unable to accept the anxieties of a contingent mortal existence, he has advanced upon hateful death, daring it to do its worst. Rather than appear fearful of death and give death the victory, he triumphs over death by bringing it upon himself. Not in love of death, but, as he says "in despite I'll cram thee with more food." The ecstasy of self-annihilation at its profoundest level, then, is not due to a feeling of surrender to death but to the triumph of the unconquerable spirit over death, achieving the Infinite in its assertion of ultimate freedom.

It is in this spirit that he views not only his own approaching death but the death of Juliet:

I'll bury thee in a triumphant grave.
A grave? O, no, a lanthorn, slaught'red youth,
For here lies Juliet, and her beauty makes
This vault a feasting presence full of light. (V, iii, 83-6)

Juliet's irradiation of the night has been but a prelude to her radiance in death. When Romeo had earlier said that "her eyes in heaven/ Would through the airy region stream so bright/ That birds would sing and think it were not night," he did not think that such irradiation made the night less real but that it converted its terrors to glory. So is it now with death. To Romeo, Juliet has not outlived death but she has overwhelmed its horror in radiance. Romeo's exhilaration at the radiance of his love in death produces a "lightning" (V, iii, 90) of his antagonistic mood. In Juliet's triumph over mortality, Romeo sees his own, her excessive beauty in death proving an irresistible goad to his own triumphant conquest of death.

Seeing her deathlike state, Romeo arrives at his final and most complex view of death:

> Ah, dear Juliet,
> Why art thou yet so fair? Shall I believe
> That unsubstantial Death is amorous,
> And that the lean abhorred monster keeps
> Thee here in dark to be his paramour?
> For fear of that I still will stay with thee
> And never from this palace of dim night
> Depart again. Here, here will I remain
> With worms that are thy chambermaids. O, here
> Will I set up my everlasting rest
> And shake the yoke of inauspicious stars
> From this world-wearied flesh. (V, iii, 101–12)

Although his first view of Juliet's radiance in death had blinded him to the detestable nature of death, his primary abhorrence of it reasserts itself. He now sees its abode not as a "feasting presence full of light" but as the "palace of dim night" in which feast only the worms. But such a vision, rather than causing a retreat from death, provides a truer support to his fatal desires by making him the more "world-wearied" and anxious to assert his own superiority to the oppressive forces of mortal existence. Romeo finally triumphs over death not through denying its abhorrent nature but through facing the ugliest facts of death and, "in despite" of them, shaking off "the yoke of inauspicious stars." But, since the courage to accomplish this defiant act has come to him only through the inspiration of Juliet's love-death, Romeo achieves a final synthesis of his double vision of death, seeing death as, at one and the same time, "amorous" and "the lean abhorred monster." Romeo's death rapture is the triumph of infinite love over the detestable facts of death, a triumph accomplished only through this clear perception of its abhorrent nature. The death to which he goes is not, as in his dream, one which "gives a dead man leave to think," but the utter finality, "A dateless bargain to engrossing death!" (V, iii, 115). It is this ultimate union with Juliet in "everlasting rest" for which he had bargained with his stars and which he now claims:

> Come, bitter conduct; come, unsavoury guide!
> Thou desperate pilot, now at once run on
> The dashing rocks thy seasick weary bark!
> Here's to my love! *[Drinks.]* O true apothecary!
> Thy drugs are quick. Thus with a kiss I die. *[Falls.]* (V,
>   iii, 116–20)

Romeo's love finds its supreme fulfillment only in "love-devouring Death." To gain that infinite freedom from mortality which Juliet, in her unearthly radiance, has ever represented, Romeo had adventured farther than "the farthest sea," his "weary bark" carrying him even to "engrossing death." And, despite the "bitter conduct" to this end, such death proves at the last infinitely desirable and Romeo transcends even his own defiance of death to die with a kiss.

Juliet's death speech has not the poetic grandeur of Romeo's but, as she was ever "light a foot" (II, vi, 16), so she has that "lighting before death" (V, iii, 90) of which Romeo spoke. Seeing Romeo dead, all previous fears are overcome and she moves to death with cheerful alacrity:

> O churl! drunk all, and left no friendly drop
> To help me after? I will kiss thy lips.
> Haply some poison yet doth hang on them
> To make me die with a restorative. . . .
> Yea, noise? Then I'll be brief. O happy dagger!
> This is thy sheath; there rest, and let me die. (V, iii, 163–9)

Meeting death with a kiss, she dies "with a restorative," the joyous restoration of her initial freedom from constraint and contingency.

The play ends on this final note of the redemptive quality of a death so amorously embraced. Romeo and Juliet had both embraced death as the redemption of their ultimate freedom from mortality's "yoke"; in so doing, their deaths prove to be redemptive as well for the living. In love with the infinite peace they could find only in death, they had spurned the world of strife that gave them being. Now, in the radiant light of their pure sacrifice, the petty futility of that strife is seen. Their deaths not only restore the peace of Verona but confer upon them the special glory of being forever upheld as the city's most shining example of admired virture. The city immortalizes the "Poor sacrifices of our enmity." (V, iii, 304) who, almost as in a religious ritual, have vicariously atoned for the multiple sins of the populace. The example of their heroic transcendence of the compromises of life and the terrors of death illuminates the more humble path of the ordinary citizen as he attempts to justify, by a more consecrated life, the martyrdom of the gloriously "faithful" (V, iii, 302). Thus does Shakespeare conclude his great tragedy of a love that has throughout been vehicle and symbol of the "immortal blessing" conferred in the kiss of death. Though the character and reactions of the lovers have been explored in all their earthly reality, they, no less than Gismund and Guiszhard, have embarked on a spiritual journey which finds its promised haven only in a death transfigured by their religious devotion to the dictates of Courtly Love.

Romeo and Juliet is, like all great romance, deceptively simple. Although I have been primarily concerned with explicating its profounder complexities, the surface appearance of the lovers is itself revealing. Shakespeare's lovers move as unquestioningly through the ritual pattern of Courtly Love tragedy as do Gismund and Guiszhard. They accept the validity of the obstructing force and, although "passion lends them power, time means, to meet,/ Temp'ring extremities with extreme sweet" (II, Pro., 13-4), they never attempt an open solution of their extremities. Whereas Gismund had at least broached the subject of marriage to her father, Romeo and Juliet are both dead before Capulet has the faintest inkling of their love. Combined with this unwillingness to contest the obstructing force is the unquestioning alacrity with which they move to death upon learning of the death of the other.

It is, in fact, this lack of essential questioning of the necessity for the obstructing force that constitutes the classic pattern of this form of love tragedy and which gives to the lovers a superficial appearance of being innocently "star-cross'd." But if this unquestioning behavior has marked the lovers of romance from the beginning of the genre, so do we find romance conventions being used throughout the genre as the vehicle for presenting profounder allegorical meaning. The more human qualities of Shakespeare's lovers may sometime shrink from and cry out against their hopeless position and the dictates of their love, but in their actions they finally do accept both. It is in these actions, combined with the symbolic import of the love poetry, that the allegorical meaning of this love emerges. It would seem that, in the *mystique* of Courtly Love, the redemptive power of love arises from a passive assent to the necessity of the obstructing force which is then transcended in a self-sacrificial love-death. It is because Romeo and Juliet never questioned the validity of the obstruction that divided and destroyed them that they can become the "poor sacrifices of our enmity" and redeem the living. In the less pure Courtly Love tragedies which are to follow, this circle of redemption dwindles to the extent that the necessity of the obstructing force is actively and openly contested. And this extent is itself determined by the degree of faith the lovers have in their love. The greater the faith in the redemptive power of Courtly Love, the less do the lovers concern themselves with contesting the opposing values of society and the more eagerly do they embrace the love-death.

In the two Elizabethan tragedies thus far considered, the truth and value of Courtly Love has been assumed as the greatest perfection of the human spirit. But it is only in Shakespeare's tragedy that the death of courtly lovers has a cathartic effect upon the living. In this high moment of Elizabethan enthusiasm, the pure sacrifice of life for such infinite love has seemed to provide a meaning for life. But as the Elizabethan age draws to its ominous close, this power of love's inspiration fails. In the years to follow, love's sacrifice provides no meaning for the living and, in losing this meaning, loses also the power to inspire an answering ardor or to rise to its death in unstained radiance. It is only in this exuberant-with-life Elizabethan moment that the purity of "a dateless bargain to engrossing death" can be inspirational—and this moment ceases to be "ere one can say 'It lightens.' "

3

Redirections of the Courtly Ideal

Soliman and Perseda

If the Elizabethan flowering of the courtly ideal proved to be ephemeral, the signs of its enfeeblement were already visible within the period of its greatness. It is to these rather than to the classic tragedies of Courtly Love that we must look to understand the new form which the ideal of pure love had to take in the Jacobean period and the dramatic pattern which it followed. These signs are first to be seen in the only other Elizabethan tragedy of Courtly Love, *Soliman and Perseda*.

Now generally attributed to Kyd, *Soliman and Perseda* was written at approximately the same time[1] as *Tancred and Gismund* and, like it, is thoroughly grounded in the Medieval conventions of Courtly Love. The early treatment of the lovers is identical with that of chivalric romance: Erastus is the long-serving, humble lover; Perseda, the cruel mistress. Though prepared to die from the sufferings of love, Perseda, like Guinevere, refuses to listen to Erastus' explanation for the lost carkanet with which she pledged her favor. And he, like Lancelot, humbly accepts his lady's justice though it be a "hard doome of death" (II, i, 167). When she learns the truth about the carkanet and that Erastus has been forced to flee as an involved result of his attempt to recover it, she has a reversion of feeling: "Ah, poore Erastus, how thy starres malign" (II, ii, 32), His stars are malevolent, however, because he has, in accordance with the ritual of Courtly Love, devoted himself to the ennobling service of a cruel mistrss. But she, too, is only playing her part in a ritual which will lead them both to a noble death.

The pattern of this love is, however, drastically altered by the introduction of a new type of obstruction in the person of the lustful tyrant Soliman. Reunited at his court, the lovers are now obstructed by Soliman's desire for Perseda, a desire which is Worldly in so far as it refuses to accept obstruction. The effect of this introduction is to shift the focus of action to the conflict between Soliman and Perseda. While the courtly lovers in the classic pattern accept the validity of the obstruction and concern themselves primarily with the joys and sufferings of love, Perseda and her Jacobean followers are chiefly concerned with an open defiance of the obstruction. In *Soliman and Perseda* such defiance becomes acceptable because the obstructing force is not the voice of society upholding worldly well-being or marriage but simply an ignoble love exercising the power of a corrupt society. Nonetheless, the essential conflict is still one between a noble love directed at other than social well-being and the spiritually corrupt or deficient forces of social power. What is significant in the change is that instead of the conflict being one between a nobly illicit love and a socially acceptable marriage, it becomes one between faithful chastity and lust. Since the obstruction to true love is presented in such vicious tears, the beset lady can contest it to its face with full sympathy from the audience:

> *Per.* My thoughts are like pillers of Adamant,
> Too hard to take an new impression. . . .
> *Sol.* Why, thy life is doone, if I but say the word.
> *Per.* Why, thats the period that my heart desires. . . .
> Strike, strike; thy words pierce deeper then thy blows. (IV,
> i, 99–100, 105–6, 114)

Although true to Courtly Love in passively accepting the worst that can be offered as "the period that my heart desires," she

differs from the purer manifestations of this love in openly placing the onus for her death upon the obstructing force. This
deathless affirmation of her love momentarily daunts Soliman and
he reunites the lovers, but his tyrannical will soon repents
of his generosity and, despite the prickings of conscience, he
executes his rival:

> O vniust Soliman: O wicked time,
> Where filthie lust must murther honest loue. (V, ii, 90–1)

In this significant statement, Soliman defines the new terms of
dramatic conflict just discussed, ascribing it to the decadent sensibility of the time.

This change from passive acceptance to open defiance is, however, the mark of the lovers' own decline from the high purity
of their models. Erastus had jeopardized his character by using
false dice to win back the carkanet, and Perseda becomes even
more morally questionable. Her open defiance soon crosses the
fine moral line into active revenge. Learning of Erastus' death,
Perseda kills Lucina (who with her husband had aided Soliman's
amorous purposes) in self-righteous vindication of Erastus' and
her own abused innocence. But in thus revenging herself against
a "wicked time," she loses her own claim to innocence. This loss
is reflected in the fact that, upon learning that Soliman is coming
to claim her, she does not simply commit suicide to affirm her
truth but plans that her death should be destructive as well to
her enemy. Appearing disguised as a knight, she challenges him
to single combat:

> Thou murtherer, accursed homicide,
> For whome hell gapes, and all the vgly feendes
> Do waite for to receiue thee in their iawes:
> Ah, periur'd and inhumaine Soliman,
> How could thy heart harbour a wicked thought
> Against the spotlesse life of poore Erastus? (V, iv, 37–42)

Though her past murder of Lucina and present plans for Soliman's death should make her as much an "accursed homicide" as he, she feels herself as spotlessly innocent as Erastus, justifying all she does by this absolute claim to abused innocence. But however pure she may feel herslf to be, she has lost contact with the true *mystique* of Courtly Love. Whereas the true courtly lover *symbolcally* poisons the oppressors' victory through suicide, Perseda has so planned her suicide that she actually kills Soliman with a poisoned kiss. This movement into open conflict marks the decadence of Courtly Love, but it is still essentially courtly in that it does not further the lovers' earthly fulfillment but is only a means of inviting and inflicting death. It is, however, the pattern here established, or at least here first employed in the Eizabethan drama, which will be followed in the Jacobean tragedies of this love.

As an indicator of dramatic tendencies, *Soliman and Perseda* is a more significant play than *Romeo and Juliet,* for it better reflects the corruption of vision which, from the beginning of the dramatic period, infected the majority of courtly lovers on the Elizabethan stage. By 1599 this corruption became so complete that it was thereafter impossible for a tragic Courtly Love to be portrayed in its conventional form.

Antonio and Mellida

Una Ellis-Fermor has shown that Elizabethan vitality gave way, in the period beginning 1599, to a new mood which took the form of "a sense of impending fate, of a state of affairs so unstable that great or sustained effort was suspended for a while and a sense of the futility of man's achievement set in." [2] Nowhere in this sense of futility and suspended effort more enervating them in the love of Antonio and Mellida, presented in Marston's two-part play, written in 1599 and 1600, which bears their names. Although this double play cannot be considered a love tragedy, insofar as the first part is a tragicomedy and the second a revenge tragedy, it is most significant for my purposes because it marks the death of conventional Courtly Love as a tragic ideal.

The change from the coarse, practical, strife-ridden but still perfectible world of *Romeo and Juliet* to the satanically evil world of *Antonio and Mellida* is a measure of the change of mood which but a few years had wrought. In such a world the idealism of love can find no fitting soil for even its ephemeral bloom. It exists in a vacuum of its own making, as a state of mind abstracted from all sense of time, space, and causality, its only possible action being the contemplation of its own suffering.

At the very beginning of the play Antonio appears in an absolute state of anguish beyond the power of circumstance to alter or increase: "Lower than hell there is no depth to fall" (I, i, 34).[3] Abhorring life and desiring death, he is fatigued at the very idea of pursuing the fulfillment of his love: "Is death grown coy . . . But I must . . . try new fortunes . . . To purchase my adored Mellida" (I, i, 25–29). When Antonio finally reveals himself to Mellida, he does so "like himself, wretched and miserable" (II, i, 270). He immediately suggests flight, saying: "thou and I will live/ Like unmatch'd mirrors of calamity" (II, i, 296–7). And she, to whom such a picture of exile is congenial, leaves her love with the words: "Farewell, bleak misery" (II, i, 301). These lovers are in the same position as Romeo and Juliet; they are children of warring families. But, unlike the hopes of Shakespeare's lovers, the prospect of union holds nothing for them beyond the unmatched calamity to which they both assent. This calamity soon overtakes them as Mellida is captured while attempting to join her lover in the marsh. Love's "antidote,/'Gainst all the poison that the world can breathe" (IV, ii, 5–6) has lost its virtue in "this bleak waste" (IV, ii, 8) where Antonio must still live.

The first part has a tragicomic ending, mercy triumphing over hate and joining the lovers in the promise of a forthcoming marriage. But the playwright, for once, is more truthful than the conventions of tragicomedy demand and in the second part, *Antonio's Revenge,* Courtly Love is denied the possibility of arriving at the "highest point of sunshine happiness" (I, ii, 179)[4] in an earthly fulfillment. In *Antonio's Revenge* Mellida's father,

Piero, emerges as a full-fledged Machiavellian villain bent, among other evils, not only on frustrating but also poisoning the lovers' purity.

Piero stops the wedding by staging the apparent proof of his daughter's lust: "Her wedding eve . . . And found even cling'd in sensuality!" (I, ii, 228, 230). Later, at Mellida's trial for lust, Piero reverses his earlier tactics and has his accomplice clear Mellida by attributing lust to Antonio. So does Piero strive to poison the faith of each in the purity of the other's love. Piero, not understanding the nature of their love, thinks he can destroy it through slandering the purity which it holds so dear. As the presentation of Courtly Love gets further away from an inspired belief in its transfiguring power, so, too, does it tend to substitute a glorification of physical purity for what was originally meant to be a spiritual purity. No longer can the spiritually pure love of Gismund and Guiszhard be presented. To Marston they would be "found even cling'd in sensuality!"

But, while Antonio and Mellida still have faith in each other's love, this faith does not bring with it the attendant power to gladden life and glorify death. The lovers manage only one meeting in the second part (II, ii, 69–125), and this meeting reveals the complete enfeeblement of their love. Antonio, venting his woes by night, chances to pass the grate of Mellida's dungeon when she, too, is bemoaning her fate. He had not sought a meeting with his beloved, and when he meets her by accident he has nothing to say to her. Their conversation is heavy with fatigue and they part as soon as possible. Their love has absolutely no need of the other's presence. Mellida, though content to die for her love, does not expect Antonio to join her in death: "To-morrow I must die. . . . For loving thee. . . . Be patient, see me die; good, do not weep;/ Go sup, sweet chuck, drink, and securely sleep" (II, ii, 97–98, 114–5). Antonio, on his part, feels no power to pursue his love, either in life or death. "Somewhat I will do" (II, ii, 110), he says; but all he can think of is to kiss her hand and feebly second her resolve to die. Despite his "crushing anguish" (II, ii, 123), he says "I'll force my face/ To palliate my sickness" (II, ii, 116–7). His anguish is so absolutely a state of mind that no circumstantial relation to his beloved, whether

her presence or her possible death, can resolve it into action. He can neither live nor die for love.

But if for Antonio there is no necessary connection between his absolute suffering for love and death, the same is true for Mellida, her death for love being as unmotivated as his continuation of life. Antonio, who had assumed the habit of a fool to escape Piero, has it given out that he has drowned himself crying Mellida's name. News of his death might be cause enough for the noble death of a courtly lover were this the first time, rather than the third, that Mellida had believed her lover dead; but since she has twice outlived his supposed death, her mortal response to this third instance seems hardly to be credited. Before she dies, however, Mellida is robbed of even this coloring for her death. Present throughout her death scene in his fool's disguise, Antonio does not reveal himself to Mellida until she is too far gone to recover and then only to wish her "soft rest" (IV, i, 309). In restoring her momentarily to witness his lively presence, Antonio completely robs her sacrifice of any meaning. Well might Mellida consider the world "too subtle/ For honest natures" (IV, i, 299–300) if even her dearly loved Antonio wishes neither to prevent her death nor join her in it.

The final impotence of Courtly Love as a tragic ideal is revealed as much in Antonio's continuing behavior as in Mellida's death. For he who is so in love with death that he has three times reveled in the image of his death never feels the least necessity to cause it. His suicidal desire is completely satisfied with its vicarious fulfillment. Rather than join his "all heavenly" (IV, ii, 5) love in death, this whining malcontent resolves to live so that he may curse others with "like misery" (IV, ii, 20). Being "the very Ooze,/ The quicksand that devours all misery" (IV, ii, 15–16), this final wrong strengthens rather than weakens his hold on life, and this despite his promise to follow her to death upon completing his revenge.

It is, in fact, the failure of his decadent Courtly Love that causes him to take up revenge. Since he lacks the faith to trancend the world's evils, he lashes out against them. This movement begins right after the complete failure of inspiration in his love, which he experienced in his chance meeting with Mellida.

His encounter with her is shortly followed by a visit to his father's tomb, where he says: "Tomb, I'll not be long/ E'er I creep in thee" (III, i, 13–4). Only then does his father's ghost appear, saying: "Thy pangs of anguish rip my cerecloth up. . . . Revenge my blood!" (III, i, 32, 36). Antonio, who professes to hate life and love Mellida, has actually brought upon himself the revenge motive which keeps him from joining Mellida in death. Though this revenge is partly made in the name of his disappointed and disappointing love, in affirming the purity of his love through revenge rather than death, he only proves the corruption of his love. And, when the revenge for which he had temporarily postponed his death is accomplished, Marston's own decadence permits the conspirators to "live enclos'd/ In holy verge of some religious order" (V, ii, 151–2). His foul revenge left unpunished, Antonio merely resolves: "For her sake, here I vow a virgin bed" (V, iii, 158). Hating the evils of life and in love with the perfection Mellida represents, Antonio has not the faith in his own spiritual truth to transcend his abhorred life in a radiant love-death.

Antonio is the mouthpiece of a generation that has lost faith in the actualization of the ideal, and in losing this faith loses also faith in the inspirational power of Courtly Love. As such, Marston's *Antonio and Mellida* is a significant play rather than a great one. For, in it, Courtly Love is no more than a relic of a former age of faith asked to perform miracles beyond its power.

Though this play marks the final impotence of conventional Courtly Love as a *tragic* ideal, it is through its various influences that the Medieval formulation of Courtly Love continues as a vital factor in the Jacobean drama. The influence of Antonio extends in two directions, that of revenge tragedy and of the Fletcherian forms of both tragicomedy and False Romantic Love tragedy. With the character of Bel-imperia in *The Spanish Tragedy*, Kyd began the association of Courtly Love with revenge [5] that distinguishes, to greater or lesser extent, the whole genre of Elizabethan revenge tragedy from its classical antecedents. The Aeschylean and typical Senecan revenger is prompted by honor to avenge the murder of an immediate member of his family. [6] While Hieronimo and Hamlet continue to operate primarily within this traditional concept of revenge, Antonio combines

this traditional motive with that of revenging the defeat of a re-
quited love; and, in *The Revenger's Tragedy,* the death of the
beloved becomes the sole motive of revenge in an entire tragedy.
Such a revenger as Vendici is an embittered and disenchanted
courtly lover and his impulse toward revenge has its primary origin in the bitterness of his disenchantment. But whereas Romeo
and Juliet's sacrifice of self redeemed both themselves and their
society, in sacrificing others rather than himself to his ideal of
good, the revenger loses the power to redeem either himself or
the society he would scourge. He has moved even beyond the
courtly lover who contests the powers of destruction, for if such a
courtly lover has lost the power to redeem society, he still has
power to redeem himself. It is, then, a completely disenchanted
Courtly Love that continues as a factor in later revenge tragedy.
And what is true of this genre is also true of the appearance of
Courtly Love in the Fletcherian genres. The essential point about
the false romantic lover is, of course, that his early idealism was
false; and the very form of tragicomedy marks a retreat from
tragic idealization. What is most significant about the Antonio
tradition is that its particular kind of romantic sensibility demands forms of expression other than that of Courtly Love tragedy proper. In their different ways, however, the various genres
peopled by the progeny of Antonio all openly proclaim the futility of idealism.

But if, after *Antonio and Mellida,* conventional Courtly
Love is no longer a viable tragic ideal, the Jacobean drama does
contain an analogous form of the tragedy of pure love, an analogy
drawn from antiquity. In the Jacobean period, it is only possible
to present the tragedy of pure love if it is formulated in terms
of either Stoicism or a stoical Neo-Platonism. Such an association
of spiritual disciplines is not surprising for, as Erich Auerbach
has shown, Stoicism, Platonism, and Courtly culture are all forms
of a similar "turning away from reality." [7] Courtly culture is,
however, distinctive in its exaltation of heterosexual romantic
love. Though Stoicism is a classical ideal, antiquity offers us no
examples of Stoic love tragedy. It is for this reason that the
Jacobean manifestations of "Stoic Love" may be considered as a
reformulation of Courtly Love.

In the Jacobean period, then, Courtly Love appears in two

forms, to both of which Marston was a major contributing factor. In the progeny of Antonio the conventional form of Courtly Love continues, but in genres other than that of Courtly Love tragedy. In *Sophonisba,* however, he revives the tragedy of pure love in the transmuted form of Stoic honor. But the redefinition of ideal love in this chastened form bears equal witness to the decline of faith in this ideal. When Marston revives Courtly Love tragedy, he does so not in terms of its "classic pattern" but of the "conflict pattern" which Kyd (?) had developed in *Soliman and Perseda.* In this he is followed by the only other Jacobean tragedy of Stoic Love, *The Second Maiden's Tragedy.* These tragedies, then, can properly be considered as part of the decadent tradition of Courtly Love.

Sophonisba

Antonio's Revenge ends with the hope that "th' immortal fame of virgin faith" may be presented more fully in the future in "some black tragedy" (V, iii, 178, 180). When, in 1605, Marston again turns to tragedy, it is to give this fuller presentation of "Womens right wonder, and just shame of men" (V, iii, p. 63).[8] Once again woman becomes symbolic of the heroic faith that men adore but can no longer emulate. But since Marston's earlier attempt to present a pure Courtly Love had only revealed the sterility of this ideal in his eyes, the nature of this faith has to be transformed before it can prove inspirational even for woman. Transmuted into the form of Stoic honor, however, love proves once again capable of inspiring an exalted death.

This transmutation is fully revealed in the words with which Sophonisba sends Massinissa into battle on their wedding night:

> Thinke every honor that doth grace thy sword
> Trebbles my love: by thee I have no lust
> But of thy glory: best lights of heaven with thee!
> Like wonder stand, or fall, so though thou die
> My fortunes may be wretched, but not I. (I, ii, p. 18)

Sophonisba's love is so equated with honor that it is only through the appreciation of honor that it can be inspired and increased. In her marriage to Massinissa she desires not earthly happiness but glory. In this Massinissa heartily assents: "Fame got with losse of breath is godlike gaine" (I, ii, p. 18). Unlike traditional courtly lovers, however, they refuse to consider physical ecstasy even as symbolic of this "godlike gaine." Sophonisba scorns the "faint pleasures" (I, ii, p. 18) of the flesh; and Massinissa, in approaching the marriage bed, had prayed that even these might be as minimal as possible. When the forthcoming consummation is interrupted by news of the war, neither of the lovers shows the slightest displeasure. Both feel that even marital pleasure is a temptation from true honor and would seem to really prefer a completely chaste love devoted exclusively to the "godlike gaine" of honorable death. It is certainly Sophonisba's greatest satisfaction and claim to honor that she dies a "Virgin wife" (V, iii, p. 61). With Marston, the identification of spiritual with physical purity becomes complete.

If Sophonisba and Massinissa seem threatened by their own physical desires, their fears are fully justified when we see the result of indulging such desires. When "lust" is not directed toward glory but, as with Syphax, toward physical satisfaction, it embraces not the highest but the grossest deformity of nature. The contrast between these "lusts" is not only thematic but the primary source of dramatic conflict. Once again we find "filthie lust" pitted against "honest loue" as Syphax' lust, aided by corrupt political power, obstructs the earthly union of pure love. While Massinissa is fighting honorably to protect Carthage against Syphax' revenge, the Carthaginian senate treacherously goes over to Syphax' side and votes to give Sophonisba over to him. She, after vigorously condemning their action, accepts their decree. Holding "lifes losse/ To be no evill" (II, i, p. 23), she eagerly embraces the worst fate has to offer as a means of winning a spiritual victory over it: "Without misfortune Vertue hath no glorie" (II, i, p. 23). While Syphax awaits his lust's satisfaction, she goes to him prepared to gain a far different prize.

In the ensuing conflict between lust and spiritual purity, Sophonisba, like Perseda, openly contests the value of Syphax' power to constrain her free spirit: "Thou maiest inforce my body but not mee" (III, i, p. 32). But, also like Perseda at that stage of her development, she seeks a passive victory through suicide. Gaining time to make a sacrifice to the gods, she prays: "all that I crave/ Is but chast life or an untainted grave" (III, i, p. 36). When, however, she discovers the secret exit through which her earthly freedom might become possible, she prays once more, this time only for death: "Harke Gods, my breath/ Scornes to crave life: graunt but a well famde death" (III, i, p. 38). Overtaken by Syphax, she faces his desire with her own: one show of force, she tells him, and "this good steele,/ Shall set my soule on wing" (IV, i, p. 45). Syphax now tries to show her that her pro-claimed spiritual victory will be meaningless and brought to eventual shame through his own triumph: "Doe strike thy breast, know being dead, Ile use,/ With highest lust of sense thy sense-lesse flesh" (IV, i, p. 45). This moves Sophonisba, in one of her rare touches of humanity, to pity him for that very depth of in-humanity which has lost even the sense of its own horor: "I shame to make thee know,/ How vile thou speakest" (IV, i, p. 45). But she tries patiently to make him understand that in actualizing "imaginations utmost sin" (IV, i, p. 45) he will bring not her but himself into utter vileness. His supposed victory, she affirms, is his true defeat and cannot touch the deathless integrity of her love: "know I live or die/ To Massinissa" (IV, i, p. 45). The force of her argument finally does impress itself upon his mind and, for the moment, he grants her an actual as well as theoretical victory: "Thinke Syphax—Sophonisba rest thine owne,/ . . . Creature of most astonishing vertue,/ . . . We dote not on thy body, but love thee" (IV, i, p. 45). For this one mo-ment, Syphax is actually inspired with love for Sophonisba, a love identified as always in this play with the appreciation of "astonishing vertue."

But, though he is momentarily carried away from himself, such love is alien to his nature. His desire for Sophonisba, as it has been presented from the beginning, did not commence in love or even in pure lust but in scorned pride at her rejection of his suit. It is his loss of reputation that causes his true suffering, as is shown when he inveighs against this universal need that "makst mortals sweat/ Bloud and cold drops in feare to loose, or hope/ To gaine thy never certaine seldome worthy gracings./ Reputation!" (I, i, p. 9). This is an important speech because it introduces the play in which the desire for "reputation" afflicts both the virtuous and vile. But where the virtuous believe that "fame" is only a "godlike gaine" when it is "got with losse of breath," the vicious think fame is to be achieved not through self-destruction but the destruction of others.

As the virtuous desire for "fame" is the source of virtuous love, so the vicious desire for "reputation" becomes the source of vicious love or lust. Thinking himself disgraced by Sophonisba's rejection, Syphax wishes her to feel the depth of such disgrace. His lust for her is born of his desire to revenge himself against her former scorn. But perhaps this is the true origin of lust, at least in a sensitive being. Malraux has offered this very explanation: "'Lust,' he thought, 'is the humiliation of oneself or of the other person, perhaps of both.'" [9] At any rate, this is the explanation of his behavior which Syphax offers Sophonisba when he finally has her in his power:

> For all thy scornefull eyes thy proud disdaine,
> And late contempt of us now weele revenge,
> Breake stubborne scilence: looke Ile tack thy head
> To the low earth, whilst strength of too blacke knaves
> Thy limbs all wide shall straine: praier fitteth slaves. (III,
>   i, p. 32)

Against such a perverted passion, Sophonisba beseeches him to "Be but a beast,/ Be but a beast" (III, i, p. 32). She rightly sees that a frankly bestial lust would be less humiliating to both their human dignities than this fruit of scorned pride.

Syphax receives the first proof of the self-humiliation effected by lust when he eagerly approaches the bed in which he expects to find Sophoniba only to find the guard, Vangue, whom Sophonisba had drugged and placed there before her escape: "Hah! can any woman turne to such a Divell?/ Or: or: Vangue, Vangue—" (III, i, p. 38). The full implications of this hellish embrace of lust are most brilliantly developed in the sequence with the witch. Immediately after Syphax' apparent succumbing to Sophonisba's forcible argument against his lust, his desires rebel and cause him to seek out the magic art of the witch. She promises to charm Sophonisba to his bed, but takes Sophonisba's place herself. As he approaches, Syphax says: "Sophonisba thy flame/ But equall mine, and weele joy such delight/ That Gods shall not admire, but even spight" (IV, i, p. 50). But discovering his delusion, he cries out in horror: "Thou rotten scum of Hell—/ O my abhorred heat! O loath'd delusion!" (V, i, p. 51). In desiring such delusive charms, Syphax has sought his hell. With full realization of the horror of such lust, he now rejects the excessive flame, earlier exalted as worth the gods' envy, as an "abhorred heat." By such symbolic use of witchcraft, Marston not only brings Syphax to witness the horror of his desires but also indicates the just reason for Sophonisba's resistance to the excessive physical fulfillment of her pure love for Massinissa. Did Sophonisba's "flame/ But equall" Syphax' even for Massinissa, it would be an equally "abhorred heat."

Sophonisba's passion, however, is far more fatal. Fleeing from the Roman legions who have defeated Syphax' troops, she stops a Lybian soldier, who later discloses himself to be Massinissa, with a plea which is a significant prelude to their reunion:

> O save me from their fetters and contempt,
> Their proud insultes, and more then insolence,
> Or if it rest not in thy grace of breath,
> To grant such freedome, give me long wishd death,
> For tis not much loathde life that now we crave,
> Onely an unshamd death, and silent grave
> Wee will now daine to bend for. (V, iii, p. 58)

Her plea for freedom from the insulting fetters of a Roman triumph is but a lesser form of the freedom from mortal constraint which she envisions in the "silent grave." Even were she granted "such freedome" to live unconstrained, she would still view it as a "loathde life." This being so, her initial plea is soon

disclaimed in favor of her true desire for "long wishd death."
At the expression of such a wish, Massinissa hails her as a
"rarity" (V, iii, p. 58). Earlier, when he had been told that his
Sophonisba had been possessed by Syphax, he had said: "Libea
hath poyson, aspes, knives, & to much earth/ To make one grave,
with mine? not, she can dye" (III, ii, p. 41). Massinissa loves
Sophonisba for the same reason that she loves him, in appreciation of her lust for glory; and as the greatest glory must be
purchased with "losse of breath," he has no doubt that she would
die before shaming her bed. When he now sees her praying for
"an unshamd death," he is thrilled by this confirmation of his
faith.

Having celebrated her desire for noble death, he now promises her the lesser freedom from Roman constraint. Her response
to this is only the negative "We cannot now be wretched" (V, iii,
p. 58). She recognizes in such a free life the lessening of misery
but not any addition of joy. But when Massinissa declares that
"this night be loves high feast" (V, iii, p. 58), Sophonisba, for the
first time in the play, becomes panicky. At the thought of the
overwhelming joys of physical consummation, she cries out for
protection to Jove: "O'rewhelme me not with sweetes, let me not
drinke,/ Till my breast burst, O Jove thy Nectar, thinke" (V,
iii, p. 58). She fears profoundly the change that might be wrought
in her own nature by her loss of chastity, that the physical consummation of her marriage would dissipate the power of her
spiritual lust for glory. Convinced that physical pleasures are
faint in comparison with spiritual joys, she now not only does
not desire but actually fears any earthly happiness as a temptation
from the greater spiritual proof she covets, a proof of the highest
honor possible only through death.

The opportunity of such a proof is soon forthcoming. Sophonisba could not achieve this proof, however, without the aid
and abetment of Massinissa, this both during and before her final
triumph. When Massinissa had Syphax in his power, instead of
killing him he said: "Rise, rise, cease strife,/ Heare a most deepe
revenge, from us take life" (V, ii, p. 55). It is true that he was
"reddy to kil him" (stage direction, V, ii, p. 55), and only relented
after Syphax informed him of Sophonisba's purity. Still, it was

through thus granting him life that Syphax was freed to commit his final treachery against Sophonisba.

Such forgiveness, moreover, is consistent with Massinissa's character. Earlier, when Asdrubal, Sophonisba's father, had come under cover of friendship to further Syphax' desires, Massinissa, being informed of the treacherous plot to have him poisoned, had said to the poisoner, Gisco:

> Gisco th' art old,
> Tis time to leave off murder, thy faint breath
> Scarce heaves thy ribs, thy gummy bloud-shut eyes,
> Are sunke a great way in thee, thy lanke skinne,
> Slides from thy fleshlesse veines: be good to men,
> Judge him, yee Gods, I had not life to kill
> So base a creature, hold Gisco ( ) live,
> The God-like part of Kings is to forgive. . . . (II, ii, p. 26)

Massinissa, like Sophonisba, is moved by the spectacle of utter depravity to a feeling of compassion which is truly "God-like." Also like her, he tries to impress upon a warped mind the logic of virtue and to reveal its quality through his own actions.

But the highly principled behavior of Sophonisba and Massinissa is lost upon the world they inhabit. A measure of its depravity is indicated by Asdrubal's action. We have seen that in almost all of the plays it is the heroine's father that proves the chief obstruction. The purest form of this is given in *Tancred and Gismund* where it is simply parental displeasure which obstructs the union. With *Romeo and Juliet,* parental displeasure becomes firmly grounded in the legitimate values of social well-being, the father trying to assure an acceptable marriage for his daughter. In *Sophonisba,* however, the father not only supports the desires of a lustful lover but tries to further this claim by having his daughter's legitimate husband murdered. This change marks the difference in the nature of the society to whose values the fathers are always dedicated. However imperfect and prosaic was the society in the earlier plays, it still represented the conditions of productive life. The society portrayed in *Sophonisba,* on the other hand, is totally corrupt.

The way in which the corruption of society undermines the honorable intentions of the lovers is early indicated when the Carthaginian senate, betrays their honorable warrior, Massinissa: "And see by this he bleedes in doubtfull fight:/ And cries for Carthage . . . When Carthage is/ So infinitely vile" (II, i, p. 22). The "seldome worthy gracings" of "reputation," against which Syphax had earlier inveighed, now prove to be equally true of honorable "fame." The ends to which it is immediately dedicated prove totally unworthy of the sacrifice. Moreover, honorable behavior in a world "so infinitely vile" dooms the virtuous, making them the easier prey of malice. It is ultimately, however, because the world proves so infinitely unworthy of their sacrifice that the truly honorable are inspired to their supreme acts of heroism. These are felt to be even more glorious when embraced for no other reward than the awareness of having remained honorable in a world so vile. Thus Massinissa praises "above the Gods" that man who can maintain his virtue against all worldly temptation, "Having no pay but selfe wept miserie,/ And beggars treasure heapt" (III, ii, p. 41).

The person who covets this "beggars treasure" may, however, become rigid in fulfilling the absolute letter of the code of honor. The rigidity which may result from the lust for glory is revealed in the final scene between Sophonisba and Massinissa. As she is praying for help to safeguard her against the temptation of physical pleasure, a messenger from Scipio enters, demanding Massinissa to surrender Sophonisba in obedience to their "mutuall league of endles amity" (V, iii, p. 59), Massinissa is now placed in the dilemma of conflicting vows, having just vowed that he would protect Sophonisba's freedom. His rigid sense of honor, which makes both claims seem equally valid, and his fear lest he lose honor by making a personal choice cause him to become almost inarticulate with panic: "Right which way/ Runne mad impossible distraction" (V, iii, p. 60). But both of these claims upon his honor are not equally valid. Scipio's order originated in the vicious misrepresentation of Syphax and was further motivated by Scipio's desire to revenge himself against Sophonisba's father, who had killed his own, and to add pomp to his triumph. On the other hand, Sophonisba not only represents the ultimate of virtue but is bound to Massinessa more closely than a "mutuall league of endles amity." But it is precisely the personal nature of his relationship to Sophonisba which prejudices him in favor of the impersonal claim as a way of proving the extreme integrity of his spirit: "tell him wee will act/ What shall amaze him. . . . Shee shall arive there straight" (V, iii, p. 59–60). His very desire to "amaze" the world with a great sacrifice for honor causes him to act dishonorably. This dishonor is not, however, that which he so strongly feels, the fact that he has been "inforcedly perfidious" (V, iii, p. 60) to his formal vow to Sophonisba; it is the fact that he is willing to literally sacrifice Sophonisba's life to uphold his honor. When Sophonisba, wishing to outdo him in an honor that will "maze all power" (V, iii, p. 60), suggests her own death as the way out of his dilemma, Massinissa's reaction marks a fall in human dignity beneath even that of Syphax: "Thou darst not die, some wine, thou darst not die" (V, iii, p. 60). In this telling speech, Marston's dramatic art reaches the level of genuine greatness. In a flash we see the total deterioration of personality caused by a rigid need for superhuman honor. In Massinissa's eager haste to conclude her death before she may change her incredible decision, an aroused "lust" for glory is illuminated in its most pejorative sense.

But if Massinissa has been betrayed by his lust for glory into the most spiritually abject behavior, sacrificing Sophonisba to the dishonorable purposes of Scipio, so is Sophonisba's sacrifice betrayed by the totally unworthy end to which it is directed: in relation to Sophonisba's pure purposes, Massinissa proves as "infinitely vile" as was Carthage to him. But it is precisely in terms of this that Sophonisba achieves the glory of that true honor which has "no pay but selfe wept miserie." Dying for the honor of a love that is specifically unworthy of her pure sacrifice, she achieves a spiritual greatness which inspired Marston to his finest speech:

> How neere was I unto the curse of man, Joye,
> How like was I yet once to have beene glad:
> He that neere laught may with a constant face
> Contemne Joves frowne. Happinesse makes us base.

[She takes a bole into which Mas. puts poison.]
. . . Deere doe not weepe.
And now with undismaid resolve behold,
To save *You, you,* (for honor and just faith
Are most true Gods, which we should much adore)
With even disdainefull vigour I give up,
An abhord life. *[She drinks.]* You have beene good to me,
And I doe thanke thee heaven, O my stars,
I blesse your goodnes, that with breast unstaind,
Faith pure: a Virgin wife, try'de to my glory,
I die of female faith, the long liv'de story,
Secure from bondage, and all servile harmes,
But more, most happy in my husbands armes. *[She sinks.]*
    (V, iii, pp. 60–1)

She embraces the opportunity to die for honor as the heaven-sent blessing for which she had recently prayed, thankful that she had so nearly escaped the earthly happiness which would have made her base to the claims of immortalizing honor. Still virgin to the joys of life, she has preserved that spiritual purity which can transcend the abhorrence of life through the "disdainefull vigour" with which it is given up. Though she so heavily underscores the fact that she is dying to save the wretched honor of Massinissa, it is not his honor but her own which, as a true god, she would worship with self-immolation. By thus sacrificing herself she will achieve the "godlike gaine" of immortal glory and, what is perhaps even more profoundly coveted, the absolute freedom "from bondage, and all servile harmes." As in her earlier plea to the unrecognized Massinissa, it is finally only this freedom for which she craves. But a desire for freedom which can be ultimately satisfied only in death does not so much represent an abhorrence of specific bondage as of the essential constraints of mortal existence.

In triumphing over these, she incidentally triumphs also over the specific enemy to her dignity: Syphax. As Sophonisba's self-sacrifice proves the impotence of his power to enforce her free spirit, his exultation turns to a torment which fully reveals the hatred that has ever motivated his vengeful lust: "Burst my vext heart, the torture that most rackes/ An enimie, is his foes

royall actes (V, iii; p. 63). If Sophonisba has redeemed herself
through self-sacrifice, its effect is not to redeem but only further
vex her enemy. This dwindling of the circle of redemption, from
the full extent achieved by self-sacrifice in *Romeo and Juliet,*
would seem to follow from the open contesting of the values
of society which defined the progress toward this final act of
self-sacrifice, and may be considered a defining characteristic
of the "conflict pattern" of Courtly Love tragedy.

Her triumph over Syphax, and all the worldly corruption
he represents, is not only that of honor over dishonor but also
of pure love over lust. Sophonisba's love was not directed toward
the happiness of an earthly fulfillment; it was a spiritual discipline through which she was "try'de to my glory." And, as
true glory can only be gained through "losse of breath," it is
only under this fatal circumstance that she can permit herself
to be "most happy in my husbands armes." In such a trial the
actual Massinissa, who now so eagerly puts poison into her cup,
is not important; what is important is the faithful purity of her
own love, a love which has served as preparatory discipline for
the radiant death embraced in its name. Stoic honor has proved
a true ally to Courtly Love.

Sophonisba is Marston's finest tragedy and an excellent work.
Eschewing the inflated rhetoric of *Antonio and Mellida,* Marston's
language here becomes the fit conveyance for the subtlety of his
thought. If none of the characters have the irritating vitality
of Antonio, they represent a far more subtle perception of the
psychological motivation of abstractly significant types. Marston's
presentation of the origin and end of lust is the most perceptive
treatment of this condition in the Elizabethan drama. In the
character of Massinissa, no less than that of Syphax, Marston
reveals the dishonorable result to which a compulsive need for
honorable repute can lead. Both characters serve to qualify the
validity of the ideal for which Sophonisba makes the supreme
sacrifice. But Sophonisba's progress toward this proof of true
honor is no less anatomized. Her fear of earthly happiness sheds
as illuminating a light on the essential character of the martyr
as Massinissa's call for wine or Syphax' embrace of the witch
shed on their characters. The desire for honor can pervert the

essential humanity of even its true devotee, but it can also exalt that intensified spirituality which affirms its unconquerable integrity even at the price of death, even in a world without honor.

Having given shape to the two major deflections of the pure current of Courtly Love, those in which the forces of obstruction are met either by revenge or Stoic honor, in his later development Marston followed the stream into the shallows of false romaticism, going further than any of his contemporaries in tracing this ultimate dissipation of the vital springs of Courtly Love. His third and last tragedy, *The Insatiate Countess* (1610). is the most depraved tragedy of False Romantic Love in the Elizabethan genre, his titular character committing an unparalleled triple infidelity to a marriage that was already an act of infidelity to the memory of her former husband.[10] But if as a tragedian Marston only approaches greatness in *Sophonisba,* his three tragedies make him the most significant figure for the study of the decadence of Courtly Love on the Elizabethan tragic stage, revealing all the possible changes that can be wrung on its theme. Though Marsten concluded as he had begun with a negative treatment of the potentialities of Courtly Love, the positive direction he defined for Courtly Love tragedy in *Sophonisba* was to be followed by a still greater playwright in *The Second Maiden's Tragedy.*

The Second Maiden's Tragedy

It is perhaps ironic that *The Second Maiden's Tragedy,* which has received almost no critical comment and whose worth has been consistently underrated even where it has been mentioned,[11] has been the center of an extensive controversy concerning its authorship.[12] Since the 1875 edition of *The Works of Chapman,* however, none of the scholars concerned with the play's authorship has given the manuscript attribution to Chapman more than the most cursory reference. As the manuscript provides the only authentic external evidnce we have with regard to the play's authorship, it may well be time to agree with Swinburne that "the claim for Chapman deserves some attention from all students of our dramatic poetry," [13] and I have elsewhere argued extensively in support of the manuscript attribution to Chapman.[14]

The Second Maiden's Tragedy, which survived its 1611 production in a single manuscript, represents a culmination of the change in the dramatic patterning of Courtly Love tragedy wrought by the successive work of Kyd and Marston. Once again the union of courtly lovers is obstructed by the political power of an ignoble lover. As in *Soliman and Perseda,* Courtly and Worldly Love are drawn in mortal conflict, but the form of Courtly Love presented here follows the reformulation of its essence into Stoic terms effected by Marston in *Sophonisba.* In this stern, intellectual work, Courtly Love appears as a Stoic ideal to be admired even if its glory is beyond the power of frailty to imitate. Surrounded by the corrupt and the weak, the Lady remains, in a world no longer attuned to the music of infinity, the "Queene of Scilence" (V, ii, 2447).[15]

The Second Maiden's Tragedy is dialectically structured on the opposing life principles of the Lady and the Tyrant, early distinguished by her as the rival claims of spiritual goodness and worldly greatness. Having usurped the throne from her lover, Govianus, when he appeared to obstruct the way to the lady's favor, the Tyrant also hopes to command her love. When he proudly summons her to share his throne, however, she enters clad in black and, to his astonishment as well as that of her lover, proclaims the integrity of her love for Govianus in terms of her general spiritual convictions:

> I haue a mynde,
> that must be shifted ere I cast of thease
> or I shall weare straung coloures;—tis not titles
> nor all the bastard-honoures of this frame
> that I am taken w^th, I come not hether
> to pleaze the eye of glorie, but of goodnes
> and that concerns not yo^u sir, you're for greatnes
> I dare not deale wth yo^u, I have found my matche
> and I will neuer loose him. . . .

fortunes are but the outsides of true worth
it is the mynde that sets his master forth; (I, i, 132–40, 189–
90)

The Lady is alone in her heroic dedication to the ideal but not
alone in espousing the superior worth of the unworldly realm
of the mind, and this worship of the intellect devoted to spiritual
perfection defines the tone of the whole play.

Govianus' brother, Anselmus, expresses this central belief
most importantly upon the Tyrant's confinement of the lovers
to prison:

why he was neuer happier . . .
h'as lost the kingdome but his mynde's restorde
wch is the larger empire? pre thee tell me.
Domynions haue their lymitts, the whole earth
is but a prisoner, nor the sea her Iailor
that wth a siluer hoope lockes in her bodie
th'eir fellow prisoners, thoe the sea looke bigger
bycause he is in office, and pride swells him:
But the vnbounded kingdome of the mynde
is as vnlymitable as heav'ne, that glorious court of spirrits
. . . my brothers well attended, peace and pleasure
arc neuer from his sighte; he has his mistris
she brought those servaunts and bestowde them on him . . . (I
ii, 264, 266–74, 278–80)

The compression of thought in this passage is so great as almost
to obscure its meaning. Using the metaphor of land and sea to
define the two human classes of the ruled or imprisoned and
the rulers or apparent jailors, Anselmus appears to be saying
that all men are prisoners and this whether they meekly surrender to their condition of limitation, as do the lovers, or
proudly appear to defy it, as does the Tyrant. The imprisoned
earthly realm is further contrasted with "the vnbounded kingdome
of the mynde," with the implication that the mind is imprisoned
in its earthly embodiment but, as pure spirit, can transcend the

prison of life and be "restorde" to an approximation of its true heavenly condition.

Anselmus is right, for the lovers, having gained a certain leniency from their guards, have no complaint against their imprisonment. The lovers' marriage—for from the temptation which follows it may be assumed that they are married—is characteristic of the marriage of courtly lovers in that it approximates the obstructed condition of adultery. They sometimes have three hours together and this, the Lady rightly says, is "as much as I would aske of libertie" (II, i, 639).

The Tyrant, however, not being able to have the Lady for his wife, hopes to gain her for his mistress and sends her father, Helvetius, to tempt her. But it is the lovers' truth which finally prevails over the old man's false orientation. When the reclaimed Helvetius refuses to continue his pandering and is also sentenced by the Tyrant to prison, he exclaims:

> Close prisoner?
> why my heart thanckes thee, I shall haue more tyme
> and libertie to vertue in one howre
> than all those threescore yeares I was a Courtier,
> so by imprisonm^t I sustaine great losse
> heavne opens to that man, the world keepes close, . . . (II,
>   iii, 1138-43)

Here the symbolic use of imprisonment is again made clear. In accepting the otherworldly values, for which the lovers themselves were imprisoned, Helvetius recognizes that the world, with all its greatness, is but the prison of the soul and, in affirming this truth, "heavne opens" to his uplifted spirit.

But this stoical Neo-Platonic resignation of the values of the world for those of the spirit has a deeper implication, one which only becomes explicit in the behavior of the lovers. Although their Stoicism enables them to continue life pure-spirited in an impure world, when the Lady's preservation of the purity of her love is no longer possible in terms of this world and she sees that "ther is no waie/ but throughe my bosome" (III, 1329–30), death suddenly manifests itself in a new light.

When all the Tyrant's efforts to woo the Lady to his bed have failed, he sends armed men to carry her forcibly to him. Though the Lady, when warned of their approach, immediately resolves upon her death, Govianus is unable to bear the thought of her loss as the price of his peace: "Tis a most miserable waye to get it,/ I had rather be content to liue w^thout it/ then paye so deer for't, and yet lose it too" (III, 1269–71). But such a compromising stance is not for the Lady. She explains that it is only through her death that they can be truly united and their love fulfilled: "his lust may part me from thee, but Death neuer" (III, 1333). Temporarily strengthened, he runs to give her the death she finds "neuer more deerly wellcome" (III, 1340), but at the last moment swoons. With the Tyrant's men now knocking insistently at the door, she resolutely meets death alone:

> my lorde, my loue,—o thow poore spirited man;
> hees gon before me, did I trust to thee
> and hast thow seru'd me so? left all the worke
> vpon my hand, and stole awaie so smoothlie;
> ther was not equall suffering showne in this,
> and yet I cannot blame thee, Euerie man
> would seek his rest, eternall peace sleep wth thee,
> thow art my servaunt now, come thow hast lost
> a fearefull master, but art now preferd
> vnto the service of a resolute ladie
> one that knowes how to imploye thee, and scornes death
> as much as SOME men feare it, wher's hells ministers?
> the Tyrants watche and guard? tis of much worthe *[Knock]*
> when wth this key the prisoner can slip forthe— *[Kills her
> self.]* (III, 1341–56)

In death, the Lady becomes another Juliet: "O churl, drunk all and left no friendly drop/ To help me after? . . . Yea noise? then I'll be brief. O happy dagger . . ." But with all her tender levity to her lord and his dagger and the resolute swiftness with which she uses it, the Lady is a Juliet with a difference. She suddenly sees and embraces the fatal implications of her philosophy: "Euerie man/ would seek his rest, eternall peace." Hitherto she had believed, in accordance with Govianus, Anselmus, and Helvetius, that the prisoning limitations of life could be satisfactorily transcended in pure mind. Now she realizes that death is the only true "key" with which "the prisoner can slip forthe."

The Lady dies in the third act but her influence continues through the remainder of the play, effecting a final victory of her spiritual love over the Tyrant's opposing worldliness. At the beginning of the play, the Tyrant had proudly summoned the Lady to share his glory with the following characteristic words: "ther is no gladnes/ but has a pride it liues by,—thats the oyle/ that feedes it into flames" (I, i, 29–31). Though all joy in his triumph deserts him when his love is spurned, the pride he lives by soon revives and his self-love deceives him into thinking that he can still win the Lady's love. But as she continues to resist his temptations of wealth and greatness, his pride becomes demoralized, and he orders her seizure. When he learns that she prefers death to him, his pride is utterly demolished:

> her owne faire hand so cruell; did she chuse
> destruction before mee? was I no better;
> how much am I exalted to my face?
> and wher I would be grac'te, how little worthye? . . .
> I cannot call this, life, that flames wthin me
> but euerlasting torment lighted vp
> to shew my sowle her beggery. (IV, ii, 1676–79, 1692–94)

In these great lines of self-awareness, he no longer sees himself in the exalted image which his pride had erected but in the true "beggery" of soul buried beneath. He can no longer exist, however, without this delusion of greatness. The flames of self-hate, which had always lurked unseen within the brighter flames of self-love, are again eclipsed by the rekindling of his pride. But it is an insane pride which now takes possession of his being.

Planning to have her body preserved in the manner Herod once used, he reclaims it from the grave and lovingly says to it:

o I could chide thee wth myne eye brym full;
and weep out my forgiuenes when I ha donne. . . .
Since thy life has left me
ile claspe the bodie for the spirrit that dwelt in't
and loue the howse still for the mistris sake,
Thow are myne now spight of distruction
and Gouianus; and I will possess thee . . . (IV, iii, 1838–39,
  1851–55)

Here the two modes of love are pitted against each other: that which in all humility finds its fulfillment in death, and that which in all pride demands its fulfillment in life. To the Tyrant it is incomprehensible that the Lady should not appreciate "how deere a treasure life and youth had bin" (IV, iii, 1843) and would willfully commit suicide. He loved her body "for the spirrit that dwelt in't," but he cannot conceive of a love of the spirit divorced from its physical embodiment. And so it is that when his love of life becomes deranged, it can be satisfied with the mere semblance of life and still find it precious. Rather than follow her spirit through death, he strives to join her spirit in the only place in which, for him, it has a meaningful existence, her body.

It is, however, this fanatic love of life long after it has lost its meaning which is to prove his destruction for, despite the Tyrant's denial of Govianus' power, Govianus is still an actor in this tragedy. Mourning at her tomb, he is prepared with philosophic calm for a long life. But this calm deserts him at the sight of the Lady's ghost and, like a true courtly lover, he wishes to follow her to death: "ile make my self/ ouer to death too, and weele walke together/ lyke loving spirrits" (IV, iv, 1975–77). But as she has left him with the duty of revenge, he defers his suicide until he can "dispatche this busines vpon earth" (IV, iv, 1979); and then he procrastinates in pursuing his revenge.

The opportunity for Govianus' revenge finally arises, however. The Tyrant, still relying on the power of human ingenuity to outwit death, sends for an artist to mend her "too constant palenes" (V, ii, 2245), and Govianus seizes this commission. He paints her lips with poison, and in kissing them the Tyrant meets his destruction—a fitting symbolic end to his love of the corruptible. At the last, he hails her revenging ghost as "thow enemie to firmeness/ mortallities earthquake" (V, ii, 2386–7). For her spiritual dedication has, indeed, been his mortality's destruction. In embracing a corrupted mortality, he has embraced the death that his worldly pride had so futilely tried to outwit. The use of necrophilia and the ghost provides a dramatic correlative to the ultimate symbolic conflict between the Tyrant and the Lady. The devotion to the embodied spirit is finally reduced to an insane adoration of pure body, whereas the devotion to spiritual purity achieves its final triumph in the form of pure spirit. Though all desire for death leaves Govianus upon the unexpected restoration of his kingdom, he ends the play by celebrating the Lady's triumph over her philosophically opposed antagonist, having her borne, in all her radiant purity, "Vnto the howse of peace from whence she came/ as Queene of Scilence" (V, ii, 2446–67).

In the nature of this final triumph, *The Second Maiden's Tragedy* is markedly similar to *Soliman and Perseda*. In both, the suicide of the ladies is but the prelude to their physical revenge against their would-be lovers. Apart from any question of possible influence, a reason for this similarity may be that in both the conflict is between Courtly and Worldly Love and that when tragedians of Courtly Love deal with Worldly Love their lack of sympathy with it seems to impel them to present it as a depraved, physical love which can only be symbolically defeated through the defeat of the body. In both tragedies, moreover, this physical defeat results from the worldly lover's fatal kissing of his beloved's poisoned lips. The difference between these two tragedies, is that, whereas Perseda accomplished her revenge directly, the Lady accomplishes her revenge through her less inspired lover. In both cases, however, their desire for revenge does not act as a substitute for the perfection of their love's fidelity in suicide, and this is also true of Gismund's desire to have her suicide revenged. Despite the impulse for revenge on the part of the tragic lover, then, these plays retain the classic courtly requirement of the love-death. It is nonetheless true that the association of Courtly Love with revenge is a profound one and pervades this type of love tragedy. Of all the plays in this category only *Romeo and Juliet* and *Sophonisba* are entirely free of it. This association becomes even more significant when we realize that none of the non-courtly lovers in the genre has this desire to be revenged against an *external* obstruction that has caused either his own death or that of his beloved.

Though the plot focus of *The Second Maiden's Tragedy* moves, after the suicide of the Lady, to Govianus' revenge, Govianus can hardly be considered the protagonist of the tragedy. The pattern of dramatic action his love follows is strikingly similar, however, to that of Antonio, the classic courtly revenger. Antonio, not finding his love sufficiently inspirational to cause him to follow Mellida's suicide with his own, chooses to live so that he can be revenged against the indignities, suffered by both of them, which had driven her to death. However different Govianus is from Antonio, both are lovers who, although desiring to die for love, are unable to do so and whose voluntary continuation of life calls down upon them the duty of revenge.

Reviewing all the tragedies thus far considered, it would appear that there are only two legitimate reactions that the surviving courtly lover can have to the death of the beloved. He can either achieve the true honor of the love-death or seek the less honorable alternative of revenge. When he does neither of these, as in the case of Massinissa, his survival is accompanied only by shame. Thus, when Govianus recovers from the thought and actuality of her death and is prepared for long life, the Lady's ghost returns to inspire him to revenge. Only when it is accomplished will she permit him to "live ever honourd here" (V, ii, 2399).

With the passing of that Elizabethan moment in which Romeo died to his glory, playwrights seem no longer able to conceive of a man dying to preserve the spiritual purity of his love. The playwrights still allow the women to die for their purity but this seems more a product of nostalgia than conviction. In the world of *The Second Maiden's Tragedy*, the Lady's pure sacrifice can no longer be inspirational. Her death can neither inspire the Tyrant to a more meaningful life nor inspire Govianus to a like immolation in death. Govianus understands the meaning of the Lady's death no more than the Tyrant does. But whereas the Tyrant's lack of comprehension was a product of his own tragic commitment to life, Govianus' bewilderment results from the weakness of his convictions. Admiring the Lady's purity but no longer able to comprehend its source or to imitate its perfection, Govianus represents that minor segment of Jacobean thought that resists the more vital Hedonism of the age with the armor of Stoicism. Govianus is no whining malcontent like Antonio. He has so controlled his desire for happiness that he can accept equally both the evils and virtues of life and so can live. Govianus reigns in "the vnbounded kingdome of the mynde," however, without ever truly perceiving that the key to this kingdom is death. And, although it is he who makes the last comment on both plots, there is something which shines through the deaths of the Lady and the Wife that Govianus cannot understand.

The conflict between the Lady and the Tryant, which makes up the main plot, presents two opposed but equally consistent attitudes of mind: the Lady's Stoic view of the imprisoned yet harmonious spirit, and the opposing Hedonistic philosophy of the Tyrant: "affection wilbe mistris here on earthe,/ the howse is hers, the Sowle is but a tenaunt" (V, ii, 2213–14). The subplot, however, is concerned with something quite different—the mind divided against itself. Votarius, the lover, presents the problem quite succinctly; and though he speaks of the husband, Anselmus, what he says can be equally applied to himself and to the Wife: "man has some enemy still y^t keepes him back/ in all his fortunes, and his mynde is his,/ and thats a mightie adversarie" (I, ii, 435–37).

The mental conflict of the characters in the subplot serves as a foil to the single-mindedness of those in the main plot. But the subplot acts as a foil to the main plot in still other ways. Where the Lady resists temptation, the Wife yields to it. Where the Lady's love relationship with Govianus is pure and socially above reproach, the Wife's love affair with Votarius is sensual and descends to the sordid level of an intrigue. Where the Lady and Govianus feel free from taint, the Wife and Votarius have a constant sense of sin and shame. And, finally, where the Lady meets her death with noble conviction, the deaths of the adulterous lovers is a tragic mistake.[16]

There is, however, in this tragic course of adultery not simply a sinful yielding to sensuality but a romantic passion which bears a close affinity to the pure, untroubled love of the Lady and Govianus. *The Second Maiden's Tragedy* is especially interesting in this regard because it is the only tragedy of its time in which both the chaste and original adulterous traditions of Courtly Love are represented. But the spiritual motivation of Courtly Love cannot shine forth unclouded in the subplot, as it does in the main, because it is here embodied in the adulterous form which English morality could not countenance, at least in its tragedies of "death-marked love."

The action of the subplot is an offshoot of the main action. Having witnessed the Lady's noble defense of her chaste love against temptation, Anselmus desires to put his own wife to a like proof. This desire to have his wife's chastity approved is a curious product of Anselmus' Courtly Love for his wife, for it enables him to forget "the waie of wedlock" (I, ii, 378). In terms of the philosophy which he shares with the Lady and Govianus, and for which he is a major spokesman, he cannot, however, express his courtly craving for obstruction and transcendent death in any way save the heroic vindication of purity. To this end he persuades his friend Votarius to undertake the temptation.

So romantic is Votarius' seduction, however, that the Wife, despite her mental anguish, finds herself yielding as she cries out: "What ist to yo^u (good sir) if I be pleazd/ to weep my selfe awaie? and run thus violently/ into the armes of death, and kisse distruction" (I, ii, 534–36). Though she may see her conflict as one between pure spirit and a sensuality that it cannot countenance, the real conflict is actually between spirit and sense. When she finally does overcome the dictates of society's morality, she abandons herself, in true Courtly Love fashion, to her "distruction."

Votarius' passion follows a somewhat different course. Having watched himself with anguished self-awareness as he fought more and more helplessly against his passion, Votarius is finally overwhelmed by an irrational lover's jealousy; he jumps to the conclusion that the Wife has another lover when he comes upon the maid's lover in the house. Enraged against the Wife, he tells Anselmus, who has now been transformed into something of a dolt, of the Wife's yielding and that he will provide the proof. When he learns the truth and begs the Wife's forgiveness, she offers the following sage comment on his behavior: "Confest me yeilding, was thy waie to free?/ why didst thow long to be restrainde?" (IV, 1, 1485–86). It is Votarius' Courtly Love passion that creates the fatal obstruction,[17] just as Anselmus' passion had created the whole situation.

The lovers now plot to convert the scene of her dishonor into a vindication of her chastity. However, through the machinations of her maid's lover, who is Votarius' mortal enemy, the flesh wound they had planned to have the Wife give Votarius proves fatal. The apparent faithlessness of his mistress cruelly undercuts Votarius' passion, therefore, at the supreme moment of his death: "y'are a most treacherous ladie; this thy glorie?" (V, i, 2116). This fatality, nevertheless, restores Anselmus' faith in his wife, and killing the maid who had informed upon his wife's infiidelity, he is challenged by the maid's lover. As they fight, the Wife "purposely runs betwene, and is kild by them both." Not hearing his wife's last words, Anselmus goes to meet the death of a chivalric courtly lover in the defense of his lady's virtue, the death which is "the deare wish of a great mans spirrit" (V, i, 2158). Lingering long enough to learn the truth his Courtly Love passion, like that of Votarius, is ironically undercut at the moment it reaches its fulfillment in death.[18]

It is only the Wife whose passion is fulfilled in death. Truer than Votarius can know, she does rise to her "glorie" when the supreme test presents itself. Throwing aside all such irrelevant considerations as the petty honor she had so fatally vindicated, she rushes onto the clashing swords crying "I come Votarius" (V, i, 2136). The greatest irony of the Wife's play-acted avowal to "ymitat my noble sisters fate/ . . . and cast awaie my life as she[19] did hers" (V, i, 2079, 2081, is not that this is false but true.

In this subplot, then, meant to serve as a foil to the pure spirituality of the Lady's sacrifice, there shines through all the guilt, shame, and criticism attached to adultery the same passion of Courtly Love which the main plot so differently manifests. But even while the lovers in the subplot conform to the dictates of their fatal passion, the course of their love does suffer from its combat with morality. In the moral atmosphere of the play, the abandonment to adultery cannot help but divide the mind against itself and corrupt the purity of its passion. And that is why this almost unique case of courtly adultery in the Elizabethan drama [20] can validly serve as a foil to the accepted form of Courtly Love, that between two young people who wish to marry or who have an obstructed marriage.

In the Lady's tragic dedication to spiritual purity, *The Second Maiden's Tragedy* affirms an ideal so high that it can only be made in terms of the most comprehensive qualifications. Assuming a greater urgency than the affirmation of the ideal itself is the lack of comprehension of such a dedication on the part of the others, whether this lack of comprehension results from an opposing orientation to life, from a lack of ultimate faith in the value of such idealism, or from a debasement of the ideal. More important even than this need for qualification is the form in which such spiritual purity is presented. It has been pointed out that in the treatments of a noble Courtly Love, the equation between spiritual purity and chastity was increasingly insisted upon. This equation has, however, a larger bearing on the Jacobean drama than has yet been mentioned. The Lady's noble suicide to avoid "a fate worse than death," rape, is but one in the increasing suicide rate of chaste Jacobean heroines. The Lady's suicide was motivated by the desire to preserve the purity of her love: "his lust may part me from thee, but Death neuer." In a special group of Jacobean tragedies, on the other hand, the honorable preservation of chastity becomes its own justification and is divorced from any consideration of love. The principal plays of this type are Heywood's *Rape of Lucrece* (1607), Fletcher's *Valentinian* (1613), and Webster and Heywood's *Appius and Virginia* (1624?). In these tragedies of Stoic Roman women. suicide is motivated simply by honor and is unrelated to the mystic fulfillment of love in death. And yet, the movement of Heywood, alone and with Webster, and of Fletcher to the Roman materials of rape and resultant suicide is another important instance of the Jacobean tension between the desire to affirm the value of purity and the awareness of a "wicked time,/ Where filthie lust must murther honest loue."

Although spiritual purity was equated with chastity before the Jacobean period, in this period another dimension is added to the equation, that of Stoicism. In the above mentioned Roman plays of rape and suicide, the value which triumphs over the unstable corruption of the age is Stoicism. Against the more powerful Epicureanism of the age, these plays present a minor Stoic note of defiance. But this also holds true for the Jacobean tragedies of Courtly Love, the only tragedies of Courtly Love to be written in the whole of the Jacobean period being the Stoic *Sophonisba* and *The Second Maiden's Tragedy*. This is the most significant development which Courtly Love undergoes in the Jacobean period, and this fact therefore casts an illuminating light upon the general temper of that age. It would seem that the Jacobean mood could not fully sympathize with any affirmation of purity which did not present itself in the form of Stoicism; its realism could not countenance an enthusiastic faith but only one which expressed itself with a proud restraint. But the very fact that there are only two such tragedies written in the whole of this long period, and that even these must be severely qualified before the nature of their affirmation can be permitted, indicates a more profound alienation of such writers from the general spirit of the age. The age that produced the great tragedies of Worldly Love had little sympathy for spiritual purity even if it was presented in Stoic terms. In such an age the affirmation of Stoic purity represents a minor note of protest. But, because it is a minor note, its force is largely dissipated in the very conflict with corruption which defines the dramatic pattern of these plays.

Section II
Tragedies of False Romantic Love

4

The Classic Pattern
of False Romantic Love Tragedy

A Woman Killed With Kindness

Shakespeare, in perhaps his most famous definition of love, has said: "Love is not love/ Which alters when it alteration finds, . . . Love's not Time's fool" (Sonnet 116). That untrue love which may be "Time's fool," but which Shakespeare was still pleased to call "love," is what I have termed False Romantic Love. This love may be "real," in the sense of being a felt emotion which causes involvement, but it cannot be "true," cannot sustain an emotional involvement by the power of a committed faith. False Romantic Love renders the lover incapable of appreciating the value of the love he receives and so liable to an act of infidelity which prohibits his return. But the tragedy of False Romantic Love is that, if and when the lover does come to appreciate the value of the love he has forsworn, this appreciation comes too late. It is in this sense that False Romantic Love renders the lover liable to the tragedy of being "Time's fool." False Romantic Love can "graduate" to either Courtly or Worldly Love, but it cannot become tragic until it has so graduated. Once it has, the fate of such a lover is far more painful than that of straight courtly or worldly lovers. They have at least known the fulfillment of their love. But even when his love has become true, this fulfillment is forever denied to the false romantic lover. The tragic irony of it is that he had lost his love in thinking it commonplace and easily attainable, when, having once gained a vision of what love's fulfillment might be and seeing his life hopelessly bereft of it, he, and only he, can have a true sense of what a precious thing it is and how exceedingly difficult to attain.

False Romantic Love emerges at the moment when Courtly Love loses its inspiration; a moment which, in the swift progress of the Elizabethan drama, came all too soon. The faith that had so recently animated the different purposes of a Romeo or a Tamburlaine finds no echo in the ominous years of Essex's execution and Elizabeth's death.[1] The tragedy of False Romantic Love makes its first dramatic appearance in Heywood's *A Woman Killed With Kindness* (1603). While Greene, in his *James the Fourth,* had hinted at it as early as 1590, tragedy was there prevented by a still efficacious miracle of goodness. In the transitional period from Elizabethan idealism to Jacobean realism, however, false romanticism finally becomes the stuff of tragedy.

The theme of infidelity repented, which is the tragedy of False Romantic Love, is nowhere treated as fully as in the work of Thomas Heywood. Besides his one masterpiece in the genre, *A Woman Killed With Kindness,* he treated the subject of tragic feminine infidelity in his later *The English Traveller* (1625) and in the earlier *Edward IV* (1599), if this "anonymous" work is, as seems indisputable, his. Heywood also treated the subject of masculine infidelity but, unless *A Yorkshire Tragedy* (1606) is truly his, never tragically. *The Wise Woman of Hogsdon* (1604) is a comedy of intrigue and *How a Man May Choose a Good Wife from a Bad* (1602), an anoymous work that has been generally ascribed to Heywood, is a tragicomedy. In the five plays mentioned which are generally ascribed to Heywood, infidelity is the greatest crime committed. And here a moral distinction between the sexes becomes significant. When it is the man who proves unfaithful, the betrayed fiancée or wife can, without censure, accept the prodigal back. But when it is the woman who proves unfaithful, even the most forgiving husband, such as Matthew Shore and Mr. Frankford, cannot accept his wife back to a shared life. She is doomed to tragedy by a societal morality which infuses her own spirit as much as her husband's. While the other tragic adulteresses of Elizabethan drama are also murderers, Heywood made simple feminine adultery the important center of his tragic work. The reason for this may lie in his Puritan affinities,[2] for his work is animated by the ideal of conjugal love preached by the Puritans, an ideal that expressed the essence of what I have termed Worldly Love in its most productive form.[3] Since he held conjugal love so high, the simple adulteress could become, for Heywood, a proper subject for tragedy.

At the wedding feast, with which *A Woman Killed With Kindness* begins, Anne Frankford appears as the image of the perfect wife:

> His sweet content is like a flattering glass,
> To make my face seeme fairer to mine eye:
> But the least wrinkle from his stormy brow
> Will blast the roses in my cheeks that grow. (i, 33–6) [4]

She looks upon marriage as a state of responsible mutual dependence, but she is still only three hours wed and has not yet experienced the meaning and demands of such a relationship.

With this image before his heart, Frankford next day muses upon his happiness. It is with a modest pride that he counts his intellectual and financial endowments, concluding:

> But the chief
> Of all the sweet felicities on earth,
> I have a fair, a chaste, and loving wife,
> Perfection all, all truth, all ornament.
> If man on earth may truly happy be,
> Of these at once possess'd, sure I am he. (iv, 9–14)

Frankford's energies are bent on gaining the "sweet felicities *on earth.*" The chief of his possessions, prize "ornament" of all his worldly blessings, is his good and loving wife. But mark that word "ornament." At the wedding feast, Sir Charles Mountford had said: "she's a chain of gold to adorn your neck./ You both adorn each other" (i, 64–5). And now Frankford repeats this conception of marriage as a mutual adornment. Though Mrs. Frankford had suggested a higher vision of marriage, she can no more understand its true implications than her husband. Since both are essentially good, kind, and generous people, their marriage bodes fair to both but, in its commitment to external attributes, it is not above temptation.

For Frankford, his "loving wife" is a precious ornament which he has bought with his own good deserts. But he does not realize that if one accepts love as an ornament, it may—like an ornament—be lost or stolen. His attitude toward his wife is of a piece with his general attitude toward the world. As he had just added up his own and his wife's attributes and thought himself happy in their possession, so immediately does he consider his acquaintance, Wendoll: "You are full of quality and fair desert. . . . I will allow you, sir, . . . all/ At my own charge; be my companion" (iv, 68–72). Assessing the attributes of his acquaintance, he decides to buy his companionship. Frankford gives not of himself but of his possessions; and though this gift is generous, he does not realize that its natural reward is not love but that which without love is most resented, obligation. As in this bargain he does not miss the hearts of his wife and friend, so is he incapable of judging their true nature.

The inevitable happens. Kept in constant and close proximity to the fair Mrs. Frankford, Wendoll at length becomes violently attracted to her. His sense of obligation rises to stay his passion and a terrible conflict ensues within his breast:

> And shall I wrong this man? Base man! Ingrate!
> Hast thou the power straight with thy gory hands
> To rip thy image from his bleeding heart?
> To scratch thy name from out the holy book
> Of his remembrance; . . . And yet I must: (vi, 44–8, 51)

His sense of damnation grows as he endows his friend with Christlike qualities and sees his own treachery in this grave context, but he can fight his desire no longer. Helpless, he confesses his love to her.

But she, significantly enough, counters his suit only with a weak reminder of Wendoll's obligation to her husband, not with the strength of a committed love. She has no thought of yielding to him but neither has she any prop to stay her own downfall. And this is speedily accomplished by the strength and sincerity of Wendoll's passionate outburst:

> O speak no more,
> For more than this I know and have recorded
> Within the red-leav'd table of my heart.
> Fair, and of all belov'd, I was not fearful
> Bluntly to give my life into your hand,
> And at one hazard all my earthly means.
> Go, tell your husband; he will turn me off,
> And I am then undone. I care not, I—
> 'Twas for your sake. Perchance, in rage he'll kill me.
> I care not—'twas for you. Say I incur
> The general name of villain through the world,
> Of traitor to my friend—I care not, I.
> Beggary, shame, death, scandal, and reproach—
> For you I'll hazard all. What care I?
> For you I'll live, and in your love I'll die. (vi, 125–39)

All of this is true. He has fought desperately to restrain his passion and, in avowing his love, does place his honor and his very life in her power. But such a desperate, overpowering love has never been offered her by her securely happy husband, and it does stir her soul as Frankford's never did:

> You move me, sir, to passion and to pity;
> The love I bear my husband is as precious
> As my soul's health. (vi, 140–2)

It is now no longer Wendoll's dishonor but her own that becomes important. She has, from the beginning, believed in the

sanctity of marriage, has tried to be a good wife, and has been
happy in this attempt because she feels she loves her husband.
But this love is a product of admiration rather than a felt sympathy. It is False Romantic Love, a good thing at its best but
one incapable of true commitment and so of absolute fidelity.
It is not a love capable of countering the passion that Wendoll
has roused in her breast, and, as he continues to do so, she can
only respond:

> [Aside] What shall I say?
> My soul is wand'ring and hath lost her way.
> . . . I ne'er offended yet;
> My fault, I fear, will in my brow be writ. . . .
> [To him.] Pray God I be not born to curse your tongue,
> That hath enchanted me. This maze I am in
> I fear will prove the labyrinth of sin. (vi, 150–1, 154–5,
>   159–61)

"I ne'er offended yet"! It is as though she has been silently
waiting all her life for this *grande passion* that she fears and
yet abandons herself to. But even as her soul loses its moorings,
it whispers to her that this passion may not be so very grand
but "prove the labyrinth of sin."

And so it does. For this passion, which seems a true instance
of Courtly Love, is as much a sham as that love with which she
married. She endows neither with full commitment, and soon the
passion for which she has risked her soul's health becomes tame
and barren of meaning. When Frankford again leaves the pair
alone and Wendoll, expecting his right, suggests that they sup
in her chamber, she responds:

> O what a clog unto the soul is sin.
> We pale offenders are still full of fear;
> Every suspicious eye brings danger near, . . . (xi, 103–5)

Rather than releasing her soul, her passion has merely proved
a clog to its honest functioning in the realm in which she yet

remains. She knows no ecstasy, but only shame. And Wendoll's
retort—"Fie, fie, you talk too like a Puritant" (xi, 109)—is only
too true. She is, in the best sense, a Puritan; but a weak one:

> You have tempted me to mischief, Master Wendoll;
> I have done I know not what. Well, you plead custom;
> That which for want of wit I granted erst
> I now must yield through fear. Come, come, let's in.
> Once o'er shoes, we are straight o'er head in sin. (xi, 110–14)

She is no longer enchanted, can no longer even understand what
impelled her to her first abandon, but neither does she appreciate
the gravity of her actions. She has, indeed, "lost her way." But
she has not yet lost her innocence, not yet recognized the true
nature of good and evil.

Frankford is the first to lose his innocence. When his trusty
servant Nicholas, the one person whose heart Frankford's generosity has truly won, informs his master that he is being deceived, his response marks the beginning of a crucial change in
his soul. For the first time his innocent heart ponders the fearful
possibility:

> Though I durst pawn my life, and on their faith
> Hazard the dear salvation of my soul,
> Yet in my trust I may be too secure.
> May this be true? O may it? Can it be? (viii, 73–6)

Incredulously he asks himself again and again how it can be
that the sum of good attributes should not produce goodness:
"Is all this seeming gold plain copper?" (viii, 101). Unable to
apprehend the essence behind the attribute and so to resolve
his spiritual doubt, he gives way to despair: "what thing mortal
may we trust. . . . O God, O God" (viii, 78, 103). His habitual
frame of reference, upon which the security of his spirit had
rested, now begins to disintegrate. He resolves to act as though
nothing had happened until he can determine the truth of the
matter, but at his next encounter with his wife and Wendoll he

feels himself breaking down and leaves them abruptly. He can put off the dreaded proof no longer and immediately plans to set a trap for them.

That dreaded night is to work a complete reversal of his spiritual nature. As he stands outside his gate fingering his keys, the key to his bedroom door rekindles his torment at the hallucinations of appearance:

> Fountain and spring of all my bleeding thoughts,
> Where the most hallowed order and true knot
> Of nuptial sanctity hath been prophan'd.
> It leads to my polluted bedchamber,
> Once my terrestrial heaven, now my earth's hell, . . . (xiii,
> 11–15)

That which had seemed to be a sanctified marriage, one that brings divine order into the everyday life of man and converts this life into a "terrestrial heaven," has proved to be a polluted value which can make a hell of earth. And, lest his trust in this most desired appearance should be completely destroyed, he is stopped by fear at his chamber door:

>   Astonishment,
> Fear, and amazement beat upon[5] my heart,
> Even as a madman beats upon a drum.
> O keep my eyes, you Heavens, before I enter,
> From any sight that may transfix my soul; . . . (xiii, 23–7)

Driven almost to madness by the fear that his whole structure of values will disintegrate at the coming confrontation, he enters, sees them "lying/ Close in each other's arms, and fast asleep" (xiii, 42–3), and, lest he "damn two precious souls" (xiii, 44),, quickly withdraws crying, "O me unhappy" (xiii, 42).

This is the end of his first spiritual movement. It had begun with his smug satisfaction, as adding up all his endowments and ornaments, he had proclaimed himself happy. Now he learns that all of these possessions have only served to bring about his unhappiness. All that had formerly been the basis of his modest pride collapses into meaninglessness. But, out of the suffering which this collapse invokes, his spirit is regenerated on a new and higher basis. This spiritual change, which occurs beneath the level of consciousness, becomes manifest in his next utterance: "O God, O God, that it were possible/ To undo things done, to call back yesterday" (xiii, 51–2). Whereas, in his earlier spiritual framework, he had asked himself "Is all this seeming gold plain copper?" now that he actually sees his marriage "prophan'd" and "polluted" by his wife's infidelity, he does not, surprisingly, reject her essential value. On the basis of his former distinction between appearance and reality, he should no longer be able to see her— even in the past—as pure in spirit. But, not only can he see her so, he longs "that I might take her/ As spotless as an angel in my arms" (xiii, 61–2).

This marks a complete change of spiritual orientation. No longer does he regard her as the sum of ornamental attributes; through his own suffering, he gains a sympathetic appreciation of her very essence. As his own spirit becomes purified, he reaches out to embrace her on a higher level. And then the dreadful realization comes: "But O! I talk of things impossible,/ And cast beyond the moon" xiii, 63–4). It is not possible "To undo things done." He has become "Time's fool."

When he sees his wife shedding the fertile tears of penitence, his torment becomes unbearable: "Spare thou thy tears, for I will weep for thee;/And keep thy countenance, for I'll blush for thee./ Now I protest I think 'tis I am tainted" (xiii, 84–6). What is most poignant about these beautiful expressions of love is that this should be the first time he has shown her such love. That true sympathy, which had tragically commenced at the very moment when he fully appreciated the meaning of her loss, now swells to such an extent that her sorrow becomes more painful to him than his own. He feels what she feels and, in the strength of this new relation of sympathetic love, assumes her guilt.

Mrs. Frankford's tragic reorientation comes about more slowly, but when it is finally achieved its effects are far more devastating. Upon discovery, her first reaction is the bewildered realization of the gravity of her thoughtless and, of late, even casual acts:

> O by what word, what title, or what name
> Shall I entreat your pardon? Pardon! O
> I am as far from hoping such sweet grace
> As Lucifer from Heaven. To call you husand—
> O me most wretched, I have lost that name; . . . (xiii, 78-82)

Blindly she gropes for the means of pardon only to realize that she has fallen irrevocably. That word of intimate relation, "husband," which had risen so readily to her lips on her wedding day that her brother had been forced to remark "How strangely the word 'husband' fits your mouth" (i, 38), now sticks in her throat. Preparing herself for sentence, she states the terrible because incontrovertible fact: "I am no more your wife" (xiii, 83).

When her husband's sympathy falls unexpectedly upon her, her sense of loss also becomes unbearable:

> I would I had no tongue, no ears, no eyes,
> No apprehension, no capacity.
> When do you spurn me like a dog? When tread me
> Under your feet? When drag me by the hair? (xiii, 90-3)

Like her husband, Mrs. Frankford wishes to be spared the full knowledge of her loss. When she had realized the enormity of her own sin, she had expected the utmost severity of his punishment. Now she almost asks for punishment as a relief from the sympathy which, in her unworthiness, she can no longer accept. Still, his sympathy draws from her the incredible sweetness of her last request:

> Though I deserve a thousand thousand fold
> More than you can inflict, yet, once my husband,
> For womanhood . . . mark not my face
> Nor hack me with your sword. . . .

I am not worthy that I should prevail
In the least suit, no, not to speak to you,
Nor look on you, nor to be in your presence;
Yet as an abject this one suit I crave,
This granted I am ready for my grave. (xiii, 94–6, 98–9,
    101–5)

The more she desires to be in his sweet presence, the more she feels her unworthiness and that the most barbarous actions would be justified in him. And so she pitiably begs him to spare her from what would be unthinkable to him.

The sweetness of each increases the sympathy of the other and, with this, comes an increase in their mutual suffering. Frankford's inner being has undergone a great change, but this change has occurred on a pre-intellectual level. It is with the vestiges of his former intellectual orientation that he asks the uncomprehending question of the false romantic lover, "Why me?" That his own moral behavior is beyond reproach, he feels certain; but he is also made painfully aware that, despite this, all he has done for her has somehow not been enough. Like every husband whose wife has been untrue, he tries to understand wherein he has been inadequate; but his true inadequacy is unconsciously made manifest in the very questions he asks of her. His first thought is to the central pillar of his pride, his material generosity. When this is denied, he questions his masculinity. It is only last that he turns to love:

Frank. Did I not lodge thee in my bosom?
    Wear thee here in my heart?
Anne.   You did.
Frank. I did indeed; witness my tears I did.
    Go bring my infants hither.
        [Exit Maid and returns with two Children.]
                O Nan, O Nan, . . . (xiii, 113–6)

The tears he sheds at the thought of his love witness much more to the depth of his present love than to that love which he had shown in the past. As the children are brought out to him, this living symbol of their marriage and love completely breaks down his emotional resistance to her. His love reaches out to her in all the intimacy of which these children are a symbol—"O Nan, O Nan"—and with this the painfully uncomprehending "why?" But it is too much for him to bear, and he retires from her sight to consider what he must do.

With the understanding bred of his own anguish, Frankford rises to the "kindness" of his final decision: he and his children must be separated from her, but she is to be given ample means to continue life. What is remarkable about this decision is that while he sees the unfortunate results of his former generosity, he does not repudiate it but raises it to a higher level. He is, however, no longer motivated to generosity by the desire to augment his own worth and happiness, but by a sympathy united to responsibility. Effusive generosity would impel him to reaccept his dearly beloved wife,[6] to forgive and forget, but responsibility places her moral salvation above their happiness, and this can only be accomplished by the harsh fact of a complete divorce. His final decision reflects the claims of both justice and mercy. If justice demands that she be made to feel the effects of her moral conduct, his mercy consists in the gift of free life, that she be entirely free to arrive at her own moral destiny.

The first effect of his decision is the mutual suffering of their separation. Now that she sees that it is only through her husband and children that her earthly happiness is possible, her loss of them makes life unbearable; she wishes to end her wretched existence right on the very road that is taking her from her family. Her servants' commiseration does not withhold her, but it is her husband's message, delivered by Nicholas with the lute, that finally instructs her spirit:

> My master commends him to ye; there's all he can find that was ever yours. He hath nothing left that ever you could lay claim to but his own heart—and he could afford you that. All that I have to deliver you is this: he prays you to forget him, and so he bids you farewell. (xvi, 21–5)

Though "his own heart" is still hers, "he prays you to forget him"! Feeling the pain of his own inability to forget her, his sympathetic love rises to the sublime level of wishing that her spirit might be freed of suffering even though it is she who is responsible for the suffering of both. For the first time the moral meaning of his gift of freedom becomes clear to her. She now accepts his gift of free life not as a good in itself, for her freedom means also her loss of him as a husband and so of earthly happiness, but as a means to redeem her fallen goodness.

And she immediately realizes that the only means by which this redemption can be accomplished is through repentant death. Whereas before she had desired death as a means of ending her misery, she now sees death as a moral instrument whereby her goodness may be redeemed and, even more important, her love prove itself worthy. Had she loved her husband less, she could have accepted his prayer "to forget him" and tried to build a wiser life on the wreckage of the old. But the more she considers her sin in the light of his sympathy, the more her hopeless love for him grows and the less she can envision such a life without him. All she now desires is to know herself once again worthy of his love, and this can be accomplished only by transcending the desire for the recovery of her earthly marriage, through a repentance so deep that it can only be satisfied by the final penance of death. If she did less than this, the depth of her repentance would be suspect even to herself. She would still be in a position where, as she had recognized while awaiting judgment, "He cannot be so base as to forgive me,/ Nor I so shameless to accept his pardon" (xiii, 139–40).

When Mrs. Frankford, true to her vow of starvation, lies dying, she sends for her husband, saying: "My soul but tarries/ His arrive and I am fit for Heaven" (xvii, 61–2). Though even the strictest Puritan moralist would say that her soul was eminently "fit for heaven" without Frankford's arrival, it is because Heywood is not simply writing a tragedy of spiritual salvation but of love that he makes her utmost concern in the last moments of life with her husband's pardon. Her sympathetic love teaches her that if she cannot endure life divorced from her husband, this divorce is also a continuing torment for him. It is not only she that needs his pardon; he needs to give it: "I lov'd her dearly,/ And when I do but think of her unkindness,/ My thoughts are all in Hell" (xiv, 4–6). Until his heart is cleared of bitterness, the effects of her sin endure despite her penitence.

This is not, however, the only reason why her hopes for heavenly pardon rest with his forgiveness; in her mind, the two are identified. Nor is she ethically wrong in this. Heywood has taken great pains to stress the Christlike qualities of Frankford, underscoring them in his relations with Wendoll. Frankford twice refers to Wendoll as "Judas," and Wendoll had likewise pictured Frankford as Christ. Frankford's mercy toward his wife and the patience with which he has endured his wrongs are certainly an emulation of the highest Christian virtues. To be worthy the pardon of such a man, therefore, is a sign of objective worth that may stand before the highest judge. But if this symbolic level exists in the play, it is not this that causes Mrs. Frankford to identify heavenly pardon with her husband's pardon. Mrs. Frankford is a wholly emotional woman. She has not her husband's breadth of vision and could never say, as he does when he enters the final scene:

> God, that had laid this cross upon our heads,
> Might had He pleas'd have made our cause of meeting
> On a more fair and a more contented ground;
> But He that made us, made us to this woe. (xvii, 69–72)

If he has lost his innocent assurance of happiness as the condition of man, he has had the moral vision to reaccept life on a higher level. Mrs. Frankford cannot do this. She cannot divine God's will directly but only through the agency of that which she feels to be most highly moral, her husband. They perfectly represent Milton's view of the spiritual relationship within the Puritan marriage: "Hee for God only, shee for God in him" (*Paradise Lost,* IV, 299). As it was in desiring her husband's pardon that she was first made to realize the gravity of her sin, so it is only though his pardon that she can feel her sin to be redeemed.

But whereas God's pardon could have been gained by living the completely reformed moral life that had been her husband's wish in granting her continued life, *his* pardon is a far more difficult thing to earn, more difficult because it is immediately needed. Living such a moral life in hopes of gaining his pardon is impossible for her, for she simply cannot live without his pardon. And herein lies her tragedy: the only way in which her husband's loving acceptance can be redeemed, and thus life sustained, is through her death. If this last scene be read merely as the story of her spiritual salvation, accompanied by a chorus of weeping friends and relations, it becomes a simple, sentimental tear-jerker. It is only by reading the story of her salvation in its context of human love that its tragic nature can be realized. What is most poignant about these last lines is not Mrs. Frankford's humble desire for salvation and Frankford's magnanimous sympathy but the love that underlies their every word, the love that cannot be satisfied in the sacrifice which its very demands have dictated because it desires its continuing fulfillment on earth. It is this tension between earth and heaven that produces the tragic force of her death.

Frankford approaches his wife with cold detachment: "How do you, woman?" (xvii, 74). Feeling her shame most intensely because of his coldness, and yet hopeful in her penitence, she tries with anxious humility to establish contact:

> Well, Master Frankford, well; but shall be better
> I hope within this hour. Will you vouchsafe,
> Out of your grace and your humanity,
> To take a spotted strumpet by the hand? (xvii, 75–8)

He takes her hand out of humanity, but this galvanic contact begins the release of his suppressed emotions. She is no longer merely an impersonal "woman," but a woman to whom he was *once* strongly bound:

> This hand once held my heart in faster bonds
> Than now 'tis gripp'd by me. God pardon them
> That made us first break hold. (xvii, 79–81)

Frankford is here at his most magnanimous. This magnanimity does not unite their broken relationship, however, but just permits him to view it with compassion. But Mrs. Frankford desires real union through pardon, that pardon for which she has already sold her life. Seizing upon his impersonal thought of pardon, she releases all the longing of her soul:

> Amen, amen.
> Out of my zeal to Heaven, whither I am now bound,
> I was so impudent to wish you here,
> And once more beg your pardon. O good man,
> And father to my children, pardon me.
> Pardon, O pardon me! My fault so heinous is
> That if you in this world forgive it not,
> Heaven will not clear it in the world to come. (xvii, 81–8)

Though she appeals to him on the ground of his goodness and of their formerly fruitful marriage, it is her love that speaks and his that answers:

> As freely from the low depth of my soul
> As my Redeemer hath forgiven His death,
> I pardon thee. I will shed tears for thee,
> Pray with thee, and in mere pity
> Of they weak state I'll wish to die with thee.
> . . . Though thy rash offence
> Divorc'd our bodies, thy repentant tears
> Unite our souls. (xvii, 93–7, 107–9)

Seeing the desperate depth of her penitence, the depth of his soul is engaged. She is more than redeemed in his sight, for such power of goodness he had not expected in her. Now that he can accept her soul, his sympathetic love flows out with its full force. As his sympathy for her suffering had earlier caused him to assume her guilt, now that he understands her desire for death as the only fitting penance, he actually feels *her* will to die. This desire for sympathetic death is the effect of his love, but his love does not actually impel him to death because neither of them considers heaven and the afterlife as a consummation of human love but exclusively of divine love. For both, the consummation of their love can only occur on earth. Frankford has always affirmed the value and dignity of earthly existence, and his disillusionment has not been with life but only with his formerly smug acceptance of it. The loss of this has, in fact, enabled him to accept life on a higher level because he can now accept its necessary evil as well as its good. When he gave his wife continued life, it was the highest gift of which he could conceive. Frankford does not divorce the divine from the human but sees the divine as working through life and sanctifying its earthly good. He sees marriage not as a venal order but as a sacrament. This love is the most sublime form of World Love. But the sacrament of marriage is imperfect if it is not imbued with the full commitment of World Love. Now for the first time their love reaches that full commitment that can "unite our souls" and so create a true marriage.

The tragedy of this marriage, meant for life, is that it can now only come into being in virtue of death. Frankford's acceptance can only make his wife "not of this world" (xvii, 113). For Mrs. Frankford's sin has been such that only an utter purgation can, in the nature of tragic paradox, fit her for the earthly marriage she craves: "Pardon'd on earth, soul, thou in Heaven art free;/ Once more thy wife, dies thus embracing thee" (xvii, 121–2). Death can be accepted as the consequence of this new marriage precisely because this love has become the highest value of life and its consummation on earth all-important. But its consummation is tragic because it is "Time's fool," bereft of continuity by the irrevocable sins of False Romantic Love on which it is predicated.

A Woman Killed With Kindness is a profound love tragedy; if the language of its characters does not always rise to the purity of its ethical instincts, it is always true to character deeply conceived. Only twice is speech woefully out of character and this is in Frankford's two speeches in which the title of the play is contained. But Heywood can be forgiven this, as he can the lengthy and inferior subplot,[7] for in this finest of domestic tragedies the pathos of everyday life, touched with moral weakness but straining for perfection, is realized with a humility and sweetness of utterance that most befit its homely theme.

Edward IV

Heywood's masterpiece marks a great improvement in the tragic handling of this theme over his first essay into domestic love tragedy, *Edward IV*. The love of Matthew and Jane Shore is fully committed, but both are also intensely loyal to their king. When it is King Edward himself who demands her favors, Jane finally yields to him rather than commit the greater fault of treason. She continues to love Shore, prostitute herself to the king's will out of a sense of duty and without any pleasure, and do continual penance for a sin for which she is not to blame. Only once does her constant longing for Shore almost give rise to her treason. It is when, accidentally coming upon her husband who is about to leave the country because of his shame, she allows herself the hope that by running away with him she can escape the king's influence. But Shore himself will not permit such a treasonous act. Her life in court is spent like an angel of mercy, and her patient fortitude in adversity is exemplary. But not even the tragedy of a saint can be hers, or Shore's either— he matching her in saintly goodness—for in the end they are broken and die of a spiritual exhaustion that is akin to despair. At the end Shore says: "Man, euen from his birth,/ Finds nothing else but misery on earth." [8] In the four years that passed between this statement and Frankford's firm "But he that made us, made us to this woe," Heywood was able to move beyond this despairing faith to a higher acceptance of life upon a tragic basis. But in 1599, the year also of Marston's equally despairing *Antonio and Mellida,* he could not yet transmute his sympathy for human suffering into tragic affirmation.

He was then, however, but twenty-five years of age; an age when despair is easy and yet cannot suppress the youthful joy that, in this same play created the endearing character of Hobs and expressed such surging patriotism and love of simple things. In his long life, Heywood's concern with simple goodness—his joy at its prosperity and sympathy for its suffering—never changed. But this concern, like all things human, suffered the transmutations of time, and his sympathy being great, these transmutations reflected the changing sensibility of the age.

The English Traveller

Late in life, Heywood again turned to his favorite tragic subject and modeled a new play upon his greatest success. *The English Traveller* (1625) bears much formal resemblance to *A Woman Killed With Kindness,* but the formal closeness of the two plays only serves to point up the vast spiritual difference between them. No longer is it a question of "the most hallowed order and true knot/ Of nuptial sanctity," but rather what form of adultery is to be cherished. Mrs. Wincott's chaste love relationship with Geraldine is absolutely condoned and her greatest sin in terms of the play is not in being untrue to her husband but, in so doing, betraying Geraldine's loving trust. But since this love is itself a betrayal of the conjugal love with whose infringement his innocence is outraged, the whole ethical core of the play is unsound, if not diseased. It is not only the terms in which this central ethical question is posed which are unsound but also the moral quality of Geraldine and Mrs. Wincott. She is a thoroughly corrupt character, carrying on her secret affair with Dalavill with an easy complacency and brazen hypocrisy. Without a qualm she has, for an extended period, been playing false to her husband, her chaste lover, and the hopes of her sister. And though Geraldine, upon discovering the lovers, spares their lives and refrains from disclosing the secret of their adultery, this seeming "goodness" is completely voided of meaning by his selfish desire for her death as a means of escape from his own chaste, adulterous vows. With no psychological realism, however, the impudent Mrs. Wincott proceeds to do just as he asks. But her repentant death draws no sympathy from those who loved her.

Pandering to the jaded imagination of an audience that required increased stimulation to sustain its interest, Heywood's own moral sensibility has hardened, his taste coarsened, his piety become rigid. Considering *The English Traveller* in its necessary relation to *A Woman Killed With Kindness,* one can only sigh at the change which twenty-two years had wrought on the spirit of this sweetest of tragic poets and on the theatre which had once produced such an artless masterpiece as his.

This earlier period, if it concerned itself with the tragedy of moral weakness, did so with full moral vitality. What is most significant about Mrs. Frankford is not her liability to temptation but the strength of her moral rebound, a strength gained from the recognition that the good irrevocably lost by her fall from innocence was a fine value capable of sustaining meaningful life. Inspired and guided by the loving forgiveness of her wronged husband, she is able, moreover, to transcend the despair arising from this recognition of loss in a final redemptive reconciliation. This redemption through a kind of vicarious atonement is a pervasive feature of the Elizabethan domestic drama, a form that *A Woman Killed With Kindness* exemplifies. But it continues to play an important, if diminishing, role in the redemptive process of the later non-domestic tragedies of False Romantic Love. In these later tragedies, however, the normative love envisioned is more the result of nostalgia than belief and thus can neither be given initial dramatic representation nor effect as genuine a final redemption. These later plays show the decadence of False Romantic Love tragedy, that in which expression, though powerfully true, is limited in ultimate implication. *A Woman Killed With Kindness* can similarly be viewed as the classic tragedy of False Romantic Love, that in which the form is given its definitive and most universal expression. It shows us a vision of mankind shackled by a romanticism without *mystique* and straining for a sense of human relatedness which the irresponsibility of sentiment has rendered it incapable of achieving. While presenting the tragedy of False Romantic Love, it projects a vision of conjugal Worldly Love whose exalted nature has never been surpassed. In the plays of Worldly Love, the tragic nature of this love will be revealed. Here, however, we are permitted one moment of grace to contemplate a vision of love that can achieve a nontragic fulfillment on earth when man learns to embrace it with full commitment in time.

5

The Courtly Pattern

Where Heywood projected a norm of Worldly Love in his tragedies of False Romantic Love, Beaumont and Fletcher mark a return to the norm of Courtly Love, but a norm accepted in the decadent form already achieved at the hands of Marston. Beaumont and Fletcher portray Courtly Love constantly in their tragicomedies and comedies, but they never build a tragedy about it. The corpus of plays that bears the names of "Beaumont and Fletcher" as authors contains three love tragedies: *Cupid's Revenge* (1608), *The Maid's Tragedy* (1610), and *The Double Marriage* (1620). Beaumont and Fletcher are the authors of the first two, Fletcher and Massinger of the third. But the three plays are no more than successive treatments of one theme conceived in one manner: the tragedy of irresponsible involvement. For Beaumont and Fletcher, love tragedy evolves from the inability of the lover to recognize or adhere to the ideal woman who has been presented to him until she is either dead or he has effectively barred himself from her. This is the only genuine tragedy that they could write about an ideal which had, even for them, no real but only desired substance.[1] Beaumont and Fletcher have been convicted by their modern critics of dramatic irresponsibility, and this is true. But when they turn to tragedy, it is the tragedy of irresponsibility that they write. *The Maid's Tragedy* is their greatest play and its greatness rests upon the authors' own awareness of the tragic limitations of their orientation.

There is one thing, however, of which neither they nor their critics were aware. Beaumont began his dramatic career, in *The Knight of the Burning Pestle* (1607), with a satire on Heywood's naive enthusiasm. He felt that he was too sophisticated to be "taken in" by it. But when he himself turned to serious drama, and especially tragedy, he approximated Heywood much more closely than he would have liked to admit. Both used every means at their command to elicit the emotional responses of their audience, and the greatest work of each was the tragedy of false romanticism. Now it is the turn of Beaumont and Fletcher to be the victims of a sophistication in their critics that precludes a full appreciation of their worth. Lawrence B. Wallis, for example, says:

> Several years before I began this study, when trying to make clear to college classes why *Hamlet* is actually superior to *The Maid's Tragedy,* I had learned that modern young readers might still succumb to the deft craftsmanship of Beaumont and Fletcher. So I had analyzed with them certain portions of the latter play in order to bring out what I have since named its "emotional patterning." In doing so, I had found that I could make students understand the means by which the drama's plausible smoothness and artistry had deceived them.[2]

Heaven forbid that we should be deceived! But heaven forbid, also, that an analysis of the means used to achieve the "plausible smoothness and artistry" or "certain portions" of the play should blind us to the meaning and value of the whole. This meaning can best be approached through a consideration of Beaumont and Fletcher's first attempt at the tragedy of False Romantic Love, *Cupid's Revenge.*

Cupid's Revenge

The allegorical device of Cupid and his cult, which Beaumont and Fletcher use to motivate the action of their first love tragedy, reveals their understanding of the nature of tragic false romanticism. Leucippus' tragic error is his denial of seriousness to love: "There is no such power:/ But the opinion of him fills the Land/ With lustful sins" (I, i, Vol. 9, p. 223).[3] It is for this sin that Cupid vows revenge against Leucippus, providing an apt description of this tragic mode when he claims him as victim:

> Leucippus thou art shot through with a shaft
> That will not rankle long, yet sharp enough
> To sow a world of helpless misery—(I, i, p. 235)

The denial of seriousness to love leads to impermanent involvements and to the further misery of their consequences. This is perhaps the most overt testimony made by dramatists of this period on the possibility of tragedy resulting from a merely transient and uninspired love.

The first important difference between the Beaumont and Fletcher and the Heywood tragic patterns of False Romantic Love is that the former begin their main action not with the innocent possession of good but after the fall to temptation has already taken place. Although Leucippus had seconded his sister's demand for outlawing the worship of Cupid, when he is next seen he is about to leave his mistress. Unable to maintain his own high standards, he had become innocently involved with a woman whose consummate hypocrisy had led him to believe that no complications would ensue from their affair. He learns, however, that even such a debased and casual involvement has a fearful power over his free integrity. Because of his innocence, Bacha is able to convince him that he has seduced her and must vindicate her honor in the face of his father's accusations. Still not understanding the seriousness of casual acts, he so overplays his

defense that he succeeds in erecting her into an image of unparalleled virtue. In so doing, Leucippus finds that he has embraced evil, first from the effects of his "conscience (never us'd
to lye)" (II, i, p. 239), and second because these lies result in
his father's hasty marriage to Bacha. In agreeing to lie on Bacha's
behalf, he had already learned that involvements carry certain
responsibilities, but these further effects imbue him with a new
respect for the seriousness of the most trivial act. Suffering, rather
than showing him the inadequacy of his earlier smug virtue, only
throws him back more rigidly into his former path. If sin makes
one vulnerable to evil, then virtue shall henceforth be his shield
of armor.

This pious hope is brutally undermined in a brilliant confrontation scene with Bacha, a type of scene that is to become
an integral part of the Beaumont and Fletcher tragic pattern
of False Romantic Love. In this scene, Beaumont[4] faces Leucippus
with a series of shifting moral appearances which gradually undermines his faith in life. When he finally learns that Bacha still
desires him as a lover and is even willing to kill his father to
effect this end, and when she realizes that she has only inspired
his loathing, their future course is unalterably determined. Bacha
vows his death and Leucippus accepts death, even at her hands,
as his only desire.

When Bacha's intrigues against his life bring him to trial,
all he can say is:

> . . . I am weary of my life,
> For Gods sake take it from me . . .
> The usage I have had, I know would make
> Wisdom her self run frantick through the streets,
> And Patience quarrel with her shadow.
> . . . my wickedness has brought
> All this to pass, else I should bear my self. (IV, i, pp. 264–5)

Patience is undermined because that which wisdom shows him
to be true, the extent of wickedness and his own responsibility
for it, drives him almost frantic. He had compromised his virtue

by following the way of the world in his involvement with Bacha, and, thus compromised, all his subsequent virtue cannot free him from her power. Accepting responsibility for the treatment he has received, since it cannot redeem his fault, can only increase his unbearable weariness with life.

Beaumont had carried Leucippus' tragic history to this point but now gives it over largely into Fletcher's hands. As Fletcher takes control of Leucippus, the character undergoes a marked change, the most important factor being his immediate disavowal of responsibility: "My innocency is my Armor" (IV, i, p. 272). But this change is echoed in Beaumont's last remaining scene with this character,[5] as evidenced by Leucippus' claim: "for I know/ My courses are most just; nor will I stain 'em/ With one bad action" (IV, i, p. 278). This disclaiming of responsibility, in which both authors concur, differentiates the pattern of False Romantic Love tragedy constructed by Beaumont and Fletcher from the classic pattern of Heywood. But such a basic shift in characterization on the part of our authors is not as irresponsible as might at first appear, for without such an evasion of responsibility Leucippus' sanity might crumble and he "run frantick through the streets." As he had earlier evaded the laws he had caused to be enforced and had become irresponsibly involved with Bacha, so again, when responsible behavior becomes too burdensome for his weak spirit to bear, he evades it.

When a people's uprising rescues him from his captors, instead of pursuing his advantage he dismisses his supporters and chooses the solitude of the wilderness where alone he will be able to preserve his spiritual purity. Alone in the wilderness, having learned through suffering the importance of moral commitment while seeing nothing on earth worthy of it save the integrity of his own soul, he is visited by the blessing of Urania's love. Symbol of that spiritual love which her name implies, yet daughter of Bacha and a world that will not allow such spiritual love an earthly fruition, she has come to die in Leucippus' presence because of her conviction that Leucippus would never accept the love of Bacha's daughter. Nor is this belief invalid on the symbolic level to which the play has risen, as Leucippus' retirement to the wilderness was a rejection of the human world.

Leucippus, showered by the selfless love that her disguise and approaching death have permitted her to manifest, has been moved, despite his desire for solitude, to an unexpected solicitude for her:

> *Ura.* I cannot eat, God thank you.
> But I'll eat to morrow.
>   *Lou.* Thou't be dead by that time.
>   *Ura.* I should be well then, for you will not love me.
>   *Lou.* Indeed I will. This is the prettiest passion that e'er I felt yet. . . . Thou wilt love me?
>   *Ura.* Yes sure till I die, and when I am in heaven, I'll e'en wish for you.
>   *Lou.* And I'll come to thee boy.
> This is a Love I never yet heard tell of: come, thou are sleepy, child; goe in, and I'll sit with thee: . . . (V, i, p. 284)

This spiritual love, death impelled yet death transcending, is indeed "a love I never yet heard tell of," surely not when he had so categorically denied the very existence of a love higher than that of "lustful sins." The tragedy of this denial is that the false romanticism that resulted from it had closed to him the earthly possibility of that higher love which he now both recognizes and desires. When Urania dies—as a result of intercepting a blow meant for him—and her identity is revealed, Leucippus' desire for her love suddenly erupts with special urgency: "I will love thee, or any thing: what? wilt/ Thou leave me as soon as I know thee?" (V, i, p. 287). With the realization that a love so strong it was capable of sacrificial death had been barred to him by the still operating effects of his own irresponsible involvement with Bacha, his last tie to life is severed: "it is no matter who/ Comes on me now" (V, i, p. 287). The supreme importance of his own spiritual integrity, which had become his only light in an ethical wilderness, now pales beside this revelation of another life, a life hallowed by love. He no longer looks upon death as a wished for escape from a world of evil but as the fulfillment of eternal love.

When, his father having died, the lords bring Bacha before him for sentencing, Leucippus understands that he must "Leave her to Heaven" (V, i, 287), a heaven now recognized as merciful. Bacha, however, rejecting this mercy which she cannot understand, uses her momentary freedom to stab Leucippus. Destroyed by the power of earthly hatred, Leucippus finds himself in death "Nearer my health, than I think any here" (V, i, 288). Rising above his false romantic involvement with life, Leucippus meets death like a courtly lover.

This marks the final difference between the Heywood and the Beaumont and Fletcher patterns of False Romantic Love. If the hero's involvement with the wicked woman had caused him to hate life, his final appreciation of the good woman causes him to love death. Broken by the evil to which his irresponsible involvement had made him vulnerable, her sacrificial forgiveness shows him a vision of death not as penance for his sin (the classic pattern) but as a release and reward for his suffering.

The Maid's Tragedy

The Maid's Tragedy marks a great dramatic advance over *Cupid's Revenge*. In the earlier play, fantasy almost completely substitutes for realistic presentation, love's tragedy being enacted in terms of the obvious allegory of Cupid and the only slightly disguised allegory of Urania; in the later play the setting and characterizations are entirely realistic.

The Maid's Tragedy perfects the dramatic method of *Cupid's Revenge* in beginning after the denial of love has been accomplished. The play opens with preparations for Amintor's marriage to Evadne, a marriage which we learn is following hard upon Amintor's broken engagement to Aspatia. Amintor had "pour'd the sweetest words/ That Art or Love could frame" (II, Vol. I, p. 15) into Aspatia's ears only to rebound from her love into new love for the more dazzling Evadne. As Amintor himself later says: "It was the King first mov'd me to't, but he/ Has

not my will in keeping" (II, p. 17). This personal motivation
may be better understood by recognizing the appearance which
Aspatia presented to him.

Aspatia does not represent a genuine Courtly Love but a
self-conscious imitation of it. Excessive reading in the literature
of Courtly Love, would seem to have developed in her a craving
for an intensely tragic love experience which held her more
genuine feelings in captivity. But Amintor, who had no such
intense cravings and longed only to "draw out/ A long con-
tented life together here" (III, p. 31), must have become dis-
pleased by such an unwonted display of intensity. That Aspatia
finally understood this is revealed in her advice to Evadne: "if
you love so well,/ Alas, you may displease him, so did I" (II,
p. 16). She had made "a Faith out of the miracles of Ancient
Lovers. . . . Such as speak truth and dy'd in't" (II, p. 24). Now
she sees herself as the only remaining miracle of true love in
an inconstant world and, both because of this "faith" and her
new knowledge of the world's inconstancy, resolves to die in
it. Dramatizing this misery to her maids, she bids them use her
as model for their needlework of the forsaken Ariadne:

> Do it again by me the lost Aspatia,
> And you shall find all true but the wild Island;
> I stand upon the Sea beach now, and think
> Mine arms thus, and mine hair blown with the wind,
> Wild as that desart, and let all about me
> Tell that I am forsaken, do my face . . .
> Like sorrows monument; and the trees about me,
> Let them be dry and leaveless; let the Rocks
> Groan with a continual surges, and behind me
> Make all a desolation; look, look Wenches,
> A miserable life of this poor Picture. (II, pp. 25–6)

In this picture, Fletcher, in one of his finest poetic flights, has
caught that curious mixture of genuine disenchantment and
self-conscious pose that characterizes Aspatia almost to the end
of her fatally determined course.

Considering his denial of Aspatia's love a small price for the happiness he expects from his new found love for Evadne, sanctioned as it is by the King's will, Amintor, eagerly awaits the wedding night and the knowledge it will bring. But our initiation into Evadne's secrets slightly precedes Amintor's, as we discover her being prepared for the wedding night by her maids. Among the attendant ladies is the heartbroken Aspatia and hearty Dula, and in Evadne's reactions to them we discover a dissonant note which will be sounded with increasing force and modulations in the events to follow. Coolly parrying Dula's unrestrained high spirits, Evadne turns to play with Aspatia's sorrow. To this Aspatia feelingly responds: "It were a timeless smile should prove my cheek,/ . . . this should have been/ My night" (II, p. 15). But as Aspatia continues in this vein, Evadne interrupts the sorrowful outburst she had provoked, saying: "Nay, leave this sad talk Madam. . . . See if you have not spoil'd all Dulas mirth" (II, p. 15). When, however, Aspatia, upon leaving, announces and embroiders upon her approaching death, Evadne is forced to remark: "Alas, I pity thee" (II, p. 17).

And so she does, both Aspatia and Dula, for their vulnerable and unadvised lack of control. But this pity is not a sympathetic emotion, rather a detached comment on the pathos that attends the lack of such emotional control as she prides herself upon. It is but the subordinate manifestation of her scorn. The primary manifestation of this scorn is the usually controlled but sometimes unrestrained sadism with which she treats all those who come within her power. She is, indeed, one who "strikes dead/ With flashes of her eye" (I, p. 3). And it was to win this Medusa that Amintor had forsaken Aspatia to her death.

Coming upon Aspatia as she is leaving, he is greeted by her sorrow:

Go and be happy in your Ladies love . . .
You'l come my Lord, and see the Virgins weep
When I am laid in earth, though you your self
Can know no pity: . . . (II, p. 17)

Having just experienced Evadne's "pity," she can expect no more from the proven inconstancy of Amintor. But the quiet desperation of her grief does touch him:

> I did that Lady wrong; methinks I feel
> Her grief shoot suddenly through all my veins;
> Mine eyes run; this is strange at such a time.
> It was the King first mov'd me to't, but he
> Has not my will in keeping—why do I
> Perplex my self thus? something whispers me,
> Go not to bed; my guilt is not so great
> As mine own conscience (too sensible)
> Would make me think; I only brake a promise,
> And 'twas the King that forc't me: timorous flesh,
> Why shak'st thou so? away my idle fears.
> Yonder she is, the lustre of whose eye
> Can blot away the sad remembrance
> Of all these things: . . . (II, p. 17)

He is pained by his sudden acknowledgment of responsibility for Aspatia's fate which he recognizes cannot be wholly laid at the King's charge. Aspatia's mortal grief seems a greater price for his freedom than his conscience can bear; and he momentarily wishes he could rectify his sin rather than ratify it by the consummation of his marriage. But his love for Evadne is greater than his sympathy for Aspatia and acts to mitigate his guilt.

In the scene which follows, Beaumont repeats his triumph of a confrontation scene which shifts appearances not merely for theatrical effectiveness but so that innocence may be initiated. In the earlier play, Leucippus had entered such a scene thinking that his own position was impaired only by the guilt born of recognizing in his father's marriage the unfortunate fruits of his own irresponsibility. So, too, does Amintor enter this scene recognizing in Aspatia's grief the unfortunate fruits of his own irresponsibility while thinking his own position to be impaired only by a "too sensible" conscience. But Evadne immediately begins to play with him as she had with Dula, cutting his enthusiastic joy with cool detachment until he begs her: "prethee put thy jests in milder looks" (II, p. 18). Searching her innocent-looking face—"I cannot find one blemish in thy face,/ Where falshood should abide." (II, p. 19)—as she says "A Maidenhead Amintor at my years? . . . 'tis not for a night/ Or two that I forbear thy bed, but for ever" (II, p. 19), he can only repeat with growing astonishment, "this cannot be. . . . I dream,—awake Amintor!" (II, p. 19). Helpless beside her cold cruelty, he falls in supplication to her:

> Have mercy on my youth, my hopeful youth,
> If thou be pitiful, for (without boast)
> This Land was proud of me: what Lady was there
> That man call'd fair and vertuous in this Isle,
> That would have shun'd my love? It is in thee
> To make me hold this worth. . . . thy heart cannot be hard.
> Come lead me from the bottom of despair,
> To all the joyes thou hast; I know thou wilt; . . . (II, p. 21)

Melantius had earlier said: "His youth did promise much, and his ripe years/ Will see it all perform'd" (I. p. 3). Favored by all so that he could not but be sure of his own worth, he now finds his hopes cruelly mocked. That no fair and virtuous lady would have shunned his love was unfortunately proven by Aspatia. Though he had rejected her with the sense of impunity that these hopes had engendered, he feels his worth insures his immunity from a similar fate. Were this not true, his rejection of Aspatia could not be justified. Since he is not ready to admit such an appalling possibility, he desperately needs the confirmation of his worth that only Evadne can give him by somehow or other unsaying the torment and the doubt. Evadne, however, not only confirms his predicament but informs him through various stages that the King is her lover.

Collapsing under the full knowledge of his misery, fortune's darling now cries out the uncomprehending, Why me?: "What Devil put it in thy fancy then/ To marry me?" (II, p. 22). Desperately clinging to his formerly smug estimation of his worth, the injustice of his punishment is all the more tormenting.

Evadne's answer, "that my sin may be more honourable" (II, p. 22), finally succeeds in numbing his spirit. In the detachment produced by this numbness, he comments: "What a strange thing am I!" (II, p. 22). This strikes a sympathetic chord in Evadne and again her strangely detached pity is elicited: "A miserable one; one that my self am sorry for" (II, p. 22). For a moment her scorn of vulnerable weakness gives place to her pity for it, but both only serve to strengthen her own pride in invulnerability. Thoroughly dejected, Amintor again makes claim on her pity. As the last remnant of an impotent violence turns in upon himself he begs: "Why shew it then in this,/ If thou hast pity, though thy love be none,/ Kill me . . . rid a lingring Wretch" (II, pp. 22–23). But Evadne's self-interest, denies him even this fulfillment of his rage at fortune: "I must have one/ To fill thy room again, if thou wert dead,/ Else by this night I would: I pity thee" (II, p. 23). The desire for death, which was the last vestige of a pride unable to countenance its wrongs, yields to a total numbness: "These strange and sudden injuries have faln/ So thick upon me, that I lose all sense/ Of what they are" (II, p. 23). Asking only that his reputation be preserved and the King kept from gloating over his wrongs, he meekly accedes to her terms. Now in this glazed state, his torment turns to self-mockery as he insists upon immediately assuming his bitter role as cockold buffoon: "Come let us practise, and as wantonly/ As ever loving Bride and Bridegroom met,/ Lets laugh and enter here" (II, p. 23).

In the morning, when Evadne's brothers come to call on them, Amintor continues to mask his "sick thoughts" (III, 28) with outward hilarity. The King is so convinced by Amintor's counterfeit that, ordering the brothers out, he takes Evadne to task: "I see there is no lasting Faith in Sin" (III, 31). But Evadne proudly replies:

> I swore indeed that I would never love
> A man of lower place; but if your fortune
> Should throw you from this height, I bade you trust
> I would forsake you, and would bend to him
> That won your Throne; I love with my ambition,
> Not with mine eyes; . . . (III, pp. 31–32)

Evadne is that rare woman who is totally lacking in feminine wiles. She needs to constantly prove to herself her superior invulnerability by pointedly proving the same to her victims, and the way in which this can be best achieved is by proving them helpless against her sadistic attacks. This mode of reaction, which we have witnessed in mounting degrees of intensity in her relations to Dula, Aspatia, and finally Amintor, we now see to be also true of her relations with the King.

When the King, still underestimating her ruthlessness, cannot believe that she has so successfully controlled Amintor's natural wrath, Evadne calls upon Amintor to prove her truth in the one way he had begged her to refrain from. Now, being forced to confront his brazen wife's equally brazen lover, he understands that "The faithless Sin I made/ To fair Aspatia, is not yet reveng'd,/ It follows me" (III, p. 33). For the first time he accepts and articulates the fact that his misery—"Alas! I am nothing but a multitude/ Of walking griefs" (III, p. 33)—is the punishment for the misery his faithlessness had inflicted upon Aspatia. Nor is there any way short of death of escaping his hopeless position, since he reverently believes "there is/ Divinity about you, that strikes dead/ My rising passions, as you are my King" (III, p. 33).

But the fact that his inescapable torment is the result of his own sin and thereby justified becomes more than his weak spirit can bear. Since his injuries are "too sad a weight/ For reason to endure" (III, p. 34) when reason justifies these injuries as fitting punishment for his crime, his happier self-estimation reasserts itself and causes him to ask the perennial question of the false romantic confronted with the effects of his own irresponsibility: "why did you choose out me/ To make thus wretched?" (III, p. 34). And when the King, according with Amintor's self-estimation, answers, "for I believe thee honest, as thou wert valiant" (III, p. 34), Amintor replies:

All the happiness
Bestow'd upon me, turns into disgrace;
Gods take your honesty again, for I
Am loaden with it; . . . (III, p. 34)

He sees that his honesty, rather than being the guarantor of happiness, not only attracts the dishonest practices of others but also leaves him unable to right himself against them. But he does not see that his honesty is a burden rather than a blessing because its very basis is unstable, that he has been betrayed to dishonesty not by the perfection of his honesty but the flaw in it, his self-flattery. It is this lack of final comprehension which enables him to lament his outraged innocence almost at the same time as he assumes responsibility for this outrage. His sense of outraged innocence causes him to pity his lot, his guilty conscience to hate his life; but these contradictory attitudes, while they alternately oppress and torment his spirit, are not organically related.

This last point is the essence of John F. Danby's excellent study of Beaumont and Fletcher, a study in which the earlier approach of Arthur Mizener and his followers is rejected as inadequate and misleading:

> The charge that Beaumont sacrifices everything to situation, combined with the acknowledgment of his skill in contriving situations, might suggest that he is not sincere. There can, however, be little doubt as to the seriousness with which Beaumont took himself and his main themes . . . The sameness of his types . . . indicates obsession rather than poverty of invention. They *are* unities, but the unity they have is schizophrenic. Beaumont insists on dividing the minds of each of his *dramatic personae*. He compels them to walk among the mirrors [of appearance]. Everyone is set amid conflicts no single one can contain. Choice for them means scission, and finally self-destruction. . . . The deepest note in Beaumont is one of negation.[6]

In *Cupid's Revenge*, this double attitude was more severely disassociated and it then appeared that this disassociation was principally due to the different approaches of the two authors: Beaumont stressing the character's responsibility for his wrongs, while Fletcher militantly asserted his innocence. In the present play, Fletcher's attitude remains unchanged. Although he has only one scene that contains Amintor, he represents him therein as "an innocent,/ A soul as white as heaven" (IV, p. 50). But Beaumont, who with this single exception controls Amintor's characterization from beginning to end, has succeeded in incorporating both of these conflicting attitudes into a unified, if "schizophrenic," portrayal. Though Amintor alternately asserts his innocence and guilt, he is always Amintor, essentially good but weakened by self-flattery. Whereas Leucippus had cracked under the strain of trying to live up to self-imposed standards too high for his nature, Amintor is a fine manifestation of standards not his own, a conformist "fair-haired boy" who falls apart when forced to make a genuine moral choice and lacks the personal moral vision which can reintegrate the pieces.

Like Leucippus, however, Amintor is unwilling to right his wrongs. When Melantius suggests that he join him in "a brave revenge" (III, p. 41), Amintor replies: "I dare not do a sin, or else I would" (III, p. 41). Amintor here most closely approximates Leucippus by retreating into a rigid sense of honor as the only means of coping with the disproportionate effects of his former real lapse of honor. Melantius therefore proceeds alone to the prosecution of his revenge, but proceeds in a manner whose disorganization can only be laid at the authors' charge. Beaumont has him scheming to gain the fort long after Fletcher has had him move Evadne to take the revenge into her own hands, which renders possession of the fort useless.

Though Fletcher's Evadne undergoes an important change of attitude, her character continues essentially unchanged. Evadne enters the confrontation scene with Melantius with her usual sense of scornful invulnerability, but this suddenly cracks as she gains the incredible knowledge that she is not invulnerable to his sword. She agrees to name her lover, and this assent marks a crucial change in Evadne's attitude and behavior. It is not, however, as profound a change as might appear. Evadne has never before been brought to her knees and it is this fact, rather than any ethical agreement with her brother, which alters her feelings. She understands that all her emotional control and royal support have not, in fact, rendered her invulnerable and that it is precisely this course which is now proving most dangerous for her.

If she is to preserve herself, therefore, she has to change. Calianax will shortly say that Melantius "has no vertue in him, all's in his sword" (IV, 57) and this is true. But since the power of his sword will ever be over her head demanding that she follow his conception of virtue, she sees that it is in her personal interest to accommodate herself to this conception. This concession, rather than freeing her from his power, only paves the way for his greater demand, the horrible suggestion that she prove her newly found virtue by revenging herself against the King. Though she cries out against the dreaded sin of regicide, it is of no avail against Melantius' "virtuous sword" and she is forced to agree.

When Amintor now enters, she sees him in a new light, as a "noble youth," "a soul as white as heaven" (IV, p. 50), with whom happiness could have been as simple as it was good. Seeing him now as her "much abused Lord!" (IV, 49), she feels the inadequacy of her repentance and confesses: "My whole life is so leprous, it infects/ All my repentance" (IV, 49). The necessity of effective repentance gains a new urgency as, recognizing the value of the heart which she had so thoughtlessly thrown away, she suddenly is filled with the desire to regain his love and esteem:

> . . . though too late,
> Though in my evening, yet perceive a will,
> Since I can do no good because a woman,
> Reach constantly at some thing that is near it; . . . (IV, p. 50)

Her will to the good is genuine, but the corruption of her nature, though its destructive futility has been fully recognized and repudiated, still has power to pervert her will from its higher course. It is "too late" for effective change. Though she may substitute a new set of values for the old, she cannot change her method of achieving them. Her need for sadistic self-vindication simply changes its direction. She becomes the revenger, acting now in the name of all that is holy.

It is in this new guise that she next appears to prosecute her revenge:

> . . . he sleeps, good heavens!
> Why give you peace to this untemperate beast
> That hath so long transgressed you? I must kill him,
> And I will do't bravely: the meer joy
> Tells me that I merit in it: . . . (V, p. 61)

It is a sad paradox that in all her formerly evil course she had never so bared her fangs in sadistic relish as she does now in carrying out, as she thinks, God's work.

She begins in her habitual manner of coolly parrying the responses to her ambiguous statements. To his bewildered "How's this Evadne?" (V, 62), she replies with cold brutality:

> I am not she: nor bear I in this breast
> So much cold Spirit to be call'd a Woman:
> I am a Tyger: I am any thing
> That knows not pity: . . . (V, p. 62)

If we had before given any credence to the possible effectiveness of her wished-for repentance, this pitilessness should dispel such a hope in our minds as it immediately does in hers: "I am as foul as thou art, and can number/ As many such hells here." (V, p. 62). It is this fact—not that she is redeemed, but still hopelessly foul—which now spurs her on to a most savage vengeance. She continues:

> . . . I was once fair,
> Once I was lovely, not a blowing Rose
> More chastly sweet, till tho(u), thou, thou, foul Canker,
> (Stir not) didst poyson me: . . . for which (King)
> I am come to kill thee. (V, p. 62)

Once purer than most, it was the defeat of this innocence by a crass mankind, perhaps even this particular man, that perverted her nature into its present coldly vindictive course.

"Thus, thus, thou foul man,/ Thus I begin my vengeance"

(V, p. 63) she cries, as she begins her stabbing. And to the King's cry to stop, she replies:

> I do not mean Sir,
> To part so fairly with you; we must change
> More of these love-tricks yet. (V, p. 63)

Here the erotic component of her sadism—first suggested at the beginning of their confrontation in the King's amorous question: "What pretty new device is this Evadne?/ What do you tie me to you by my love?" (V, p. 61)—becomes overt. Inflamed by murderous desire, she refuses his bid for pity, as, with an orgy of "love-tricks," she completes her revenge. Then, secure in her triumph, her strange compassion is again elicited: "Die all our faults together; I forgive thee" (V, p. 63).

While Aspatia desires her own death to revenge herself against the conscience of a cruel world, Evadne desires to revenge herself not by taking her own life but the life of another. Together they comprise what might be called the sado-masochistic perversions of Courtly Love,[7] a phenomenon also present in *Antonio's Revenge.*

The fatal hour now arrives in which the delusions of love are exchanged for the reality of death. Aspatia begins this triple threnody, saying:

> This is my fatal hour; heaven may forgive
> My rash attempt, that causelesly hath laid
> Griefs on me that will never let me rest:
> And put a Womans heart into my brest;
> It is more honour for you that I die;
> For she that can endure the misery
> That I have on me, and be patient too,
> May live, and laugh at all that you can do. (V. p. 67)

To be patient, to live and laugh at the grievous infliction of life is to be devoid of all that honors heaven—man's spirituality —is to be no more than an animal. Evadne had rejected "a

Womans heart" for that of a tiger, had learned to live and laugh life's miseries to scorn, but such a solution seems more horribly inhuman, to Aspatia, than all the misery that heaven can so causelessly inflict. She has chosen Amintor to be her executioner not so much to revenge herself against his conscience since, though she would like to believe this possible, she is really convinced that he has no conscience, but simply because it seems fitting to her fevered brain that he should finish the task he had begun and quit her of her mortal injury.

Announcing herself as brother to "the wrong'd Aspatia" (V, p. 68), she is greeted sympathetically by Amintor. But, though he understands the full weight of her wrongs by those he himself has received, he is yet uncomfortable in his dual role as "wronger wronged." However great the pain of injuries causelessly received, the knowledge of having deserved his wrongs is greater than his weak spirit can bear. He would do anything that might overcome his guilt except the one thing needful, to face it:

> . . . for thy Sisters sake,
> Know that I could not think that desperate thing
> I durst not do; yet to enjoy this world
> I would not see her; for beholding thee,
> I am I know not what; . . .
> Thine eyes shoot guilt into me. (V, p. 69)

But since the disguised Aspatia refuses to be gone, and continues to provoke him by more and more degrading means to her purposed death duel, his patience, no greater than Aspatia's own, finally gives out. They fight and Aspatia is mortally wounded: "I have got enough,/ And my desire; there's no place so fit for me to die as here" (V, p. 70).

At this moment, with his greatest wrong upon his head, Evadne flies in, still radiant from her blood orgy, saying: "Joy to Amintor, for the King is dead" (V, p. 70). At this Amintor suddenly gains an insight into the nature of human love which serves to explain all that has transpired:

> Those have most power to hurt us that we love,
> We lay our sleeping lives within their arms. (V, p. 70)

As it has been with the King, so also has it been with Aspatia
and himself. This truth of the vulnerability that attends the
surrender of love, while it is true for all human love, would
only have been perceived as the most essential truth of love by
a false romantic lover. Only he experiences the vulnerability of
love without its redeeming fulfillment. Amintor's romantic intanglements have revealed nothing but the vulnerability that
laid bare the poverty of his spirit. This is the highest truth to
which Beaumont and Fletcher can rise in their dramatization of
human love, nor has this truth ever been more beautifully or
more profoundly expressed, but they do not stop here.

Coming upon the body of the disguised Aspatia, as he has
been retreating from the blood-stained Evadne, he suddenly sees
himself surrounded by the wantonly shed blood of all that is
holy, Aspatia's honor and the King's divine life, and all of this
blood is on his hands. Seeing in this blood the broken pieces
of his life, the fatal fruits of his irresponsibility which have also
poisoned his own life, he sees no exit from the black night of
his despair: "this keeps night here,/ And throws an unknown
wilderness about me" (V, p. 71). Evadne continues to pursue
him in the desperate and deluded hope that she can regain his
love, but, in his despair, the thought of possible future happiness
through Evadne's love—even if she were still only a repentant
adulteress instead of a cruel murderess—is too irrelevant to his
spiritual concerns to really engage his attention, to appear to
him as more than some incomprehensible distraction reminiscent
of a former life.

As he leaves, Evadne's own mind clears of the delusions that
since her crucial encounter with Melantius had clouded her self-
perception. Melantius had made her recognize the corruption
of her nature, but he had also convinced her, because of his own
false standards, that repentence and redemption was a simple
matter. Now Amintor's unexpected rejection has shocked her
into an instant reappraisal which justifies the truth of his charge:
"Thou hast no intermission of thy sins,/ But all thy life is a

continual ill" (V, p. 70). Unable to free herself from the "disease" (V, p. 70) which not only has warped her nature but continues to thwart any attempt at real change, death offers the only possibility of peace; and it offers too the pathetic hope that Amintor may be brought to realize that she has at least tried, however futilely, to become worthy of him:

> Amintor, thou shalt love me once again;
> Go, I am calm; farewell; and peace for ever.
> Evadne whom thou hat'st will die for thee. (V, p. 71)

Hearing, as he is leaving, the words with which she stabs herself, he returns:

> *Amin.* I have a little humane nature yet
> That's left for thee, that bids me to stay thy hand.
> *Evad.* Thy hand was welcome, but came too late;
> Oh I am lost! the heavy sleep makes haste. (V, p. 71)

He has seen too much of blood to suffer another death on his account, but it is "too late," far too late for any human kindness to have effect upon Evadne's fate. She is as "lost" in death as she was in life and dies a pathetic, broken woman.

But now the spectacle of blood, the death of everything his "hopeful youth" had touched and been touched by overwhelms him:

> This earth of mine doth tremble, and I feel
> A stark affrighted motion in my blood;
> My soul grows weary of her house, and I
> All over am a trouble to my self; . . . (V, p. 71)

His weariness with life is so complete that he is even too weary to lie: 'I am cold;/ Be resolute, and bear'em company" (V, pp. 71–72). In the listlessness that accompanies exhaustion, his memory lights upon the unredressed wrongs of the still living Aspatia and

his conscience is irritated into activity by this last obligation to the
land of the living:

> There's something yet which I am loth to leave.
> There's man enough in me to meet the fears
> That death can bring, and yet would it were done; . . .
> Though she may justly arm with scorn
> And hate of me, my soul will part less troubled,
> When I have paid to her in tears my sorrow:
> I will not leave this act unsatisfied,
> If all that's left in me can answer it. (V, p. 72)

"And yet would it were done"! This duty call, hitherto an impossibly perilous undertaking, now seems a matter of indifference
to him. As he had never really loved Aspatia, the thought of her
has no power to reclaim him to life; his apology will merely
make his inevitable death less troubled, if, that is, he can muster
the energy to accomplish it.

But now the miracle occurs which carries his soul beyond
despair to make a higher affirmation of value. Aspatia interrupts
his departure to reveal her true self:

> Th'art there already, and these wounds are hers:
> Those threats I brought with me, sought not revenge,
> But came to fetch this blessing from thy hand, I am Aspatia
> yet. (V, p. 72)

"Dare my soul ever look abroad agen?" (V, p. 72) Amintor res-
sponds. This statement of awe, of total guiltiness miraculously
united to a humble hope, marks the transition to his greater
health. If he has unwittingly completed his earlier selfish destruction of Aspatia, despite his single sustaining desire to comfort her, then his soul is incapable of effecting its good intents
and he may never dare look abroad again. If, however, his final
and unbearable guilt is miraculously turned into blessing, his
murder of all that is good forgiven him by the divine power
of love, then his newly humbled and reverent soul may dare

to hope. Both movements of his soul are equally present in this moment of wonder until hope is given the ascendance by the comfort that Aspatia's love blindly promises them: "I shall live Amintor; I am well:/ A kind of healthful joy wanders within me" (V, p. 72). For the first time he responds to the supreme value of something external to himself yet deeply important to him, and, forgetting himself, he desires only to care for her needs: "The world wants lines to excuse thy loss:/ Come let me bear thee to some place of help" (V, p. 72). Nor should it be forgotten that in the scene with Evadne, while he had remembered only his own spiritual despair, he had let Aspatia's repeated moans go unheeded. Now that Aspatia is no longer an unrelated moaning thing but a person recognized as uniquely valuable and bound to him in a relation that gives his life its only meaning, he can forget his own needs for hers.

As Aspatia's love had saved Amintor from despair, the like returns upon her with heightened effect:

Amintor thou must stay, I must rest here, . . .
How does thou my best soul? I would fain live,
Now if I could: would'st thou have loved me then? (V, p. 72)

Knowing that she must die, her thoughts are only of Amintor's welfare. And as she forgets herself for the first time in a true love for Amintor, her own "best soul" is revealed. Hitherto held in captivity by her craving for an intensely tragic love experience, the ministrations of Amintor's love reveal a new Aspatia—warm, tender, eager, and artlessly genuine. Newly born in lovely innocence are her wondering surmise and the desire it engenders: "I would fain live,/ Now if I could: would'st thou have loved me then?" But as such a surmise and desire were impossible to the self-conscious morbidity that had led her hither, she could not have known the pathetic inadequacy and falseness of her former love and the course it dictated. Now that true love has been born, and with it the desire for life, it is too late; she has destroyed all chance for happiness by her own willfulness and "must rest here."

But her true loveliness, so tragically revealed, inspires Amintor's love to still greater dimensions. If before he had responded gratefully to a loving forgiveness which saved him from despair, now that he perceives not only her love but her loveliness, his desire for her and simultaneous sense of his own unworthiness for such a blessing are immeasureably increased. And as he watches the sole blessing of his life rapidly declining, his response is touched by frenzy: "Alas! all that I am's not worth a hair from thee" (V, p. 72). But the dreadful fact of her death finally impresses him despite his utmost efforts to repress its possibility and, at the same time, overcome its actuality: "Oh she is gone!" (V, p. 73). And it is dreadful precisely because he too no longer desires death but life with Aspatia: "I'le call it mercy if you'l pity me,/ You heavenly powers, and lend for some few years,/ The blessed soul to this fair seat agen" (V, p. 73). His deepest wish is not even to "chain life for ever to this frame" (V, p. 73) but, more modestly, to be granted "some few years" in which her blessedness might be returned to him and his love for her allowed to be realized on earth, for without this expression of heavenly pity he cannot live. But "No comfort comes, the gods deny me too" (V, p. 73). Though he despairs of being able to continue life without love's blessing, his love does enable him to transcend his former despair and to die affirming the vision of love which she has granted him:

> The soul is fled for ever, and I wrong
> My self, so long to lose her company.
> Must I talk now? Here's to be with thee love. *[Kills himself.]*
>   (V, p. 73)

Their hope for an earthly love cruelly thwarted by the still operating effects of their own human failings, there is nothing for him but to join her there where human failings no longer hinder the hopeful heart.

While the conclusions of Beaumont and Fletcher's tragicomedies are generally unconvincing, the greatness of *The Maid's Tragedy* is that it is not content with the happy ending it could so easily have had. It is to Beaumont and Fletcher's everlasting credit that they were not tempted to make this final evasion of moral responsibility in favor of a redemptive forgiveness in which they might hope but could not, at their most profound level, believe. Even in the splendid realization of the love finally achieved by Amintor and Aspatia, there is a nostalgic quality; it is the love that might have been were man and his world differently constituted.

The Double Marriage

This study of Beaumont and Fletcher's earlier tragedies of False Romantic Love has shown an increasing understanding on their part of the nature of this love. In *Cupid's Revenge* the authors first surmised that the denial of importance to love is a tragic error; in *The Maid's Tragedy* they further realized that this initial denial causes any love relationship that is based upon it to be vulnerable. When, however, Fletcher returned in his last tragedy to the subject that had crowned his joint achievement with Beaumont ten years earlier it was to complete this progression of understanding. In *The Double Marriage* Fletcher appears to discern that the initial denial of importance to love, which causes the vulnerability of False Romantic Love, is itself the result of a lack of integration in the lover. Fletcher gives support to Danby's analysis of the schizophrenic unity of the Fletcherian hero in a most important speech of his last hero, Virolet:

> When we are little children,
> And cry and fret for every toy comes cross us;
> How sweetly do we shew, when sleep steals on us!
> When we grow great, but our affections greater,
> And struggle with this stubborn twin, born with us;
> And tug and pull, yet still we find a Giant:
> Had we not then the priviledge to sleep,
> Our everlasting sleep? he would make us idiots; . . . (II,
>   Vol. 6, pp. 347–8)

Like Amintor, Virolet is shortly to say: "O my fortune!/ That I must equally be bound to either" (III, p. 371). The "Giant," who would make them idiots and whom they cannot overcome, is the unrestrainable "affection" with which their innate greatness of soul is in continual and unsuccessful struggle. However good they would be, their intentions are always undermined by the greater power of their affections which "cry and fret for every toy comes cross us." "This stubborn twin, born with us" makes their life a trouble to themselves from which death is the only release.

This final insight into the fundamental lack of integration of the false romantic lover comes, however, after all hope of integration has passed. While Leucippus and Amintor had died cleansed of their sins by the faith that love brought them, the miraculous power of love has been lost for Virolet. Although he fully perceives the goodness of his first wife and that he lost it because he was "too weak a guard for that great treasure" (IV, p. 382), when he lies dying, an accidental victim of his good first wife's attempt to protect him against the revenge of his evil second wife, he says to her:

> . . . weep not dear, shed not those sovereign Balsames
> Into my blood; which must recover me;
> Then I shall live again, to do a mischief,
> Against the mightiness of love and virtue,
> Some base unhallowed hands shall rob thy right of. (V, p.
>   397)

He had come to fetch his death because he fully realizes that continued life can only mean continued mischief, that the "base unhallowed hands" of the "stubborn twin" shall always rob him of that good which his better self is not strong enough to hold. Begging Juliana to forgive him and pray for him, he faints under the burden of his faults; but she soon follows him, exhausted alike by life's cross-purposes. Whereas Urania was able to save Leucippus' life and inspire his death, and Aspatia at least the latter, in this third tragedy the ideal of love itself fails, Juliana actually causing Virolet's death and being unable to relieve either his or her own despair. But such irredeemable and uninspired weakness is to be the final permutation of the genre of False Romantic Love tragedy.

6

The Final Pattern

The Changeling

The tragedy of False Romantic Love reaches its final Jacobean form in the hands of Middleton.[1] While primarily a study of Beatrice-Joanna's False Romantic Love, *The Changeling* (1622) goes beyond this single concern to give comprehensive treatment to all three modes of love. In the portraits of her two lovers, Alsemero and De Flores, Middleton has pictured the Stoic form of Courtly Love and the Hedonistic form of Worldly Love. The three main actors in this tragedy represent, then, the three modes of love, and each follows the course appropriate to his love.

The powerful study of Beatrice-Joanna, which marks the final vagary in the history of False Romantic Love tragedy, is not, however, Middleton's own final statement on love as a tragic value. It is, rather, the Worldly Love of De Flores, here subsidiary to the tragic false romanticism of Beatrice-Joanna, that becomes the final value embraced by Bianca Capello in Middleton's last tragedy, *Women Beware Women*.[2] Though the threefold division of this study makes it impossible to consider Middleton's tragic production in one piece, it is important to realize that the tragic value affirmed in his second tragedy, that of Worldly Love, is also the norm of his first.

It is important because the lack of this realization has led

to a general misinterpretation of Middleton's tragic vision. While
the specific tragedy of Beatrice-Joanna has been remarkably well
understood by all of the good modern critics of Middleton, this
masterly portrait has tended to obscure their vision of the positive potentialities of Middleton's tragic universe. Modern criticism
of Middleton may be said to begin with Eliot, who has contributed
both the basic understanding of Beatrice's tragedy and the view
that Middleton "has no message."[3] The view that Middleton
has nothing—or nothing positive—to say has been strangely allied to the view that he has the same thing to say in both of his
tragedies, that *Women Beware Women* is "also a study of the
progressive deterioration of character."[4] While it has been generally granted that "In the central scene (III, iv) Middleton has
carried Beatrice, as he does Bianca in the corresponding scenes
of *Women Beware Women,* from ignorance to experience, from
a romantic sleepwalking to an awakening in the midst of horrors,"[5] nothing is made of the subsequent differences of behavior. The positive quality of the death of Bianca, and also of
De Flores, when it is noted, is noted without comment.[6] And
the view persists that "Middleton's men and women gradually
disintegrate as moral beings"[7] while Middleton, who "refuses to
compromise with sin,"[8] underlines "the irony that invests the
sinner's career."[9]

Irony there is, but the irony is just that man must "compromise with sin" and outgrow the romantic delusions of inept
and bungling innocence. As in the early comedies the gallant
must finally find his happiness in a marriage to his own whore,
so his later women—Beatrice, Bianca, and Clara (in *The Spanish
Gipsy)*—must compromise their innocent expectations to the
fact of enforcement and rape, and build a wiser life on the wreckage of the old. Middleton brings his false romantic innocents to
a confrontation with the flawed reality of existence, which can
only be redeemed through their acceptance of it. He uses, to
better purpose than any other Elizabethan tragedian, the myth
of Original Sin,[10] the belief that man's very nature bars him
from realizing a paradise on earth. But this fact does not, for
Middleton, preclude earthly values; rather it is the basis on
which earthly values can be achieved. This is the "message" that

Middleton puts into the mouth of De Flores. If Beatrice's understanding of it finally brings her to the despair of self-knowledge,
it leads as well to the tragic fulfillment of De Flores and Bianca.

It is, then, with tragic irony that Middleton begins *The
Changeling* on a note of purified Courtly Love. Although Alsemero's friend tells him, "Lover I'm sure you're none; the stoic
was/ Found in you long ago" (I, i, 36–7),[11] the love to which
Alsemero unexpectedly succumbs is the devotion to purity that
we would expect of a Stoic, and not a contradiction of his Stoicism:

'Twas in the temple where I first beheld her. . . .
The place is holy, so is my intent:
I love her beauties to the holy purpose;
And that, methinks, admits comparison
With man's first creation, the place blessed,
And is his right home back, if he achieve it.
The church hath first begun our interview,
And that's the place must join us into one;
So there's beginning and perfection too. (I, i, 1, 5–12)

Alsemero conceives of love as a holy union, which can bring
man back to his perfection before the fall. This is not to say
that Alsemero denies the general corruption of man's present
state. On the contrary, he specifically says:

There's scarce a man amongst a thousand found
But hath his imperfection . . .
Myself, I must confess, have the same frailty. (I, i, 119–20,
  128)

But Alsemero believes that it is not only possible to control man's
natural frailty through the exercise of Stoic restraint but that
he can transcend it through the perfection of holy love. This
love of perfection, Alsemero rightly sees, is no contradiction of
his former Stoicism but "the same church, name devotion" (I,
i, 35). It is Courtly Love.
    Beatrice also believes that natural frailty should be guided

by judgment, but the counsel she gives him against his love "at first sight" (I, i, 69) might better be applied to herself: "Our eyes are sentinels unto our judgments . . . But they are rash sometimes, and tell us wonders / Of common things . . ." (I, i, 74–7). As she silently realizes, her own eyes have been injudicious. Five days earlier she had believed herself to be in love with Piracquo, and had become engaged to him. Now she finds herself even more attracted to this amorous stranger: "I shall change my saint, I fear me; I find/ A giddy turning in me" (I, i, 158–9). Though she appropriates the devotional language of Alsemero to both of her loves, her feelings for Alsemero are no less false romantic than her now repented feelings for Piracquo had been. She has simply changed the object of her love because Alsemero appears worthier to her: "Methinks I love now with the eyes of judgment,/ And see the way to merit, clearly see it" (II, i, 13–4). Never do the eyes of judgment fail to give their support to the eyes of desire, and never are they sufficient to ensure the real commitment of love.

Though her father's haste in preparing for the marriage "scarce allows me breath/ To speak to my new comforts" (II, i, 25–6), Beatrice manages to arrange a clandestine meeting with Alsemero. She greets him with the words:

> I have within mine eye all my desires:
> Requests that holy prayers ascend Heaven for,
> And brings 'em down to furnish our defects,
> Come not more sweet to our necessities
> Than thou unto my wishes. (II, ii, 8–12)

And Alsemero replies:

> We're so like
> In our expressions, lady, that unless I borrow
> The same words, I shall never find their equals. (II, ii, 12–4)

This similarity of expressions is what confuses not only Alsemero's perception but also Beatrice's own self-awareness. Both appear to desire the same holy perfection through love. Alsemero believes that the achievement of love enables man to return to the condition of his "first creation," and Beatrice believes that the satisfaction of her desires enables her to rise above her natural "defects." The difference is that her "desires" reflect a "giddy turning" from one supposed "saint" to another whereas his involve a strenuous personal achievement of purity. Beatrice looks upon love as an external solution to her defects, the desired effects of love flowing wholly from her lover and requiring nothing of her. She has only to accept the most worthy lover and then happiness is assured.

To this proper satisfaction, however, her engagement to Piracquo presents a serious obstacle. Desiring an easy dissolution of her rashly contracted engagement she thinks of De Flores: "Why, men of art make much of poison,/ Keep one to expel another; where was my art?" (II, ii, 46–7). As, for Beatrice, her own desires are the only reality that need be considered, she treats all other individuals, whether those she loves or hates, as instruments towards the satisfaction of these desires. She blames herself only for her former lack of "art," with no thought to the evil of murder, even to one who loves her as passionately as does Piracquo. Nor does she question De Flores' motive in his constant haunting of her.

But De Flores' motive, were it known, is indeed ominous:

    I know she hates me,
Yet cannot choose but love her: no matter:
If but to vex her, I will haunt her still;
Though I get nothing else, I'll have my will. (I, i, 237-40)

His is a case "of human bondage," the compulsive love a deformed man may develop for a beautiful, scornful woman. It is her scorn that first fired his love:

    Will't never mend this scorn,
One side nor other? must I be enjoin'd
To follow still whilst she flies from me? well,

> Fates, do your worst, I'll please myself with sight
> Of her at all opportunities,
> If but to spite her anger: . . . (I, i, 102–7)

Once her scorn has produced his passionate desire "to spite her anger," however, he hopes this scorn will mend, whether through indifference or love. Her indifference would free him from the torment of his love, but her yielding to him, stooping from her height of scornful beauty to embrace his ugliness, would crown his happiness as nothing else could. He would love her the more tenderly for the sweet revenge she has given him in making him her victor. But the only means by which he could conquer her despite her loathing, and it is her loathing that has produced his compulsive need to conquer her, is by lowering her in her own eyes, by making her feel so unworthy of love that she will embrace his acceptance of her defective nature as her greatest good. De Flores is the only one of Beatrice's lovers who really perceives her true nature, who perceives that she not only can be humbled but needs to be humbled as the sole condition by which she can really give herself:

> I'll despair the less . . .
> Wrangling has prov'd the mistress of good pastime;
> As children cry themselves asleep, I ha' seen
> Women have chid themselves a-bed to men. (II, i, 82, 86–8)

> Hunger and pleasure, they'll commend sometimes
> Slovenly dishes, and feed heartily on 'em.
> Nay, which is stranger, refuse daintier for 'em:
> Some women are odd feeders. (II, ii, 152–55)

De Flores perceives that, despite Beatrice's supposed desire for a perfect romantic love, she is really just such an "odd feeder." He perceives that a defective nature underlies her unwarranted scorn:

> I know she had
> Rather see me dead than living; and yet
> She knows no cause for't but a peevish will. (I, i, 107–9)

Yet he alone can accept her love as his greatest good, despite her faults. Piracquo had said: "I can endure/ Much, till I meet an injury to her,/ Then I am not myself" (II, i, 149–51). Alsemero will cast her from him when he perceives her true nature. Only De Flores knows and loves her true self. But he also knows that the only means by which he can gain her love is to chide her "a-bed" and that this can only be accomplished if he catch her in some conscious guilt which he can use to overcome her scorn. And so he haunts her, delighting even in her lovely scorn, and waiting for his moment. His "bless'd occasion" (II, ii, 114) comes sooner than he expects.

That she should want him to commit a murder for her provides him with a hold over her greater than he had ever dreamed possible. Sure of this power, he cares not that it is for love of another man that she wishes his services and kneels to beg this service from her. This were enough to warn a person of more perception and less "art" that De Flores was not one whose will could be simply bought and sold as her occasions served. But, blinded by her selfish desires, she dismisses this warning. She leaves believing: "I shall rid myself/ Of two inveterate loathings at one time,/ Piracquo, and his dog-face" (II, ii, 146–8), but he can "feel her in mine arms already" (II, ii, 149).

As the great confrontation scene is to begin, she awaits De Flores, pleased with her artful handling of her affairs: "So wisdom, by degrees, works out her freedom" (III, iv, 13). But, as her expectations are more and more rudely shooked, she is to find herself hopelessly enmeshed. The first shock of seeing the dead man's finger—"Bless me, what hast thou done?" (III, iv, 30)—is quickly succeeded by De Flores' wrathful refusal to accept cash payment. Her nameless fear grows as he says: "Nor is it fit we two, engag'd so jointly,/ Should part and live asunder" (III, iv, 89–90). She tries to counter his demands with her habitual scorn—"Take heed, De Flores, of forgetfulness,/ 'Twill soon betray us." (III, iv, 95–6)—but that last word "us" betrays her gradual realization that they are indeed "engag'd so jointly." This partial realization makes it imperative for her to fend off the implications of such an engagement. With growing imperiousness, she says: "I would not hear so much offense again/ For such another deed" (III, iv, 105–6). Playing her now with ease, De Flores reminds her: "Soft, lady, soft!/ The last is not yet paid for" (III, iv, 106–7). And now, with great relish, he clearly states the reward he demands; but she, no longer able to doubt his intentions, is still unable to fully assimilate their horror:

> Why, 'tis impossible thou canst be so wicked,
> Or shelter such a cunning cruelty,
> To make his death the murderer of my honour!
> Thy language is so bold and vicious,
> I cannot see which way I can forgive it
> With any modesty. (III, iv, 121–6)

In this remarkable speech, Beatrice begins, for the first time, to see beyond the amorality of her own desires in an actual confrontation with another independent individual, not a tool for her use, but a person with his own demands. Confronting this knowledge utterly confuses the whole structure of her former "wisdom." What seems to her so "impossible" that she "cannot see which way" to react is that he should presume to make demands upon her from which all her "wisdom" and "art" cannot free her, though this is as yet only understood consciously as an attack upon her "honour" and "modesty."

De Flores immediately brings her to a deeper recognition: "Push! you forget yourself;/ A woman dipp'd in blood, and talk of modesty!" (III, iv, 126–7). Now her inner conflict becomes conscious, though still not resolved:

> O misery of sin! would I'd been bound
> Perpetually unto my living hate
> In that Piracquo, than to hear these words!
> Think but upon the distance that creation
> Set 'twixt thy blood and mine, and keep thee there. (III,
>   iv, 128–32)

As all false romantic lovers eventually do, she realizes that she is "Time's fool," but with a difference. It is not that she values

Piracquo any more than formerly but that she now realizes that, in attempting to free herself from her rash bond to him, she has become vulnerable to a world of evil against which all her former arts are powerless.

In De Flores' great reply, the ethics of responsibility are brilliantly clarified:

> Look but into your conscience, read me there;
> 'Tis a true book, you'll find me there your equal:
> Push! fly not to your birth, but settle you
> In what the act has made you; you're no more now.
> You must forget your parentage to me;
> You are the deed's creature; by that name
> You lost your first condition, and I challenge you,
> As peace and innocency has turn'd you out,
> And made you one with me. (III, iv, 133–41)

He tries to show her that it is not his wickedness that has turned her deed against her but the very nature of that deed itself, that there is no such thing as freedom from responsibility. Entering too easily into a contract with Piracquo, she had thought to escape it as easily only to find that she must finally face a true accounting for her persistent rashness. Had she stood behind her initial commitment, she would have "been bound/ Perpetually unto my living hate/ In that Piracquo," this the true payment due for that initial rashness. In trying to escape this payment, she has exposed herself to a more dire penalty which she can only escape by shameful death: "She that in life and love refuses me,/ In death and shame my partner she shall be" (III, iv, 154–5). Though Beatrice claimed the dispensation of her birth as sufficient justification for her behavior, she learns that by eating of the forbidden fruit she has lost "man's first creation." In Middleton's language there can be no further doubt that the pattern of tragic irresponsibility is a reenactment of the Original Sin.

It is this difference in self-awareness that distinguishes De Flores from Beatrice. She refuses to identify herself with him as a "foul villain" (III, iv, 141), whereas he has accepted the corruption of his nature as the premise of his existence. Unlike Beatrice, De Flores has not purchased his pleasure irresponsibly. Though he has ventured dangerously for his prize and is willing to pay for it with his life, he counts the highest payment cheap recompense for the pleasure he has purchased by it. He is not "the deed's creature" but its master, and the master not the creature of Beatrice as well:

> Let this silence thee;
> The wealth of all Valencia shall not buy
> My pleasure from me;
> Can you weep Fate from its determin'd purpose?
> So soon may [you] weep me. (III, iv, 159–63)

Beatrice, however, in trying to escape the fate for which she bargained, has discovered that her true fate is De Flores, a fate to her much worse than perpetual bondage to Piracquo.

But her discovery is only partial:

> Vengeance begins;
> Murder, I see, is follow'd by more sins:
> Was my creation in the womb so curst,
> It must engender with a viper first? (III, iv, 163–6)

If she realizes that through some Original Sin she "must engender with a viper first," she still feels that, having given the Devil his due, she will be freed thereby to partake the full "joys of marriage" (III, iv, 149) with Alsemero. If murder has a higher price than she had expected, she still does not see it as an insuperable barrier to her coveted happiness. But when De Flores said, "Thy peace is wrought for ever in this yielding" (III, iv, 169), the peace he promised her was one which could only be achieved were she to settle herself in what the act has made her, "one with me. . . . engag'd so jointly." It cannot be achieved with Alsemero because she is now "the deed's creature," however unsettled she may still be in this fact. But De Flores also knows that he will be able to make her capable both of guilt and love: "thou'lt love anon/ What thou so fear'st and faint'st to venture on" (III, iv, 170–1). And he embraces her tenderly, understanding her awful guiltiness more deeply than she can herself.

Beatrice soon realizes that De Flores' embraces are not nearly so fearful a prospect as the wedding embrace of Alsemero, now that she has lost her "first condition." Her distress is not caused, however, by her own consciousnes of guilt but by her fear of Alsemero's discernment: "Before whose judgment will my fault appear/ Like malefactors' crimes before tribunals" (IV, i, 7–8). Having the false romantic notion that marriage to a desirable man produces a miraculous happiness which solves all problems, her principal task is to hide her faults until the marriage is assured, at which point she believes her faults will somehow disappear or cease to matter. Since the principal fault which Beatrice recognizes is her loss of virginity, she resolves on the unhappy expedient of substituting her maid on her wedding night. She does not recognize that by this trick she had already spoiled the purity of her marriage, just as she did not recognize that the murder that was necessary to assure this marriage had spoiled whatever peace and innocency she might have brought to it. For all expedients, she has only one response: "Necessity compels it; I lose all else" (IV, ii, 125). And her ethical blindness convinces her that she still has something to lose.

It is later shown that Beatrice slept a second time with De Flores, on her wedding night (IV, iii, 163, 165). But this does not keep Beatrice from an ever-increasing jealousy as her maid continues to delay her departure from Alsemero's bed: "This strumpet . . . Devours the pleasure with a greedy appetite,/ And never minds my honour or my peace" (V, i, 2–4). Her moral blindness assumes staggering proportions as Beatrice penalizes Diaphanta for a crime similar to her own—"she pays dearly for't . . . That cannot rule her blood to keep her promise" (V, i, 5, 7) —while believing that she still has an "honour" that need be respected.

But De Flores loves her so deeply that he is willing to support her delusions if it will help him gain her love. Alsemero is later to call them "you twins/ Of mischief!" (V, iii, 145–6), and nowhere else are they "engag'd so jointly" as in the following conference:

> *De. F.* Ay: is she not come from him yet?
> *Beat.* As I'm a living soul, not!
> *De. F.* Sure the devil
> Hath sow'd his itch within her; who would trust
> A waiting-woman?
> *Beat.* I must trust somebody. . . .
> *De. F.* You are so rash and hardy, ask no counsel;
> And I could have help'd you. . .
> *Beat.* Advise me now to fall upon some ruin;
> There is no counsel safe else.
> *De. F.* Peace! I ha't. . . . 'tis proper now,
> But she shall be the mark.
> *Beat.* I'm forc'd to love thee now,
> 'Cause thou provid'st so carefully for my honour.
> *De. F.* 'Slid, it concerns the safety of us both,
> Our pleasure and continuance. (V, i, 12–5, 20–1, 26–8, 45–50)

Adjusting his tone exactly to meet her own annoyance and guessing thereby her desire to have Diaphanta killed, he wins her complete confidence with the gentle chastisement: "You are so rash and hardy, ask no counsel." With him Beatrice need hide nothing and yet can feel perfectly safe. He sees and accepts the faults she herself recognizes and tactfully supports her delusions of pride. After the distress of having to hide her faults from Alsemero, the relief of being able to expose her worst faults and desires before De Flores, and have him accept them as natural, causes her to open her heart to him with true gratefulness. Never before has she felt grateful for the love she aroused in anyone, feeling it her due; but now, in recognizing the value of his totally accepting love, she is forced to return it. And he, happy to have gained her heart with all its selfishness, dismisses her thanks with the thought of their continuing pleasure. As he later says: "I lov'd this woman in spite of her heart" (V, iii, 168). Happy that his service will be rewarded with her love, he goes about his commissions while she remains behind, glowing with the joy of her new love:

> Already? how rare is that man's speed!
> How heartily he serves me! his face loathes one;
> But look upon his care, who would not love him?
> The east is not more beauteous than his service. . . .
> Here's a man worth loving! (V, i, 68–71, 75)

Realizing that his previous tactics of awakening her self-awareness, which alone could produce a genuinely reciprocal love, would destroy her if continued, and preferring her happiness to her pain, he accepts the highest love of which she is now capable and resolves to service her desires with all his power. And she basks in his total servicing, regarding him now as "a wondrous necessary man" (V, i, 90).

But Beatrice cannot settle herself in this love for DeFlores because it does not conform to her falsely romantic notions about love. What she may actually do or be is not as important to her as how she may appear in the eyes of society, and as, in these eyes, De Flores would never be an acceptable husband, so he cannot win final approval in her eyes. She can only meet him in "a back part of the house" (IV, ii, 92), where her faults can be accepted if discerned. For her socially acceptable facade, however, she desires a husband like Alsemero, "one who's ennobled both in blood and mind" (IV, i, 5). But, since she cannot show her actual self before him, his very ennoblement bars their truer union—"that's my plaque now" (IV i, 6)—and she must take "the back door" (V, iii, 11) to find total acceptance for her real self. Her preferred image of herself, however, forces her to disown the self De Flores loves and to find only Alsemero worthy of her. Whatever release she may find through "the back door" must not be allowed to interfere with her rightful marriage, which alone she can justify to her pride. She is as much a fractured personality as any Beaumont and Fletcher portrayed and must ever "struggle with this stubborn twin." One side of her yearns for the pure wedding with Alsemero of which she is incapable, and the other is fatally engaged " 'mongst things corruptible" (V, iii, 158).

But Alsemero's friend has shattered these hopes by proving her infidelity to her reluctant husband. As she tries vainly to maintain a confident face before her husband at their next meeting, Alsemero quickly cuts short her pleasantries with the charge: "You are a whore!" (V, iii, 32). For a moment she collapses before this indictment: "What a horrid sound it hath!/ It blasts a beauty to deformity" (V, iii, 32–3). Seeing herself through his eyes, with that judgment she most fervently respects, she sees herself as unworthy of his love. But in the desolation which accompanies her sense of unworthiness, he appears to her so truly fine that she cannot bear to give him up if by any means she can still assure him. And immediately she forswears that moment of self-hate in a desperate effort to outface his suspicious. Convinced that he has certain knowledge of her meetings with De Flores, she resolves to shield the lesser with the greater crime, still believing that the two murders she has so easily perpetrated cannot really be so terrible.

But it is no good. Alsemero is as horror stricken as was Amintor when Evadne triumphantly announced the King's murder, and, like him, now exclaims:

> O, the place itself e'er since
> Has crying been for vengeance! the temple,
> Where blood and beauty first unlawfully
> Fir'd their devotion and quench'd the right one;
> 'Twas in my fears at first, 'twill have it now:
> O, thou art all deform'd! (V, iii, 73–8)

All the religious imagery with which Alsemero and Beatrice have clothed their love is now seen as a false idolatry. Alsemero realizes that the holiness he has sought cannot be found in human love. Turning from her love in despair, he cries: "O cunning devils!/ How should blind men know you from fair-fac'd saints?" (V, iii, 109–10). Beatrice, in trying to actualize his "holy intent" without holiness of feeling, had destroyed not only Alsemero's holy love for her but also his Stoic's faith in such a possibility. In the world of the play, the impediments to a holy love are so great that it were better for the Stoic not to attempt it, for, once attempted, the ideal will manifest itself to his moral vision as a corrupted reality. Alsemero realizes his moral error in idolizing love as a way of life and, his eyes now opened, he returns with enlightened resignation to the Stoic attitude with which he had begun.

Rejecting her last pathetic argument, he dismisses her while he decides upon his rightful course of action. But Beatrice still cannot accept his image of her as "all deform'd" because the only deformity that she recognizes is her loss of the outward name of "honour." She still holds her obstinate conviction that all would not yet be lost could she but convince him of her chastity. When De Flores is tricked into confessing her adultery, she yells from her confinement: "He lies! the villain does belie me!" (V, iii, 111).

But, hearing her desperate denial of guilt and love, De Flores asserts his rights to her, as one "engag'd so jointly," saying to her husband: "let me go to her, sir" (V, iii, 112). Though the ensuing confrontation is not revealed to the audience, its essence can be deduced from the changed behavior which follows this scene. De Flores must have tried, once again, to break down her delusions, so that she would see their kinship; and he must have succeeded better than he wished. With her new appreciation of Alsemero's personal worth, the image of her true self, which she now recognizes in De Flores, becomes all the more hateful. Seeing both herself and De Flores with new clarity, she rejects them both as totally despicable. De Flores had earlier said: "She that in life and love refuses me,/ In death and shame my partner she shall be." Now, when Beatrice refuses him her love and utterly rejects him, he makes good his threat. Though it could only be in "death and shame," he finally claims her as his own, stabbing himself too—"Nay, I'll along for company" (V, iii, 141)—because life without her is meaningless.

Hearing her cries, Alsemero says: "Come forth, you twins/ Of mischief!" (V, iii, 164), and De Flores comes forth triumphantly dragging his maimed prize. To her father's amazed cries, however, Beatrice answers:

> O, come not near me, sir, I shall defile you!
> I am that of your blood was taken from you
> For your better health; look no more upon't,
> But cast it to the ground regardlessly,
> Let the common sewer take it from distinction:
> Beneath the stars, upon yon meteor
> > *[Pointing to De Flores.]*
> Ever hung my fate, 'mongst things corruptible;
> I ne'er could pluck it from him; my loathing
> Was prophet to the rest, but ne'er believed:
> Mine honour fell with him, and now my life. (V, iii, 152–61)

Too late she realizes the meaning of her former loathing for De Flores. Once she recognizes that she is identified with him " 'mongst things corruptible," she knows that she was incapable of realizing that higher love with Alsemero for which her best self really yearned. Since the only means she had to achieve the good were antipathetical to it, she was defeated before she began. This is the real importance of her prohibitive engagement to Piracquo. It symbolizes the insurmountable obstruction within her own spirit to its highest realization. Since neither factor could completely integrate her spirit, in trying to realize herself she split in two and began more and more to lead a double life. As long as she feared to acknowledge the true circumstances of her life and come to responsible terms with them, the more did each successive expedient further entrench her in her difficulties and the more did her dream life tend to isolate itself from her actual existence until nothing that took place on that lower plane of reality could disturb the somnambulistic calm in which her finest feelings had encased themselves. When she is fatally awakened by De Flores to the actual life she had been leading, her finer self desires only its own destruction. Turning in her death to Alsemero, she begs him to forgive the sins which shame the truest part of her: "Forgive me, Alsemero, all forgive!/ 'Tis time to die when 'tis a shame to live" (V, iii, 181–2).

It is only in De Flores that love's power triumphs at the last. However Beatrice may despise him, he knows that she is sold to him beyond redemption, and he rejoices in this fact:

> I lov'd this woman in spite of her heart:
> Her love I earn'd out of Piracquo's murder. . . .
> Yes, and her honour's prize
> Was my reward; I thank life for nothing
> But that pleasure; it was so sweet to me,
> That I have drunk up all, left none behind
> For any man to pledge me. . . .
> Make haste, Joanna, by that token to thee,
> Canst not forget, so lately put in mind;
> I would not go to leave thee far behind.
> > (V, iii, 168–9, 170–4, 178–80)

Though Beatrice can no longer love her own heart, it is still precious to De Flores. His love for her was the highest value in his life, and its satisfaction has been so unutterably sweet that he cannot regret it though it has caused his destruction. De Flores can accept his life and love triumphantly precisely because he has never been afraid, as has Beatrice, to face his own deformity. Facing this, he has been able to face life without illusions, to know his own true powers and desires and commit himself to their realization at whatever the cost. His was a Worldly Love in its most corrupt form. It was corrupt simply because he did accept his defective nature as it was and made no attempt to correct it. Even in this, however, he made a better bargain than did Beatrice. She was "the deed's creature" even though she refused to acknowledge the deed. When final acknowledgment brought repudiation of self rather than acceptance, she was still powerless to effect a real change of nature. Her belated and revolted acknowledgment only brought her grief, whereas his never-flinching acceptance brought him final joy.

In the world of the play, it is, then, only to a corrupted ideal of love that man can relate himself in life. For the Stoic, ideal love, and all ideals worthy to engage the spirit, are incapable of realization, and the only morally permissible way of life is to retreat altogether from any attempt to achieve the ideal. For the Hedonist, on the other hand, love is possible; but it is so far from being ideal that the sensitive nature coming in contact with it cannot triumph but meets a sordid destruction. Although such a love can only grow in an already deformed spiritual state, it can, however, achieve success in its own terms. De Flores anticipates Bianca Capello for, like her, he has drained the "cup of love" and dies with the cup still raised to his lips.

The Witch of Edmonton

A year before Rowley's collaboration with Middleton in *The Changeling,* he collaborated with Dekker and Ford on another tragedy of False Romantic Love, *The Witch of Edmonton* (1621). Although critical opinion is generally agreed that Rowley's main contributions to these two works were in their comic portions, the similarity of pattern between the Frank Thorney plot of *The Witch of Edmonton* and the Beatrice-Joanna plot of *The Changeling* is remarkable and may be the most important fruit of Rowley's collaboration in both works. If Rowley did not contribute to the formulation of the Frank Thorney plot, the authorship of which has been generally ascribed to Ford—although I have elsewhere argued Dekker's primary responsibility for the conception [12]—he may very well have suggested its general pattern to Middleton.[13] This pattern will be discussed in the conclusion immediately following, in terms of both these plays.

The Frank Thorney plot marks a return to the domestic tragedy of False Romantic Love, a form of tragedy not utilized since the much earlier *A Woman Killed With Kindness,*[14] and it is the most brilliant study of erotic irresponsibility in the whole literature of domestic drama. As a domestic tragedy it is unique in allowing an erring husband to have a tragic ending. It is also unique in being the love tragedy of a man who could not love. Nowhere else in the whole corpus of Elizabethan love tragedy do we find a character who is destroyed by love involvements without ever being motivated by even the delusion of love.

Frank is not a malicious miscreant. On the contrary, he is a man who, trying to be good to everybody, sins against all. Though unable to bear either his own or another's pain, he has no clear conception of his own good beyond the necessity of avoiding beggary. Since he wishes to be good, the best he can do, therefore, is to accommodate himself to other people's conceptions of his goodness and try to act as they desire. When his relations with Winifred bear unexpected fruit and she demands that he act like a man of honor, he marries her. And when his father demands that he marry Susan, to whom he had been engaged, so that their estate might be freed from debt, he is willing to do this too.

To quiet Winifred's objections, he explains that the necessity for his departure "Is onely but to gain a little time/ For our continuing thrift" (I, i, 14–5).[15] He believes himself to be a past master at the subtle art of winning the favor of those whom, "to gain a little time," he has had to wrong:

> Fathers are
> Wonne by degrees, not bluntly, as our masters,
> Or wronged friends are; and besides, I'll use
> Such dutiful and ready means, that ere
> He can have notice of what's past, th'inheritance
> To which I am born Heir, shall be assur'd:
> That done, why let him know it; if he like it not,
> Yet he shall have no power in him left
> To cross the thriving of it. (I, i, 24–32)

His technique is, by "dutiful and ready means," to satisfy whatever demands are made upon him, receive the reward "to which I am born heir" in the time thus gained, and then move out of danger. This mode of behavior exactly describes the way he has acted towards Winifred. Her claim had been "a business soon dispatch'd" (I, i, 1) and, before she could "have notice of what's past," he is ready to leave and she powerless "to cross the thriving of it."

But the reason he can be so easily pressured into bigamy would seem to be that, all evidence to the contrary, Frank does look upon himself as a man of honor; he does have "the true part of an honest man" (I, i, 6) for which Winifred commends him—a "true part" that needs to be flattered by the approval of others; and the chorus of "honest Frank" (I, i, 116) is easier on his ears than would be the just recriminations of those he has wronged. Thus, when his father charges him with the report of his marriage to Winifred, he only thinks "I must out-face it" (I, ii, 164), and outface it he does: "Am I become so insensible of losing/ The glory of Creations work? My soul!/ O I have liv'd too long" (I, ii, 178–80). Words, all words, but still words that have power to evoke in him a tinge of weariness with life because of his inability to conform to them. And again the reason he is willing at—for all he knows—the hazard of his soul, and certainly of his present peace, to "make the Marriage-bed an Inne" (I, ii, 175) is that he really does want to satisfy his father's will so that he may hear him say: "My good Son,/ I'll bear with many faults in thee hereafter" (I, ii, 200–1).

But he now begins to realize that in trying to be the good boy to everyone he has placed himself in an impossible position: "On every side I am distracted:/ Am waded deeper into mischief,/ Then virtue can avoid. But on I must" (I, ii, 191–3). And so, to gain the time which he hopes will somehow unravel his complicated affairs and prove his pure intent, he says: "The peace is soon concluded" (I, ii, 202).

After a distracted sleep on his wedding night he finds himself unable, however, to maintain the farce of smiles before Susan's simple trust. Assuming that the inadequancy must be hers, Susan begins to weep. When neither evasions nor exaggerated flattery will dispel her anguished concern, Frank finally admits: "In mine own bosom: here the cause has root;/ The poysoned Leeches twist about my heart,/ And will, I hope, confound me" (II, ii, 112–4). This new confession of inability to cope with his situation, and the wish it engenders that it may destroy him so that he will at least be out of it, has resulted from his realization of the terrible grief he is causing the lovely Susan, since he cannot allow her the pleasure of pleasing him. And now he is further tormented by the thought that his inconstancy has barred the return to the simpler happiness he might have had with Susan: "she has't before thee,/ And that's the Fiend torments me" (II, ii, 126–7). Suddenly appreciating her value, he realizes his own baseness, and the disparity between them is too great for him to endure: "thou art so rare a goodness. . . . But we, as all things else,/ Art mutable and changing" (II, ii, 138–41). Unable to continue living with her knowing his constant violation of her pure love, he suddenly decides to leave Susan and run away with Winifred.

This act was certainly not his original intention when he left Winifred. At that time he had told her she might expect to see him "once every month at least" (I, i, 44). To which Winifred had sadly replied:

> I, I, in case
> No other Beauty tempt your eye, whom you
> Like better, I may chance to be remembred,
> And see you now and then. Faith, I did hope
> You'ld not have us'd me so: 'tis but my fortune. (I, i, 46–50)

But if Winifred's unerring perception of his essential dishonesty had discomfited him, it had released him from guilt; and the fact that, seeing through him, she is yet able to accept him—in fact, desires to be with him—enables him to accept her. With Susan, on the contrary, he would have to live a lie, for if she were ever to admit to herself that he was not the man of her dreams, that however much she might search for her own inadequacies they could not ultimately excuse his, then she could not accept him even if the admission meant her own destruction.[16] Though he has not the respect for Winifred that he has for Susan, it is finally only to Winifred that he can say: "While we together are, we are at home/ In any place" (III, ii, 19–20). With her he need not watch himself because he knows that, though she can easily see through all his pretenses, she will always have "one hours patience" (III, ii, 13) left for them.

But this truer marriage is now as barred to him as the other,

for Susan, coming for her final farewells, cannot bear to part
with him. In the painful scenes which follow, the conflict between
Susan's clinging love and Frank's indifferent irritability soon
reaches its fatal end. Frank first resorts to perfunctory kisses in
an effort to rid himself quickly of his clinging bride, all her
simple yearning only increasing his irritability towards her:

> What a Thorne this Rose grows on? parting were sweet,
> [*Aside.*]
> But what a trouble 'twill be to obtain it?
> Come, again and again, farewel. Yet wilt return?   [*Kisses.*]
> All questions of my journey, my stay, imployment,
> And revisitation, fully I have answered all.
> There's nothing now behinde, but nothing. (III, ii, 118–23)

When Frank discovers that the "roses" he has plucked as his
natural patrimony carry with them thorns of responsibility, his
only response is an offended surprise. Entering too easily into
binding relations, he thinks he can find his way out of them
just as easily, almost as payment for his initial compliance; and
he has no empathy for the more genuine emotions of those with
whom he becomes involved. As he treats his own compliance
as no more than a perfunctory duty, so does he regard the emotions of others as an irrelevant trouble from which he desires
only to be free. But the perfunctory politeness which Frank
considers to be a great concession on his part is that which most
pains Susan: "And that nothing is more hard then any thing,/
Then all the every things" (III, ii, 124–5). So, too, under a
similar circumstance, did Winifred say: "All these are nothing/
Without your company" (I, i, 42–3). And, on both occasions,
Frank simply cannot understand what these wives of his are
talking about. Though he knows that he has answered them
falsely, he does think that he has fully "answered all" the immediate objections to his behavior. He cannot understand, therefore, why, once they have accepted his answers, they should not
allow him to depart without further ado. The more Susan demands some show of parting affection, the more does his hostility

towards her grow until it crosses that incredibly short distance between betrayed trust and murder: "Then I'll ease all at once./ 'Tis done now: what I ne'er thought on" (III, iii, 15–6).

The deeper he had waded into mischief, the more urgent was his flight from reckoning; and the more heedless his flight, the more mischief he must accomplish to free his path for the increasing acceleration of his flight, until he comes to resemble Spenser's knight fleeing from Despair: "Still as he fledd, his eye was backward cast,/ As if his feare still followed him behynd" (*The Faerie Queene*, I, ix, 21). As circumstances begin to catch up with him, he weakly muses: "Would I had Wings but to soar up yon Tower: But here's a Clog that hinders me" (IV, ii, 141–2). There is always some clog that hinders him from being the good boy to everyone that he would wish to be, and life itself bears his weak spirit down. He had desired to make people happy and to gain their approval, and he never fully realizes how it came about that, in trying to satisfy all demands upon him, he has turned good into evil: "To please a Father, I have Heaven displeas'd./ Striving to cast two wedding Rings in one,/ Through my bad workmanship I now have none" (IV, ii, 102–4).

Frank has never been able to see further into the future than "a little time" and, in this time, he has tried to satisfy the moral demands made upon him as best he could. His flight has really been from the moral demands made by that looming future which he feared to face. But in prison he feels the full relief of his death sentence as, in its light, he is freed at last from form-less fears to scrutinize his soul. Freed from his desperate flight, self-scrutiny brings with it an increasing inner peace, and since he cherishes this peace, he is grateful to the law for having per-mitted him the only moral regeneration of which he was capable:

> He is not lost
> Who bears his peace within him: had I spun
> My Web of life out at full length, and dream'd
> Away my many years in lusts, in surfeits,
> Murthers of Reputations, gallant sins . . .
> You might have mourn'd for me indeed; . . . (V, iii, 73–7, 81)

His tragedy is not only that his moral understanding has come too late but that without the legal punishment, which made further evasion useless, it would never have come at all. But, though "A Court hath been kept here, where I am found/ Guilty" (V, iii, 87–8), this new self-knowledge does not bring with it the desire, however vain, to relive a weary life. He is too exhausted by his aimless life even to feel the sharp pain of loss, and love no longer rises to direct his end. Though his feelings for Winifred deepen at the last, he is already far too advanced on the road of no return for this love to desire continuance: "Thou much wrong'd woman, I must sigh for thee,/ As he that's onely loath to leave the World,/ For that he leaves thee in it unprovided" (V, iii, 63–5). This is the most negative, the most contracted form of both False Romantic Love and of its tragedy. Usually we find superficial and irresponsible flights of amorous rapture; here, nothing but constriction; but the pattern of this "love" is always the same, always unstable, always unrewarding, always too easily and never deeply enough involved.

In the decadent tragedies of the early 1620's, the false romantic lover renounces the evil into which he has fallen, sees and desires the good he has lost, but, unlike his predecessors, is no longer able to experience a potent love for that lost good. Virolet, Beatrice, and Frank Thorney gain no final vision which can integrate the cleavage between what they are and what they would wish to be, and their final desire is that death may extinguish the despair which their ultimate self-recognition has brought them.

Conclusion: Patterns of False Romantic Love Tragedy

In this study of the sub-genre of False Romantic Love tragedy, we have seen that there were three successive moments in which this form of tragedy manifested itself: 1) 1603, *A Woman Killed With Kindness;* 2) 1608–10, *Cupid's Revenge* and *The*

Maid's Tragedy; 3) 1620–5, *The Double Marriage, The Witch of Edmonton, The Changeling* and *The English Traveller.* We have also seen that during this historical progress there was a steady decline of redemptive vision. During the first period, Heywood clearly perceived and dramatized those values which the tragic figure only recognized too late. During the second period, Beaumont and Fletcher dramatized the sense of loss without clearly perceiving the nature of that which was lost. The final redemption of their characters, therefore, had a quality of nostalgia which was not present in the more genuine redemption achieved by Mrs. Frankford. In the third period, even the nostalgia has departed, and redemption is as unconvincing as positive loss.

As Beaumont and Fletcher had played a transitional role in this historical devolution of tragic vision, so did they play a transitional role in the historical development of the tragic pattern of False Romantic Love. Heywood had established a simple pattern moving from the possession of an unappreciated good, through the loss of this good, to an obstructed return transcended in ultimate tragic redemption. Beaumont and Fletcher had altered this pattern by beginning after the original good had already been lost through denial. The simple love triangle is still adhered to, but Beaumont and Fletcher begin their dramatization with the second stage of what is essentially a three-stage process, revealing the first stage only through narrative comment.

In the third historical period, however, the tragic pattern is substantially and, it would appear, almost simultaneously changed by Dekker and Ford, on the one hand, and Middleton, on the other. As Fletcher's final play in this genre repeats the pattern he had previously developed with Beaumont, it need not be considered in this discussion. Both *The Witch of Edmonton* and *The Changeling* begin, as did *The Maid's Tragedy,* with the establishment of a love contract which is, in fact, an instance of infidelity; but then—and here is the significant change—they return to the original threefold pattern established by Heywood, the contracting of a love relationship to which the lover will prove unfaithful and to which he will desire too late to return. The grotesque result of this synthesis of tragic patterns is that the possessed good of the first pattern becomes identified, in this third pattern, with the infidelity of the second.

Let us now consider these patterns more concretely. In the first pattern, Mrs. Frankford moves dramatically from Frankford to Wendoll back to Frankford. In the second pattern, Amintor moves dramatically only from Evadne back to Aspatia, who we have previously learned was actually his first love. In the third pattern, Frank and Beatrice move dramatically from Winifred and Alsemero, to Susan and De Flores, back to Winifred and Alsemero, although we have previously learned that they were first contracted to Susan and Piracquo. Nor is there any great difficulty about the fact that, in Frank's case, the original engagement and second infidelity are to the same person while, in Beatrice's case, they are to different people. In both cases, the original pre-contract has determined the need for the second infidelity. Since the purpose of this second infidelity is to establish the first infidelity by vitiating the original contract, it makes little difference how this is accomplished. Frank attempts to silence Susan's claims first by marriage (bigamy) with her and then by murdering her; whereas Beatrice attempts to silence Piracquo's claims first by having De Flores murder him and then by commiting adultery with De Flores. In both cases, however, the same momentary sense of remorse occurs between the first and second of these actions, Frank experiencing it when he beholds Susan's tears and Beatrice when she is faced with De Flores' "impossible" demands. At their first partial recognition of the evil they have embraced to establish the first infidelity, they both wished that they might still be free to return to their original love. But this momentary remorse is soon dispelled, and both further entrench themselves in evil in order to stabilize the more important first infidelity. In this attempt, however, they prove that a love contract that is based upon infidelity is essentially unstable. It is unstable because of the inadequacy of the love which is brought to its support, an inadequacy which results in persistent infidelity. In this new pattern, then, the lover is tainted with infidelity in establishing his most important love relationship and his further infidelity proves him irredeemable.

This change in formal patterning to accommodate a change in vision is a beautiful instance of the essential unity of form and content in a truly creative work of art. What has actually happened is that a new vision has created a form suitable for its revelation. A tragic vision which reveals man to be hopelessly corrupt has created a pattern of action which has man entering sinfully into his finest relationships, destroying his dearest hopes by a persistence in sin, and, though brought to recognize his tragic persistence in sin by this destruction, incapable of real change and redemption despite his recognition and remorse. The historical importance of this perfect union of form and content is attested to by the fact that Dekker and Ford in collaboration and Middleton, perhaps from a suggestion made by Rowley, adopted it almost simultaneously and that even Heywood, in *The English Traveller,* later adopted this new form to convey his altered vision.

Even more significant than this successive historical change of form to accommodate a changing vision, however, is a more profound union of form and content in the whole genre of False Romantic Love tragedy. I have repeatedly shown that the pattern of this tragic genre reveals an essential triadic structure of both action and characters. The tragic figure, torn between two opposing lovers, is tempted from his best love to embrace his worst only to find that this embrace bars him from returning to that best love which he has learned to appreciate too late. Now this three-part dramatic action involving three essential characters corresponds symbolically to the analysis I have also repeatedly made of the false romantic lover's own character.

In Beatrice's typical avowal—"Let the common sewer take it from distinction"—a fundamental personality split can be seen which characterizes each successive false romantic lover. Fletcher, who returned three times to the depiction of this type of character, finally expressed his understanding of this fact in a striking theoretical statement:

> When we grow great, but our affections greater,
> And struggle with this stubborn twin, born with us;
> And tug and pull, yet still we find a Giant:

> Had we not then the privilege to sleep,
> Our everlasting sleep? he would make us idiots. *(The Double Marriage)*

Like Beatrice, Fletcher's Virolet distinguishes between the true self who is speaking and that other self who is impersonally characterized as "it," and "Giant." The recognition that this other repudiated self is "born with us" and can only be overcome by a general self-destruction brings with it the desire "to sleep/ Our everlasting sleep," because living with this knowledge "would make us idiots." This knowledge only "would make us idiots," however, as long as it is opposed by an equally strong conviction of the essential purity of that divorced self who is speaking. As long as the two selves remain unintegrated, the baser self will be free to continue its irresponsible behavior and the purer self will be forced to greater evasions to preserve its sanity. As the result of this lack of integration is persistent irresponsibility, the only means by which the potency of the best self can be redeemed from its evasive dreams is for it to face its essential unity with that other maddening self and assume responsibility for it with new personal integrity. This solution Middleton discerned as clearly as Fletcher had diagnosed its cause:

> Push! fly not to your birth, but settle you
> In what the act has made you; you're no more now.
> You must forget your parentage to me;
> You are the deed's creature; by that name
> You lost your first condition, and I challenge you,
> As peace and innocency has turned you out,
> And made you one with me. . . .
> Thy peace is wrought for ever in this yielding.
>   *(The Changeling)*

This new peace can only be wrought, however, by facing the knowledge which "would make us idiots" and yielding to the ritual destruction of the old unintegrated self.

Fletcher's diagnosis explains the persistent three-character formula of our plays, the "stubborn twin" within the central figure accounting for the two opposing loves which he alternately experiences. Middleton's prescribed cure likewise explains the persistent three-stage pattern of action which our plays have followed. The first stage, in which the true love is possessed without real appreciation, corresponds to Middleton's "first condition" in which true "peace and innocency" is possesssed. The second stage, in which the lover is tempted to forswear his true love for the embraces of his evil genius, corresponds, to the loss of this original peace as a result of a cleavage within the self which permits irresponsible behavior without true acknowledgment. Although this irresponsibility has made the whole self "the deed's creature," part of the self still persists in claiming the sanctity of its "first condition" by flying to its birth rather than acknowledging its actual loss. The third stage, in which the lover, recognizing and disavowing the evil he has rashly embraced, regains his lost good through penitent self-destruction, corresponds, finally, to Middleton's prescription: "but settle you/ In what the act has made you; you're no more now. . . . Thy peace is wrought for ever in this yielding."

The pattern of False Romantic Love tragedy, which is telescoped in Middleton's illuminating lines, has, finally, two most significant analogues. For the road which Middleton suggests to this "peace" is comparable to the processes by which both psychoanalytic "health" and religious "redemption" may be realized. It is the psychological truth of the religious pattern of sin and redemption which perhaps best explains the moral and psychological profundity of these tragedies. Although out dramatists were not vouchsafed the revelations of Freud and his followers, the teachings of the religious doctors were as common to their thinking as the former are to ours, and, it must be admitted, served very much the same purposes. Accepting the theological premises of Original Sin and salvation as a pattern for human tragedy, such diverse tragedians as Heywood, Beaumont and Fletcher, and Middleton could not fail to touch the highest moral truth.

Section III
Tragedies of Worldly Love

7

The Elizabethan Genesis

If the Elizabethan period produced the classic tragedies of Courtly Love, it gave little evidence of the future greatness of Worldly Love tragedy. The most impressive Worldly Love tragedy of this period is Marlowe's *Dido* and even this is a minor work. Though Marlowe was the first great playwright to make a high ideal of Worldly Love, he was not the only playwright to attempt this form of tragedy during this early period. Two groups of playwrights also made this attempt: the anonymous domestic tragedians, and the closet dramatists of the Countess of Pembroke's coterie. But they as well as Marlowe were hampered in the expression of this new ideal by their use of alien literary models. The reason for this may be that, unlike the writers of Courtly Love tragedy, they had no literary precedents to guide them. Marlowe was working with a pattern of love tragedy that Vergil had employed for a different mode of love. The closet tragedians of Worldly Love, Daniel and Lady Elizabeth Carey, used the classical form which, in telescoping the action into the prescribed one-day limit, prohibited any real development. The domestic tragedians were likewise hampered by their bondage to the conventions of domestic tragedy which, as we know from Heywood and Dekker, were concerned with a pattern of sin and redemption. But with all their dramatic faults, these pioneers laid the groundwork for the later achievements of Shakespeare, Webster, Massinger, and Middleton; and this not only in their dramatic experimentation but also in their subject matter.

Despite the different methods of the domestic and closet tragedians, they were alike in looking to the same source for the subjects of Worldly Love tragedy, history. While the domestic tragedians turned to Holinshed and Stow, Daniel and Lady Carey turned to Plutarch and Josephus and found there the two greatest examples of actual Worldly Love tragedy in antiquity: Antony and Cleopatra, and Herod and Mariamne. If Daniel and Lady Carey failed in their attempts to divert the course of Elizabethan drama into classical channels, they did add to the store of dramatic subjects two stories which were later to be treated by Shakespeare and Massinger. They may even have suggested lines of treatment to those later dramatists, for in their interpretations of these subjects, Shakespeare's *Antony and Cleopatra* (1607) is markedly similar to Daniel's *Cleopatra* (1593) and Massinger's *The Duke of Milan* (1621), a fictionalized version of the Herod and Mariamne story, to Lady Carey's *Mariam* (1604).

While the closet dramatists were absorbed with the grandeur of ancient history, the domestic dramatists were equally fascinated by a variety of "true and home-born tragedy." [1] Though Worldly Love did not become a literary subject until the 1590's, this mode of love had already led to actual tragedy in two notorious English criminal cases. In 1552 Alice Arden with her lover Mosbie, and in 1573 Anne Sanders with her lover George Browne, were sentenced to death for the murder of their respective husbands, and two anonymous playwrights in the last decade of the sixteenth century found in their cases a subject to "build a matter of importance on." [2] Their tragic potential is later confirmed by the fact that the first of these, *Arden of Feversham* (1591), bears a marked resemblance to Webster's *The White Devil* (1612), while the second, *A Warning for Fair Women* (1599), seems equally to anticipate Middleton's *Women Beware Women* (1622).[3] Beyond their similarity of tragic pattern, however, is the more striking fact that all four of these tragedies were based upon nearly contemporaneous events, the earlier two plays upon events in England, the later two upon events in Italy. As we can see, the source of almost all of the Worldly Love tragedies is historical rather than literary, and this because the ideal of love they depict was not that which had been extolled by centuries of poets but the actual mode of love which was then just coming into its full realization.

In order to clarify the dramatic similarities between these early Elizabethan tragedies and their more brilliant Jacobean counterparts, it will be necessary to make a preliminary definition of the various patterns of Worldly Love tragedy. Although the central distinction made among worldly lovers in the Introduction was that between those whose self-love was based upon genuine self-esteem and those for whom it was simply narcissistic, this is not the major distinction from which the separate patterns of Worldly Love tragedy develop. What does seem to determine this pattern is the spiritual position of the worldly lover on a continuum which ranges from complacency to despair. The first pattern concerns the stage of Worldly Love that is basically narcissistic and develops out of the lover's sense of complacency towards his position in the world, a complacent self-satisfaction which the rival claims of love will seem to threaten and which will cause his desire for revenge against the beloved. The third pattern develops out of the lover's sense of despair, a despair which leads him to murder anyone who hinders his only hope of salvation through love. The second pattern seems to represent a meridian between these two potentially destructive extremes, in which Worldly Love achieves its noblest fulfillment. *Dido* and the somewhat later *Mariam* exemplify the first pattern, *Cleopatra* the second pattern, *Arden of Feversham* and *A Warning for Fair Women* the third pattern.[4] As the Elizabethan period proper is most deficient in its expression of the nobler second pattern,[5] the primary concern of this chapter will be with the more brilliant examples of the first and third patterns, *Dido* and *Arden of Feversham*.

Dido

Marlowe was the only Elizabethan tragedian of Worldly Love who turned to classical poetry as a source for his love tragedy, and the love he found depicted there had to be completely altered before it could serve his purposes. The love of Vergil's Dido proceeds in its fatal course to the death that will release it from suffering. This is indicated from the first description of Dido's love: "Now the queen, already suffering from the sharp pangs of love, nursed a wound in her veins and was consumed by a hidden flame." [6] The sufferings of ceaseless desire, which characterize Dido's love from its inception, are, however, intimately related to death: "That day was the prime cause of her death. . . . overcome by grief, she became mad and decided to die." [7] As she is finally consumed by the flame she nursed, she jumps into an actual fire crying: "Relics, so dear as long as Fates and Heaven allowed, receive this spirit and free me of this anguish." [8] Although Vergil condemns this love as a cursed madness while the troubadours glorify it, it will be seen that it represents the same kind of passion. Marlowe's Dido, in contrast, represents an original characterization which is informed throughout by the opposing mode of Worldly Love.

The tragic blindness of Courtly Love is that it carries the individual beyond the realm of his rational safety. The complementary blindness of Worldly Love, especially in its first pattern, is that it is so concerned with its personal interests that it cannot see beyond them. Once Dido has determined upon Aeneas' fitness for her—"Is not Aeneas worthy Dido's love?" (III, i, 67) [9]—and has said "Stout love, in mine arms make thy Italy" (III, iv, 56), she believes this settles the matter: "Speak of no other land, this land is thine;/ Dido is thine" (IV, iv, 83–4). But the love she offers him in exchange for Italy is perfectly revealed in her next words: "henceforth I'll call thee lord./ Do as I bid thee" (IV, iv, 84–5).[10] In these incredible words we see the form of love that results when total sovereignty is preserved. Dido is willing to give everything she has to Aeneas but herself. Similarly, it is not Aeneas' real self that she desires but only her image of what it should be: "let me gaze my fill./ Now looks Aeneas like immortal Jove" (IV, iv, 44–51).

There are two faces to her sovereign will, however: one smiling and one angry. She smiles when she proclaims her will but is easily angered if its wisdom or goodness is questioned.

When Dido wins back Aeneas after his first attempt to escape her, she becomes rhapsodic: "the stars fall down,/ To be partakers of our honey talk" (IV, iv, 53–4). But when, having decided to parade her lover through the streets as the new king, it is asked "What if the citizens repine thereat?" (IV, iv, 70), her "honey talk" gives way to venom:

> Those that dislike what Dido gives in charge
> Command my guard to slay for their offence.
> Shall vulgar peasants storm at what I do?
> The ground is mine that gives them sustenance,
> The air wherein they breathe, the water, fire,
> All that they have, their lands, their goods, their lives;
> And I, the Goddess of all these, command
> Aeneas ride as Carthaginian King. (IV, iv, 71–84).

Her self-inflation is so complete that she believes herself to be a goddess placed among peasants without rights. But if her peasant subjects (considered "citizens" with the right to "repine" by others) have no rights in her eyes because they enjoy their estate at her bequest, this is equally Aeneas' position. Though she may endow him with godlike attributes so that he may be a fitting mate for her own "Goddess" nature, she grants him no legitimate rights:

> Henceforth you shall be our Carthage gods.
> Ay, but it may be he will leave my love,
> And seek a foreign land call'd Italy. . . .
> I must prevent him; wishing will not serve. . . .
> What if I sink his ships? O he'll frown!
> Better he frown than I should die for grief. (IV, iv, 96–8,
>   104, 110–11)

Though she says that "in his looks I see eternity" (IV, iv, 122), in trying to keep him in this way, she will never see anything in his looks but a projected reflection of her own desires.

Aeneas's reaction to Dido's imperious love is, in fact, to run away from her: "I may not dure this female drudgery:/ To sea, Aeneas, find out Italy" (IV, iii, 55–6).

Although her love, up to this point, had suffered a gradual corruption in trying to cope with Aeneas' persistent discontent by imperial fiat rather than understanding, she at last learns the terrible truth that Aeneas has an independent will. Waiving his supposed obedience to the gods as a poor excuse, she has the courage to face the truth directly, that "It is Aeneas calls Aeneas hence" (V, i, 132) in violation of her own proclaimed will. But once she recognizes the fact of his rebellion, she returns to her habitual response to such malefactors:

> Ah foolish Dido to forbear this long!
> Wast thou not wrack'd upon this Libyan shore
> And camest to Dido like a Fisher swain?
> Repair'd not I thy ships, made thee a King. . . .
> I hope that that which love forbids me do
> The rocks and sea-gulfs will perform at large
> And thou shalt perish in the billows' ways,
> To whom poor Dido doth bequeath revenge. (V, i, 160–3,
>   170–3)

She no longer sees Aeneas as a god but as a peasant, "a Fisher swain," who is beholden to her for all he has and, therefore, owes her absolute obedience upon pain of death. Although her love forbids her in this special case to command her guard to slay him, in her heart she does condemn him to death and prays that he will be punished for his ungratefulness. This desire to be revenged against him is different, however, from that of Courtly Love, for she does not wish to be revenged against an eternal obstruction but to destroy the beloved. This desire is an essential factor in the first pattern of Worldly Love tragedy, for in this pattern the insistence upon sovereignty will first corrupt and finally destroy the rival claims of love, only to be itself destroyed by its loss.

Aeneas' stark rejection of Dido begins to work a partial change in her. Before this she had never made the slightest sacrifice for her love, insisting that it accommodate itself entirely to her royal will. However, now that this love has been withdrawn from her, she suddenly realizes its importance, that it alone can really give her happiness. She who had never sacrificed the slightest prerogative to her lover would now be willing to sacrifice everything to win him back: "Now bring him back and thou shalt be a queen,/ And I will live a private life with him" (V, i, 197–8). Perceiving that Dido is losing her proper dignity in pure futility, her sister abruptly puts an end to Dido's fantasies of recovery: "Ah sister, leave these idle fantasies;/ Sweet sister, cease; remember who you are" (V, i, 262–3). And Dido does remember: "Dido I am, unless I be deceiv'd" (V, i, 264). Dido's tragedy lies in the fact that, while the insistence on preserving her sovereignty has destroyed her love, it is the destruction of her love that deprives this preservation of meaning. It is the conflict between love and sovereignty, neither of which she can live without, which destroys her. But if sovereignty has destroyed her love, it is finally to sovereignty that she returns. She will show the world that the love of a queen is not to be abused:

> Now Dido, with these relics burn thyself,
> And make Aeneas famous through the world
> For perjury and slaughter of a queen. . . .
> And from mine ashes let a conqueror rise
> That may revenge this treason to a queen. . .
> Live, false Aeneas! Truest Dido dies; . . . (V, i, 292–4, 306–7, 312)

Her death will prove her value and revenge her loss of honor by the greater loss that Aeneas will be made to suffer when the falseness of his nature is made "famous through the world." Dido she is and, spectacular in death as ever she was in life, she dies to affirm the truth and dignity of her being.

Far different is the death of a courtly lover:

> Cursed Iarbus, die to expiate
> The grief that tires upon thine inward soul!
> Dido, I come to thee: ay me, Aeneas! (V, i, 316-8)

Though Dido and Iarbus are both impelled to death by unre-
quited love, Dido dies to affirm the dignity of her life, Iarbus to
find expiation in death. That Marlowe understood the meaning
of Courtly Love is clear from his characterization of Iarbus with
his "delight of dying pensiveness" (IV, ii, 44). For his own Dido,
however, Marlowe rejected this Vergilian element completely,
substituting for it a totally different conception of character and
love. The death of Iarbus, for which there is no basis in the original, serves the important thematic function of affirming the
value of Dido's love. If Aeneas' rejection of Dido be thought to
imply the author's rejection of her character and love, Marlowe's
conclusion on the note of Iarbus' death for love of her dispels
this impression. Though Marlowe has spared no truth in his portrait of her tragic pride, a pride destructive of love and resulting
in death, it is precisely the love of such a character that he is
affirming as a value in this play. It is the love of a sovereign
nature, seeking a companion with whom it can be happy in this
life, which is, with all its tragic deficiencies, the only form of love
that has meaning to Marlowe. The tragedy of Dido's love is the
same as that which would have befallen Tamburlaine had he
been ready to invest love with primary meaning and Zenocrate
been less obliging. It is the love of all of Marlowe's earlier heroes
made central and explored to its ultimate conclusion.

But if Marlowe affirms the tragic love of a woman, he is not
prepared to do so for a man. Although Aeneas was pulled by the
rival attractions of love and a great destiny, he saw Dido's love
as a temptation from the proper object of his aspiration:

> Grant she or no, Aeneas must away,
> Whose golden fortunes, clogg'd with courtly ease,
> Cannot ascend to fame's immortal house
> Or banquet in bright honour's burnish't hall
> Till he hath furrow'd Neptune's glassy fields
> And cut a passage through his topless hills. (IV, iii, 7-12)

In his first play, Marlowe presents his Renaissance aspiring man with the first temptation, love. Its impact upon his soul is slight. In this dawning of a tragic age, love, at least Wordly Love, is not seen as the ultimate fulfillment of a masculine spirit.

Arden of Feversham

The distinction between the sexes revealed in *Dido* is also true for the only other important Worldly Love tragedy of this early period, *Arden of Feversham,* an example of the third pattern. The desperation of this third type of worldly lover is perfectly exemplified by Alice Arden. Though the playwright sticks closely to Holinshed's account, he develops his own portrait of Alice in such a way that it best explains the desperate quality of her love for Mosbie which drives her to murder for its preservation. Both treatments begin with Mosbie's message to Alice that he will see her no more. Though the chronicler shows that after his return Mosbie stayed with her for another two years, before his second rejection of her and subsequent return, the playwright eliminates this long interval between Mosbie's rejections so that the picture of their relationship which emerges is one in which Mosbie is ready to leave her at the slightest opportunity and Alice must constantly sue for his grudging favor.

It later becomes clear that Mosbie has entirely ceased to love Alice and that her only remaining attraction for him is the wealth that will be hers if she can be persuaded to the murder of her husband. Like Aeneas, Mosbie accepts love as the means of his material advancement but soon grows weary both of love and the woman. His rejection of her, however, finally confirms in her mind the necessity for her husband's death as the only means of saving her love: "Nay Mosbie let me still inioye thy loue,/ And happen what will, I am resolute" (I, 225–6).[11] Alice's desperate attempt to preserve their love at any cost, despite Mosbie's loss of true feeling for her, only leads to the greater corruption of their love. Although she differs from Dido in the high valuation she gives to love from the beginning, she is like her in using desperate expedients to hold her lover, expedients which only reinforce his dissatisfaction with her nature. This becomes clear in Mosbie's soliloquy:

> But whether doeth contemplation carry me.
> The way I seeke to finde where pleasure dwels,
> Is hedged behinde me that I cannot back . . .
> Then Arden perish thou by that decre. . . .
> And then am I sole ruler of mine owne:
> Yet mistres Arden liues, but she's my selfe . . .
> But what for that I may not trust you Ales,
> You have supplanted Arden for my sake, . . . (III, v, 1285–9,
>   1302–6)

Realizing this growing corruption and that for it they are becoming inextricably involved in an evil that has already robbed them of their peace and endangers their very lives, both grow nostalgic for the uncomplicated lives they led before their meeting and turn against each other with bitter recriminations. Her agreement to the murder has cost her not only her own self-esteem but his respect. Before the murder is even accomplished, their relationship has deteriorated beyond repair. But even this recognition cannot destroy Alice's love: "Nay heare me speake Mosbie a word or two,/ Ile byte my tongue, if it speake bitterly" (III, v, 1375–6). To a love so desperate that it will not only countenance murder but believe Mosbie to be worthy such a sacrifice, the blatantly unworthy Mosbie coldly replies: "I will forget this quarrel gentle Ales,/ Prouided Ile be tempted so no more" (III, v, 1414–5). Though Mosbie to the end is ever ready with a curt reply, Alice never again falters in her love. Stabbing her husband to death with the words "Take this for hindring Mosbies loue and mine" (V, i, 2260), she affirms her sovereign right to love. Worldly lovers of the third pattern dramatize Aquinas' observation that "he who desires something intensely, is moved against all that hinders his gaining or quietly enjoying the object of his love" (*Summa Theologica*, II, I, 28, 4). They, of all worldly lovers, are most opposed to courtly lovers in that they move to overcome all obstructions to their love, even to the point of murder. Their desperation has hardened them to any value but the love in which they see their only salvation. Though the sight of her husband's body reduces Alice to tears, the sweeter sight of Mosbie is so great a fulfillment that it excuses any evil: "Sweete Mosbie art thou come?/ Then weepe that will./ I have my wishe in that I ioy thy sight" (V, i, 2368–70).

A decisive change in her attitude takes place, however, when she is sentenced to death. If before she had accepted the price of murder for the fulfillment of her love, when this fulfillment is denied her the futility of such a terrible murder weighs so heavily upon her that her only remaining wish is to atone for it. Though she continued to affirm her love as long as there was hope for its fulfillment in life, death brings with it different concerns. In the light of death, Alice sees the futility of the love that has inspired her life. With the worldly defeat of her love (for Worldly Love is defeated by death) the desperation born of this love also vanishes, and she addresses herself with new calmness of spirit to her God: "Leaue now to trouble me with worldly things./ And let me meditate vpon my sauiour Christ" (V, iii, 2524–5). It is only Mosbie's exclamation, "Conuey me from the presence of that strumpet" (V, iii, 2528), that breaks her spiritual calm, "Ah but for thee I had neuer beene strumpet" (V, iii, 2829); but her concern is not now for lost love but lost virtue. At the last she rejects Mosbie as completely as he does her. Like Dido, she returns to her proper self and rejects the love that had driven her to distraction.

Although these early feminine worldly lovers differ in the quality of their commitment to love, they come at the end to approximate their uncommitted lovers. In this pre-classical period of Worldly Love tragedy, the inspiration of Worldly Love finally fails even for women. And this may be the reason why this earliest period of the Elizabethan drama yields no important example within the specific genre of love tragedy of the nobler manifestation of Worldly Love, that mutual love which is neither the product of complacency nor desperation. Since Worldly Love has not yet proved inspirational for men, it cannot prove sufficiently inspirational even for women. Their lovers' dissatisfaction with love spoils their own love, leading them to take measures that rob them of their self-respect and ultimately cause a revolt of their own pride against such love.

We are left, then, simply with a distinction between the capacity for commitment to love. While Aeneas and Mosbie are wholly uncommitted to love, Dido, Alice, and Daniel's Cleopatra are only partially committed to the love that has made their death inevitable. George Browne, in *A Warning for Fair Women* (1599),[12] is a unique figure among the early worldly lovers in that he is the only male to remain dedicated to his love until his death.[13] He cannot, however, qualify as a significant artistic expression of his age, being the work of a hack catering to a public demand for lurid crime stories. And yet, as the latest of these male lovers, he perhaps anticipates the later masculine affirmation of Worldly Love which continues unabated from Shakespeare's *Antony and Cleopatra* to the end of the Jacobean period.

The general distinction between the sexes in the earlier period of the drama is only true, however, for the tragedies of Worldly Love. In the three tragedies of Courtly Love written or revised between 1590-5, *Tancred and Gismund, Soliman and Perseda,* and *Romeo and Juliet,* the affirmation of love is mutual. But the love these tragedies affirm is a dying ideal, the highest tragic ideal of the Medieval period, while the love affirmed in the tragedies of Worldly Love breathes the fresh air of the Renaissance. If, despite their equal numbers, the tragedies of Worldly Love are completely overshadowed by the brilliance of *Romeo and Juliet,* it is the force of Worldly Love that finally triumphs. Those dramatists who affirmed the weaker ideal were, naturally enough, most conscious of the significance of the conflict between these rival conceptions of love. In *Soliman and Perseda,* the villain, Soliman, who causes the destruction of the courtly lovers is himself a worldly lover. And, if the value of this rival love is denied, its power is yet well attested to. So also with the most important Courtly Love tragedy after *Romeo and Juliet, The Second Maiden's Tragedy.* When Courtly Love raises its head in the Jacobean period, it is largely to view the greater power of Worldly Love.

Worldly Love is the last of the three forms of love to be given full tragic expression in the Elizabethan drama. As the classical period of Courtly Love tragedy may be said to be the 1590's, and of False Romantic Love the early 1600's, so the classical period of Worldly Love tragedy occurs in the later 1600's. As can be seen, the movement of Elizabethan love tragedy is towards the final affirmation of Worldly Love. But if Worldly Love is to become dominant in the Jacobean period, its future power is no more than hinted at in the Elizabethan. In this earlier period, the masculine spirit is still too much obsessed with aspiration to turn its full attention to the love that best suits the expansive nature. In this period it is only women who bear the promise of the new ideal of love tragedy which, through Shakespeare, Webster, and Middleton, is to dominate the later drama.

8

The First Pattern: Othello

If Worldly Love is to become the final tragic value of the Elizabethan drama, it is Shakespeare who gave this value immortal form. Perhaps the most significant single fact of Elizabethan love tragedy is Shakespeare's shift of allegiance from Courtly to Worldly Love, a shift that bore witness to the changing values of his age. His triumphant affirmation of this value in *Antony and Cleopatra* was in part dependent, however, upon his having first tested the initial difficulties of this new vision of love in *Othello*. Since the first pattern of Worldly Love tragedy, which *Othello* exemplifies, concerns the initial difficulties that block a full affirmation of this love, a study of this pattern may serve beside the earlier consideration of the Elizabethan genesis as an introduction to the fully affirmative phases of Worldly Love tragedy.

Recent criticism has tended to reject the romantic reading of *Othello* exemplified in the following remarks by Coleridge:

Othello does not kill Desdemona in jealousy, but in a conviction forced upon him by the almost superhuman art of Iago, such a conviction as any man would and must have entertained who had believed Iago's honesty as Othello did. . . . Othello had no life but in Desdemona:—the belief that she, his angel, had fallen from the heaven of her native innocence, wrought a civil war in his heart. She is his counterpart; and, like him, is almost sanctified in our eyes by her absolute unsuspiciousness, and holy entireness of love.[1]

Through Bradley's concurrence,[2] this view has become the traditional interpretation of *Othello*. Perhaps the most important effect of this interpretation has been the tendency to allegorize the contents of the play, a trend that has reached full expression in Bernard Spivack's study.[3] In Coleridge's reading, Othello believes what "any man would" and the opposing influences of the "superhuman art of Iago" and "his angel," Desdemona, cause "a civil war in his heart." Coleridge's interpretation, then, sees Othello as Everyman torn between the powers of supernatural good and evil. The long persistence of this view is understandable, for the imagery of the play certainly suggests such an added dimension to the play's total meaning and effect. But while this is true, the allegorical dimension is yet wholly separate from the realistic surface of the play; Othello does not, like Romeo, endow his beloved with symbolic implications in the very act of loving. A further and, from my perspective, even a more drastic effect of this allegorizing tendency is that it excludes the possibility of viewing Othello as a love tragedy. If Othello is the soul of Everyman and Desdemona his good angel, a human love and marriage is hardly possible between them. Thus Franklin Dickey, for instance, excludes *Othello* from a book exclusively concerned with Shakespeare's love tragedies, and this even though he takes his title from *Othello*.[4] The final effect of the Coleridgean interpretation, even among those critics who have focused upon the human qualities of the characters, has been the carryover of his view that Othello and Desdemona are "almost sanctified in our eyes" by their "holy entireness of love." But this view of the noble Moor and his faultless bride has come under increasing attack.

The first important attempt to show "the inadequacy of Othello's passion, and the fact that it precedes his tragedy," [5] was made by D. A. Traversi. His analysis of Othello's character and its development reveals the essentials of the first pattern of Worldly Love tragedy, that which derives from the lover's spiritual complacency:

This complacency directly affects his love. . . . for him a condition of "circumscription and confine." . . . For Othello is rarely able to get sufficiently far from himself fully to love Desdemona. His happiness in the opening scenes is, like everything else in his character, self-centred, naive, even egoistic . . .[6]

Othello approaches love with a feeling of complacency resulting from the independent satisfactions of his personal power, and his acceptance of Desdemona is due "in no small part because she ministered to his self-esteem." [7] It is this egoism that makes him vulnerable to Iago's temptation and causes him to seek revenge: "[Iago] makes him visualize the sin by which Desdemona is offending his self-esteem. . . . Thwarted in love, his egoism will be consistent in revenge." [8] It can be seen that the nature and progress of Othello's love closely parallels that of Dido.

This analysis of Othello is developed at much greater length by G. R. Elliott and Robert Heilman, both of whom finally grant *Othello* the status of a great love tragedy.[9] While both of these critics accept the larger outlines of Traversi's analysis of Othello, Elliott emphasizes his pride [10] while Heilman emphasizes his insecurity.[11] The essential accord of these three critics also extends, though in a different way, to their treatment of Desdemona. Traversi eliminates her completely from the tragedy, not discussing a single one of her actions or speeches. Heilman does discuss her but leaves her in "the heaven of her native innocence" where Coleridge had placed her. Elliott treats her with greater understanding of her significance. In his treatment of the Venetian courtroom and Cyprus reunion scenes, he stresses and illuminates the distinction between their concepts and modes of loving.[12] But Elliott does not stress the way in which Desdemona's consecration to her vision of marital interdependence [13] effects her later behavior and its further effect upon Othello. Although he says that "her goodness, while real and strong, has all along had in it a vein of self-will that could easily render it vulnerable," [14] and although he notes that in her last words "she is deeply aware how much 'myself' has been to blame for Othello's jealousy," [15] Elliott does not himself find her blameworthy in any respect, believ-

ing that all of her actions conform to the ideal of married love
which her words express and her heart intends. If these three
critics have desanctified Othello, they have not seriously touched
the earlier canonization of Desdemona.

Robert Speaight, however, poses, with much qualification, a
question which he himself does not undertake to answer: "was
Desdemona perverse even while remaining pure?" [16] This question had already been forcibly answered in the affirmative by
Richard Flatter:

> Desdemona, to put it as mildly as possible, is not a good
> diplomatist. . . . What makes her arrogate the right to meddle
> in her husband's military affairs? . . . Her insistence on
> having things all her own way, although she wraps it in a
> grace of manner and sweetness of words, is a remarkable
> feature in her. It has its peculiar function in the scheme
> of the play, which without that trend in her character would
> be in danger of losing its probability. . . . Shakespeare refused
> to make Desedemona a being "without blemish" . . .[17]

Although Flatter still holds to the "noble Moor" interpretation
of Othello, he shows the way in which Desdemona's willfulness
contributes to Othello's violent reaction against her. This view
of Desdemona is becoming more widely accepted. Davis S. Berkeley stresses that "for each gaucherie she pays heavily," [18] while
M. L. Renald, in detailing her departures from the courtesy-book
precepts of wifely behavior, recognizes "Desdemona's partial responsibility for the tragic action." [19] But however imperfect Desdemona's behavior may be, it still seems hard to account for
Othello's murderous reaction to it unless we bring to these newer
analyses of the interrelation of Desdemona and Othello the view
of the other critics concerning Othello's flawed nature. It is this
combination of modern views on *Othello* that I find most acceptable for an adequate illumination of the play.

We may well begin by pondering Brabantio's question, "Are
they married, think you?" (I, i, 168).[20] Othello and Desdemona
are no sooner wed than separated, and the consummation of their

wedding is twice prevented by external conflicts. This external disunity is accompanied, moreover, by indications of internal conflict which suggest a symbolic interpretation of the action, namely that Othello and Desdemona are not married in spirit.

When their marriage is first put in question, Othello rests on his conviction that "My parts, my title, and my perfect soul/ Shall manifest me rightly" (I, ii, 31–2). It is this sense of independent perfection that causes him to look upon marriage as a circumscription:

> But that I love the gentle Desdemona,
> I would not my unhoused free condition
> Put into circumscription and confine
> For the sea's worth. (I, ii, 25–8)

He has accepted this circumscription, however, because his love did not seem to endanger but rather to support the proper manifestation of his "perfect soul": "She lov'd me for the dangers I had pass'd/ And I lov'd her that she did pity them" (I, iii, 167–8). Yet, in his exclusive concern for his personal excellence there is a self-centered quality which may prove to be of greater danger with respect to love than it has been in his former condition:

> For since these arms of mine had seven years' pith
> Till now some nine moons wasted, they have us'd
> Their dearest action in the tented field; . . . (I, iii, 83–5)

"Othello's occupation" (III, iii, 357) and his "dearest action" have been in the "pride, pomp, and circumstance of glorious war!" (III, iii, 354). Though he had, in nine wasted months of peace, been moved to responsive love for a gentle lady, who seconded his own estimation of "his honours and his valiant parts" (I, iii, 255), he still remains a man "all in all sufficient" (IV, i, 276), one who expects his love to accommodate itself to his otherwise self-sufficient life. When, on his wedding night, Othello is ordered to the war, he accepts it with the "natural and prompt alacrity/ I find in hardness" (I, iii, 233–4), begging only "fit disposition for my wife" (I, iii, 237). Othello now has his "occupation" to attend to, that in which his true self-estimation lies, and Desdemona is to be put aside until the wasted time of peace returns.

His first decision with regard to their marriage, however, provokes Desdemona's immediate objection, an objection based upon her differing conception of their marriage:

> That I did love the Moor to live with him,
> My downright violence, and storm of fortunes,
> May trumpet to the world. My heart's subdu'd
> Even to the very quality of my lord.
> I saw Othello's visage in his mind,
> And to his honours and his valiant parts
> Did I my soul and fortunes consecrate.
> So that, dear lords, if I be left behind,
> A moth of peace, and he go to the war,
> The rights for which I love him are bereft me,
> And I a heavy interim shall support
> By his dear absence. Let me go with him. (I, iii, 249–60)

"Heaven had made her such a man" (I, iii, 163), the longed-for completion of her being to whom she could "consecrate" her soul. She hopes to supplement and succor his spirit in its inmost concerns, to be there when he needs her and not to be "left behind,/ A moth of peace, and he got to the war." But this is exactly what he will not allow. He rigidly excludes her from his dearest concerns, resenting her interference therein and accepting her only as the "moth of peace" which she has scorned to be.

Though he immediately seconds her desire to go with him, he makes it quite clear that it is not his desire that she accompany him, that though he wishes "to be free and bounteous to her mind" (I, iii, 266) in this request, he will do everything in his power to minimize the effects of her presence. He does not see Desdemona's presence as a help but only a hindrance to his "serious and great business," and in a striking vow promises not to allow her to "corrupt and taint my business" nor to "Make head against my estimation" (I, iii, 268, 272, 275). In his self-centered manifestation of his worth he has no need of Desdemona. She is casually assigned "With what else needful your good Grace shall think/ To be sent after me" (I, iii, 287–8).

Beneath this casual assignment, is Othello's growing concern, as reflected in his vow, lest Desdemona gain an influence over him greater than that of a "light-wing'd toy" (I, iii, 269). In her forthright demand to go with him, despite his public announcement that she is to remain behind, he sees an emergent individuality which confounds his conception of Desdemona and threatens his sense of personal sovereignty. In reducing her to the status of, in the Duke's words, "such things else of quality and respect/ As doth import you" (I, iii, 283–4), he is trying to force her conformity to his preconception. Since the Duke does not prohibit Desdemona from going directly with him and since she actually does arrive before him, it is Othello's own decision that causes the wedding-night separation. It is his inner dissatisfaction, both with her independent nature and its power over his will, that causes him to act in this secretive way to frustrate her intent. This pattern of open acceptance and secret frustration of her will is, moreover, followed with fatal consistency in the sequel.

Reunited in Cyprus, the omens of discord rise once more in their very words of greeting, omens given a symbolic import by the fact that their second attempt to consummate their marriage will also be interrupted by violence:

> *Oth.* O my fair warrior!
> *Des.*   My dear Othello:
> *Oth.* It gives me wonder great as my content
> To see you here before me. O my soul's joy!
> If after every tempest come such calms,
> May the winds blow till they have waken'd death!
> And let the labouring bark climb hills of seas
> Olympus-high, and duck again as low
> As hell's from heaven: If it were now to die,
> 'Twere now to be most happy; for I fear
> My soul hath her content so absolute
> That not another comfort like to this
> Succeeds in unknown fate.
> *Des.*   The heavens forbid

> But that our loves and comforts should increase
> Even as our days do grow!
>   *Oth.*   Amen to that, sweet powers!
> I cannot speak enough of this content;
> It stops me here; it is too much of joy.
> And this, and this, the greatest discords be *[They kiss.]*
> That e'er our hearts shall make! (II, i, 184–201)

The discord which Othello tries to transcend with his passionate kisses had once more come perilously close to the surface when his passionate declaration was met by Desdemona's shocked outcry, "The heavens forbid." The sight of his "fair warrior," who had risked tempests of his love, had suddenly overjoyed his spirit. Though he had accepted her only as a "moth of peace," he had not expected that her presence would convert the wasted time of peace into "such calms," calms of such momentous joy that, for them, even death is not too great a price. But even this greatest fulfillment of his love is utterly self-centered and self-contained. It is "my content . . . my soul's joy . . . my soul hath her content so absolute." His being gains no enrichment from Desdemona's love even in his excessive love for her. It is this dimly sensed factor of his over-extension into the "unknown" that inspires his "fear." The unknown future suddenly becomes ominous to him because it is not only his bride's nature that is unknown to him but also the very excessive quality of his love for her.

Desdemona has no fear that a married future must diminish the strength of their love, since she "did love the Moor to live with him." She does fear, however, that his present absolute content precludes the possibility of her influence increasing their mutual comfort. "Our loves" and "our days" betoken to her a meaningful and sustaining serenity rather than a passion whose irrationality can only be accepted in brief moments containing "too much of joy" for enduring comfort. His self-centered joy in the moment causes her sharply contrasted concern for their increasing mutual happiness, but he cannot partake of her vision. Evading her concern as well as his own, he takes comfort in precisely that joy which is the cause of their differing fears for him: "I cannot speak enough of this content."

This growing tension of fear beneath their joyous greetings now causes Othello's highly keyed emotions to relapse from their intensity:

> Honey, you shall be well desir'd in Cypress;
> I have found great love amongst them. O my sweet,
> I prattle out of fashion, and I dote
> In mine own comforts. (II, i, 206–9)

This relapse, however, marks a return to his safer feelings for Desdemona. Again he shallowly regards her as a mere appendage to his "own comforts" and considers excessive feeling for her as dotage. Once again he finds true comfort to reside in a general love for his own parts. But in this reduction of her importance from a power that can waken death to a harmless "honey" and sweetness, he represses both his real fear and joy in his bride under a false assumption of personal security. Again he has faced the threat of her independent personality by a reductive evasion which produces a more comfortable but false image of Desdemona and of his relation to her. It is this evasive tactic which provides the real danger in their discord. It prevents the possible resolution of their differences by permitting Othello to withdraw from real participation in their love.

It is in this state of suppressed discord that the wedding finally reaches its most unquiet consummation. The interruption of the wedding night, while symbolizing this disharmony, is not, however, the most important symbolic use made of Cassio's drunken brawling. As is clearly indicated in Iago's description, the brawl symbolizes the very nature of the consummation it interrupts:

> . . . Friends all but now, even now,
> In quarter, and in terms like bride and groom
> Devesting them for bed: and then, but now
> (As if some planet had unwitted men)
> Swords out, and tilting one at other's breast
> In opposition bloody. (II, iii, 179–84)

As Cassio's drunken friendliness, in divesting him of his self-control, gave way almost immediately to violence, so does the consummation of marriage require of Othello a similarly dangerous divesting of his self-sufficiency which, in causing him to fear for his "estimation," will lead to more tragic conclusions.

All the signs of discord which we have witnessed between Othello and Desdemona, first in the Venetian courtroom and then at the Cyprus reunion, are ominously present in the first early morning conversation of the marriage, as reported to Cassio by Emilia:

> The General and his wife are talking of it,
> And she speaks for you stoutly. The Moor replies
> That he you hurt is of great fame in Cyprus
> And great affinity, and that in wholesome wisdom
> He might not but refuse you. But he protests he loves you,
> And needs no other suitor but his likings
> To take the safest occasion by the front
> To bring you in again. (III, i, 46–53)

Cassio is no more satisfied with this reply than Desdemona. Just as Desdemona, in the pride of her consecrated love, had objected to Othello's first decision with regard to their marriage, that she remain behind while he attends to his occupation, so she now "stoutly" objects to the way in which he has handled his first professional duty. He explains that he has acted in accordance with "wholesome wisdom" and "needs" no advice on this matter from her. Here, then, the lines of opposition are drawn between his occupation and hers, between his desire to remain "all in all sufficient" (IV, i, 276) and her desire to be a full partner in his life.

Desdemona believes that if the marriage is to develop in the spirit of mutuality which she had envisioned she must not simply accept Othello's total disregard for her opinion but must succeed in her principled defense of Cassio:

> Do not doubt that. Before Emilia here
> I give thee warrant of thy place. Assure thee,
> If I do vow a friendship, I'll perform it

To the last article. My lord shall never rest;
I'll watch him tame and talk him out of patience;
His bed shall seem a school, his board a shrift;
I'll intermingle everything he does
With Cassio's suit. Therefore be merry, Cassio,
For thy solicitor shall rather die
Than give thy cause away. (III, iii, 19–28)

She would rather die than yield Cassio's cause because it is her cause too, the crucial test for the marriage to which she has consecrated her life. But in her determination to force Othello's acceptance of the rightness of her counsel and, therefore, of her individual importance, she forgets to consider Othello's own individuality. To say "I give thee warrant of thy place" is to deny Othello any voice in his own professional concerns, which is a far graver fault than Othello's unwillingness to share his professional affairs with her. Her decision to use his bed and board to "talk him out of patience" will not "tame" her husband but go far to destroy their marriage.

Though Othello had politely told her not to interfere, Desdemona meets him with the words: "If I have any grace or power to move you,/ His present reconciliation take" (III, iii, 46–7). The question of whether Desdemona has "any grace or power to move" Othello is of central importance to both of them. If Desdemona has not the power to "sue to you to do a peculiar profit/ To your own person" (III, iii, 79–80) then her marriage cannot be the consecration of her soul. If, on the other hand, Desdemona does have this power, then Othello will view his marriage as a power to "corrupt and taint my business" by not permitting the proper manifestation of his parts, title, and perfect soul. A successful marriage between these two is only possible, therefore, if either or both were to modify their inflexible positions. But both are doomed by their innocent self-righteousness, which makes them refuse to adjust to the realities of their situation. Desdemona does not realize that she cannot transform Othello in a day, and Othello will not admit that Desdemona's genuine love and concern might be a help to him.

As in their simpler disagreement of the early morning, Othello tries to counter her pleading by causually putting her off: "Not now, sweet Desdemon; some other time" (III, iii, 55). If Desdemona had heeded his resistance to her will she might have saved their marriage, even though it would have been less than the ideal she had envisioned.

But Desdemona cannot relinquish her ideal. She sees his resistance not as a warning but as a challenge to be overcome if her own hopes are not to be defeated. Refusing to be pacified, her demands take a form that would seriously circumscribe his will: "let it not/ Exceed three days (III, iii, 62–3). She follows this demand by upholding the convictions of her private judgment as "our common reason" (III, iii, 64) and, therefore, of superior weight to the rules of war upon which Othello has been acting. Not understanding why Othello does not accede either to her demand or her arguments, she concludes that he still does not love her with a dedication equal to her own love for him: "I wonder in my soul/ What you could ask that I should deny/ Or stand so mamm'ring on" (III, iii, 68–70). She does not realize that in disputing his "wholesome wisdom" and demanding a proof of his love, which goes against his best convictions, she has denied him the simple submission which is all he has ever asked of her love. As if this were not enough, she now reminds him that "many a time" she has spoken of him "dispraisingly" (III, ii, 71–2), that she has never accepted the manifestations of his parts, title, and perfect soul as uncritically as he would like, however consecrated she may be to her own vision of "his honours and his valiant parts."

When she follows this by saying "trust me, I could do much" (III, ii, 74), Othello suddenly agrees to do anything she might wish: "Prithee no more. Let him come when he will!/ I will deny thee nothing" (III, iii, 75–6). He has capitulated to her and proven to both of them that his love does give her the "grace or power to move" him. But this capitulation also means that he has lost the precious freedom of action that he considers necessary to the proper manifestation of his being. Desdemona's victory is her defeat. His desire, following his capitulation, to be "but a little to myself" (III, ii, 85) reveals the sudden resurgence of his sense of sovereignty.

This immediate background to his discussion with Iago provides a partial explanation for the ease with which he is ensnared by Iago's suggestions. In combination with his lack of knowledge of the opposite sex, it allows his misplaced credence to Iago's "worst of thoughts" (III, iii, 132). Though he had earlier accepted Desdemona's love uncritically, the implications Iago draws from her dissembling before her father move him to probe more deeply into the quality of her love. But this otherwise desirable impulse is unfortunately undertaken under the wrong tutelage and for the wrong reasons. It is the sign of his effective estrangement from the influence of her love: "I am bound to thee for ever" (III, iii, 213). Othello's statement, the first product of his growing jealously, is not only an expression of his extreme gratefulness for Iago's disclosures but a symbolic act of infidelity to Desdemona through the embrace of another's love. And now it is Othello who eagerly pushes forward the exploration of her defective nature:

> *Oth.* And yet, how nature erring from itself—. . . . .
> *Iago.* Foh! one may smell in such a will most rank, . . .
> Her will, recoiling to her better judgment,
> May fail to match you with her country forms,
> And happily repent. (III, iii, 227, 232, 236–8)

The independent will which Iago describes as a symptom of potential infidelity is the very characteristic of Desdemona that has most surprised him since their marriage. If he had earlier felt that it jeopardized the proper manifestation of his being in his official capacity, the new suggestions of her power to "make head against my estimation" through sexual infidelity become intolerable.

Othello's passionate jealousy is, then, a product of the mere suggestion of its possibility. This alone so disturbs his judgment that he needs little proof to seal his conviction of her guilt:

> *Oth.* O monstrous! monstrous!
> *Iago.*   Nay this was but his dream.
> *Oth.* But this denoted a foregone conclusion.

'Tis a shrewd doubt, though it be but a dream.
    Iago. And this may help to thicken other proofs
That do demonstrate thinly.
        Oth.   I'll tear her all to pieces! (III, iii, 427–31)

From the end of their first interview, Othello no longer needs
Iago to provide proof but rather encouragement. He, too, has
a "foregone conclusion" of her guilt which required no more
than "a shrewd doubt, though it be but a dream." Othello leaped
so early to this conclusion, however, because of the earlier seeds
of distrust that Desdemona's behavior had sown in him, seeds
which Iago was able to redirect into the course of sexual jealousy
because of Othello's naiveté. His violent desire to destroy this
danger to his "good name" (III, iii, 159) stems from the nature
of his original acceptance of Desdemona.

In marrying, Othello had wished only to add to his pleasure
while maintaining his self-sufficiency. He was sure of his own
ability "not to outsport discretion" (II, iii, 3), but he was not
aware that it was not only his own but also his wife's discretion
upon which his well-being depended. Desdemona looks upon this
mutual dependence of marriage as a mutual fulfillment. Othello
does not conceive of marriage in these terms, but he is suddenly
made aware of the fact that marriage does entail this dependence
and that he has over-extended himself. His wife not only has
a power over his will but also a free will of her own, and both
powers are injurious to him. It is this realization that forces
him to exclaim: "Why did I marry?" (III, iii, 242). It is finally
against marriage itself, that institution which confines his independent action, that he cries out:

I am abus'd, and my relief
Must be to loath her. O curse of marriage.
That we can call these delicate creatures ours,
And not their appetites! (III, iii, 267–70)

While his jealous love for Desdemona is directed toward his
image of her as a delicate possession and totally rejects any sug-

gestion of her individuality, the strong suggestion that he does not possess her exclusive interest can only be interpreted by him as an illegitimate abuse of his faith. It is, however, *his* faith that is deficient. With his growing realization that he does not know this creature that love has bound his life to, his impulse is not to increased understanding but to self-preservation. In his resistance to her influence, he loses that sympathy which, properly informing his perception of her, would have guarded him against misinterpretation.

When he now meets Desdemona he curtly rejects her attempt to medicate his ills: "Your napkin is too little" (III, iii, 287). In rejecting the adequacy of the handkerchief to minister to his spiritual needs, Othello is also rejecting the adequacy of her concept of wifehood to satisfy his spirit. This symbolic identification is central to the tragedy and clearly stated:

That handkerchief
Did an Egyptian to my mother give.
. . . She told her . . . if she lost it
Or made a gift of it, my father's eye
Should hold her loathly, and his spirits should hunt
After new fancies. . . .
To lose't or give't away were such perdition
As nothing else could match. (III, iv, 55–6, 58, 60–63, 67–8)

The loss of the handkerchief, let it be noted, does not betoken the infidelity of the wife but of the husband, who then "should *hunt*/ After new fancies." When Othello had first rejected Desdemona, she had replied: "Be as your fancies teach you" (III, iii, 88). These fancies had led him to search out Iago's "worst of thoughts" and, when he had them, to swear: "I am bound to thee for ever." It is only after Othello had bound himself to his new fancy that Desdemona loses the symbolic token of their union, a loss caused by the distraction of being unable to comfort him. Desdemona loses the symbol of wifehood after she has lost her status as helpmate. Othello views this loss as a sign of *her* infidelity, however, because he had perceived the performance of her wifely functions as a sign of disloyalty to his image of himself. He had rejected her ministrations, and thereby caused the loss of the handkerchief, because he felt that Desdemona's dedication was, like the handkerchief, "too little." In transferring his infidelity to her, he also hopes to transfer the "perdition" that attends such a loss of faith.

Yet, as he is later to testify, this "perdition" could never have come to him but for his unwitting over-extension of self through love:

> Had it pleas'd heaven
> To try me with affliction . . .
> I should have found in some place of my soul
> A drop of patience. But, alas, to make me
> A fixed figure for the time of scorn
> To point his slow unmoving finger at!
> Yet could I bear that too; well, very well.
> But there where I have garner'd up my heart, . . . (IV, ii,
>   47–8, 52–7)

Othello's stoic self-sufficiency could have maintained itself against any affliction, even to the highest scorn, because his inward being could still have been secure in its knowledge of personal perfection. In an involvement of emotional dependency, however, the question of self-perfection is simply irrelevant. What is alone important is the full acceptance of another's being and faith in it, and Othello's very saving self-sufficiency has precluded this. He has over-extended himself but with no new vision of anything save himself, and so her love is incapable of sustaining his faith. That he could not understand and felt no need for what she had to offer, he does not appreciate. All he feels is that "I am abus'd, and my relief/ Must be to loath her."

Unable to bear the suggestion of this vulnerability, his abused will rises to overthrow his love. It is his need to return to his "unhoused free condition" (I, ii, 26) which causes his fatal vow. His revenge will be "Like to the Pontic sea,/ Whose icy current and compulsive course/ Ne'er feels retiring ebb" (III, iii, 453–5). No new factors can alter his "compulsive course" until it has been fulfilled.

During this period, however, Desdemona undergoes as drastic an alteration of behavior as did Othello before his course was set. This change began at the time of their mutual farewells. When Othello's capitulation caused his need to withdraw from the sphere of her influence, his request that she leave him "but a little to myself" was followed by an equally important capitulation on her part: "Shall I deny you. No. Farewell, my lord./ . . . Be as your fancies teach you./ Whate'er you be, I am obedient" (III, iii, 86, 88–9).

As Desdemona becomes aware that she has somehow estranged Othello's love, she strives to regain it by conforming to his image of submissive obedience. This image is, however, so alien to her that she immediately reverts to her earlier pattern of personal assertion, overriding his discomfort even to the point of openly criticizing him:

> *Oth.* The handkerchief!
> *Des.* In sooth, you are to blame.
> *Oth.* Away! (III, iv, 96–8)

She refuses to heed his open antagonism until his rude dismissal suddenly opens her eyes to his true condition: "I ne'er saw this before" (III, iv, 100). Finally forced to the admission that "My lord is not my lord; nor should I know him,/ Were he in favour as in humor alter'd" (III, iv, 124-5), she gains an equally important insight into one cause of his altered behavior: "I have . . . stood within the blank of his displeasure/ For my free speech!" (III, iv, 127, 128–9). Although she does not suspect the added machinations of Iago, she does realize that the freedom she had assumed to be proper to a wife has produced only his extreme displeasure, that Othello utterly rejects her concept of marital consecration. Though she cannot herself reject it, she realizes that criticism, however loving it may be, is injurious to Othello's well-being and that she must not try to change him but to accept him as he is. This recognition becomes so instantly internalized that, whereas a few minutes earlier she had openly blamed him to his face, she now feels that she must not even criticize him to herself. It is this new attitude that prevents her from truly getting at the roots of his disturbance:

> Something sure of state . . .
> Hath puddled his clear spirit, . . .
> Nay, we must think men are not gods,
> Nor of them look for such observancy
> As fits the bridal. (III, iv, 140, 143, 148–50)

Recognizing and accepting the fact that her marriage is less than the ideal she had envisioned, Desdemona reconsecrates her soul to the all-too-human man she married. Once more she means to subdue her sovereign heart "even to the very quality of my lord," that "clear spirit" which she discerns even in its present eclipse.

Whereas Desdemona had earlier vowed to tame her husband, she now puts her own fiercely independent spirit to school, and this is as difficult a task as the other. Though she no longer dares to blame her husband for his acts, she cannot help protesting her innocence. When Othello strikes her before the Venetian ambassadors, she protests: "I have not deserv'd this" (IV, i, 252). This does not prevent her, however, from being resolutely submissive to his will: "I will not stay to offend you" (IV, i, 258). Since Desdemona has forbidden herself the privilege of criticism, her attempts to understand her predicament always reach the same awful contradiction. Justifying Othello's behavior, she must accept the validity of his treatment of her, must try to find and eradicate the fault for which she is being so severely punished. But even while she accepts the burden of error so that she may justify her lord, she nonetheless feels herself to be guiltless. This is the true tragedy of faith for a sovereign being. This is the challenge that Job faced, when God, out of the whirlwind, demanded: "Wilt thou condemn me, that thou mayest be justified?" (*Job* 40:8). Since both Job and Desdemona wish to be justified by the perfection of their consecration, they cannot condemn the object of their faith. They can only be perfect in their faith by admitting their imperfection: "Wherefore I abhor myself, and repent in dust and ashes" (*Job* 42:6). Thus, when Othello leaves Desdemona's spirit numb—"half asleep" (IV ii, 97)—after the horrors of the "brothel" scene, she accepts the importance of this training, objecting only to the severity of the discipline which he is demanding of her still unschooled spirit:

> Those that do teach young babes
> Do it with gentle means and easy tasks.
> He might have chid me so; for, in good faith,
> I am a child to chiding. (IV, ii, 111–4)

While Desdemona cannot help weeping over her treatment, she accepts it: "It is my wretched fortune" (IV, ii, 128). This acceptence is motivated by her desire to regain Othello's confidence through absolute obedience to his will. Though she cannot help being aware of the total nature of his estrangement from her and of the inefficacy of her attempts to be reconciled with him, this awareness only causes her to search her own inadequacies, to believe that something further is required of her though she cannot presently discern it:

> O good Iago,
> What shall I do to win my lord again?
> Good friend, go to him; for, by this light of heaven,
> I know not how I lost him. Here I kneel.
> If e'er my will did trespass 'gainst his love, . . .
> Or that I do not yet, and ever did,
> And ever will (though he do shake me off
> To beggarly divorcement) love him dearly,
> Comfort foreswear me! Unkindness may do much;
> And his unkindness may defeat my life,
> But never taint my love. (IV, ii, 148–52, 156–61)

Not knowing how "to win my lord *again*," since all her attempts to win his full love have only led to the loss of that love which he had formerly given her, she can only reconsecrate her soul to him in the simple faith that, if her love does not ultimately justify her, it will at least sustain her.

Her spirit has been so schooled to obedience that, as she prepares for her final ordeal, she can say "My love doth so approve him/ That even his stubbornness, his checks, his frowns/ (Prithee unpin me) have grace and favour in them" (IV, iii, 19–21). Beyond concern for her personal outcome, "All's one" (IV, iii, 23), she desires only that her love may be perfect in its obedience to his unfathomable will. The tragedy of Desdemona's painful reorientation toward her love is that she has become the Desdemona of his dreams only after he has forsworn them.

In the final moment of her life, Desdemona rises to the supreme consecration of her love. If harm has come to her as a result of her consecration, it is she who is to blame for the "downright violence" with which she attempted to actualize her vision. She still sees in him that spiritual nobility for which she loves him, and she knows that when he comes to realize what he has done this abused nobility will cause him greater torment than she has received. Accepting responsibility for her destruction, her only remaining desire is that he may be saved. Who has killed her? "Nobody,—I myself. Farewell./ Commend me to my kind lord. O farewell!" (V, ii, 124–5).

This ultimate consecration of her "soul and fortunes" to "his honours and his valiant parts" begins to work a change in Othello's spiritual regard for her and, thereby, for himself as well. Though his compulsive hatred had blinded him to her tortured attempts to conform to his most exacting requirements, his eyes are suddenly opened not only to her final conformity with his ideal image, but also to the loving individual behind that image who could achieve this conformity in the face of his brutal antagonism. And now the sense of his own loss seizes him:

> Nay, had she been true,
> If heaven would make me such another world
> Of one entire and perfect chrysolite,
> I'ld not have sold her for it. (V, ii, 143–6)

If he could have her again as a thing, however precious and easy to possess, he could no longer value it beside the higher truth of a consecrated individual. As the full knowledge of his loss comes more and more violently home to him, he is made to accept a new image of himself: "O gull! O dolt!/ As ignorant as dirt!" (V, ii, 163–4).

The self-sufficiency, whose destruction he feared in his necessary dependence on Desdemona, had rested on his conviction that "my perfect soul/ Shall manifest me rightly." Now he suddenly realizes that his soul is not perfect and that his self-sufficiency, rather than guaranteeing his soul's perfection, has acted as a positive barrier to it. In trying to repress his partial imperfections, he had produced a total imperfection, a rigidity of spirit that tended to make his perceptions shallow and his actions rash. His peremptory dismissal of Cassio and promotion of Iago were products of this rigidity and proved that his imperfect soul could not manifest him rightly. Most serious of all, to maintain this rigid self-sufficiency, he had had to close his spirit to the enriching influence of love.

He now begins to understand Desdemona's vision of a perfect fulfillment through mutual dependence, to see the influence of her love as a power, not to harm, but "to do a peculiar profit/ To your own person." But as he comes to see life with Desdemona as his greatest good, he also sees it irrevocably barred to him and, what is most unbearable, by his own willful stupidity. He who was so proud is nothing but a "fool! fool! fool!" (V, ii, 323). "Othello's occupation" (III, iii, 357), the loss of which had once stirred his spirit into a frenzy of hate, now holds no meaning for him: "Tis not so now. . . ./ Man but a rush against Othello's breast,/ And he retires. Where should Othello go?" (V, ii, 265, 270–1). Where, indeed? He cannot go back for, in his blind destruction of his greatest good, he has destroyed even that goodness that was formerly his. Nor can he go forward to embrace that new vision granted him by Desdemona's love. His own will has annihilated this hope forever.

In his first anguish he had wanted nothing but to live once more with Desdemona, to be able to love her with his very soul, and it was the impossibility of this happiness that tormented him. But as he begins to fully comprehend his awful guiltiness, he sees that such undeserved happiness would be the greatest torment. He is too guilty. Now he insists that this loss must never be redeemed. He must be punished, punished everlastingly and with ever more fury for he has sinned against her unpardonably: "Whip me, ye devils,/ From the possession of this heavenly sight!/ Blow me about in winds! roast me in sulphur!" (V, ii, 277-9).

He goes to meet his desired damnation through suicide with a new dignity born of his dearly gained moral wisdom. Of his once precious "occupation," he has only a word: "I have done the state some service, and they know't—/ No more of that" (V, ii, 339-40). What he must explain to the assembled representatives of the state is why he killed Desdemona and must now kill himself. For understanding him rightly, they then must speak:

> Of one that lov'd not wisely, but too well;
> Of one not easily jealous, but, being wrought,
> Perplex'd in the extreme; of one whose hand
> (Like the base Indian) threw a pearl away
> Richer than all his tribe; of one whose subdu'd eyes,
> Albeit unused to the melting mood,
> Drops tears as fast as the Arabian trees
> Their med'cinable gum. (V, ii, 344-51)

Unused to love and so unprepared for the way it might work upon his hitherto unjealous, self-sufficient nature, he had not returned Desdemona's love wisely but, perplexed by it in the extreme, had allowed his emotions to run their perverted course too well. He had destroyed her only to learn that he had irrevocably lost his own greatest good. But though he had not allowed her while living to influence his rigid spirit, her death has taught him that fulfilling sympathy which now enables him to weep for her. These are the important things of which they must speak. But they may "say besides":

> . . . that in Aleppo once,
> Where a malignant and a turban'd Turk
> Beat a Venetian and traduc'd the state,
> I took by th' throat the circumcised dog
> And smote him—thus. (V, ii, 352-6)

Realizing that it was his malignancy that had destroyed Desdemona, the truer part of him which her love has finally released will now wreak vengeance on that malignancy in his soul which has destroyed all their mortal hopes.

Now that his own awful justice has, as at least he believes, doomed his soul to hell, his truest self, tragically released only for this one triumphant moment, flies to its momentous "possession of this heavenly sight":

> I kiss'd thee ere I kill'd thee. No way but this—
> Killing myself, to die upon a kiss. (V, ii, 359–60)

At the last Othello affirms the love to which Desdemona had consecrated her soul and experiences that final forgiveness she bestowed upon him which graces his own soul. But the worldly union that might have been, had they learned to respect each other's true sovereignty in time, is tragically annulled by death.

In *Othello,* Shakespeare has presented us with the profound tragedy of two sovereign beings who do not know how to love, how to give the love that they feel or to receive the love that they need. When the love they offered each other with initial generosity was rejected, they did begin the painful process of learning the art of Worldly Love, but by this time the bridge of confidence has been irrevocably destroyed. Desdemona learns how to express her loving concern so that it will not violate his pride, but only after her independence and criticism have helped to estrange his love. Othello finally learns that her loving concern does not threaten his pride, but only after he has destroyed her. But love is the most fragile seed that can be planted in the human heart. If its initial cultivation is not handled with care, it will not survive. Once withdrawn, love can never again be revived with its initial generosity but only with a resistance equal to its early heedlessness, a resistance that contorts its natural spontaneity into a wary distrust. Though Othello and Desdemona ultimately prove that they could have made a good marriage, their initial faults in loving led only to "the tragic loading of this bed" (V, ii, 363). *Othello* is a tragic lesson in the art of love.

It is at such a lesson that the fully developed first pattern of Worldly Love tragedy aims. This pattern is logically first because in it the lover does not affirm love as the only value capable of sustaining meaningful life but tries to accommodate his love to an otherwise sovereign life. He desires a love that will not endanger or violate his sovereignty and for which he need make no sacrifice. As soon as he learns, however, that his sovereignty is endangered by dependence, deference, or, what is most important, the possibility of rejection with a consequent loss of pride, the lover tries to preserve the threatened bases of his self-esteem, and to this end he can easily be tempted into destroying the beloved. The tragedy of his love is that, because its true importance was not originally granted, its unexpected effects prove so drastic that the only solution by which imperiled sovereignty may be preserved is the murder of the beloved. Only after the murder does he realize that a healthy sovereignty was not really endangered, that rejection was not really threatened, and that in the panic caused by fear of such a loss, panic because such possible loss was not expected when love was originally accepted, the lover has destroyed the true bases of his self-esteem. Whether or not suicide is the result of such a realization, the lover begins by sacrificing nothing for his love and ends by murdering the beloved. The prime examples of this first pattern are Othello and the Duke of Milan, but Dido and the Tyrant in *The Second Maiden's Tragedy* conform as well to its large outlines. All cause or wish to cause the death of the beloved since they do not sufficiently value the individuality of the beloved when it conflicts with their own will and vision of love. All begin with a complacent narcissism which destroys and is itself destroyed by the love that it did not sufficiently value in its highest terms.

In the case of *Othello* and *The Duke of Milan,* this pattern also traces the process of vicarious atonement by which the murdered wife's vision of love finally redeems her slayer. If Desdemona and Marcelia betray a tragic lack of sympathy in their early attempts to correct their husband's faults in loving, they finally come to represent the ideal form of Worldly Love. Though they are destroyed by their inept attempts to give their love realization, they do achieve a final compassion for their tortured husbands which redeems Othello and Sforza from a destructive narcissism.

In the commitment of a sovereign nature to love, the first difficulty encountered is the resistance of this sovereignty to being fulfilled by love, a difficulty that cannot be overcome as long as the independent satisfactions of sovereignty persist. The full gratification of Worldly Love cannot begin until these rival satisfactions have ceased to be valued independently of their fulfillment in love. But the fulfillment of a sovereign nature in love bears within it the seeds of the second tragic pattern of Worldly Love. Having tested its initial difficulties, Shakespeare can now proceed to the difficulties encountered in a full affirmation of Worldly Love.

9

The Second Pattern: Antony and Cleopatra

Antony and Cleopatra is not only the greatest tragedy of Worldly Love ever to have been written but the only such tragedy of the period to be unreservedly considered a tragedy of love. Since the question of love is largely disregarded in the criticism of Webster and Middleton, it is primarily in the criticism of *Antony and Cleopatra* that we may see the general inadequacy of critical standards to deal with Worldly Love tragedy. With one exception, even the most perceptive of the play's recent critics have been unable to fully free themselves from the standards of love tragedy imposed by Courtly Love.

The difficulties caused by this alien standard can be seen in G. Wilson Knight's otherwise unexceptionable analysis. His study of Shakespeare's imagery in this play had led to the following illuminating conclusions: "The vision is eminently a life-vision and a love-vision. . . . Humanity is in truth 'crowned' here by potency of love's vision transfiguring mortality. . . . 'A race of heaven': such is our transcendent humanism."[1] In his study of the lovers' characters as well as of the imagery, Knight shows that "The poet never shirks the more sordid aspects of things divine."[2] Knight shows that the theme is one of loyalty, profound at base but imperfect in action, the imperfection of Antony being due to his wavering between opposing loyalties, of Cleopatra to her surface insincerities.[3] When he comes to a final evaluation of Cleopatra and the vision of love she represents, however, he illogically reverts to Coleridge's view that "the sense of criminality in her passion is lessened by our insight into its depth and energy." [4] Knight shows Cleopatra as prepared to sacrifice Antony to Caesar only to argue for the cancellation of this blot through the glory of her love-death: "the Arabian perfume of a Cleopatra's death can at last sweeten to all eternity the nightmare agony of that other blood-stained hand." [5] This is, however, a perverse justification of Cleopatra since she neither betrays Antony nor dies for him, and it violates all that his earlier analysis had proven of the "transcendent humanism" of the lovers and the "life-vision" of their love.

Willard Farnham shows the same inability to affirm what his own analysis has disclosed. Arguing for the influence of Daniel's *Cleopatra* upon Shakespeare's treatment of her death, he shows that "Daniel builds his drama on the theme of Caesar's triumph. . . . Daniel's Cleopatra flees to her love when she dies, but the thought of that from which she flees has determined her to die." [6] But having shown that this interpretation of Cleopatra's death is supported not only by Daniel but by Plutarch, such other Elizabethan writers as Richard Reynolds, and finally by the facts of Shakespeare's play, Farnham proceeds to pose the following crucial question: "Will love for him be the actual cause of her suicide and will she, then, die in the odor of sanctity as one of Cupid's saints?" [7] His answer reveals his inability to accept his own verdict:

> Perhaps it is the Devil's advocate who in the way of reason can make the better case. He has an advantage in that he argues from both words and actions of Cleopatra's, not merely from words, as his opponent does. But by following reason coldly the Devil's advocate may arrive at a condemnation of Cleopatra that Shakespeare will not support.[8]

Farnham's problem is that he believes that a death not motivated by Cleopatra's love must imply Shakespeare's condemnation of her, and this condemnation is obviously lacking. For Farnham, only courtly lovers can be "Cupid's saints," and since Cleopatra's love has been glorified, it must, against all reason, be forced into the alien mold of Courtly Love. Farnham's dilemma runs through almost all of the contemporary criticism of the play. Those critics who have responded to the splendor of the play have been able to justify their reaction only by misinterpreting the nature of the love it glorifies. Critics like Franklin Dickey,[9] who have seen that this love is not courtly, become Devil's advocates who condemn this love in full violation of the play's tone.

Only one critic of whom I am aware has been able to throw off the prejudice of Courtly Love and see in *Antony and Cleopatra* the affirmation of a totally different form of love. Harold Wilson's concluding statements on this love fully render its true quality:

> Cleopatra remains true to herself. She is the living, and dying, embodiment of earthly love, with all its energy of variety and enchantment; . . . for the dream of the lovers of meeting in Elysium is the symbol of the lasting human memory of their final reconciliation and their faith. That reconciliation and that faith embody for us the most enduring value of human life. It is a shared fulfilment. . . . they have lived greatly; they are not pitiable in defeat; rather, they achieve the utmost human grandeur in their tragic eclipse and in their deaths affirm for us the supreme value—in this world—of human love. . . . It is not too much, perhaps, to say that the play contains the greatest affirmation of this value in the world's literature.[10]

Wilson resolves Farnham's dilemma by showing that Cleopatra represents a different mode of love, what Wilson terms human or earthly love and I term Worldly Love, and for Wilson this different mode is not less glorious than Courtly Love but the supreme value in this world. Where Knight and Farnham were unable to trust their own analyses when they seemed to go counter to the tradition of Courtly Love, Wilson finally does face the differing truth of this love. If his analysis of the play differs from mine in focus and particulars, it arrives at a similar conclusion.

It might be said that *Antony and Cleopatra* begins where *Othello* ends. Both tragedies are concerned with the internal conflicts of generals in love and with the women who wish to win their full hearts. The difference is that while Othello had not learned to value his own love, nor Desdemona how to hold his love, until it was too late, Antony and Cleopatra have learned these lessons perhaps too well.

In his second consideration of Worldly Love, Shakespeare once again focuses his attention upon the central problem of this love, that which evolves from the lover's desire to preserve his sovereignty. As was shown in the study of *Othello,* this desire can take two forms: Desdemona's wish to preserve her sovereignty within love, and Othello's to preserve his sovereignty apart from love. In the strategy of *Antony and Cleopatra,* these two modes of sovereign expression are symbolized by the opposed societies of Egypt and Rome,[11] respectively; and, whereas Cleopatra's orientation to love is identified with Egyptian values, Anthony's is only partially responsive to Roman values. Though he affirms from the first that the noblest expression of sovereignty is through love, he retains something of the traditional masculine belief that holds its proper exercise to be the pursuit of worldly power. This residue of feeling creates an inner resistance toward his love that renders it essentially unstable.

It is the power of Rome over Antony's spirit that is the chief weakness of their love, and Cleopatra has just cause to fear it. It is this fear which prompts her opening question:

> *Cleo.* If it be love indeed, tell me how much.
> *Ant.* There's beggary in the love that can be reckon'd.
> *Cleo.* I'll set a bourn how far to be belov'd.
> *Ant.* Then must thou needs find out new heaven, new earth.
> (I, i, 14–7)[12]

Cleopatra's first words provide the clue to her subsequent behavior. They reveal that she is unsure of the nature and extent of Antony's love. The reason for her insecurity lies in the very nature of Antony's affirmation. Here and throughout the play,

Antony affirms that his love cannot be defined by the ordinary usage of this world—which for him is the Roman usage—since it has found "new heaven, new earth." Though it is Cleopatra who has revealed this new heaven and earth to Antony, she knows that the ties to his old world are still strong within him and wishes him to assess his love for her in relation to them. This generalized conflict becomes particularized by the arrival of a Roman messenger, whom Antony refuses to hear. Cleopatra taunts him with the power that his old world has over him despite his rejection of it, a power that she cannot adequately fight until she has brought him to face it: "Call in the messengers. As I am Egypt's Queen,/ Thou blushest, Antony, and that blood of thine/ Is Caesar's homager!" (I, i, 29–31).

Antony answers this charge by rejecting the values of Rome and affirming his equal sovereignty in love:

> Let Rome in Tiber melt and the wide arch
> Of the rang'd empire fall! Here is my space.
> Kingdoms are clay; our dungy earth alike
> Feeds beast as man. The nobleness of life
> Is to do thus *[embracing];* when such a mutual pair
> And such a twain can do't, in which I bind,
> On pain of panishment, the world to weet
> We stand up peerless. (I, i, 33–40)

In these lines Antony makes the most profound affirmation of Worldly Love that we are to find in the drama of the period. It is the affirmation that comes after the values of worldly power have been tried and found wanting. Antony has attained the highest pinnacle of worldly power, has become "the triple pillar of the world" (I, i, 12), only to realize that "Kingdoms are clay," that all his power does not raise him above the level of the poorest beast who feeds upon the refuse of the earth. He sees that it is not the power built of clay upon dung that ennobles man's life but his ability to love another human being who can "stand up peerless." It is only between two such sovereign beings that a bridge of meaningful love can be built, a bridge that stands more truly for the "nobleness of life" than "the wide arch/

Of the rang'd empire." In this affirmation of the superior value of love, Antony expresses his most profound conviction, one which he will not always have the strength to support but which nonetheless motivates his most crucial behavior.

Thinking that he has fully answered her objections, Antony continues to evade the careful scrutiny of Rome's power over him which Cleopatra desires. This escapist quality in his love rightly disturbs Cleopatra, but she does not fully recognize that it is her power to transport him to a "space" beyond the cares of Rome that gives love its great value to Antony and constitutes her ultimate hold over him:

> *Ant.*   Now for the love of Love and her soft hours,
> Let's not confound the time with conference harsh:
> There's not a minute of our lives should stretch
> Without some pleasure now. What sport to-night?
>   *Cleo.* Hear the ambassadors.
>   *Ant.*   Fie, wrangling queen!
> Whom every thing becomes—to chide, to laugh,
> To weep; whose every passion fully strives
> To make itself, in thee, fair and admir'd!
> No messenger but thine, and all alone
> To-night we'll wander through the streets and note
> The qualities of people. Come, my queen,
> Last night you did desire it.—Speak not to us. (I, i, 44–55)

The love that Antony affirms here and at the end is one that confers nobility on life through the unique pleasure that only a "mutual pair" can experience. This mutuality can best be seen in their descriptions of each other. The above description of Cleopatra by Antony is matched by hers of him: "O heavenly mingle! "Be'st thou sad or merry,/ The violence of either thee becomes,/ So does it no man else" (I, v, 59–61). As she is "my queen" to him, so is he to her: "the demi-Atlas of this earth, the arm/ And burgonet of men" (I, v, 23–4). These two, who "stand up peerless" both in their own and in the world's eyes, need no other wordly glory than that which they themselves bestow upon their meanest acts. In that "space," over which

Cleopatra presides, and which Antony has elected as his own, they can wander through the streets "all alone" and still be noble: "for vilest things/ Become themselves in her, that the holy priests/ Bless her when she is riggish" (II, ii, 243–5).

However ultimate may be the "strong toil of grace" (V, ii, 351) in which she has caught Antony, Cleopatra's immediate fears are soon justified: "He was dispos'd to mirth; but on the sudden/ A Roman thought hath struck him" (I, ii, 86–7). Antony's blind renunciation of Rome only made him, as she had feared, the greater prey to its actual power over him, a power which, though less than that of his love, gains strength from his habitual refusal to meet it directly. When he is finally forced to face it directly, therefore, he has no adequate defense against it and immediately capitulates:

> These strong Egyptian fetters I must break
> Or lose myself in dotage. . . .
> I must from this enchanting queen break off.
> Ten thousand harms more than the ills I know
> My idleness doth hatch. (I, ii, 120–1, 132–4)

Looking at her now through the eyes of Rome, he sees his love as mere "dotage" and "idleness." Antony's inability to reconcile his two worlds, while it cannot defeat the greater power of his love, does impair his ability to preserve it from attack by his other world. His Roman thoughts now attack Cleopatra's love at its most vulnerable point: "She is cunning past man's thought" (I, ii, 150).

This doubt about the genuineness of Cleopatra's love is echoed by her maid:

> *Char.* Madam, methinks, if you did love him dearly,
> You do not hold the method to enforce
> The like from him.
>   *Cleo.*   What should I do, I do not?
>   *Char.* In each thing give him way, cross him in nothing.
>   *Cleo.* Thou teachest like a fool. The way to lose him!
>   *Char.* Tempt him not so too far; . . . (I, iii, 6–11)

Cleopatra's "cunning," while it does inform her behavior with Antony, does not discredit the genuineness of her love. On the contrary, it is the very depth of her love that motivates her constant use of cunning. The doubt which had inspired her initial question is always with her, so that she is forever striving to gain his love no matter how vehemently he may protest it. As she never can assume his love, she can never relax her own self-control when she is with him and express her love straight-forwardly. She knows it is only by means of vigilant cunning that she can hold Antony. But, while this belief is generally warranted, there are moments in which her hold over him is greater than she suspects; at such times, her continued use of cunning does tragically tempt him "too far." Yet that very cunning which, when his own commitment to his love falters, feeds his suspicions about the adequacy of her love is actually the quality for which he loves her and which will always bring him back to her:

> *Maec.* Now Antony must leave her utterly.
> *Eno.* Never! He will not.
> Age cannot wither her nor custom stale
> Her infinite variety. Other women cloy
> The appetites they feed, but she makes hungry
> Where most she satisfies; . . . (II, ii, 238–43)

Though it was her ability to employ a cunning past his thoughts that won his heart, it was *his* nature as well as her own that dictated its use. However much he may protest his constancy in absence—"My precious queen, forbear,/ And give true evidence to his love, which stands/ An honourable trial" (I, iii, 73–5)—Cleopatra knows that once she is absent, she will be forgotten: "oblivion is a very Antony,/ And I am all forgotten" (I, iii, 90–1). The long separation which ensues tests the constancy of both and proves that it is Cleopatra, for all her cunning, who is truly committed to their love and that the intensity of Antony's love is essentially unstable.

If the difficult task of handling the wayward Antony had caused her to use cunning, when he is absent Cleopatra reveals the fullness of her love: "He's speaking now,/ Or murmuring 'Where's my serpent of old Nile?'/ . . . Now I feed myself/ With most delicious poison" (I, v, 24–7). The enthusiasm of her own love causes her to imagine that she is as much the constant object of his thoughts as he is of hers, but she immediately realizes that she is only humoring herself.

When Fulvia died, the possibility of marrying Cleopatra presented itself and, much to the surprise of the most ingrained Romans, Antony rejected it. Menas quite casually said: "We look'd not for Mark Antony here. Pray you, is he married to Cleopatra?" (II, vi, 112–4). And even Caesar, when the possibility of Antony marrying his sister was raised, exclaimed: "Say not so, Agrippa./ If Cleopatra heard you, your reproof/ Were well deserv'd of rashness" (II, ii, 122–4). But if other Romans can reconcile the idea of Cleopatra with marriage, Antony can not. For better or worse, she is his "serpent of old Nile," a temptation to renounce the stability of Rome for a different and possibly nobler life, but in no case a support for his Roman ambitions. It was in the hope of repairing his broken fortunes that Antony had returned to Rome, and both to further and hold him to this purpose he needs such a wife as Octavia: "If beauty, wisdom, modesty, can settle/ The heart of Antony, Octavia is/ A blessed lottery to him" (II, ii, 246–8). But as Cleopatra could not settle him in his renunciation of Rome, so Octavia cannot settle him in his purposed renunciation of Cleopatra. Enobarbus' knowledge of Antony causes him to foretell the failure of Antony's attempt to reform:

> *Eno.* Octavia is of a holy, cold, and still conversation.
> *Menas.* Who would not have his wife so?
> *Eno.* Not he that himself is not so; which is Mark Antony.
> He will to his Egyptian dish again. . . . (II, vi, 130–3)

Antony also thinks that a wife should be "of a holy, cold, and still conversation," but he cannot long abide such a one. His truest impulses respond to the sensual verities and respond with all the greater vehemence for his internal resistance. But this

resistance is always present and sometimes gathers enough strength
to demand reform.

Realizing that his stay in Egypt had hatched "ten thousand
harms" at home, Antony returned to Rome with every intention
to reform: "that to come/ Shall all be done by th' rule" (II, iii,
6–7). But Antony does not have that inner compunction which
can hold him to the rule of continence, as does Caesar. Their
behavior on Pompey's galley is a good instance of the truth of
the soothsayer's earlier analysis:

> Thy daemon, that thy spirit which keeps thee, is
> Noble, courageous, high, unmatchable,
> Where Caesar's is not; but near him thy angel
> Becomes a fear, as being o'erpow'r'd. Therefore
> Make space enough between you. . . .
> If thou dost play with him at any game,
> Thou art sure to lose; and of that natural luck
> He beats thee 'gainst the odds. Thy lustre thickens
> When he shines by. (II, iii, 19–23, 25–8)

Caesar shines above Antony in Rome because he exemplifies the
rules of Roman behavior, which Antony feels he should accept
but which he cannot follow. When a difference of reaction develops between them, Antony feels forced to reject his own
natural promptings in Caesar's favor. But such a forced attempt
to abide by the rules of Rome only hinders the true expression
of his genius and robs him of his full power. His inner resistance
to Egyptian values, therefore, is a less serious impediment to the
expression of his noblest self than is the unnatural constraint
which Roman values enforce upon his spirit. Though he needed
to return to Rome to discover this truth, Antony now fully realizes
that, for better or worse, his true place is in Egypt: "He hath
spoken true. . . . I will to Egypt;/ And though I make this marriage for my peace,/ I' th' East my pleasure lies" (II, iii, 33, 38–
40). Though he needs to pacify Rome in order to be able to fully
enjoy his Eastern pleasure, he is willing to risk this new-made
peace for the superior satisfactions of his pleasure. Before this
he had not affirmed Egyptian values for better or worse, but only

for better; and when he saw the harm that resulted from this affirmation, he had rebounded from it. Now he resolves to return to Egypt with the full awareness that there can be no turning back. The result of his long internal conflict is his final concesssion that Egypt has achieved "full supremacy" (III, xi, 59) over his spirit. He returns to Egypt with the full commitment to his love that Cleopatra has long desired.

But, while Antony was moving toward this full commitment in Rome, Cleopatra was painfully reconciling herself to the fact that he would never achieve it. It is true that when Antony had first left, Cleopatra had permitted herself to hope that a new era of their love was beginning, an era in which it would no longer be constrained by the existence of marital bonds which Antony's conscience would not long permit them to forget. Fulvia's death had opened for Cleopatra a realm of freedom such as she had hitherto believed impossible: "Can Fulvia die?" (I, iii, 58). Though she did not expect or require Antony to marry her, their changed circumstances promised much good to her heart. It is, then, with bitter resignation that she finally accepts the truth of Antony's remarriage:

> *Cleo.* In praising Antony I have disprais'd Caesar.
> *Char.* Many times, madam.
> *Cleo.*   I am paid for't now.
> Lead me from hence,
> I faint. O Iras, Charmian! 'Tis no matter.
> Go to the fellow, good Alexas. Bid him
> Report the feature of Octavia, her years,
> Her inclination; let him not leave out
> The colour of her hair. Bring me word quickly. *[Exit Alexas.]*
> Let him for ever go!—let him not—Charmian,
> Though he be paintetd one way like a Gorgon,
> The other way's a Mars.—*[To Mardian]* Bid you Alexas
> Bring me word how tall she is.—Pity me, Charmian,
> But do not speak to me. Lead me to my chamber. (II, v,
> 108–19)

Cleopatra feels justly rebuked for the over-enthusiasm of her own love at the thought of Antony's freedom. She now sees that she should have known better than to expect such constancy from him. Now that her gravest doubts as to the quality and extent of his love have been confirmed, she wishes she could rid herself of all love for him—but she cannot. She must accept his mingled nature, the inconstancy which kills her heart with the nobility which has inspired it to love as never before. She sees herself as a truly pitiable figure, constrained to love a man who cannot return her full love. And yet she desires no consolation. She must see her fate clearly and resign herself to it, must even pain herself further with the full knowledge of the woman who has won him away from her.

As she listens to the description of Octavia, however, her knowledge of Antony convinces her that "he cannot like her long" (III, iii, 17). Furthermore, it is the answer given to her most significant question which assures her of her superior attractiveness to Antony:

> *Cleo.* What majesty is in her gait? Remember,
> If e'er thou look'dst on majesty.
> *Mess.*   She creeps!
> Her motion and her station are as one.
> She shows a body rather than a life,
> A statue than a breather. (III, iii, 20–4)

Octavia lacks that superb vitality which was Cleopatra's chief revelation to Antony, a vitality that can ennoble even the "vilest things." This is the essential quality of Cleopatra's majesty, that which raises it above the ordinary level of this "dungy earth." Cleopatra reveals life as "a wonderful piece of work" (I, ii, 159–60), a noble thing of "infinite variety." It was this revelation that enabled Antony to affirm "the nobleness of life," an affirmation that could only be stifled by Octavia's "holy, cold, and still conversation." In Octavia's presence, as well as Caesar's, his "angel/ Becomes a fear, as being o'erpow'r'd." What is truly "noble, courageous, high, unmatchable" in Antony's spirit can only be released by its galvanic contact with Cleopatra's life force. Cleopatra knows that Antony's need for this release is his most powerful motivating force. Realizing that with Octavia he will not be able to achieve it—"This creature's no such thing" (III, iii, 42)—she finally permits herself to hope that "All may be well enough" (III, iii, 50).

But this "well enough" is as well as she can hope, not as well as she might wish. Her earlier experience with Fulvia had taught her the extent to which Antony's conscience bound him to the claims of a wife, claims he might disregard for a while but could not ultimately deny. Since his love for her had proven itself to be such a weak and unstable thing that it could throw away the precious gift of freedom that had been granted them, she does not see how she can expect him to be any different upon his probable return than he was before he left. She expects him still to be Janus-faced. Though her love for him makes it impossible for her to "let him for ever go," her self-love cautions her against abandoning herself for the love of anyone as untrustworthy as Antony, especially since she has been "paid" so dearly for indulging her earlier hopes. The tragedy of Antony's final commitment to love is that it comes only after Cleopatra has fortified her heart against believing in its possibility. It is not only Cleopatra but Antony who is "paid" for his infidelity. It is Antony's past infidelity that corrupts the heart of their relationship even as it moves towards its final moment of truth.

Upon his return, Antony reveals the totality of his new commitment to love by means of a ceremony which legitimizes their relationship:

> Contemning Rome, he has done all this and more
> In Alexandria. Here's the manner of't:
> I' th' market place on a tribunal silver'd
> Cleopatra and himself in chairs of gold
> Were publicly enthron'd . . . Unto her
> He gave the stablishment of Egypt. . . .
> I' th' common show-place, where they exercise.
> His sons he there proclaim'd the kings of kings:
> . . . . She
> In th' habiliments of the goddess Isis
> That day appear'd; . . . (III, vi, 1–5, 8–9, 12–3, 16–8)

In this ceremony, Antony not only condemns the power of Rome but also its forms. Theirs is not a Roman marriage but a unique union suited only to "such a twain." Self-sanctioned, it ennobles and sanctifies the commonplace; truly a "kingly seal/ And plighter of high hearts!" (III, xiii, 125–6).

But such a marriage can neither be sanctioned nor tolerated by Rome. Having made and proclaimed his choice to the world, Antony knows that he must now defend his choice against the aroused ire of Rome, must still battle to win the right to love as he wishes. Without waiting to learn the reaction of Rome, therefore, he proceeds to levy "the kings o' th' earth for war" (III, vi, 68), making "these wars for Egypt" (IV, xiv, 15). And Rome's wrath is as he had expected. To Rome, Antony's relationship is still "adulterous" (III, vi, 93), and however much Antony may renounce the claims of his Roman marriage they do assert themselves against his freedom to love.

This fact is never absent from Cleopatra's mind. Once before Antony had renounced Rome with full affirmation of his love for her, and yet had proved that she had no power over him. Now she believes they are simply repeating the same game with more dangerous stakes. It is, in fact, the high cost of affirming their love that especially causes Cleopatra to fear for the stability of Antony's love, to fear that when he is once engaged in the coming civil war, his loyalties to Rome may cause him to rebound to the other side. It is this fear that motivates her behavior throughout the war. It causes her, in the first place, to insist upon going to the war with Antony. Like Desdemona, she fears that if she allows him to depart alone, at this crucial point in their relationship, she will lose what influence she does have over his heart. But even being with him cannot still her fears that he may betray her, that she cannot rely upon him but must take pains to preserve herself. This would seem to be the reason why "i' th' midst o' th' fight,/ When vantage like a pair of twins appear'd/ Both as the same" (III, x, 11–3), Cleopatra, suddenly overcome by this fear, "hoists sails, and flies" (III, x, 15).

When confronted with the disastrous consequences of her flight, therefore, Cleopatra is genuinely bewildered:

> *Ant.* O, whither hast thou led me, Egypt? See
> How I convey my shame out of thine eyes
> By looking back what I have left behind
> Stroy'd in dishonour.
>   *Cleo.*   O my lord, my lord,
> Forgive my fearful sails! I little thought
> You would have followed.
>   *Ant.*   Egypt, thou knew'st too well
> My heart was to thy rudder tied by th' strings,
> And thou shouldst tow me after. O'er my spirit
> Thy full supremacy thou knew'st, and that
> Thy beck might from the bidding of the gods
> Command me.
>   *Cleo.*   O, my pardon! (III, xi, 51–61)

Cleopatra "little thought" he "would have followed" because the one thing she did not know was her "full supremacy" over his spirit. It was her very uncertainty over the course he might take that had caused her to be "fearful." She now sees, however, that the caution resulting from her underestimation of his love had undermined the power of their love to withstand attack, that she is now as guilty of having betrayed their love as he.

The mode of infidelity that Antony and Cleopatra have both been guilty of is common only to Worldly Love. It is the infidelity to love caused by fidelity to self. Worldly lovers are sovereign beings who do not wish to lose themselves but to find another. They do not desire to achieve union but to remain "such a twain," a "mutual pair." As in their love they affirm, rather than deny, the values of their personal sovereignty, not the least of which is the power it gives them to achieve meaningful relations, so does their sovereignty retain prime importance. Should their love *appear* to be violating this sovereignty, they will fly from their love in the attempt to preserve it. Antony had returned to Rome because he thought that love was undermining his personal power. This return taught him, however, that the only personal powers he really valued were those which were released by his love. So, too, with Cleopatra. She had fled from Actium because she had felt that in following the dictates of her love and standing beside Antony she would endanger her life. But she was to learn that only by defending her love unwaveringly could she have saved not only her love but her very life, that her love did not threaten the isolated preservation of her life but was its great support. But the love that both Antony and Cleopatra have come to value fully is one that now bears the liability for their former errors. Their mutual infidelities in the name of sovereignty have corrupted their love and further jeopardized their sovereign preservation. Had Antony not married, they might have loved in freedom and not needed to battle for their right to love. Had Cleopatra fought firmly, they might have won that battle. Now they must bear instead the penalty for defeat, that loss of power which not only afflicts them from without but also makes them irritable and suspicious of each other. But this very loss of power also draws them closer to each other than they had ever been before. Imprisoned for their love, they now have nothing but each other and that love for which they have paid so dearly.

It is not Caesar's sentence that now worries Cleopatra, but Antony's. Only his pardon can redeem their defeat and place their love above the power of fortune. And, as she tearfully begs for "pardon, pardon!" (III, xi, 68), Antony replies:

> Fall not a tear, I say. One of them rates
> All that is won and lost. Give me a kiss.
> Even this repays me. We sent our schoolmaster.
> Is 'a come back? Love, I am full of lead.
> Some wine, within there, and our viands! Fortune knows
> We scorn her most when most she offers blows. (III, xi,
>   69–74)

Though Antony had been in "despair" (III, xi, 19), believing that in following Cleopatra's lead he had "lost my way for ever" (III, xi, 4), he now realizes that wherever Cleopatra has led him, there is his "space," a space in which all losses are repaid. But, while this truth enables both of them to scorn Fortune's blows, the fact that their love must wait upon Caesar's pleasure drains it of its life-giving power: "Love, I am full of lead." As Cleopatra is later to say: "Our strength is all gone into heaviness:/ That makes the weight" (IV, xv, 33–4).

In their straitened circumstances, Antony and Cleopatra had been forced to send their children's schoolmaster as an ambassador to inform Caesar of their jointly agreed upon requests:

> Lord of his fortunes he salutes thee, and
> Requires to live in Egypt; which not granted,
> He lessens his requests and to thee sues
> To let him breathe between the heavens and earth,
> A private man in Athens. This for him.
> Next, Cleopatra does confess thy greatness,
> Submits her to thy might, and of thee craves
> The circle of the Ptolemies for her heirs,
> Now hazarded to thy grace. (III, xii, 11–9)

From this it will be seen that neither of them feels that the affirmation of their love requires their death. They are quite prepared to live, even apart if necessary, as long as they can preserve their lives from the utter disgrace of being brought in triumph to Rome, and both feel that Cleopatra should remain Queen of Egypt if this is possible. They do not feel that such an arrangement would destroy their essential sovereignty or betray their love. What would betray their love is Cleopatra's willingness to perform Caesar's will. Hearing of the terms, Antony almost dares Cleopatra to fulfill them:

> *Ant.*   Let her know't.
> To the boy Caesar send this grizzled head,
> And he will fill thy wishes to the brim
> With principalities.
> *Cleo.*   That head, my lord? (III, xiii, 16–9)

To such a preposterous idea, however, Cleopatra will give no consideration, and when a messenger from Caesar shortly arrives desiring to negotiate privately with her, she refuses:

> *Thyreus.* Hear it apart.
> *Cleo.*   None but friends. Say boldly. (III, xiii, 47)

Cleopatra will not negotiate her own peace privately at the expense of Antony. What she does feel perfectly entitled to do, however, is to use her utmost cunning to secure that which Antony also considers to be valid, the preservation of her royal power in Egypt. She proceeds to act with great cordiality towards Caesar's ambassador, even allowing him to kiss her hand, though ever refusing the assurance of Antony's doom which Caesar desires. But Antony, coming upon this scene, becomes unreasonably angry: "He makes me angry;/ And at this time most easy 'tis to do't" (III, xiii, 143-4).

Their circumstances have, indeed, become difficult:

> *Cleo.* What, no more ceremony? See, my women! . . .
> *Ant.* Approach there!—Ah, you kite!—Now, gods and
>   devils!
> Authority melts from me. (III, xiii, 38, 89-90)

As authority melts from them, they both sink to unbecoming practices: Cleopatra to compromising behavior, Antony to a peevish jealousy:

> *Ant.* You were half blasted ere I knew you. Ha!
> Have I my pillow left unpress'd in Rome,
> Forborne the getting of a lawful race,
> And by a gem of women, to be abus'd
> By one that looks on feeders?
> *Cleo.*   Good my lord,—
> *Ant.*   You were a boggler ever.
> But when we in our viciousness grow hard
> (O misery on't!) the wise gods seel our eyes,
> In our own filth drop our clear judgments, make us
> Adore our errors, laugh at's while we strut
> To our confusion.
> *Cleo.*   O, is't come to this? (III, xiii, 105-15)

As their situation becomes increasingly difficult, they start to view each other once again with suspicion, suspicion which only increases the corruption of their love. Antony had pardoned her flight from Actium, but this flight had stirred his old suspicion that "she is cunning past man's thought." Though she tries to calm his rage, Cleopatra herself becomes alarmed by his reversion to Roman values, a reversion which indicates to her that, despite his action at Actium, he is still not totally committed to his love for her. But this time she is wrong, for this reversion is only the nostalgia of impotence. Though he speaks with the language of Rome, it no longer has the power to cause his renunciation of love. Whereas his earlier reversion had compelled him to reject Cleopatra, and this is what she now begins to fear anew, his present reversion is tortured by the knowledge that he cannot reject her, that he adores the "filth" which he sees once again through the eyes of Rome, that he has "forborne the getting of a lawful race" for the sake of a woman who will continue to abuse the love he cannot control. It is his very powerlessness in this regard that causes him to become jealous rather than to reject her. But it is only these mutual suspicions that they have to fear, for never were both Antony and Cleopatra so fully commited to their love as now. The tragic result of their earlier infidelities is that they can no longer be absolutely sure of the actual truth of the other. Confirmed in their own love, they both feel abused by the other:

> *Cleo.*   Not know me yet?
> *Ant.*   Cold-hearted toward me? (III, xiii, 157–8)

But their position is so desperate that, against all reason, they must believe in the truth of the other's love. They have nothing else, but, with this, have enough.

    Their love had never burned as brightly as it now does in the fever of desperate hope. Though their hearts are heavy, their love reaches a new height of playful tenderness. Antony must "drown consideration" (IV, ii, 45) to keep up his hope, but when Cleopatra plays at arming him, his heart is truly joyed. And when Antony returns triumphant they are given one moment of pure happiness:

> *Ant.*   O thou day o' th' world,
> Chain mine arm'd neck! Leap thou, attire and all,
> Through proof of harness to my heart, and there
> Ride on the pants triumphing!
>   *Cleo.*   Lord of lords!
> O infinite virtue, com'st thou smiling from
> The world's great snare uncaught?
>   *Ant.*   My nightingale,
> We have beat them to their beds. What, girl! though grey
> Do something mingle with our younger brown, yet ha' we
> A brain that nourishes our nerves, and can
> Get goal for goal of youth. (IV, viii, 13–22)

Though it had formerly shamed and will soon madden him, he
has this one moment to truly glory in her "full supremacy" over
his heart, to abandon himself wholly to her "triumphing." And,
as she is the "day o' th' world" to him, his smile brings "infinite
virtue" into her world. They are not benighted but, "with
Phoebus' amorous pinches black/ And wrinkled deep in time"
(I, v, 28–9), can still "get goal for goal of youth." Their love has
grown to mellowness and gained new virtue from its power to
transcend the corruption of their trust.

But this corruption inevitably overtakes them. When his
army betrays him, his suppressed suspicions of Cleopatra erupt
with tragic violence:

> *Ant.*   All is lost!
> This foul Egyptian hath betrayed me!
> . . . when I am reveng'd upon my charm,
> I have done all. Bid them all fly; begone!
> O sun, thy uprise shall I see no more. . . .
>   *[Enter Cleopatra]*
>   Ah, thou spell! Avaunt!
> *Cleo.* Why is my lord enrag'd against his love?
> *Ant.* Vanish, or I shall give thee thy deserving . . .
>   (IV, xii, 9–10, 16–18, 30–32)

Cleopatra's total dedication to their love, since her flight from
Actium, has come too late to allay the new suspicions aroused by

that fatal flight, and Antony's vengeful thoughts against her turn to fury upon her appearance. At "the very heart of loss" (IV, xii, 28) all values are obscured:

> Here I am Antony;
> Yet cannot hold this visible shape. . . .
> I made these wars for Egypt; and the Queen—
> Whose heart I thought I had, for she had mine,
> Which, whilst it was mine, had annex'd unto't
> A million moe, now lost . . . (IV, xiv, 13–8)

Yet, even at "the very heart of loss" values do emerge. The greatest loss he feels is not his own dissolution but the loss of Cleopatra's love. His heart can still reach out to her and feel that, had he but her love, *all* would not be lost.

When his deepest wish is granted him, therefore, all thoughts of revenge are past and he can accept his own loss in peace. Mardian's false message that "my mistress lov'd thee and her fortunes mingled/ With thine entirely" (IV, xiv, 24–5) strengthens his heart for the terrible task that still remained, his self-slaughter:

> I will o'ertake thee, Cleopatra, and
> Weep for my pardon. So it must be, for now
> All length is torture. Since the torch is out,
> Lie down, and stray no further. Now all labour
> Mars what it does; yea, very force entangles
> Itself with strength. Seal then, and all is done.
>   (IV, xiv, 44–9)

If he has ever criticized Cleopatra for the impurity of her love, he must now beg her pardon. It was enough that she was the "torch" which illuminated for him the greatest gift of life, the spiritual power which is released and fulfilled by love. He cannot now repent the destruction to which Cleopatra had led him, since without her "all length is torture." His "very force" is without purpose and blindly "entangles itself with strength."

But Antony does not choose to die simply because his love

for Cleopatra does not permit him to outlive her. His love had
been fulfilled in life, and death can assure it no greater truth or
fulfillment. No, he must die for the same reason that he believes
Cleopatra has died—and, in fact, shortly will:

> Since Cleopatra died
> I have liv'd in such dishonour that the gods
> Detest my baseness. . . . less noble mind
> Than she which by her death our Caesar tells
> 'I am conqueror of myself.' (IV, xiv, 55-7, 60-2)

It is not his love which is dishonored in outliving Cleopatra, but
his sovereign pride which was outdone, as he supposes, by Cleopatra's zeal in defeating Caesar's victory. Antony had been prepared to do as much before he had received this "proof" of
Cleopatra's firmness. But news of her death allows him to accept
the defeat of his glory because it restores his faith in the love that
had brought it about.

Now he hopes to join Cleopatra after death, in a "space" no
better than that which they enjoyed on earth, but where they
can still "stand up peerless":

> Eros!—I come, my queen.—Eros!—Stay for me.
> Where souls do couch on flowers, we'll hand in hand
> And with our sprightly port make the ghosts gaze.
> Dido and her Aeneas shall want troops,
> And all the haunt be ours. (IV, xiv, 50-4)

Cleopatra is later to say:

> It were for me
> To throw my sceptre at the injurious gods,
> To tell them that this world did equal theirs
> Till they had stol'n our jewel. (IV, xv, 75-8)

Cleopatra also hopes to meet Antony after death, eagerly awaiting
"that kiss/ Which is my heaven to have" (V, ii, 305-6). But the

"heaven" to which Antony and Cleopatra look forward is one made blessed by the kisses they can exchange, kisses for which "this world did equal theirs." This is one of the essential characteristics of Worldly Love, that it *can* achieve its perfect fulfillment in life. Worldly Love does not seek in death a perfect union freed from the corruptions of life; it embraces and ennobles all that is vital even to the "vilest things." It rejoices in the "day o' th' world," in the "nobleness of *life*." But Worldly Love can so fully embrace the values of life only because of its prior acceptance of the validity of personal sovereignty, of the values inherent in the individual human life, and it is only the defeat of these values which can compel a worldly lover to choose death. Antony and Cleopatra choose death not that their love may be fulfilled but because the conditions of their life have become such that they can no longer "stand up peerless."

But the love that has caused the defeat of their sovereignty has, to the very end, been corrupted by the powerful claims of both their sovereign natures. Cleopatra, seeing that he was temporarily "mad" (IV, xiii, 1) and intent upon her death, had fled to preserve her life while employing what she thought to be a suitable cunning for bringing him around:

> To th' monument!
> Mardian, go tell him I have slain myself.
> Say that the last I spoke was 'Antony'
> And word it, prithee, piteously. Hence, Mardian,
> And bring me how he takes my death. To th' monument!
> (IV, xiii, 6–10)

For, again, she "little thought" he "would have followed." Three times he had, since Actium, reverted to his old Roman values and turned against her. The first two times she had finally been able to reason with him, but this time he would not hear her and she was forced to revert to her old cunning. But as soon as she had put her policy in motion, she realized that it was no longer justified and might prove fatal: "Lock'd in her monument. She had a prophesying fear/ Of what hath come to pass" (IV, xiv, 120–1).

Though she could not have assumed the extent of his love before Actium, his action there had proven that any underestimation of his love could be dangerous. The doubts which his rage had renewed are forever banished at the same time that Antony is also reaffirming his own faith in their love. Both reaffirm their faith in the other even at the moment in which it has been most abused and thereby redeem their love from its own corruption.

Though the false news of Cleopatra's death had helped him in his fatal resolution, he does not now repent that it was so. As he could no longer expect any mercy from Caesar, it was necessary for him to end his own life nobly. Cleopatra also has vowed to do the same when there was no further hope of avoiding "Th' inevitable prosecution of/ Disgrace" (IV, xiv, 65–6). With traitors daily appearing among their own followers, Cleopatra is afraid to leave the one sanctuary in which she may be assured of a noble death. Begging his pardon for what might seem to be a lack of total dedication to their love, she resolves, therefore, to draw him up to her:

> Dear my lord, pardon! I dare not,
> Lest I be taken. Not th' imperious show
> Of the full-fortun'd Caesar ever shall
> Be brooch'd with me! . . . But come, come, Antony!
> Help me, my women. We must draw thee up.
> . . . welcome, welcome! Die where thou hast liv'd!
> Quicken with kissing. (IV, xv, 22–5, 29–30, 38–9)

She shall prove her honor in love by robbing Caesar of his triumph, show that the love that could "quicken with kissing," and produce a nobler life on earth than that which "full-fortun'd Caesar" can boast, can hold its nobility to the end. And Antony, who can die for Cleopatra because it was through her that he had truly lived, supports her resolution to live while sovereignty is hers. In his last moments his concern is all for her future, and he brushes aside her protestations as unimportant:

    Ant.   One word, sweet queen.
Of Caesar seek your honour, with your safety. O!
    Cleo.   They do not go together.
    Ant.   Gentle, hear me.
None about Caesar trust but Proculeius.
    Cleo. My resolution and my hands I'll trust;
None about Caesar.
    Ant. The miserable change now at my end
Lament nor sorrow at; but please your thoughts
In feeding them with those my former fortunes,
Wherein I liv'd the greatest prince o' th' world,
The noblest; and do now not basely die,
Not cowardly put off my helmet to
My countryman—a Roman by a Roman
Valiently vanquish'd. Now my spirit is going.
I can no more. (IV, xv, 45–59)

Antony's magnanimity to his followers, trusty and traitorous alike, was but a prelude to his great magnanimity in death. He does not feel that love should prompt Cleopatra to die with him but that she should still derive pleasure from their love, remembering their happier times and his true nobility in life and death. He would have her live, if she can preserve her life with honor, and continues to advise her to this end until he "can no more."

    As Antony had felt all earthly values to vanish with Cleopatra's death, so does Cleopatra react to Antony's death:

    The crown o' th' earth doth melt. My lord!
    O, wither'd is. the garland of the war,
    The soldier's pole is fall'n! Young boys and girls
    Are level now with men. The odds is gone,
    And there is nothing left remarkable
    Beneath the visiting moon. (IV, xv, 63–8)

Though she had led him to this death in an effort of self-preservation, Antony's death has left the world so void of meaning that even the ultimate value of her sovereignty seems questionable.

Despite Antony's hopes, she cannot believe that Caesar will allow her to preserve her honor with her safety and, weighted down by loss, can barely summon the energy to play what she already considers to be the futile game of sounding Caesar's purposes: "All's but naught./ Patience is sottish, and impatience does/ Become a dog that's mad" (IV, xv, 78–80). But, though it would be easier to "rush into the secret house of death" (IV, xv, 81) like a mad dog, she will try to summon the patience to play out this sottish game. She will maintain her "resolution" to the end, but only effect it when she is assured that Caesar vows her shame. "Then, what's brave, what's noble" she will do "after the high Roman fashion" (IV, xv, 86–7).

Not wishing to be long in doubt, she sends a messenger to Caesar to learn his "intents" (V, i, 54), and later informs Caesar's messenger "That majesty, to keep decorum, must/ No less beg than a kingdom" (V, ii, 17–8). Though hoping that Caesar may allow her to remain sovereign, she places no faith in his promises and, when she is surprised by Caesar's men, resolves upon immediate death rather than captivity:

> *Char.* O Cleopatra! thou art taken, Queen!
> *Cleo.* Quick, quick, good hands! *[Draws a dagger.]*
> *Pro.*   Hold, worthy lady, hold! *[Disarms her.]*
> *Cleo.* . . . This mortal house I'll ruin,
> Do Caesar what he can. Know, sir, that I
> Will not wait pinion'd at your master's court . . . (V, ii,
>   38–40, 51–53)

She would preserve her life as long as she can be sovereign, but no longer. And in this endeavor her cunning finally does stand her in good stead. As she is now in Caesar's power, she must immediately discover his intentions and then so manage matters that she can regain the power to dispose of herself.

In Dollabella she immediately recognizes a genuine attraction which she can use to ascertain Caesar's intentions, and she loses no time in gaining his devotion to her cause. As soon as she is assured of this, she asks her great question:

> *Dol.*   I do feel,
> By the rebound of yours, a grief that smites
> My very heart at root.
>   *Cleo.*   I thank you, sir.
> Know you what Caesar means to do with me?
>   *Dol.* I am loth to tell you what I would you knew. . . .
>   *Cleo.* He'll lead me, then, in triumph?
>   *Dol.* Madam, he will. I know't. (V, ii, 103–7, 109–10)

Her doubts finally resolved as she had expected, her course is now unalterably fixed. There remains only the task of pacifying Caesar so that he will leave her in temporary possession of the monument. While her doubts were still unresolved, however, she had deliberately omitted a fortune from the list of her possessions which she had prepared to give Caesar at this meeting. Now she must play this scene with the added burden of concealing a fortune which she no longer needs. When her treasurer, upon whose faith she had relied, betrays her, however, she bursts into a spontaneous rage: "must I be unfolded/ With one that I have bred? The gods! It smites me/ Beneath the fall I have" (V, ii, 170–2). She is willing to accept her defeat with dignity but not with such a lapse of decorum, "a wounding shame" (V, ii, 159) as great in kind as the Roman triumph that she means to prevent. But her presence of mind is strong, even with this unforseen mishap, and she manages to carry matters as she had planned. She had wished to "look him i' th' face" (V, ii, 32) and, having done so, now concludes: "He words me, girls, he words me, that I should not/ Be noble to myself! But hark thee, Charmian" (V, ii, 191–2). And she immediately orders the mortal asp.

As soon as we rid ourselves of the notion, derived from Courtly Love, that Cleopatra's love is somehow imperfect if she does not kill herself immediately upon Antony's death, it will be seen that Cleopatra has been guilty of no procrastination in the execution of her purposed death. Though she thought she would have "no friend/ But resolution and the briefest end" (IV, xv, 90–1), she was nonetheless committed to "seek" an honorable friendship with Caesar. It was only when this attempt failed that she felt obliged to turn to her true 'friend" and execute her resolution in the briefest possible time. Once we have accepted the fact that Worldly Love does not view death as the supreme fulfillment and voucher of its truth, we can understand why neither Antony nor Cleopatra should consider it ignoble for her to outlive him *if* she can do so with honor. It is, rather, by the firmness of her final attempt to preserve life with honor, despite all personal sorrow, that she pays her supreme tribute to "the nobleness of life."

Though Antony's death makes it easier for her to meet death undaunted, it is not this but the desire to escape and so defeat Caesar's triumph that impels Cleopatra, as it did Antony, to death. Having tried those means prescribed by the decorum of nobility whereby she might preserve her life with honor, and failing in these, she can now meet death, not as a mad dog, but a sovereign queen:

> Give me my robe, put on my crown. I have
> Immortal longings in me. Now no more
> The juice of Egypt's grape shall moist this lip.
> Yare, yare, good Iras; quick. Methinks I hear
> Anthony call. I see him rouse himself
> To praise my noble act. I hear him mock
> The luck of Caesar, which the gods give men
> To excuse their after wrath. Husband I come!
> Now to that name my courage prove my title! (V, ii, 283–91)

She proves her title to their higher marriage not by having *finally* died for love of him but by dying as he would have wished her to, nobly mocking the luck of Caesar, asserting the inviolability of her sovereignty to the end. As he had wished to "please" her with the remembrance that he had "liv'd the greatest prince o' th' world,/ The noblest; and do now not basely die," so does she hope to please him by affirming in her death the value of her life, that sovereign quality which had enabled both of them to become "such a mutual pair," and in death, as in life, to "stand up peerless." It was this quality that, however much it may have corrupted their love, still gave their love the triumphant power which proves "great Caesar ass/ Unpolicied!" (V, ii, 310–11):

> I am fire and air; my other elements
> I give to baser life. . . . Dost fall?
> If thou and nature can so gently part,
> The stroke of death is as a lover's pinch,
> Which hurts, and is desir'd. Dost thou lie still?
> If thus thou vanishest, thou tell'st the world
> It is not worth leave-taking. . . .
> As sweet as balm, as soft as air, as gentle—
> O Antony! Nay, I will take thee too:
>   *[Applies another asp to her am.]*
> What should I stay—[*Dies.*] (V, ii, 292–3, 296–301, 314–6)

For what should she stay in a world that neither allows her to enjoy her love nor to exercise her sovereignty? As long as she could find the total fulfillment of her nature in love, she proclaimed that "this world did equal theirs [the gods]." It is not the nature of the world, then, but this specific loss that renders it "not worth leave-taking." The world has left her but one right and this she seizes, the right to die as she has lived, reveling in her sensuous sovereignty. For even her sensuality is touched by a nobler fire and can transcend the stroke of death as easily as it had the baser elements of life. She had said of Antony that "His delights/ Were dolphin-like: they show'd his back above/ The element they liv'd in" (V, ii, 88–90), and so may it be said of her. Her death was, as her life, "well done, and fitting for a princess/ Descended of so many royal kings" (V, ii, 329–30).

Worldly Love has been tried to its truth and triumphed. In Shakespeare's first tragic exploration of Worldly Love its difficulties seemed insuperable, and he could affirm no more than a dream of what might be possible through this love. Both Othello and Desdemona are so intent upon preserving their own sovereignty from violation that they do not experience that enrichment from the other's love that could enable them to transcend their fears in the fulfillment of their love. Their individual loves are defeated before they can create a mutual life, and they die not for the values by which they lived but by which they should have lived. Shakespeare, more than any other tragedian of Worldly Love, concerned himself with this internal problem of Worldly Love, with the corrupting effects of sovereignty upon that love which would preserve it. In *Antony and Cleopatra,* Shakespeare retraces the dilemma of *Othello* in the light of its solution, showing that the fidelity to self that corrupts Worldly Love also creates its possibility for achieving a nobler life. Antony and Cleopatra are no less intent upon preserving their sovereignty than were Othello and Desdemona, but they have learned to value the offerings of their mutual love. Its value differs, however, from that projected in *Othello.* Where *Othello* projected an exalted ideal of Worldly Love, which finally identified it with the height of Christian charity, *Antony and Cleopatra* exudes a radiant Epicureanism.

Worldly Love reaches its noblest fulfillment in the second tragic pattern as it is exemplified in *Antony and Cleopatra* and *The Duchess of Malfi.* In this pattern the lover accepts from the beginning the single all-important value of love and is willing to sacrifice everything he has for the fulfillment of his love. In striving for the full realization of his individuality divorced from love, he had reached its necessary limits and, feeling the unbearable loneliness of his self-containment, now desires the communion with another person that can bridge this loneliness and make valuable his personal survival. Since the satisfactions of sovereignty have ceased to fulfill his spiritual needs, he turns to love and attempts to live a private life with his beloved. But he cannot so easily evade the responsibilities of sovereignty and society turns on him to demand its account. Both lover and beloved become joint victims of a society aroused to wrath by the lovers' reckless surrender of all for love.

If the classic expression of an art form is that in which its noblest values are realized in a living, rather than ideal, representation, then the classic period of Worldly Love tragedy becomes identified with the full enunciation of its second pattern. This classic period occurs, however, at the moment in which the drama as a whole is on the point of decline. Though Worldly Love provides the most inspired tragic value of this final period, it had first to await the decline of the earlier masculine faith in worldly power, just as Shakespeare had first to write not only *Othello* but also *Macbeth* before he could make his full affirmation of Worldly Love in *Antony and Cleopatra*. The desire for prestige or power, which had tormented Othello and Macbeth, is finally resolved by this turning from the sphere of aspiration to that of love. Where the historical development of the other two tragic modes of love is marked by a steady decline from the vision that had been most perfectly realized at the very start of these separate dramatic traditions, the historical progression of Worldly Love tragedy describes not a downward line but a curve. The moment of faith is a later development in the progress of Worldly Love than of the other two modes of love, but its endurance is as brief. In the whole history of Western literature, this bright moment occurred only in the Elizabethan tragic drama and, most radiantly, in *Antony and Cleopatra*.

Antony and Cleoptra is mankind's supreme poetic tribute to Worldly Love, to that love which can achieve a noble fulfillment in life because it glorifies all that contributes to its finite existence, the corruptions and compromises with the human sovereignty which these help to define. For the only basis upon which Worldly Love can be built is the lover's prior acceptance of the unique significance and value of his own life, of that particularly human individuality which sets him apart as a sovereign entity. If he is not at home in mortality, if he shudders at impurity and sees his finite individuality as the great evil of creation, an evil which he would overcome through some ecstatic fusion, he will turn from the celebration of life and, in pursuit of a deathless ideal which is but a mask of death, never see the true "nobleness of life" which has its source and being in finitude. It is only his prior acceptance of the unique value of his own sovereignty that can enable him to see those values which are peculiar to life and to find true fulfillment through them. He accepts the imperfect in his nature because this is a necessary concomitant of his freedom and separateness, and it is only through his freedom that he can achieve true nobility, through his separateness true relation. For his sovereignty does not condemn him to isolation but rather is his sole means of achieving fellow-ship. It is only by affirming and preserving his sovereignty that he is enabled to love another human being compounded of the limitations and virtues that are native to life. It was said of Antony that "A rarer spirit never/ Did steer humanity; but you gods will give us/ Some faults to make us men" (V, i, 31–3). It is the ability of Worldly Love to accept those faults, which make pos-sible the existence of a rarer spirit, that is its great achievement. Shakespeare's achievement and that of his fellow Elizabethan tragedians is no less.

10

The Third Pattern: The White Devil

Webster, the greatest tragedian of Worldly Love after Shakespeare, inherited a spiritual world more shrunken than that which his predecessor inhabited. When Shakespeare turned from the realm of power to that of love, the realm of power still had some remaining vitality. This manifested itself both in the continuing production of important non-romantic tragedies and in the role that power played within the love tragedies. In Shakespeare's first Worldly Love tragedy, the love of Othello came into conflict with his unassimilated drive for power; in Shakespeare's second tragedy of Worldly Love, Antony had resolved this internal conflict, but the power drive still expressed itself through his antagonist, Caesar. When Webster wrote his two great tragedies, however, the drive for power has ceased to be a tragic value. After 1610 there is no important tragedy that is not a love tragedy. In Webster's dramatic world the desire for personal power still continues but it has lost its vitality. Those who have power—Francisco, Monticelso, Ferdinand, and the Cardinal—are no longer inspired by it and use their power only for destructive ends; those who aspire to power—Flamineo and Bosola—are "rogues that are most weary of their lives" (*WD*, III, iii, 128).[1] Though the aspirants to power and love both manifest the same "integrity of life" (*DM*, V, v, 145), it is only the lovers who can affirm the value of anything beyond it: "Where's this good woman? had I infinite worlds/ They were too little for thee" (*WD*, V, iii, 18–9).

The desire for worldly success or "preferment" continues, but in Webster's dramatic world the aspirants to power can no longer speak with the true accent of tragedy and are forced to assume a satiric voice. To continue to present the conflicting values of love and power in a world in which power can no longer appeal to the best in man, Webster has had to abandon the straightforward tragic manner of Shakespeare and adapt to new uses the satiric tragedy of Marston and Tourneur. Webster's integral use of satire in tragedy is, however, totally different from that of Marston and Tourneur. In their tragedies of revenge, the tragic action serves as a satiric scourge. Webster, on the other hand, uses his Machiavellian satirists much as Shakespeare had used Iago, as a voice antagonistic to the vision embraced by the tragic lovers. His satirists reveal an untrue picture of life produced by the satiric negation of compassion, a version of reality as it would be if it were totally uninspired by love and one which best serves to explain only the satirist's own behavior. In Webster's tragedies the tragic and satiric visions do not work in unison, as Travis Bogard has argued,[2] but through opposition, and the function of the tragic action is to refute the adequacy of the satiric reduction by revealing its spiritual bankruptcy.

Flamineo is disturbed to realize that "I have a strange thing in mee, to th' which/ I cannot give a name, without it bee/ Compassion" (*WD*, V, iv, 107–9), and Bosola reveals why compassion must be strange to such as they: "where were these penitent fountaines,/ While she was living?/ Oh, they were frozen up" (*DM*, IV, ii, 392-4). They have had to freeze the fountains of their compassion in order to preserve that simplified knowledge of reality that brings some peace and order into a thing "of so infinit vexation/ As mans owne thoughts" (*WD*, V, vi, 206–7). For, to admit the validity of love, whether on earth or in heaven, is to "confound/ Knowledge with knowledge" (*WD*, V, vi, 259–60), and so to lose even their partial certainty. But the partial certainty, which comes from rejecting the existence of good and attending only to the appearances of evil, is "a Perspective/ That showes us hell" (*DM*, IV, ii, 386–7). Bosola finally admits that there is an alternative to the satiric perspective, that the admission of love can bring an ennobling fulfillment to man's life even in a world of evil, and that this ignoble course was not inevitable but "another voyage" (*DM*, V, v, 129) made necessary only because of his exclusion of love.

It is not, however, any form of love that can wrest some fulfillment from a world of despair and thus qualify as a tragic value in Webster's world. The lovers who become Webster's tragic heroes are all worldly lovers, and it is over the value of this form of love that the battle between the tragic and satiric positions rages—the lovers affirming that it enables their sovereign natures to find a compassionate fulfillment in a corrupt world, the satirists maintaining that the lovers' protestations are "but the superficies of lust" (*WD*, I, ii, 18). It can only be regretted that this partial satiric view has influenced the judgment of too many modern critics,[3] for this satiric position is qualified by the dramatic action. The battle of values is finally won by the advocates of Worldly Love when the satirists, after a fevered attempt to degrade or destroy this love, are converted to its truth.

Yet it is the satiric context that gives added power to Webster's tragedies of Worldly Love by presenting a negative picture of the world when it is deprived of such love. Webster is as much concerned with exploring the spiritual bankruptcy of the satiric position as he is with revealing the basis of a tragic affirmation. In plotting his tragedies he does little more than outline the main features of the tragic action while painstakingly observing its subtle effects upon the satiric characters. For it is through these effects that the value of Worldly Love receives its most profound confirmation.

The tragic action of *The White Devil* begins on a note of despair as Brachiano, watching Vittoria depart without having given him any sign of her favor, feels himself to be "quite lost" (I, ii, 3). But Flamineo, who has engineered the meeting between his sister and his lord in the hope of gaining preferment, has no use for Brachiano's ardor:

I must not have your Lordship thus unwisely amorous—
I my selfe have loved a lady and peursued her with a great
deale of under-age protestation, when some 3. or 4. gallants
that have enjoyed would with all their harts have bin glad
to have bin rid of: Tis just like a summer bird-cage in a
garden, the birds that are without, despaire to get in, and
the birds that are within despaire and are in a consumption
for feare they shall never get out. (I, ii, 37–44)

Flamineo would have Brachiano see love as he does, as a base
entanglement. He constantly satirizes the love of Brachiano and
Vittoria, trying to degrade it to the level of his own love experiences but succeeding only in revealing the sterility of his emotional responses.

But Brachiano's desperate need of love is of a profounder
nature than Flamineo's depraved imagination can comprehend.
It is only Vittoria who can truly appreciate the quality of despair
which bids him say: "Loose me not Madam, for if you forego
me/ I am lost eternallie" (I, ii, 197–8). The remedy of this "sweet
Phisition" (I, ii, 199), suggested by way of a recounted dream,
reveals the similar quality of her despair:

Methought I walkt about the mid of night,
Into a Church-yard, where a goodly Eu Tree
Spred her large roote in ground—under that Eu,
As I sat sadly leaning on a grave,
Checkered with crosse-sticks, their came stealing in
Your Dutchesse and my husband—one of them
A picax bore, th'other a Rusty spade,
And in rough termes they gan to challenge me,
About this Eu. . . . and for that they vow'd
To bury me alive: my husband straight
With picax gan to dig, and your fell Dutchesse
With shovell, like a fury, voyded out
The earth & scattered bones—Lord how me thought
I trembled, and yet for all this terror
I could not pray. . . .
When to my rescue there arose me thought
A whirlewind, which let fall a massy arme

> From that strong plant,
> And both were strucke dead by that sacred Eu
> In that base shallow grave that was their due. (I, ii, 222–45)

Life presents a sad and gloomy prospect to Vittoria, leading only to a grave whose decorative "crosse-sticks" cannot assuage the "terror" of the "scattered bones" beneath. From this prospect there can be no salvation through prayer but only through "that sacred Eu" (with the pun on "you" intended). As Vittoria can save Brachiano from total loss, so does he appear to her as the only thing sacred in life. But his power to "rescue" her from despair is constrained by the antagonism of their respective mates and the "base shallow" claims that their conventionality can raise against their sacred right to love. They cannot be truly rescued by the saving power of love unless he free them from their would-be persecutors by giving them "their due."

Brachiano, inspired by her vision of redemption, replies in accents which, like hers, are beyond good and evil:

> Sweetly shall I enterpret this your dreame,
> You are lodged within his armes who shall protect you,
> From all the feavers of a jealous husband
> From the poore envy of our flegmaticke Dutchessse—
> I'le seate you above law and above scandall,
> Give to your thoughts the invention of delight
> And the fruition; nor shall government
> Divide me from you longer then a care
> To keepe you great: you shall to me at once,
> Be Dukedome, health, wife, children, friends and all.
> (I, ii, 249–58)

The powers of law, scandal, and personal aspiration have lost their hold over Brachiano, who sees in the "fruition" of his love for Vittoria "all" that is truly valuable in the world. Compared to this fruition, the claims of "a jealous husband" and "flegmaticke Dutchesse" are hollow, and can be crushed without any moral qualms.

A love that can redeem despair is obviously not the "violent lust" (I, ii, 210) that Vittoria's mother Cornelia takes it for, and when she bursts in upon them, Vittoria appeals to her mother for understanding. When her appeal is answered by a mother's curse, Vittoria departs feeling deeply injured. It is the special paradox of this love that, while its saving power allows the lovers to disdain all other values, they truly believe that the goodness they derive from it should excuse them before the world's judgment. Brachiano echoes Vittoria's wronged feelings:

> Uncharitable woman, thy rash tongue
> Hath rais'd a fearefull and prodigious storme,
> Bee thou the cause of all ensuing harme. (I, ii, 298–300)

Cornelia voices the condemnation of respectable society, and it is precisely because society is so "uncharitable" to their love that Vittoria and Brachiano are forced to take a criminal course to preserve it against society's spite. If they act uncharitably to Isabella and Camillo, it is because the world's lack of charity has driven them to it. They feel themselves innocent.

Isabella's method will not serve:

> I do beseech you
> Intreate him mildely, let not your rough tongue
> Set us at louder variance—all my wrongs
> Are freely pardoned, and I do not doubt
> . . . these armes
> Shall charme his poyson, . . . (II, i, 10–3, 15–6)

Were Brachiano and Vittoria to follow Isabella's example of turning the other cheek, their love would have no greater chance for worldly success than hers. They do not live in a world of Isabellas but of Monticelsos and Franciscos where, with such mildness, "The wolfe may prey the better" (III, ii, 188). Indeed, even Isabella could not charm these wolves from their purposed attack. But Brachiano responds to Francisco's growing venom with a display of his own power to resist such attack:

Uncivill sir ther's Hemlocke in thy breath
And that blacke slander—were she a whore of mine,
All thy loud Cannons, and thy borrowed Switzers
Thy Gallies, nor thy sworne confederates,
Durst not supplant her. (II, i, 61–5)

Brachiano gives no trace of internal conflict, of hesitance in pursuing his amoral course; but, when he is attacked for this course, he feels himself to be wronged by incivility. He not only feels that he is "above law and above scandall" but that he has the power to turn malice against itself and prove it ineffectual.

When such a defiantly sovereign soul can no longer find his fulfillment in the isolated realm of power but must turn to love to overwhelm the despair of his existential loneliness, it is not to the love of an Isabella that he can turn:

> *Brac.* You are in health we see. *Isa.* And above health
> To see my Lord well—*Brac.* So!—I wonder much,
> What amorous whirlewind hurryed you to Rome.
> *Isa.* Devotion my Lord. *Brac.* Devotion?
> Is your soule charg'd with any grievous sinne?
> *Isa.* 'Tis burdened with too many; and I thinke
> The oftner that we cast our reckonings up,
> Our sleepes will be the sounder. *Brac.* Take your chamber.

Despite his resolution to smooth matters over for the moment— "You have charm'd mee" (II, i, 149)—when Isabella enters and begins her pious protestations, he is so revolted by her that he cannot endure her presence. His revulsion towards his "flegmaticke Dutchesse" is of an even profounder nature than that which caused Antony to reject Octavia, for Isabella is not merely inadequate to his needs and harmful to the expression of his better self, as was Octavia to Antony, but a contributing cause to his despair. The sources of her faith are so alien to him that they only increase his appalling spiritual loneliness. As she turns from pious speeches in the attempt to kindle his romantic instincts, he cannot contain himself:

> *Isa.* You are as welcome to these longing armes,
> As I to you a Virgine. *Brac.* O your breath!
> Out upon sweete meates, and continued Physicke!
> The plague is in them. (II, i, 165-8)

The "plague" is in her sweetness, for he needs something more
bracing to fortify his soul in its struggle to wrest meaning from
life. Confirmed by this interview in his need for Vittoria, he
vows that he shall divorce himself totally from Isabella. Bidding
her to "take your course" (II, i, 228), he immediately begins to
plan "the murder" (II, i, 288) of his "loathed Dutchesse" (II, ii,
4) and of Camillo. Observing its success through the help of a
necromancer's art, he coldly comments, "Excellent, then shee's
dead" (II, ii, 24), and of Camillo's murder, "'Twas quaintly done"
(II, ii, 38). In the combat to preserve his love, he can permit
himself no greater charity to others than he himself has received,
must steel himself against all other considerations but the one
thing needful.

So, too, with Vittoria. "Shee comes arm'd/ With scorne and
impudence" (III, ii, 124-5) to the first trial of her mettle. Although her accusers seek to try her on the grounds of lust and
murder, she accepts trial only of her sovereign quality. Whether
or not Vittoria is technically guilty of the crimes with which
she is charged, she is free of any sense of guilt and defies the
court to prove that she should feel otherwise. The values which
her spirit manifests may be beyond good and evil, but they are
not counterfeit:

> *Vit.* . . . in a cursed accusation
> . . . my defence of force like Perseus,
> Must personate masculine vertue—To the point!
> Find mee but guilty, sever head from body:
> Weele part good frindes: I scorne to hould my life
> At yours or any mans intreaty, Sir.
> *Eng. Emb.* Shee hath a brave spirit.
> *Mon.* Well, well, such counterfet Jewels
> Make trew [ones] oft suspected. *Vit.* You are deceaved.
> For know that all your strickt-combined heads,

> Which strike against this mine of diamondes,
> Shall prove but glassen hammers, they shall breake—
> These are but faigned shadowes of my evels.
> Terrify babes, my Lord, with painted devils,
> I am past such needlesse palsy . . . (III, ii, 138–52)

The accusation is "cursed" because, with "faigned shadowes,"
it presumes to question her essential nobility and her sovereign
right to find fruition in accordance with her nature. If she were
found guilty of ignobility in the pursuit of this goal, she would
indeed scorn to hold her life at their entreaty, but it is not "with
painted devils" that they can convict her nor break her diamond-
hard will. It is because she is "past such needlesse palsy" that
she can believe that death was the "due" of Isabella and Camillo,
but is not her due. Her measure is not that of good and evil,
but the ability to preserve integrity in a corrupt world and to
wrest meaning therefrom. In her performance of this primary
spiritual obligation of life she has not been guilty and, when
the character of a whore is expounded to her, can truly say: "This
carracter scapes me" (III, ii, 105). When she is nonetheless convicted for this "fault,/ Joyn'd to'th condition of the present time"
(III, ii, 266–7), her response proves how far removed she is from
the character of a whore: "I will not weepe,/ No I do scorne
to call up one poore teare/ To fawne [on] your injustice" (III, ii,
295–7). No form of outward oppression, whether it mean prison or
death, can force Vittoria to lower her dignity, to shed one base tear
in hope of pardon or fear of punishment. When she cries, and
she does so on two significant occasions, it is because something
even more valuable than her life, her love, has been touched.
Vittoria can bear unflinchingly the consequences of her pursuit of love; what she cannot bear is the loss of this love.

     This fact, so important to an understanding not only of
Vittoria but of Webster's tragic vision, first becomes clear in the
one great scene given to the lovers. Though this is the first time
we see them alone since they met, in their separate acts of defiance for the sake of their love, they have proved themselves truly
worthy of each other. But their ability to outface external antagonism is nothing compared to the ability of their love to rise

above internal conflict and corruption. For a love that murders compassion is essentially corrupt, whether the cause of this corruption is in the character of the lovers or in the "condition of the present time." When Brachiano falls into the trap laid for him by Francisco's planted love letter to Vittoria, we see what an unsteady base despair is on which to build a love:

> Bra. Your beautie! ô, ten thousand curses on't.
> How long have I beheld the devill in christall!
> Thou hast lead mee, like an heathen sacrifice,
> With musicke, and with fatall yokes of flowers
> To my eternall ruine. Woman to man
> In either a God or a wolfe. *Vit.* My Lord. *Bra.* Away.
> We'll bee as differing as two Adamants;
> The one shall shunne the other. What? do'st weepe?
> Procure but ten of thy dissembling trade,
> [W]ee'ld furnish all the Irish funeralls
> With howling, past wild Irish. *Fla.* Fie, my Lord.
> Bra. That hand, that cursed hand, which I have wearied
> With doting kisses! O my sweetest Dutchesse
> How lovelie art thou now! *[to Vittoria]* Thy loose thoughtes
> Scatter like quicke-silver, I was bewitch'd;
> For all the world speakes ill of thee. (IV, ii, 88-103)

The pressure of the world's opinion has begun to tell on Brachiano. If it is true that she is a base whore, a "wolfe" like Flamineo's mistress rather than a "god" who can save him from being "lost eternallie," then all his defiance of the world, which led him to murder his "sweetest Dutchesse," was but the road to his "eternall ruine" and he is indeed lost to despair. It is the extent of his "heathen sacrifice" of all Christian values that causes him to fear that perhaps it is he who is being sacrificed on an altar of false values.

The fear which has prompted Brachiano's rejection of Vittoria now plunges her into as deep as despair. She, who had unflinchingly accepted murder and shame for the sake of her love, dissolves into tears as he turns upon her in the hated language of Flamineo, degrading their love and her truth. Like

Brachiano, she has sacrificed everything for the saving value of their love, but if this has proved to be but a delusion born of despair, she will cut it from her with the same ruthlessness with which she had earlier rejected the false values of society:

> *Vit.* No matter.
> Ile live so now Ile make the world recant
> And change her speeches. You did name your Dutchesse.
> *Bra.* Whose death God pardon.
> *Vit.* Whose death God revenge
> On thee most godlesse Duke . . .
> What have I gain'd by thee but infamie? . . .
> Fare you well Sir; let me heare no more of you.
> I had a limbe corrupted to an ulcer,
> But I have cut it off: and now Ile go
> Weeping to heaven on crutches. For your giftes,
> I will returne them all; and I do wish
> That I could make you full Executor
> To all my sinnes— o that I could tosse my selfe
> Into a grave as quickly: for all thou art worth
> Ile not shed one teare more;—Ile burst first. [*She throwes
> her selfe upon a bed.*]   (IV, ii, 103–9, 121–9)

If Vittoria's last hope of finding value in life seems to have come to naught, she still rejects the possibility of suicide. Her response to his death will be the same as to his rejection, tears. Though Webster has altered much in the tragic history of the actual Vittoria to make it more dramatically effective,[4] this is his most significant alteration, for on the two occasions in which he brings his dramatic Vittoria to tears, the historical Vittoria did attempt suicide. Since, to Webster, it was this world which, for better or worse, "was made for Man" (V, vi, 63), it is here where man must seek fruition or, failing this, maintain at least the "integrity of life." However much Vittoria may prize her reputation and her life, she will not weep at their loss as long as she knows that she has borne herself in all with integrity. It is only the loss of love which she accepts with profound sorrow because this loss renders her very integrity a sterile value. The loss of reputation or life cannot touch the essential value of her integrity; the loss of love can. It therefore assumes a value even greater than that of integrity, a value to which integrity can be dedicated.[5]

Though Vittoria had rejected conventional Christianity, she still had some form of personal religion with which her love was in accord. Love was, in fact, the "limbe" that could best carry her to the "heaven" envisioned by this religion. It is in these terms that Brachiano's rejection of love makes him "most godlesse." Painfully rejecting him for his lack of faith, she must now "go weeping to heaven on crutches," on an integrity unsupported by vitalizing love. Her religion is not concerned with the rewards of death but of life; it prescribes a *modus vivendi* based upon integrity and its fulfillment in this world, not another. Her devotion to this creed had enabled her to accept not only "infamie" for the sake of love but even the apparent failure of her attempt to find love. Failure is "no matter" as long as she has tried nobly to fulfill her nature. But her love, otherwise in accord with her sovereignty, offers momentary resistance to her proud repudiation of Brachiano. Since he still appears to her as a man of "worth," despite his rejection of her truth, she cannot adhere to her resolution to "burst" before she will "shed one teare more" and throws herself upon a bed weeping.

This witness to the profundity of her love restores Brachiano's faith in her and assures him that the saving value of her love is not a delusion: "I have drunke Lethe./ Vittoria! My dearest happinesse! Vittoria!/ What doe you aile my love? why doe you weepe?" (IV, ii, 130–3). As with her tears, so has his jealousy revealed his extreme reliance upon their love for his ultimate happiness. But now that he is assured that Vittoria can bring him this "dearest happinesse," he must fight her resistance to accept his renewed faith: "What dar'st thou doe, that I not dare to suffer,/ Excepting to bee still thy whore?" (IV, ii, 145–8). More than anything else, it was his addressing her as "A statelie and advanced whore" (IV, ii, 77) which had steeled her resolve to "live so now Ile make the world recant/ And change her speeches." She could bear the world's speeches as long as they did not proceed from Brachiano, but if her position makes her susceptible to insult even from him, she will not give the world or Brachiano opportunity to call her "whore" again. No protestations will be able to convince her of his renewed faith unless he gives proof of this by changing her status. His earlier words had forced her to couple him with Flamineo as "yee dissembling men!" (IV, ii, 185), for Flamineo's language, as he tries to reconcile them, only succeeds in picturing a form of love with which she refuses to associate herself. Nothing could be further removed from their profound lover's quarrel than Flamineo's degraded picture of Vittoria as sullied ware, and Brachiano conclusively gives it the lie when he says: "Bee thou at peace with mee; let all the world/ Threaten the Cannon (IV, ii, 176–7). It is this affirmation of his love that weakens Vittoria's resistance to the point where it can be overcome. Though she had been rewarded only with curses, she still believes in his "good heart" (IV, ii, 189), and in this belief she is right for Brachiano now proves the fullness of his love by offering her his name: "Vittoria,/ Thinke of a Dutchesse title" (IV, ii, 222–3).

No happiness that Vittoria had hitherto brought him could compare with the expansive joy with which he makes his "dearest happinesse" his wife. As he invites his guests "to furnish out our Dutchesse revells" (V, i, 50), his words are imbued with a new sense of well-being. His love reaches its fruition in that open union which allows him to name her "our Dutchesse." In naming his former duchess, he had always used an adjective. With Vittoria, however, the fact of union is so sweet that it stands sufficient. To requite the joy she gives him is his only care. He wishes the revels to be in her name, so as to bring her joy, and he uses his utmost care to preserve her from pain. When Flamineo kills his brother, it is this tender care which bids him say: "wee commaund that none acquaint our Dutchesse/ With this sad accident" (V, ii, 70–1).

How removed is this love from Flamineo's which, from this point to the end, serves to counterpoint the tragic action. Though Flamineo had said, "I doe love that Moore, that Witch very constrainedly . . . just as a man holds a wolfe by the eares" (V, i, 147–9), when his brother, Marcello, questions his right to be involved with her, he feels his sovereignty to be abused. And when Marcello kicks his mistress, Flamineo feels that "strange thing . . . compassion" at her being maltreated for loving him.

However little he may think of her, he thinks less of the conventional morality that permits Marcello to kick her and attack his own behavior. Against this morality, he will fight as staunchly as Brachiano did when similarly attacked by his brother-in-law, and with the same sense of indignity: "Hee wrongs me most that ought t' offend mee least" (V, i, 195). If he is to receive no charity, he will return none: "I have brought your weapon backe. [*Flamineo runnes Marcello through.*]" (V, ii, 14).

It is not, however, Flamineo's love but his violated sovereignty that prompts him to the murder; nor is Zanche worthy of a greater love. Immediately after Flamineo has accepted a mortal challenge for her honor, she accosts Francisco, in his Moorish disguise, with words of love. As Flamineo's quarrel took place before the murder of Brachiano, so does Zanche's pact with Francisco take place before Vittoria's murder, and the behavior of both is suggestively similar to that of their nobler masters. As Vittoria had used a dream to further the purposes of her love, so does Zanche; and Zanche is as willing to perpetrate any evil for the sake of love as was Vittoria. She even follows her mistress in inverting the meaning of religion, making her assignation "about midnight in the Chappel" (V, iii, 275). But between the bravery of Flamineo and Zanche and that of Brachiano and Vittoria there is a vast gulf, which these surface similarities only make the clearer. For the bravery of the former is indeed spent upon a delusion, while that of the latter is upon a truth. Zanche's infidelity places her honor beneath defense, and her love is vainly expended upon one who uses her love while he mocks it. Francisco had met Zanche with the words, "You're passionately met in this sad world" (V, iii, 223). As Brachiano and Vittoria go to their doom, this caricature of their love serves to illuminate its contrasting nobility, to show that a passionate meeting "in this sad world" can provide a value capable of redeeming its corruption.

This redemptive power of love reveals itself most strikingly in the new feeling of charity with which it inspires Brachiano. His cup so runneth over with the joy of his marriage that it reaches out to embrace even the strangers at his court with "proferr'd bountie" (V, i, 46). This is the true fruition of his love

for Vittoria, a joy so great that it converts "this sad world" into a
sphere of bountiful goodness. It is not, however, the world but
only Brachiano whom love has so converted and the world which
he now accepts as good retains its evil and will not requite his
charity. As Brachiano's love becomes more healthy, it tragically
loses the power to preserve itself in an evil world. The beneficiaries
of his "proffer'd bountie," beneath their kindly disguises, are his
sworn enemies and the disastrous effects of his charity are to render
him vulnerable to them.

It is this situation that gives to Cornelia's universal elegy
its great poignancy:

> Call for the Robin-Red-brest and the wren,
> Since ore shadie groves they hover,
> And with leaves and flowres doe cover
> The friendlesse bodies of unburied men.
> Call unto his funerall Dole
> The Ante, the field-mouse, and the mole
> To reare him hillockes, that shall keepe him warme,
> And (when gay tombes are rob'd) sustaine no harme,
> But keepe the wolfe far thence, that's foe to men,
> For with his nailes hee'l dig them up agen. (V, iv, 89–98)

Voiced by a woman who had been driven insane by the sense-
less destructiveness of evil—"Why here's no body shall get any
thing by his death. Let me call him againe for Gods sake" (V,
ii, 30–1)—this sublime call for charity in a world where God
does not reign, and her grief at its futility, express the essential
ground of Webster's tragic vision. For Webster, while recognizing that the Christian ideal of redemptive love might have saved
the world, saw that the world was hopelessly damned, that Christian values, however noble and necessary, did not apply to the
actual conditions of life and that the attempt to apply them
could lead only to loss. That Christianity can have any effect
upon this world or upon man's ultimate fate, he concluded to
be a delusion, a subject for pathos or bitter satire, though it
was his recognition of the desperate need of man and his world
for Christian charity that provided the source of his tragic com-

passion. But Christian charity could not be a tragic ideal for Webster because he viewed its simple practice as leading to a pathetic rather than a noble failure. Though it was the failure of Christian charity that created the tragic condition of the world, this condition made necessary the establishment of a dif- ferent ethical basis for tragic action, a basis whose congruity with the realities of life made possible the attempt of a few noble souls to reach a genuinely rewarding fulfillment. For Webster, this basis was a Stoic adherence to a personal integrity which was beyond the terms of Christian good and evil, the tragic value to which such morality aspired being the fulfillment of Worldly Love.[6]

For Webster, the fulfillment of Worldly Love could be a genuine tragic value because it was only this that could make acceptable "that which was made for Man,/ the world" (V, vi, 63–4). It succeeds in making the world acceptable, however, only because in the fruition of Worldly Love the instinct for charity is truly realized. A devotee of Christian charity, such as Isabella, might be better off dead: "would I had given/ Both her white hands to death . . . when I gave thee/ But one" (II, i, 66–9). Nor does her charity succeed in making the world any more tolerable to her: "Unkindnesse do thy office, poore heart breake" (II, i, 278). It is only in the fulfillment of Worldly Love that anything approaching an effective form of charity can be realized, effective not because it offers a better protection against the wolves but because it succeeds, where Christianity fails, in making the values of this world acceptable. Not only does the lover's charitable disposition make the world acceptable to him, it even succeeds in inspiring some charity in the heart of his murderer: "Hee cals for his destruction. Noble youth,/ I pitty thy sad fate" (V, ii, 79–80). Whereas the Christianity of Isabella and Marcello neither made their own lives happier nor inspired pity in their murderers, the charity of Worldly Love does both. Webster, then, did not reject charity as an ultimate good but rejected the Christian means of achieving it. For Webster, the ultimate value of Worldly Love was that it is able to realize, through its amoral methods, the healthy charity of a loving heart which is the true intent of Christianity.

The nature of the charity born of Worldly Love is fully revealed as Brachiano is suddenly faced with death:

Oh I am gone already: the infection
Flies to the braine and heart. O thou strong heart!
There's such a covenant 'tweene the world and it,
They're loath to breake. . . .
Where's this good woman? had I infinite worlds
They were too little for thee. Must I leave thee? . . .
I that have given life to offending slaves
And wretched murderers, have I not power
To lengthen mine owne a twelve-month?
Do not kisse me, for I shall poyson thee. *[To Vittoria.]*
                          (V, iii, 13–6, 18–9, 24–7)

Perhaps the most singular aspect of Brachiano's charity is that it pardons murder. When Francisco gloried in his fatal punishment of Brachiano, he had said: "This shall his passage to the blacke lake further,/ The last good deed hee did, he pardon'd murther" (V, ii, 81–2). But, for Brachiano, the "lease of your life" (V, ii, 73) which he had given to Flamineo was not a further sign of his wickedness but a true act of charity, one which he believes a charitable world should award to him as well. Nor is the punishment which he now receives for his murder of Isabella motivated by the demands of justice:

    Lod. Why now our action's justified.
    Fra. Tush for Justice!
What harmes it Justice? we now, like the partridge,
Purge the disease with lawrell: for the fame
Shall crowne the enterprise and quit the shame. (V, iii,
    275–80)

If murder is a "sad accident" (V, ii, 71), revenge for murder, whether by individuals or legally constituted authority, is a graver fault. So does Brachiano's charity rise above the greater brutality of his world only to be defeated by it. But, if the meaner counsels of the world will not suffer his charity, it can still find its own reward in that love which gave it being. As his death approaches, he rises to a magnanimous care of his beloved which equals that of Antony and Desdemona: "Do not kisse me, for I shall poyson thee." The fact of death, rather than destroying, only floods his consciousness with gratitude towards Vittoria, that "good woman," for whose love the loss of "infinite worlds . . . were too little."

But, though Worldly Love has "such a covenant 'tweene the world and it,/ They're loath to breake," it has no covenant with death. Not being "a dateless bargain to engrossing death," as engrossing death displaces the "integrity of life," so does it displace the love to which it is bound. As the poisonous fumes attack his "braine and heart," Brachiano cannot attend to the voices that come to him from life but only to the deathly pains which are consuming the last vestiges of his spirit:

> *Vit.* I am lost for ever.
> *Brac.* How miserable a thing it is to die,
> 'Mongst women howling! What are those? *Fla.* Franciscans.
> They have brought the extreame unction.
> *Bra.* On paine of death, let no man name death to me,
> It is a word infinitely terrible. . . .
> What's hee? *Fla.* A Divine my Lord.
> *Bra.* Hee will bee drunke: Avoid him: th' argument
> Is fearfull when Church-men stagger in't (V, iii, 35-40,
>   117-22)

Though he could accept death as the price of his love's worldly fulfillment while his spirit was whole, with its progressive destruction all else becomes irrelevant beside this terrible power of death. And soon this too becomes irrelevant. He has slipped over to the other side, and as he looks through death's eyes at the world to which his "strong heart" had been so recently bound, he sees the vanity of life. But most fearful is the corrupt hypocrisy of the church, which instead of comforting man betrays his dying hopes.

The Franciscans who have come to give Brachiano extreme unction prove to be his murderers in disguise, and it is through them that Webster reveals the final mockery of Christian consolation:

> *Lod.* Pray give us leave; *Attende Domine Brachiane—*
> *Fla.* See, see, how firmely hee doth fixe his eye
> Upon the Crucifix. *Vit.* O hold it constant.
> It settles his wild spirits; . . .
> [*Heare the rest being departed Lodovico and Gasparo discover themselves.*]
> *Lod.* Devill Brachiano;
> Thou are damn'd. *Gas.* Perpetually. . . .
> *Lod.* And thou shalt die like a poore rogue. *Gas.* And stinke
> Like a dead flie-blowne dog.
> *Lod.* And be forgotten before thy funerall sermon.
> *Bra.* Vittoria! Vittoria! *Lod.* O the cursed devill,
> Come to himselfe againe! Wee are undone.
> [*Enter Vittoria and the attendants.*]
> *Gas.* Strangle him in private. What! will you call him
> againe
> To live in treble torments? for charitie,
> For Christian charitie, avoid the chamber. [*Exeunt.*]
> *Lod.* You would prate, Sir. This is a true-love knot
> Sent from the Duke of Florence. [*Brachiano is strangled.*]
> (V, iii, 130–6, 150–51, 167–76)

Though the word "charity" appears throughout the play, it is only in connection with this black mass that the phrase "Christian charitie" is used. Christian charity can only be a perversion "when Church'men stagger in't." Nor can the crucifix settle Brachiano's "wild spirits" when it has fallen into the power of uncharitable men. It is, rather, their brutality, greater even than that of death, that restores him from the insanity of death's vision. Seeking to escape man's inhumanity, he remembers the one source from which his former rescue from despair had come: Vittoria. Only she can save him from the torments alike of life and death. "Come

to himselfe againe" for one last moment, his restored sovereignty
affirms the value of her who had fulfilled it; and in his final call
to her, his love triumphs over the power of hate. If death shall
reduce him to the level of a "flie-blowne dog," his life had a
nobler fulfillment.

His death, however, robs their love of its saving power.
Brachiano goes to a death, Vittoria to a life, from which there
can be no rescue:

> *Omn.* Rest to his soule.
> *Vit.* O mee! this place is hell.
> [*Fra.*] How heavily shee takes it. *Fla.* O yes, yes;
> Had women navigable rivers in their eies
> They would dispend them all; (V, iii, 181–5)

Again the loss of love brings Vittoria to tears, and it is Francisco,
who had pitied Brachiano even while he sent him "a true-love
knot," who realizes the true profundity of her grief. Once again
her response is accompanied by a rejection of suicide and the
resolve to "go weeping to heaven." Finding her at her private
devotions, Flamineo informs her of his vow to Brachiano that
"Neither your selfe, nor I should out-live him,/ The numbring
of foure howers" (V, vi, 35–6). But Vittoria easily penetrates
the deception: "This is your melancholy and dispaire" (V, vi, 43).
Vittoria neither believes that her love requires her to join Brachiano in death, nor accepts the idea that he might have wished
it. He who had said, "Do not kisse me, for I shall poyson thee,"
would have desired her to find the strength to outlive him.
Whatever Brachiano's shortcomings, he, like all of Webster's
characters, is totally devoid of narcissism. He would never reduce her individuality to that of a possessed thing because it
was his respect for the value of her existence that enabled her
love to fulfill his own sovereign being. Though his death is "infinitely terrible" to both of them, they are both agreed that she
must be left to live, however terrible such a life may be. It is
this conviction of the enduring value of life, even when all
other values have forsaken it, that informs her reply to Flamineo:

Are you growne an Atheist? will you turne your body,
Which is the goodly pallace of the soule
To the soules slaughter house?
. . . forsake that which was made for Man,
The world, to sinke to that was made for devils,
Eternall darkenesse. . . . I prethee yet remember,
Millions are now in graves, which at last day
Like Mandrakes shall rise shreeking. (V, vi, 57–68)

The religion that sustains Vittoria in her moments of desolation is, as was suggested earlier, of a very personalized nature. It accepts from Christianity only that which can be assimilated by her deeper convictions: the sanctity of one's own life and the moral obligation to seek its fulfillment in this world. Her curse to Monticelso, "That the last day of judgement may so find you,/ And leave you the same devill you were before" (III, ii, 290–1), is attended by no fear that the last day of judgment will find her so. But if the day of judgment finds her free of sin, it will not be presided over by the God of Christianity, for to Christianity murder is still a sin and can be redeemed only by repentance. It is not merely that she has an "innocence-resembling boldness," as Charles Lamb noted, but that she fully considers herself to be innocent, innocent in her own eyes and in the eyes of her God.

Flamineo, on the other hand, does feel a guilty remorse but cannot accept the reality of a God to whom he might make atonement. Earlier he had said:

I have a strange thing in mee, to th' which
I cannot give a name, without it bee
Compassion. . . .
And sometimes, when my face was full of smiles,
Have felt the mase of conscience in my brest. . . .
Pray, Sir, resolve mee, what religions best   [*Enter*
For a man to die in? or is it in your knowledge   *Brachiano's*
To answere mee how long I have to live?   *Ghost.]*
That's the most necessarie question. (V, iv, 107–9, 114–5,
    122–5)

Faced with the uncertainty of death, his conclusion comes close to that of Vittoria in its final affirmation of the sufficient value of life. In *The Devil's Law-Case*, Webster was to assert this conclusion even more emphatically:

> *Capuchin.* Pray tell me, do not you meditate of death?
> *Romelio.* Phew, I tooke out that Lesson,
> When I once lay sicke of an Ague: I doe now
> Labour for life, for life! . . .
> Who has hired you to make me Coward?
>   *Cap.* I would make you
> A good Christian.
>   *Rom.* Withall, let me continue
> An honest man, which I am very certaine,
> A coward can never be; (*DLC,* V, iv, 60–3, 74–9)

The prospect of death only convinces Flamineo—as it had Romelio—that "the most necessarie" answer is not to be "a good Christian" but to "labour for life" with undaunted courage. Perhaps, for Flamineo as well as herself, Vittoria has found "what religions best for a man to die in," at least in Webster's world. For as Flamineo faces death he is finally converted to the religion of life that had motivated all of Vittoria's efforts:

> I am ith way to study a long silence,
> To prate were idle, I remember nothing.
> Thers nothing of so infinit vexation
> As mans owne thoughts. . . . I doe not looke
> Who went before, nor who shall follow mee;
> Noe, at my selfe I will begin and end.
> "While we looke up to heaven wee confound
> "Knowledge with knowledge. ô I am in a mist. . . .
> 'Tis well yet there's some goodnesse in my death,
> My life was a blacke charnell: I have c[a]ught
> An everlasting could. I have lost my voice
> Most irrecoverably: Farewell glorious villaines, . . . (V, vi,
>   204–7, 256–60, 269–72)

He now rejects the importance of such questions as he had asked Brachiano's ghost, questions which had been of such "infinit vexation" to him. No longer confounded by the fruitless attempt to search the heavens for meaning, he ends by affirming the sufficient meaning of his own existence. Beyond this there is only "a long silence . . . in a mist." It is this final conviction of the value of his life that transmutes the negation of satire into an affirmation which uniquely combines the tragic vision with an exalted humor. Whereas his earlier satire was humorless, his tragic acceptance of the value of life releases the healthy spontaneity of feeling which enables him to "laugh" (V, vi, 195) and to love: "Th'art a noble sister,/ I love thee now" (V, vi, 241–2). Bidding a gay farewell, he demands an exalted tribute to the passing of his nobility: "Strike thunder, and strike lowde to my farewell" (V, vi, 276).

Although Flamineo faces death with a courage equal to Vittoria's, he cannot, like her, look back upon a life well spent; nor can he relate the behavior that faces death to that which had faced the equally despairing prospect of life:

> Behold Brachiano, I that while you liv'd
> Did make a flaming Altar of my heart
> To sacrifice unto you . . . Now am ready
> To sacrifice heart and all. (V, vi, 84–7)

Though Vittoria had expressed this in a dramatic context,[7] which might make it suspect, it genuinely conveyed her conviction that the religion of life must be based upon a passionate devotion to love. Integrity can provide "crutches" for this faith, but only love can give it sound support. Though Flamineo finally does feel "compassion" for his brother and mother, and "love" for Vittoria, it has come too late to permit him anything but a thorough repudiation of his former life: "My life was a blacke charnell." When death becomes an inescapable reality to Vittoria, however, she *is* "ready to sacrifice heart and all" for the love that had brought fulfillment to her life.

Nevertheless, Worldly Love places no premium on death.

Not only will Vittoria not commit suicide but she tries to evade death as long as she can do so without violating her integrity. As she tried to outwit Flamineo's apparently lethal designs, so does she try to win pardon from her murderers:

> *Vit.* O your gentle pitty. . .
> *Cas.* Your hope deceives you. (V, vi, 184, 187)

Like Cleopatra, Vittoria will not resign herself to death until she has tried all honorable means to avoid it. When her appeal for charity is rejected, however, she is ready to accept death, sorry only that the means must be so ignoble: "If Florence be ith Court, would hee would kill mee!" (V, vi, 188). But if the means are base, her own nobility will transcend them:

> *Lod.* O thou hast bin a most prodigious comet,
> But Ile cut of[f] your traine: kill the Moore first.
> *Vit.* You shall not kill her first. behould my breast,
> I will be waited on in death; my servant
> Shall never go before mee. *Gas.* Are you so brave?
> *Vit.* Yes I shall wellcome death
> As Princes doe some great Embassadors;
> Ile meete thy weapon halfe way. *Lod.* Thou dost tremble,
> Mee thinkes feare should dissolve thee into ayre.
> *Vit.* O thou art deceiv'd, I am to[o] true a woman:
> Conceit can never kill me: Ile tell thee what,
> I will not in my death shed one base teare,
> Or if looke pale, for want of blood, not feare.
> . . . *[They strike.]* 'Twas a manly blow,
> The next thou giv'st, murder some sucking Infant,
> And then thou wilt be famous. . . .
> My soule, like to a ship in a blacke storme,
> Is driven I know not whither. (V, vi, 215–27, 233–5, 248–9)

Whether or not her desire to "be waited on in death" results from Webster's direct imitation of the death of Shakespeare's Cleopatra, the parallel is significant. If her life as a duchess has been tragically curtailed, she will nonetheless die, "as Princes doe," sovereign to the last. She meets her final trial as she did the earlier, scorning tears, asserting that they are "deceiv'd," who consider her bravery to be counterfeit, and affirming her true innocence. Perhaps the greatest tribute to Vittoria is that she confounds our moral "conceit," that her noble consistency to her vision of righteousness baffles our normal judgment and forces the admission that we also "know not whither" she goes.

This moral ambiguity is a product of Webster's own despair; but as its intensity waned, he was able to readmit the importance of other values besides a fulfillment for which murder could be condoned. It was only when Webster had progressed to this point, however, that he could celebrate Worldly Love in its most humane aspect. In his next tragedy, he arrived at that healthier manifestation of Worldly Love that Shakespeare also achieved in his second tragedy of Worldly Love; but he arrived there by a different route, by the route back from despair. In the spiritual world which Webster first inhabited, it was not the demands of sovereignty that could infect the health of Worldly Love but the fact that there were no other values to which the lovers could pay even partial tribute. "Passionately met in this sad world," they reject the validity of any claims that might obstruct the meeting in which alone they can find value. Their despair in all other worldly values produces an amoral devotion to their love which places them beyond good and evil. In a world divided between wolves and sheep, they will not relinquish their only hope of good through sheepish acquiescence but adopt wolfish tactics to preserve their love from the attacking wolves. They inhabit a middle ground between the pathetic weakness of the sheep and the uninspired strength of the wolves. If their renunciation of weakness causes them to lose the goodness of the sheep, their evil strength, unlike that of the wolves, is partially redeemed by the love that has enabled them to wrest some fulfillment from a world of despair.

If the second pattern began with a disillusionment in the value of an isolated preservation of sovereignty, the third pattern moves beyond disillusionment to despair. While the lovers of the second pattern are reckless with regard to their own

property and position, the lovers of the third pattern are crimin-
ally disregardful of the lives and property of others. They are so
desperately in need of the fulfillment of love, so totally scornful
of any other value, that they overcome all obstructions to their
love. In this they are exactly opposed to the courtly lovers, who
require obstruction for the intensification of passion. Where the
second type of worldly lover risked the flagrant overcoming
of societal censure as an obstruction to his love, the third type
acts to destroy the obstructions in his path. As the primary
obstruction in the plays that fall within this category is the
husband of the beloved, the lovers murder the husband and
for this are themselves destroyed. Whereas the lover of the first
type had murdered his beloved to preserve a sovereignty he
feared was imperiled by his love, the lovers of the third type
murder that their sovereign natures may be completed by the
communion of love. Like the lovers of the second type, they
think that in love they can find or create a shared meaning
which is impossible for either alone. The lovers of the second
and third types approach love more or less desperately and are
willing to defy or destroy any obstruction that stands in the
way of the only self-fulfillment which retains a meaning for
them. But these obstructions may have valid claims for consideration that will eventually arise to undermine the foundations of the love. In being pressed too hard for inspiration, this
love proves inadequate and becomes corrupt. The corruption
may enter into the very fabric of the love and cause fights and
recriminations, or it may impair the ability to preserve a love
so dearly won from outside attack. Though the attitudes of lovers
in the second and third categories are basically similar, there
is an important difference in degree, both of desperation and its
consequent corruption of love, in that lovers of the third type
will murder anyone who stands in the way of their love's fulfillment. Though disillusioned with the rewards of sovereignty,
they still presume upon their sovereign rights; in fact, they have
become hardened to any value that is opposed to the satisfaction
of their sovereign will through love. Where disillusionment has
weakened the second category of worldly lovers, despair has
hardened lovers of the third type. The examples of this third

type of worldly lover in addition to Brachiano and Vittoria, are Alice Arden, in *Arden of Feversham;* George Browne, in *A Warning for Fair Women;* Bianca Capello and the Duke of Florence, in *Women Beware Women;* and De Flores, in *The Changeling.* But Brachiano, and also the Duke of Florence, go beyond the other examples of this pattern in the final flowering of their love into a healthier generosity of spirit.

In *The Duchess of Malfi* Webster develops this final growth of Brachiano's spirit into a vision of compassionate love which, in its greater universality, transcends even Shakespeare's triumphant affirmation of Worldly Love. Although Webster's tragedies cannot compare with Shakespeare's in dramatic brilliance, it is in his hands that Worldly Love moves beyond the confines of love tragedy and even, as in the case of *Othello,* beyond the deeper consideration of personal good and evil to become the basis of a major orientation toward the relation of man to the universe.

11

The Compassionate Vision of The Duchess of Malfi

The inhospitable features of the rocky Amalfi coastline form a fitting setting for Webster's final tragic vision. If the tone of *The White Devil* seemed to issue from the despairing cry of a drowning man, that of *The Duchess of Malfi* seems to come from one who has survived the raging seas only to be shipwrecked on just such a coast. After the passionate struggle to survive despair, the shipwrecked has only such force left to "save my selfe by halves" (V, iii, 62).[1] In "this gloomy world" (V, v, 124), even the most noble Duchess fears to "venture all this poore remainder/ In one unlucky bottom" (III, v, 71–2). Though she says, "if all my royall kindred/ Lay in my way unto this marriage:/ I'll'd make them my low foote-steps" (I, i, 382–4), she is not a Brachiano to mount the bodies that would oppose the public proclamation of her choice. But that very lack of despair which allows her to take her compromising course also insures its greater moral health. Virtue replaces *virtu*, though it accompanies but a "poore remainder" of the splendid vitality that had animated her sister, Vittoria. For, as Leech has shown,[2] the Duchess is the true sister of Vittoria rather than of Isabella. Her virtue does not spring from self-denial but from a sovereign nature that even to her death would be "Duchesse of Malfy still" (IV,

ii, 139). It is, indeed, from this need to preserve her sovereignty
in love that her tragedy springs, hers a true tragedy of Worldly
Love.

Cariola pinpoints the source of the Duchess' tragedy when
she says:

> Whether the spirit of greatnes, or of woman
> Raigne most in her, I know not, but it shewes
> A fearfull madnes. I owe her much of pitty. (I, i, 576–8)

The Duchess' "fearefull madnes" lies in her desire to fulfill both
the claims of her greatness and of her femininity. A sovereign
with true nobility of spirit, she is yet a woman who, as a woman,
asks:

> Why should onely I,
> Of all the other Princes of the World
> Be cas' de-up, like a holy Relique? I have youth,
> And a litle beautie. (III, ii, 160–3)

The vital promptings of her youth and beauty demand as much
expression as does her "spirit of greatnes." Her longing is not,
however, for a "great romance," an overwhelming passion, but,
more poignantly, for a return to simplicity in which she can
"let her hair down." Significantly enough, in the one scene in
which we see the happily married couple she literally does just
that. Nor does she wish to make a life of love; rather she wishes
to find, through love, the peace and harmony that can revitalize
and strengthen her spirit to meet the more varied demands of
the full life she is healthy enough to desire. Since the spirit of
greatness and of woman reign equally in her, and since society
will only allow her to achieve greatness if she yields the right
to domestic happiness, she resolves upon a more daring course,
like Antonio, to "save my selfe by halves." She will be both
sovereign by day and secret wife by night. Her courage, that
"fearefull madnes" for which Cariola owes "her much of pitty,"
resides in permitting herself under such circumstances to love

at all. Aware of the dangers in her unconventional course—"I am going into a wildernesse,/ Where I shall find nor path, nor friendly clewe/ To be my guide" (I, i, 404–6)—she nonetheless "wincked, and chose a husband" (I, i, 390).

But it is the Duchess' misfortune to have such healthy desires in a sick society. Her two brothers, who represent society's repressive definition of woman's role in its most extreme form, are inwardly unsound. Of the Cardinal, Antonio says: "Some such flashes superficially hang on him, for forme: but observe his inward Character: he is a mellancholly Churchman" (I, i, 157–9). Of Ferdinand, Antonio adds that he has "a most perverse, and turbulent Nature—/ What appears in him mirth, is meerely outside" (I, i, 169–70). The superficial bravado of the Aragonian brethren hides an inner melancholy which, in the case of Ferdinand, bears the seeds of future madness. And, indeed, an all-pervasive melancholy seems to hang over the "gloomy world" of Amalfi. Antonio observes that Bosola is diseased by it: "This foule mellancholly/ Will poyson all his goodnesse" (I, i, 77–8). Even Antonio, for all his rational clarity, is not altogether free of it: "My banishment, feeding my mellancholly,/ Would often reason thus" (I, i, 453–4). In *The White Devil*, Francisco had one moment of real melancholy while planning his sister's revenge, and Flamineo had need after his sister's disgrace to *feign* melancholy. But here melancholy is a persistent state of mind. The hearty vitality which—whether for love or revenge—could murder without a qualm and glory when the deed was done has vanished, leaving scruple in its wake, scruple, which forces the best to save themselves only "by halves" and the worst to bring both their enemies and then themselves "by degrees to mortification" (IV, ii, 179). In that "miserable age" (I, i, 33) when vitality seems to have made a general retreat, leaving men standing "like dead wals, or vaulted graves" (V, v, 121), it is only the Duchess who has miraculously retained both her cheer and a healthy awareness of her "flesh, and blood" (I, i, 519). But just barely.

Before the Duchess' entrance, satire has painted for us a picture of the general corruption of the age; but both the malicious satire of Bosola and that of the more judicious Antonio ring hollowly beside the Duchess' hearty cheer. To her brothers' ominous warnings against marriage, she replies: "I thinke this speech betweene you both was studied,/ It came so roundly off" (I, i, 367–8). It is in this spirit of undaunted vitality and cheer that she "wincked, and chose a husband." And nowhere is this spirit better revealed than in her efforts to fire the enthusiasm of the man she has chosen:

> You doe tremble:
> Make not your heart so dead a peece of flesh
> To feare, more than to love me: Sir, be confident,
> What is't distracts you? This is flesh, and blood, (Sir,)
> 'Tis not the figure cut in Allablaster
> Kneeles at my husbands tombe: Awake, awake, (man) . . . (I, i, 516–21)

She has much need for these labors; with all his rational integrity, Antonio is "so dead a peece of flesh" that he is better suited to be an onlooker than an active participant in life. Indeed, he has already indicated his emotional sterility on the main point: "Say a man never marry, nor have children,/ What takes that from him?" (I, i, 456–7). Though he had adored her from afar, the flame of his devotion was quite cold. Her efforts to awaken the man in him only lead to still another scruple on his part: "But for your Brothers?" (I, i, 535). *Her* scruples extended only to not owning her marriage; his, to not marrying at all. But to scruples that would prevent the full realization of her potential for living, she will not attend:

> Do not thinke of them,
> All discord, without this circumference,   *[She puts her arms*
> Is onely to be pittied, and not fear'd: *about him.]*
> Yet, should they know it, time will easily
> Scatter the tempest. (I, i, 536–40)

Her tragic error lies not in choosing to love but in overestimating the ability of a hostile world to accept her vision of moral health. Though her brothers are to be pitied, they are also to be feared; and if refusal to let fear prevent the fullest living be noble, to underestimate the threat is "a fearefull madnes."

Her vision of moral health through love is not, however, a vision of passion but of harmony. Love provides a sphere of harmony in a world of "discord." If ever there was a love that could be disassociated from lust, it is that of the Duchess: "We'll onely lie, and talke together, and plot/ T'appease my humorous kindred" (I, i, 570–1). Antonio's rational coldness does not bar the way to love but is actually the ground on which a stable harmony can be built, a harmony so firm that it can extend itself outward in the effort to "appease" external "discord." Here Webster suggests a new definiton of Worldly Love, a communion based upon mutual respect whose result is a harmony in which the sensuous and the rational are fused. To "lie, and talke together" might not have appealed to Brachiano and Vittoria, but it is for this new vision of love's fulfillment that the Duchess is willing to pay the ultimate price.

Against the Duchess' vision of love, however, Webster now counterpoints Bosola's question: "What thing is in this outward forme of man/ To be belov'd?" (II, i, 47–8). If Antonio had questioned the wisdom of giving expression to his love and of bearing children in such a world, he never went so far as to deny the possibility of love itself; and it was his love that finally allowed the Duchess to override his scruples to such a point that, in his wedding vows, he can pray "That we may imitate the loving Palmes/ (Best Embleme of a peacefull marriage)/ That nev'r bore fruite devided" (I, i, 555–7). In Bosola, however, we meet a total incapacity for love, a sense of the world's corruption so great that it makes contact with another human body repulsive. It is between the Duchess and Bosola that the dialectic of the play takes form: between her belief that it is only through love that life can achieve its fullest meaning and his sense of the meaninglessness of love. In *The White Devil*, Webster presented this same conflict of vision in the persons of Vittoria and Flamineo, but there Flamineo merely hovered about the lovers, surrounding them with a barrage of degrading comments. In his second play, Webster makes the conflict more dramatically effective by turning the voice antagonistic to love into a dramatic agent whose function it is to defeat the Duchess' love.

Antonio has, indeed, become converted to the joys of "peace-full marriage." This is nowhere better seen than in his later advice to Cariola: "O fie upon this single life: forgoe it:/ We read how Daphne, for her peevish [f]light/ Became a fruitlesse Bay-tree" (III, ii, 31–3). But with all this new accent on fertility, his is a strange marriage:

> *Duch.* Why should not we bring up that fashion?
> 'Tis ceremony more then duty, that consists
> In the remooving of a peece of felt:
> Be you the example to the rest o'th' Court,
> Put on your hat first.
>   *Ant.* You must pardon me:
> I have seene, in colder countries then in France,
> Nobles stand bare to th'Prince; and the distinction
> M[e] thought show'd reverently. (II, i, 126–34)

The Duchess, big with his child, wishes somehow to mitigate his subservience to her by day; but it is just this refusal of his to presume in public upon his private prerogatives that makes him such an admirably suited husband for the Duchess. This very weakness which, when circumstances seem propitious, al-lows his strange marriage to be peaceful, renders him incapable, however, of protecting his marriage with sufficient vigor and resourcefulness when it is threatened. When the Duchess falls into premature labor, this fatal lack is first revealed. Collapsing before the first threat of danger, he is not only incapable of con-ceiving the very simple plan that Delio suggests but almost unable even to put it into effect. Rather than act, he stands "lost in amazement" (II, i, 195).

These positive and negative sides of his weakness are again revealed in the scene that shows their marriage by night. This scene takes place some years later, the Duchess having borne two other children in the interim. Knowledge of her children, coming to Ferdinand through Bosola, has brought Ferdinand to his sister's castle. The Duchess and Antonio, seeing that "The Lord Ferdinand . . . Doth beare himselfe right dangerously" (III, i, 21–2) have greater cause for tension than ever before; yet even this cannot dampen the joyous comfort that they still find in each other:

> *Dutch.* Bring me the Casket hither, and the Glasse;
> You get no lodging here, to-night (my Lord.)
> *Ant.* Indeed, I must perswade one: . . .
> *Duch.* Must? you are a Lord of Misse-rule.
> *Ant.* Indeed, my Rule is onely in the night. . . .
> *Car.* Wherefore still when you lie with my Lady
> Doe you rise so early?
> *Ant.* Labouring men
> Count the Clocke oftnest Cariola,
> Are glad when their task's ended.
> *Duch.* I'll stop your mouth. *[Kisses him.]*
> *Ant.* Nay, that's but one, Venus had two soft Doves
> To draw her Chariot: I must have another: . . . *[Kisses her.]*
>   (III, ii, 1–3, 9–10, 21–8)

If Antonio's raillery betrays any dissatisfaction with his position, a kiss from his wife is enough to quiet him and cause him to desire only more of the same. While she, in her turn, can desire no other than such an ardently compliant husband. Yet their conjugal joy does not have its source in passion but in their easy companionship. When, combing her graying hair amid this happy banter, the Duchess asks, "I pre-thee/ When were we so merry?" (III, ii, 60–1), the fulfillment of this peaceful marriage is complete.

Talking gaily to herself while Antonio and Cariola steal from the room to chaff her, she suddenly turns to see the grimly armed Ferdinand:

> 'Tis welcome:
> For know whether I am doomb'd to live, or die,
> I can doe both like a Prince. (III, ii, 77–9)

Though she had winked at danger, this firm commitment to her chosen life was always with her and rises immediately to the fore when called upon. She can die "like a Prince" because she has had the courage to live like one, even in love fulfilling rather than yielding her sovereignty.

Far different is the response of Antonio:

> . . . how came he hither? I should turne   [*He points the*
> This, to thee, for that. . . .   *pistol at Cariola.*]
> I would this terrible thing would come againe,
> That (standing on my Guard) I might relate
> My warrantable love: . . . (III, ii, 168–9, 174–7)

Remaining concealed while Ferdinand shouted irrational curses at him, he reenters, brandishing his pistol after the danger has passed, only to release his impotent rage against the innocent, defenseless Cariola. Even his "warrantable love" cannot stir "so dead a peece of flesh" to self-originated action. He can accept the position the Duchess has made for him, but it is her strength of mind that must preserve it.

And yet it is this man that the Duchess has chosen with a firm commitment which nothing can alter. If Webster makes his deficiencies all too obvious, the Duchess winks at them, too, rather than betray her love. Where Vittoria and Desdemona rebuke their lovers for their faults, the Duchess never judges Antonio. Her sympathetic acceptance extends even to his frailties, and though objective eyes deem him her inferior, his years of humble devotion deserve no less. She had chosen an inferior though good man rather than "Be cas'd-up, like a holy Relique." If the years of happiness he has given her are to have a tragic end, she will hold no one responsible for this but herself. Toward him she feels so true a gratitude that beside it his faults are nothing.

Her tragic error lies, however, in just this evasion of the whole truth, in winking at all that would obscure her clear perception of the good. It was tragic blindness that made her believe: "All discord, without this circumference,/ Is onely to be pittied, and not fear'd." A charmed circle it was for her, for within its magic confines she found a cheerful peace which was beyond even the imagination of the discordant outside world; but it held no virtue against the unbeliever. It is the incaution bred of this blindness that proves her undoing in the fatal interview with Bosola.

Thinking that she had cleverly covered her traces by dismissing Antonio in public disgrace, she was not prepared for the righteous indignation of the malcontent Bosola. But if she was unprepared for his reaction, he was as unprepared for hers:

> *Bos.* Both his vertue, and forme, deserv'd a farre better
> fortune:
> His discourse rather delighted to judge it selfe, then shew
> it selfe.
> His breast was fill'd with all perfection,
> And yet it seem'd a private whispring roome.
> It made so little noyse of't. . . .
> *Duch.* Oh, you render me excellent Musicke.
> *Bos.* Say you?
> *Duch.* This good one that you speake of, is my husband.
> *Bos.* Do I not dreame? Can this ambitious age
> Have so much goodnes in't, as to prefer
> A man, meerely for worth: without these shadowes
> Of wealth and painted honors? possible?
> *Duch.* I have had three children by him.
> *Bos.* Fortunate Lady,
> For you have made your private nuptiall bed
> The humble, and faire Seminary of peace,
> No question but: . . . (III, ii, 294–98, 315–26)

Bosola's "Character" of Antonio is meant to be taken as an objective portrait. We see in it the unassuming if weak virtue that has enabled the Duchess' marriage to him to be "The humble, and faire Seminary of peace." Hearing her own partial vision of him so unexpectedly echoed from the discordant outside world dispels all caution and causes her to place her confidence in Bosola. Again the Duchess has had eyes only for the good, for Bosola's

enthusiasm for Antonio is as genuine as his reasons for expressing it are dubious. The malcontent *is* a true lover of virtue,
though a disenchanted lover who has been too often betrayed
to trust the appearances of good. Loving the good with distrust
has given him eyes only for the evil which distorts and degrades
the goodness his best self would worship. The Duchess' dismissal
of Antonio had fired his usual wrath against the abuse of goodness. But, just as this "excellent Musicke" had unexpectedly caused
the Duchess to embrace his confidence, so does her confidence
momentarily confute his prejudices. If he suspected the Duchess
of "cunning" (II, ii, 206) in dismissing Antonio, he never suspected the true nature of their relationship, a relationship which
is impossible in terms of his vision of life. In his questioning
speech, we see him hesitatingly confronting a new realm of moral
possibility which he unexpectedly resolves in the affirmative:
"No question but." He sees and embraces a realized goodness
that he had not even dared to "dream . . . possible." But this
momentary vision is not strong enough to dispel the prejudices
of a lifetime which have taught him to trust nothing but the
evil which cannot betray. As Antonio has said of him: "You
would looke up to Heaven, but I thinke/ The Divell, that rules
i'th'aire, stands in your light" (II, i, 97–8). So, having given
best counsel to the Duchess, he resolves:

> . . . what rests, but I reveale
> All to my Lord? oh, this base quality
> Of Intelligencer! why, every Quality i'th'world
> Preferres but gaine, or commendation: . . . (III, ii, 374–7)

Hating that "base quality" in himself that hurries him on to
what he most deplores, the betrayal of the good, he justifies
himself by reasserting the just disproven fact that "every Quality
i'th'world" is equally base. In the thematic conflict between the
visions of the Duchess and of Bosola, both have won a partial
victory. Though Bosola has betrayed the Duchess' truth, his own
vision has been momentarily shattered and its pieces insecurely
refitted into the old frame.

But if the Duchess' behavior has disturbed Bosola's vision of evil, Bosola's betrayal has caused a reciprocal enlargement of her awareness. "Banish'd Ancona" (III, v, 1), and helplessly awaiting her fate, the Duchess finally sees that truth which she had before so futilely "wincked" away:

> *Duch.* Me thought I wore my Coronet of State,
> And on a sudaine all the Diamonds
> Were chang'd to Pearles.
> *Ant.* My Interpretation
> Is, you'll weepe shortly, for to me, the pearles
> Doe signifie your teares:
> *Duch.* The Birds, that live i'th field
> On the wilde benefit of Nature, live
> Happier then we; for they may choose their Mates
> And carroll their sweet pleasures to the Spring: . . . (III,
> v, 17–28)

The "diamonds" in her "Coronet of State" result in "teares" because they signify the vast gulf between her isolating sovereignty and the happier birds whose life she had vainly imagined she could imitate. If Bosola imagined himself to be dreaming when he learned of the Duchess' marriage, it was because the Duchess had been living in a dream to imagine that life could permit her such happiness. Now she begins to emerge from this dream. Thinking that safety may be possible through separation —"Let us not venture all this poor remainder/ In one unlucky bottom." (II, v, 71–2)—she yet reflects:

> I know not which is best,
> To see you dead, or part with you: Farewell Boy.
> Thou art happy, that thou hast not understanding
> To know thy misery: For all our wit
> And reading, brings us to a truer sence
> Of sorrow: In the eternall Church, Sir
> I doe hope we shall not part thus. (III, v, 79–85)

Like her young son, she too had been happy when she lacked understanding of the true misery of her position. But even with this understanding, the thought of parting with Antonio seems almost more painful than the death she is trying to protect him from. Though life may not permit her such love, she loves. And it is just this impossible conviction of the ultimate goodness of love that now causes her, as life brings her "to a truer sence/ Of sorrow," to project an ideal order in which they may "carroll their sweet pleasures to the Spring." Though she had not allowed the earthly church to obstruct the fulfillment of her love—"How can the Church build faster?" (I, i, 562); "Thou art a superstitious foole" (III, ii, 67)—she now gains a vision of an "eternall Church" in which such fulfillment will be granted. The Duchess' religious consolation springs from the same source as will Ferdinand's, a sense of life's sorrow so great that sanity can only be maintained, or in Ferdinand's case regained, by the ability to "vault credit, and affect high pleasures,/ Beyond death" (V, v, 86–7). If this is a final, albeit sublime, manifestation of the Duchess' ability to evade a starker reality, its source lies in her continuing conviction that the absolute goodness of love must be given fulfillment. But alongside this sublime affirmation of the rightness of her love remains the tragic awareness that in reaching for it she went beyond her given portion: "And yet (O Heaven) thy heavy hand is in't" (III, v, 92).

It is, however, her recognition that the ultimate contradiction within her nature cannot be resolved "by halves," and her unwillingness to forego either demand of her nature, that causes her final disillusionment with life. The belief that life would permit this total fulfillment had given her the necessary cheer to seek some realization of her dream. With the destruction of her charmed circle, she becomes a prey to the surrounding melancholia, but still a unique prey: "Her mellancholly seemes to be fortifide/ With a strange disdaine" (IV, i, 12–3). Though the supposed deaths of her loved ones have made "this world a tedious Theatre" (IV, i, 99), she curses the fact that it is so:

> *Duch.* I could curse the Starres.
> *Bos.* O fearefull!
> *Duch.* And those three smyling seasons of the yeere
> Into a Russian winter: nay, the world

To its first Chaos.
 Bos. Looke you, the Starres shine still: IV, i, 115–20)

If she curses the world, it is because a world that does not permit that peculiarly worldly fulfillment which she deemed her due would make more sense if it were truly a chaos. If she curses the stars, it is because they can shine so implacably down upon her tragedy, which is also the world's.

But however great her disillusionment with the world, there is still something within her that defies all Ferdinand's attempts "to bring her to despaire" (IV, i, 140). She "nobly" (IV, i, 3) endures even the swirling chorus of madmen:

> *Cari.* Yes, but you shall live
> To shake this durance off. *Duch.* Thou art a foole,
> The Robin red-brest, and the Nightingale,
> Never live long in cages. (IV, ii, 13–6)

The difference between her fate and that of the happier birds is that they live "On the wilde benefit of Nature" (III, v, 26) while she must depend upon the "charity" of man:

> *Bos.* Your brothers meane you safety, and pitie.
> *Duch.* Pitie!
> With such a pitie man preserve alive
> Pheasants, and Quailes, when they are not fat enough
> To be eaten. (III, v, 128–32)

Caught between the opposing forces of society and nature, it is with "compassionate nature" (IV, i, 43) that she identifies herself. But perhaps, for Webster, man's tragedy lies precisely in his necessary alienation from "compassionate nature." [3] Though the Duchess tried to bridge the gap, she was "Duchesse of Malfy still." To her had been given the splendor of a lonely sovereignty. Her futile attempt to claim her right to a simple woman's happiness had only led to this awareness of the inevitable "cage" that must forever separate her from "the wilde benefit of Nature." If the attempt only made her vulnerable to her brothers' lack of charity, it was because her "Coronet of State," with all its grief, could never be truly renounced.

She turns from thoughts of the cage to surmises about an afterlife. This turn of thought does not signify her hopes for release from her personal sovereignty, but for release from a life that prevents the full realization of both individuality and of relatedness:

> *Duch.* Do'st thou thinke we shall know one another,
> In th' other world? *Cari.* Yes, out of question.
>   *Duch.* O that it were possible we might
> But hold some two dayes conference with the dead,
> From them, I should learne somewhat, I am sure
> I never shall know here: I'll tell thee a miracle—
> I am not mad yet, to my cause of sorrow.
> Th'heaven ore my head, seemes make of molt[e]n brasse,
> The earth of flaming sulphure, yet I am not mad: . . .
>   (IV, ii, 20–8)

The afterlife for which she longs is one in which "we shall know one another" in all our earthly individuality, but such a hope seems as remote as the possibility of the worldly fulfillment of her love. If the earth appears to be a sphere "of flaming sulphure," "Th'heaven ore my head, seemes made of molt[e]n brasse." The realization of her vision of a companionate love seems equally impossible on earth and in heaven, and it is this tragic fact that makes them both appear a hell. And yet she is "not mad," for however impossible her vision is of realization, it still sustains her.

With the defeat of her love, "There is not betweene heaven, and earth one wish/ I stay for" (IV, i, 72–3). But though it was her inviolable sovereignty which proved the ultimate barrier to her happiness in love, it is nonetheless this fatal sovereignty that she affirms to the last:

> *Duch.* Thou art not mad sure, do'st know me?
> *Bos.* Yes. *Duch.* Whom am I?

Bos. Thou are a box of worme-seede . . . our bodies are weaker then those paper prisons boyes use to keepe flies in: more contemptible: since ours is to preserve earth-wormes: didst thou ever see a Larke in a cage? such is the soule in the body . . . the Heaven ore our heades . . . onely gives us a miserable knowledge of the small compasse of our prison.

Duch. Am not I, thy Duchesse?

Bos. Thou art some great woman sure, for riot begins to sit on thy fore-head (clad in gray haires) twenty yeares sooner, then on a merry milkemaydes. Thou sleep'st worse, then . . . a little infant . . .

Duch. I am Duchesse of Malfy still. (IV, ii, 121–39)

Here Webster profoundly contrasts the satiric and tragic visions with their alternate degradation and affirmation of the same stuff of life. But if the Duchess can be associated with the satirist's degraded portrait of natural corruption, it is in her transcendence of it. As with Cleopatra, "vilest things/ Become themselves in her." If she rejected the social hierarchy for the natural nobility of man, it was by thus going back to its roots that she reached the very heights of humanity. It was only by an unconventional throwing off of the false cloak of nobility, by being associated first with the mortality of mankind and then with the cares of greatness that she reached the true wellsprings of nobility and can proclaim, even in the face of death: "I am Duchessse of Malfy still."

Her defiant sense of identity has persisted through all Bosola's efforts to bring her "By degrees to mortification" (IV, ii, 178) because there also persisted within her that impossible vision of the fulfillment of her individuality in love. And this vision is so powerful that, at the last, it forces her to "vault credit, and affect high pleasures,/ Beyond death":

Bos. Doth not death fright you?

Duch. Who would be afraid on't?
Knowing to meete such excellent company
In th'other world.

Bos. Yet, me thinkes,

> The manner of your death should much afflict you,
> This cord should terrifie you? *Duch.* Not a whit—
> What would it pleasure me, to have my throate cut
> With diamonds? . . . any way, (for heaven sake)
> So I were out of your whispering: Tell my brothers,
> That I perceive death, (now I am well awake)
> Best guift is, they can give, or I can take—
> (IV, ii, 215–23, 228–31)

Now that she is "well awake," she fully perceives that the charmed circle, within which she had experienced a meaningful worldly fulfillment, was but the false projection of a dream. She must finally accept the justice of Bosola's observance: "A long war disturb'd your minde,/ Here your perfect peace is sign'd" (IV, ii, 186–7). It was a dream that she could act like "merry milke-maydes" while remaining "Duchesse of Malfy still," and the long internal war between the spirit of greatness and of women had not even permitted her to dream peacefully: "For she's the sprawlingst bedfellow" (III, ii, 17). A long war had disturbed her mind in trying to save her sovereign womanhood "by halves"; now that she is "well awake," she perceives that total salvation can be hers only in death:

> Yet stay, heaven gates are not so highly arch'd
> As Princes pallaces—they that enter there
> Must go upon their knees: Come violent death, *[She kneels.]*
> Serve for Mandragora, to make me sleepe;
> Go tell my brothers, when I am laid out, *[They strangle her.]*
> They then may feede in quiet. (IV, ii, 237–44)

She dies with the same democratic vision by which she had lived, seeing no essential difference between a neck broken by rough ropes and one cut by diamonds, and kneeling humbly before the simpler majesty of heaven.

But if her hope to "appease" her kindred by showing them the realization of her dream had proved vain, the magnanimity born of her final vision accomplishes more than it would wish. Ferdinand, realizing that in his impassioned desire for her death he "was distracted of my wits," goes mad indeed, his lycanthropy giving powerful symbolic form to Webster's earlier imagistic use of the wolf. In that lucid interval which produces his final madness, however, he undergoes a total reversal of values:

> Cover her face: Mine eyes dazell: she di'd yong. . . .
> Why didst not thou pitty her? . . .
> I bad thee, when I was distracted of my wits,
> Goe kill my dearest friend, and thou hast don't.
> . . . I hate thee for't: . . . (IV, ii, 281, 292, 298–9, 309)

The hatred for Bosola, inspired by the conversion to love of Ferdinand's tragic hatred for his sister, now causes Bosola to appreciate fully the value of his service to evil.

As Bosola's ministrations in the cause of evil led to the Duchess' awakening, so do the results of her death affect him: "I stand like one/ That long hath ta'ne a sweet, and golden dreame./ I am angry with my selfe, now that I wake" (IV, ii, 349–51). If her awakening resulted in sadness, while his resulted in anger, it was because no matter how much external discord might disturb her dream it was still a good dream, while his was a dream of evil. His brutality proved to her how futile was the attempt to create a sphere of love in a world of evil, but the result of her death is to prove to him how much more futile was his ignoble service to discordant hate. Though the Duchess' goodness had been defeated, it had found its own reward, whereas the destructiveness of evil remains unrewarding. It is through Ferdinand's betrayal of his evil hopes that the Duchess' hopes for a better world gain power over Bosola's spirit, triumphing in death over the ruins of his misspent life:

> *Bos.* What would I doe, we[r]e this to doe againe?
> I would not change my peace of conscience
> For all the wealth of Europe: She stirres; here's life:
> Returne (faire soule) from darkenes, and lead mine
> Out of this sencible Hell: She's warme, she breathes:
> Upon thy pale lips I will melt my heart

> To store them with fresh colour: . . . her Eye opes,
> And heaven in it seemes to ope, (that late was shut)
> To take me up to mer[c]y.
>   *Duch.* Antonio.
>   *Bos.* Yes (Madam) he is living,
> The dead bodies you saw, were but faign'd statues;
> He's reconcil'd to your brothers: the Pope hath wrought
> The attonement.
>   *Duch.* Mercy!   *[She dies.]* (IV, ii, 365-71, 373-81)

He finally sees the truth which, from the beginning, had been so apparent to the Duchess that it had blinded her vision to the evil he witnessed, the truth that "all the wealth of Europe" is valueless if it is unaccompanied by love. The love that had made valuable her preservation as a sovereign being is the final reality to which she attests, a love so powerful that it can momentarily revive her spirit from the death to which it had doomed her. Calling to her beloved with her last strength, the knowledge that he is not only alive but also reconciled to her brothers fills her soul with gratitude and causes her to reaffirm her earliest and deepest conviction that a merciful order of love is possible on earth.

It is Bosola himself who justifies her conviction. Realizing that his vision of evil, which caused him to destroy all evidences of love whether within or without himself, had made of his world a "sencible Hell," he finally understands, through its loss, the saving value of love. As much as he had formerly wished to mortify her disturbing vision of love he now embraces her vision and hopes for an equally impossible realization of it. The seeming miracle of her revival awakens the vestiges of his own compassion—"where were these penitent fountaines,/ While she was living?/ Oh, they were frozen up" (IV, ii, 392-4)—and causes him to minister to her body in the spirit of purest love: "She's warme, she breathes:/ Upon thy pale lips I will melt my heart/ To store them with fresh colour." Seeing that her return to life might blessedly cancel his guilt and prove his salvation, it is he who rises to that very height of mercy that he could not dare to hope from her.

But the lie which gives the lie to his former vision of evil proves the greater torment, for it is Bosola's torment to have verified that merciful love for which the Duchess lived at the very moment in which her death must forever mock its good intentions: "that we cannot be suffer'd/ To doe good when we have a mind to it!" (IV, ii, 387–8). Love cannot have a saving value for Bosola because the good he would see and do is outweighed by the angry destructiveness of his character, which gives him "a Perspective/ That shows us hell" (IV, ii, 386–7). Though his act of mercy was a final justification of the vision for which she died, her death vindicates as well the truth of his vision of evil. But this is a new and more terrible vision of evil; not of degradation that knows not that there is good, but of damnation that knows that it has destroyed goodness. And with this new vision of evil comes a new anger, an anger placed in the service of that vanquished goodness.

In the earlier discussion of the character of the revenger, it was shown that the impulse to revenge, when motivated by righteous anger at the defeat of *love*, is a perversion of Courtly Love. Like Lodovico—the admirer of Isabella who joins her brother in revenging her death, and whom Bosola resembles even more than he does Flamineo—Bosola's desire for revenge springs not from a true understanding of the nature of the Duchess' love but from the perversion of his own Courtly Love for what she represented to him, a "sacred Innocence" (IV, ii, 383) so superficially like that of Isabella that other critics have also mistaken the Duchess for Isabella's double. In the figures of Isabella and of Lodovico/Bosola, Webster has given us his own version of the extremes of Courtly Love: on the one hand in its transfigured form of Christian self-sacrifice, on the other in the traditional figure of the revenger freed at last of special pleading and presented in the truer light of his spiritual damnation. But neither extreme of Courtly Love can find the meaningful fulfillment in Webster's universe that is alone possible to Worldly Love. In *The Devil's Law-Case*, he again presents the contrasting potentialities of Courtly and Worldly Love in the persons of Jolenta and Leonora, respectively, and there he rewards Leonora with an uncensured "last merryment fore Winter"

(*D.L.C.*, III, iii, 284) even at the expense of her daughter Jolenta's madness.

That Bosola is at heart a courtly rather than a worldly lover is indicated by the fact that it is not the Duchess' presence but only her eternal absence that permits Bosola to love her and dedicate himself fully to the selfless vindication of her memory. But his is a perverted Courtly Love, one which can only find expression in a destructive hatred of all that has led to his eternal banishment from the grace of a more fruitful love. If the Duchess' example has converted him from the satiric negation of love to its affirmation, the love that her death inspires in him is unlike her own and, by its very dissimilarity, doomed to a meaningless and ignoble fate. It is not only her death but his nature that bars him from experiencing her mode of love, and it is only this that can save him. Her love was able to accept the world and envision a more humane social order which would permit its worldly fulfillment. His very love prevents him from accepting the world and its fulfillment, permits him only the hollow glory of his twisted anger.

As Bosola makes his first uncertain movements in the direction of a virtuous revenge, he becomes increasingly aware of his ultimate divorce from virtue:

> . . . Well (good Antonio)
> I'll seeke thee out; and all my care shall be
> To put thee into safety from the reach
> Of these most cruell biters, that have got
> Some of thy blood already. It may be,
> I'll joyne with thee, in a most just revenge.
> The weakest Arme is strong enough, that strikes
> With the sword of Justice: Still me thinkes the Dutchesse
> Haunts me: there, there! . . . 'tis nothing but my mellancholy.
> O Penitence, let me truely tast thy Cup,
> That throwes men downe, onely to raise them up. (V, ii,
>   373-83)

His wistful desire for alliance with Antonio, which he hardly dares even to suggest to himself, immediately raises to his mind

the admonishing spectre of the Duchess, the haunting awareness of his unworthiness for such an alliance. Instinctively, he
feels that this new desire to vindicate the Duchess' love through
a just revenge is far from the purpose of such a love; and he
becomes melancholy from the reflection that even his best efforts
do not lessen his estrangement from the Duchess' higher vision.
He knows that, for all his remorse and good intentions, he has
not experienced that true penitence that can completely change
his nature and bring it into sympathy with the Duchess and
Antonio.

The futility of Bosola's desire for alliance with Antonio
becomes even more apparent when we consider Antonio's plan
to surprise the Cardinal at night in his chamber:

> It may be that the sudden apprehension
> Of danger (for I'll goe in mine owne shape)
> When he shall see it fraight with love, and dutie,
> May draw the poyson out of him, and worke
> A friendly reconcilement; if it faile . . .
> Yet, it shall rid me of this infamous calling,
> For better fall once, then be ever falling. (V, i, 75–81)

However incompetent Antonio may still be when the need comes
for decisive, self-originated action, his foolish plan is redeemed
by the end which it proposes, that of "friendly reconcilement."
If Antonio desires to "draw the poyson" from the Cardinal and,
by his "love," convert it to charity or lose his life in the attempt,
his reason is that life is only valuable in such a sphere of charity
as love can create. Looking upon his earlier passivity as an "in-
famous calling," even while seeing that an active course could
not save him, he nonetheless resolves that he had "better fall
once, then be ever falling." He can propose no other good to
himself now save that doomed action which is dictated to him
by love. When, in coming to his midnight tryst, Bosola mistakenly
stabs him "In a mist: I know not how" (V, v, 118), Antonio
informs him of his identity by saying:

> A most wretched thing,
> That onely have thy benefit in death,
> To appeare my selfe. (V, iv, 55-7)

It is because of his resolution that "I will not henceforth save my selfe by halves" (V, iii, 62), that Antonio can appear in death as "my selfe." Learning of the Duchess' death, Antonio concludes:

> . . . I would not now
> Wish my wounds balm'de, nor heal'd: for I have no use
> To put my life to . . .
> Pleasure of life, what is't? onely the good houres
> Of an Ague: meerely a preparative to rest,
> To endure vexation: . . . (V, iv, 71-5), 78-80)

Having redeemed his value through final resolution, he finds that his wife's death makes his redeemed self valueless because there is no use to which he would put his regenerated self but that of love. That the conditions of life should destroy this love causes him to realize as well that the love that had enabled him "to endure vexation" and which, even now, can "kindle a little life in me" (V, iv, 69), was "onely the good houres/ Of an Ague," a dream of happiness beside the massive reality of that mortal disease which is life. No sublime lie comes to his aid, as it did to the Duchess, to relieve his perception of life's evil. But if the happiness of love seems meaningless in a world that is bent on its destruction, the dream of love can still be vindicated by the integrity it develops in those who aspire to its vision. However cruelly life treated their dream of love, Antonio and the Duchess are the only characters in this play who die at peace with themselves.

It is in this last that the paradox of the final act is to be found. The fourth act ended with the apparent victory of the Duchess' vision in the conversion of Bosola, though the fact of her death through his agency seemed equally to vindicate his vision of evil. In this act, however, Bosola's vision seems all but proven:

> *Bos. [to the Servant]* Smother thy pitty, thou are dead
> else: Antonio?
> The man I would have sav'de 'bove mine owne life!
> We are meerely the Starres tennys-balls (strooke, and banded
> Which way please them). (V, iv, 61–4)

That the desire for the good, whether in the Duchess, Antonio, or his own unworthy self, should meet with such fatal crosses argues a malignant and meaningless universe rather than the heaven of the Duchess' final vision. Antonio had also come to accept the ancient view that it is "impossible/ To flye your fate" (V, iii, 43–4). But, opposed to Bosola's feeling of helplessness, Antonio had also retained the classical ethic that man can redeem his fate by the way in which he faces it: "Contempt of paine, that we may call our own" (V, iii, 72). To these concepts, Ferdinand adds the Sophoclean note that character is fate: "Whether we fall by ambition, blood, or lust,/ Like Diamonds, we are cut with our owne dust" (V, v, 91–2). And the stars' bandying with Bosola's good intentions certainly seems to reveal his primary character flaw, which is his inability to do good. The final deduction from these scattered comments would seem to be that the universal doom of mankind works itself out through the weaknesses of a man's character but that he can transcend his fate if his tragic vulnerability springs from a "sacred Innocence" of character combined with "noble suffrings" (V, iii, 71). The Cardinal may be "puzzell'd in a question about hell" (V, v, 1), and Ferdinand may "vault credit, and affect high pleasures/ Beyond death" (V, v, 86–7), but the Christian cosmology seems hardly to account for man's fate as Webster presents it in this last act.

Bosola's feeling of helplessness before a malignant fate may be due in part, however, to his growing awareness of his inability to change his malignant character. Having tried to unfreeze the fountains of his compassion only to learn that he could not "truely" taste the cup of penitence, he now reverts to his earlier mode in the advice he gives to Antonio's servant: "Smother thy pitty, thou art dead else." In the end there is nothing but for him to convict himself as unreservedly as the thoroughly vicious

Cardinal, who wished to "Be layd by, and never thought of" (V, v, 113). He dies, saying:

> We are onely like dead wals, or vaulted graves,
> That ruin'd, yeildes no eccho: Fare you well—
> It may be paine: but no harme to me to die,
> In so good a quarrell: Oh this gloomy world,
> In what a shadow, or deepe pit of darknesse,
> Doth (womanish, and fearefull) mankind live!
> Let worthy mindes nere stagger in distrust
> To suffer death, or shame, for what is just—
> Mine is another voyage. (V, v, 121–9)

It is in the death of Bosola, after all events had conspired to prove the futility of love and compassion and the need to smother pity in order to endure, that the values embraced by the lovers are paradoxically vindicated. If Bosola says of himself that "We are onely like dead wals, or vaulted graves,/ That ruin'd, yeildes no eccho," the echo which came "from the Dutchesse Grave" proves that this need not always be the case. At the end Bosola grants the Duchess' vision as modified by Antonio, that man can transcend his fate if his death or shame is suffered "for what is just." But such a transcendence is only possible for those whom love inspires with a vision of harmony and mercy on earth, however blind such a vision may be. To those who only attend to the appearances of evil, however valid, death presents another prospect, a "perspective/ That showes us hell." Though this is Bosola's voyage, he ends by telling the lovers not to "stagger in distrust" of their vision. If the Duchess died believing a sublime lie, hers was a better voyage than that which resulted from his distrust.

Webster's world is a tragic habitat because man has become alienated from "compassionate nature," an alienation that only the worldly lover is, by his love, enabled to transcend, and for which transcendence he is destroyed by his non-compassionate fellow man. With the exception of Heywood, none of the other tragedians of love has so completely identified love with compassion as the defiantly anti-Christian Webster; but it is perhaps because Webster lacks the simple faith of Heywood that he sees man's condition as brutally mocking his need for compassion.

For Webster, Worldly Love is a compassionate relationship, so defined from its very inception. Brachiano's first words to Vittoria are an appeal for compassion: "Loose me not Madam, for if you forego me/ I am lost eternallie"; and she turns to him with a similar appeal for "rescue." In a like despair, they extend the hands of compassion to each other, though it is not until this sympathetic love has made them whole that Brachiano's compassion can embrace the world. This general compassion, which is the final product of Brachiano's love, is already true of the Duchess at the start of her love: "We'll onely lie, and talke together, and plot/ T'appease my humorous kindred." Their love immediately extends itself into an impulse of general reconciliation, an impulse which the Duchess believes, in her last moments, to have been gratified and which Antonio pursues to his death.

While the relation of Worldly Love to compassion was stressed by Shakespeare in both of his Worldly Love tragedies, it was Webster who focused his tragic inquiry exclusively upon this point and thus clarified our understanding of it. Webster confronts the universe with the single question of whether it admits compassion and, though his general conclusion is negative, affirms that a tragic dignity is nonetheless possible for those who try to realize a personal compassion in a universe composed of malevolent men and stars.

12

Final Tragedies of Worldly Love

The closing years of James I's reign also see the end of the brilliant reign of Worldly Love tragedy, a reign unique in the annals of literary history. After its Marlovian dawn, its Shakespearean noon, and the waning radiance of Webster, the sun of Worldly Love sets with the less inspired efforts of Massinger and Middleton. Massinger's *Duke of Milan* is the final example of the first pattern of Worldly Love tragedy; Middleton's *Women Beware Women* of its third pattern. In this last period, Worldly Love appears only in its more corrupt forms.

The Duke of Milan

Massinger's greatest tragedy is one of three Jacobean tragedies based on the historical story of Herod and Mariamne,[1] the other two being Lady Elizabeth Carey's *Mariam* (1604)[2] and *The True Tragedy of Herod and Antipater* (1622) by Gervase Markham and William Sampson.[3] In Massinger's treatment, however, the traditional story is provided with the Italianate setting so popular in Jacobean tragedy. In the relations of Francesco Sforza to Francis I and Charles V, Massinger found a parallel to the relations of Herod with Antony and Augustus, which gave an historical base to his adaptation, though he used the father,

Ludovico Sforza, rather than Francesco as titular character. Dunstan suggests that he made this adaptation to avoid the popular conception of Herod left by the Mysteries;[4] but while Massinger's Duke has none of the wanton cruelty of the traditional Herod, or of Ludovico Sforza for that matter, it is precisely the bombastic quality of the popular Herod (which, in Hamlet's words, "out-herods Herod") that most interested him.

When Sforza is informed of the crucial battle, we see his characteristic straining after an unnatural emotional intensity:

> All my hopes depending
> Vpon this battailes fortune; In my Soule
> Me thinkes there should be that Imperious power,
> By supernaturall, not vsuall meanes,
> T'informe me what I am. (I, iii, 98–102)[5]

In achieving the emotional power which he feels properly belongs "In my Soule," his most important means is the exercise of his unusually vivid imagination, and this he now sets in motion by concentrating on the effects the battle might have on his wife, Marcelia. Sforza gradually works himself up through imaginary scenes of horror until he is satisfied that, compared to the suffering he feels, "euen those the damn'd/ Houl for in Hell, are gentle strokes" (I, iii, 194–5). For Marcelia's attempts to bring him to reason he feels little short of contempt, and he tries to make her contemplate the same images so that she too can experience his intemperate horror. The thought that she should suffer on his account was his first image of horror, but it is finally his suffering rather than hers that he wishes her to share imaginatively: "Thinke, thinke Marcelia, what a cursed thing/ I were, beyond expression" (I, iii, 207–8). Though Sforza readily finds bombastic expression for all his simulated feelings, he contemplates with special relish a depth of feeling so true that he would no longer need to give it verbal expression to convice himself of its reality. But the rational Marcelia, rather than indulging his imagination, advises him sharply against such a course: "Doe not feed/ Those iealous thoughts" (I, iii, 208–9).

Opposed to her husband's emotionally impotent striving for
feeling, Marcelia strives to reduce all emotion to rational control. As he tries to bring her into his vicarious emotional experience, so does she try to bring him forth into her rational sphere.
But just as he refuses to heed her counsel, so does her rational
nature make it impossible for her to understand the extent of
his irrationality. It is from the mutual exclusiveness of their
basic orientations that their relationship will result in tragedy.

Refusing to follow her advice, he continues privately to
"feed/ Those iealous thoughts" while preparing for a dangerous
conference with Charles V that might prove fatal to him. Greater
than the suffering he would bear to see her ravished, he now
thinks, is the thought that she might love another after his death,
that she might be capable of a life independent of his own. This
thought so tortures him that he finally resolves that his peace
can only be achieved by assuring himself of her death in the
event of his. Just as in the early stages of his previous imaginative
experience he was still able to conceive of the suffering in her
terms, so now his first reaction to his decision is one of horror.
In giving Francisco the secret order, he tries to make him share
his imaginative horror just as he had earlier tried to do with
Marcelia: "'twill I know appeare so monstrous to you,/ That
you will tremble in the execution" (I, iii, 287–8). But "such
my state,/ And strange condition is" (I, iii, 294–5) that he cannot keep himself from destroying the object of his idolatry, despite his full awareness of the evil he intends: "Her greatest
enemy is her greatest louer,/ Yet in that hatred, her Idolater"
(I, iii, 337–8). As he continues, however, to contemplate, the compulsion that destroys his better instincts as it would his idol, the
very strength of his compulsion seems to be an unarguable
justification: " 'Tis more than loue to her, that markes her out"
(I, iii, 351). What this "more" is appears to be a selfish need
for her eternal presence: "There is no heauen without her; nor
a hell,/ Where she recides. I aske from her but iustice,/ And
what I would haue payd to her" (I, iii, 356–8). The fact that
he would do the same for her seems a perfectly valid argument
for imposing a reciprocal compliance upon her with no consideration of her personal wishes. As he becomes more convinced of

the justice of his cause, and so loses his sense of shame, his self-love finally mounts to the height of self-idolatry:

> The slauish Indian Princes when they dye
> Are cheerefully attended to the fire,
> By the wife, and slaue, that liuing they lou'd best,
> To doe them seruice in another world:
> Nor will I be lesse honor'd that loue more. (I, iii, 361–5)

He here reveals that the essence of his unmatched love is no other than self-adoration through the person of the beloved, the very intensity with which he adores his adorer justly entitling him, he feels, to be "cheerefully attended to the fire."

Sforza may find such an expression of love perfectly acceptable, but it is otherwise with Marcelia:

> But that my Lord, my Sforza should esteeme,
> My life fit only as a page, to waite on
> The various course of his vncertaine fortunes . . .
> Will slack the ardor that I had to see him
> Returne in safetie. (III, iii, 58–60, 65–6)

Though she had earlier been alarmed by the excess of his jealous devotion to her, she now understands that he was not devoted to her as an individual but as an appendage to his own proper person. But if she can no longer love him on his terms, she still hopes that their marriage may be saved by teaching him a truer affection based upon actual respect for her person:

> And some thing I may doe to try his temper,
> At least to make him know a constant wife,
> Is not so slau'd to her husbands doting humors, . . . (III, iii,
>   78–80)

When she next meets him, rather than answering his ardor she tries to redirect it into more temperate channels, answering his startled "why can there be/ A meane in your affections to Sforza?" (III, iii, 107–8) with the plea: "Let vs loue temperatly" (III, ii, 129). But her desire enrages him for he can accept only the excessive expression of love as genuine, that excess on which he prides himself and on which he bases all his demands on her. When he finds, therefore, his "excesse of feruor,/ Which [yet] was neuer equal'd, growne distastfull" (III, iii, 145–6), he can only conclude that she is a "most accursed woman" (II, iii, 152). Her refusal to conform to the image of his deserts immediately converts her from a woman "blest" (I, iii, 75) to one "accursed" and he orders her from his sight like a disobedient "page." Here again we see the two faces of narcissistic love which were noted in the case of Dido, one beaming at admiration, the other almost instantaneously raging at the least questioning of its worth. Yet both are consistent to this type of personality because the outside world is evaluated only on the basis of its conformity to an idolatrous image of self.

In ordering her from him in this way, he finally gives expression to that base estimate of her which, as Marcelia recognized, underlay his secret order for her death, and this living expression serves to harden Marcelia's attitude towards him: "Command me from his sight, & with such scorne/ As he would rate his slaue" (IV, ii, 1–2). Not appeased by his envoy's reports of his changed humor, she tells them: "till I haue digested some sad thoughts,/ And reconcil'd passions that are at warre/ Within my selfe, I purpose to be priuate" (IV, ii, 15–7). Although she would like to salvage something from her former happiness, she knows that she must first make some compromises with her present antagonism before she can present a suitable face to him, and so she tragically delays their reconciliation.

This delay is tragic because Marcelia is not aware that she had made a genuine impression on him and that it was this that had motivated his repentance: "But you will say she's crosse, 'tis fit she should be/ When I am foolish, for she's wise" (IV, iii, 41–2). She was right in assuming that much of his sorrow was mere self-indulgence—"Now I haue cause to grieue, I must be sad,/ And I dare shew it" (IV, iii, 15–6)—but she could

not have expected this quiet recognition of his error. Such glim-
merings of reason and true feeling have appeared in him before,
when he did consider her suffering under enemy attack and the
horror of the murder he proposed. In each case, however, this
potentially healthier reaction gave way before the diseased requirements of his self-love, as though these impulses towards
a genuine valuing of another somehow robbed him of his own
value. Had Marcelia accepted him back before this reaction set
in, she might have been able to strengthen the impulses of his
truer self and lead him to that genuine esteem, both for himself
and her, upon which a true marriage could have been based.

But she loses her moment. The sadness which also made
her want to try again was not yet "reconcil'd" to the just antagonism which his recent behavior had aroused in her, and so she
provides Francisco with the time to dissipate these reciprocal
impulses towards a higher reconciliation. While Sforza anxiously
awaited her answer, Francisco was falsely informing her of Sforza's
jealousy with regard to himself; then after Sforza received the
negative reply, Francisco as falsely informed him of the wanton
overtures she had made to him. These machinations serve to
dissipate the frail impulses of their love which, nourished, might
have produced a harmony between their affections. The basic
difference between her overly rational and his irrational nature
can be bridged only by a bond of sympathy. With the hardening
of their mutual resentments, they both lose this power, thus
permitting the worst sides of their loves to manifest their fatal
discord. Because there are no logical grounds for Sforza's jealousy,
Marcelia scorns his irrational response and decides to teach him
a lesson. Had her sympathy been more active she would have
recognized that just because his reaction was not sound, he
would only be further inflamed by the rational course she is
taking. But her sympathy is as cold as his and cannot counter
the murderous rage that has been building up in him.

Though Francisco has apparently given Sforza considerable
grounds for jealousy, the terms in which this expresses itself
indicate a more profound reason for his sense of abuse, and this
becomes more overt in their encounter:

> *Marc.* Where is this Monster? . . .
> This horned beast that would be? . . . Which of my vertues,
> My labours, seruices, and cares to please you . . .
> Inuites this barbarous course? Dare you looke on me
> Without a seale of shame?
> > *Sf.*   Impudence,
> How vgly thou appear'st now? (IV, iii, 261–71)

As Marcelia once again rejects his behavior as shameful and bids him rather examine her virtues and the justness in her treatment of him, his true sense of abuse at her "impudence" becomes articulate. If he had earlier conceded that her crossness might be the result of wisdom, it now appears to him impossibly "vgly." But Marcelia is so caught up by her own sense of abuse that she does not heed the menace in his aspect and continues with her plan to give him what he deserves. Admitting to "This horned beast that would be" what he wants to hear, she encounters the irrationality her own reason had fatally discredited:

> > *Sf.*   I begin now   *[stabs her.]*
> In this my Iustice.
> > *Marc.*   Oh, I haue fool'd my selfe
> Into my graue, and only grieue for that
> Which when you know, you haue slaine an Innocent
> You needs must suffer.
> > *Sf.*   An Innocent? Let one
> Call in Francisco. . . .
> > *Marc.*   We are both abus'd.
> And both by him vndone. . . .
> Indeed the vnkindnesse to be sentenc'd by you
> Before that I was guiltie in a thought,
> Made me put on a seeming anger towards you,
> And now behold the issue; as I do,
> May heauen forgiue you.   *[dyes.]* . . .
> > *Sf.*   O my heart-strings. (IV, iii, 286–315)

She fatally learns that all her reason was without wisdom as long as it lacked sympathy and has only "fool'd my selfe/ Into a graue." But with this recognition the sympathy that had been deadened by abuse quickens into final life and causes her to grieve more for the suffering he will experience than for her own loss. She realizes that he has felt as abused as she but also that their mutual sense of abuse had causes anterior to Francisco's final manipulation, that it was the combination of his "unkind-nesse" and her "seeming anger" that really produced this tragic issue. If she had loved less wisely and he not so well, they could not have been abused by their mutual failure in sympathy. It is her own sense of final inadequacy which gives her compassion for his failings in love and causes her last hope that heaven will forgive him his sins.

Having lived the better part of his emotional life in the fantasies of his imagination, his first reaction to Marcelia's death is that this too must be a fantasy, for "heauen . . . Would neuer be so cruell as to rob . . . so much sweetnesse" (V, ii, 19–22). When he finally realizes, however, that heaven has been cruel enough to turn his fantasies into reality, the knowledge of his guilt proves too painful and he reverts to the fantasy that she is not dead. But if he gives way to this final self-indulgence, his intense desire for her revival springs from a new ability to love her for herself and as she would have wished:

> Carefully I beseech you,
> The gentlest touch torments her, & then thinke
> What I shall suffer. . . . How slow her pulses beat to?
> Yet in this temper she is all perfection,
> . . . Shee was euer kind
> And her displeasure though call'd on, short liu'de
> Vpon the least submission. O you powers . . .
> Let her behold me in a pleasing dreame,
> Thus on my knees before her . . . guilty,
> As she is innocent; . . . (V, ii, 47–9, 65–6, 103–5, 108–9,
>   115–6)

Though he had murdered her for her "impudence," he now fully understands that he was guilty of denying her a life of inde-pendent worth, a denial that resulted in the far greater guilt he now experiences. For the first time, he speaks with true feeling; and, significantly, this feeling is one of humility and concern. He now considers her "perfection" to reside in her temperance and realizes that she was "kind" to put up with his excesses as long as she did, that her "displeasure" was always "call'd on" by his own guilt. Loving her truly now, his only wish is to be able to live with her once more and make up for all the pain he had caused her. This need is so intense that he even tries to make his dream a reality for her.

But it is not reality, and reality now calls him to account for all his sins. Francisco, revenging Sforza's dishonor of his sister, Eugenia, comes on the scene with a trick—borrowed from *The Second Maiden's Tragedy*—to bring about his death. As his indulgence of Sforza's hyper-sensitive imagination had led to Marcelia's murder, so does he lead Sforza to his own death through the same indulgence. Sforza has so fatally substituted fantasy for reality that, in kissing the dead lips of Marcelia that Francisco had painted with poison, his disease becomes mortal. But as dream and reality finally merge, he awakens from his fatal dream:

> *Sf.* I come death, I obey thee,
> Yet I will not die raging, for alas,
> My whole life was a phrensie. Good Eugenia
> In death forgiue me. As you loue me beare her
> To some religious house, there let her spend
> The remnant of her life, when I am ashes
> Perhaps shee'll be appeas'd, and spare a prayer
> For my poore soule. Bury me with Marcelia
> And let our Epitaph be—*[Dies]*
>   *Tibe.*   His speech is stop'd. (V, ii, 256–64)

If the death of Marcelia caused him to face his own failings and thereby to develop a true capacity for feeling, this feeling was still expressed through the delirious world of his imagination. It is his own death that finally causes his full awakening to reality and the sad realization that his "whole life was a phrensie." As death had shown Marcelia the failure of her vaunted reason, so does death show Sforza the reciprocal failure of his vaunted emotions. He realizes that the only contact with reality of the frenzy he had called love was its power to cause actual destruction. Awakening from his final delirium to find Marcelia dead and himself dying, he experiences his one sane moment of true feeling and this is one of weariness with his life. Uttering a simple "alas" for his "poore soule," the "speech" that for so long had been filled with bombast "is stop'd."

Massinger's exploration of the traditional Herod character is a consummate study of the bombastic quality in his nature. The reason that Massinger was able to endow this bombastic character with such reality, however, may lie in the nature of Massinger himself. Many critics have pointed out the "impoverishment of feeling" [6] that makes Massinger "in his height bombastic" [7] and accounts for his general "failure to draw a moving character." [8] But where the serious concern with virtue and vice in his other tragedies results in a rhetoric that is more or less bombastic, in his one profound study of the tragic effects of a bombastic nature he did create a moving character.

Though Massinger's rhetoric becomes bombastic when he attempts to convey powerful feeling, it is a very impressive vehicle for noble sentiments and, here again, there is an important similarity between Massinger and both the historical Herod and his own Sforza. The most paradoxical feature of Herod's personality was his verbal ability to ingratiate himself first with Antony and then Caesar, with the result that he kept his crown despite the change in empire. Massinger's rendering of the speech recorded by Josephus is close both in content and tone and this fact argues a special interest of the speech for him. The inclusion of this stately and noble speech, however, is regarded by some critics as the most serious dramatic fault of the play.[9] Nevertheless when we consider that Massinger's reason for setting the play in Milan was the fact that the relations of Sforza (Francesco) to Francis and Charles paralleled that of Herod to Antony and Augustus Caesar, we must conclude that the speech was an essential part of his original concept of the character and not an intrusion. Between the bombastic side of Herod's character, which had been exclusively exploited in the Mysteries, and his ability to make such a noble speech, Massinger saw an important inner connection. In the historical Herod, Massinger saw a character who was able to give convincing expression to the most abstract sentiments and yet collapsed into bombastic raging in giving expression to his emotions. In such a character Massinger might well have recognized his own plight as a dramatist.

Massinger must also have realized, as did Meredith in *The Egoist,* that where a bombastic nature might be very successful in impersonal matters and relationships, this nature became intolerable in a love relationship; further, that it was only through the rejection of his love that the self-love of such a character could be destroyed and he be brought to tragic confusion. Massinger's other independent treatments of love in tragedy degenerate into a rhetorical conflict between lust and chastity.[10] It is only through his searching analysis of a bombastic character that he produced a genuine love tragedy.

But there is an even more significant distinction between the profound reality of this tragedy and the artificiality of his others. From his other tragedies it would appear that he was temperamentally prone to a norm of Courtly Love, though in its disguished forms of Stoic honor or Christian piety, a preference which seems reflected in Sforza's final commendation of Eugenia to a convent. The most satisfactory solution of this seeming paradox may lie in the simple dominance of the ideal of Worldly Love in the final period of the Jacobean drama, a dominance so powerful that, despite Massinger's preference for courtly values, it drew him within its orbit. Where his conflict with the values of his age led to emotionally sterile dramas, his reapproachment with these values released the deepest potentialities of his talent and produced his tragic masterpiece.[11]

Women Beware Women

The new ideal of Worldly Love, which had gradually shrunk in inspirational power even while its nature and value were being more perfectly defined, receives a fitting end under the dispassionate eye of Middleton. In his tragic masterpiece, *The Changeling*, Middleton had projected the ideal of Worldly Love against the ruins of a tragic false romanticism which his critical genius had searched to its foundations. In *Women Beware Women*[12] he fulfills the promise of his earlier tragedy by giving us his tragedy of Worldly Love. But Middleton's treatment of Worldly Love differs from the more usual third pattern in that it begins with an initial false romantic situation.[13] As such it is a sequel to his earlier effort and cannot be considered apart from it. Bianca Capello achieves that breakthrough from a desperate false romantic situation to the affirmation of Worldly Love which Beatrice, his earlier heroine, was unable to make. This final breakthrough is prompted, however, not by an inspired faith but a cynical appraisal of reality.

Women Beware Women commences on a note of idealism, though a note so chastened as to be hardly recognizable as such. Leantio begins the play just as Alsemero had opened *The Changeling*, with an expression of timorous hope:

> As often as I look upon that treasure,
> And know it to be mine—there lies the blessing—
> It joys me that I ever was ordain'd
> To have a being, and to live 'mongst men;
> Which is a fearful living, and a poor one,
> Let a man truly think on't: (I, i, 14–9) [14]

The "learnèd" (III, i, 145) Leantio has been inspired by love to affirm as joyous the life that had hitherto seemed to him impoverished. Yet even at this moment of exultation, when he has finally brought his beloved home as his bride, he cannot fully

quiet the fears his knowledge of life has instilled in him. Though
he vows, "I'll prove an excellent husband" (I, i, 107), he fears
not only his wife's constancy but even his own, feeling forced
to disclaim a possibility that should have been beyond consideration: "I find no wish in me bent sinfully/ To this man's sister,
or to that man's wife" (I, i, 28–9). The reason why he embraces
his "treasure" with fear of loss, however, is that he recognizes
that his possession of it is the result of theft: "'tis theft, but
noble. . . . If it be known, I've lost her" I, i, 37, 47). Like
Jacob, he has stolen a "blessing." Apart from the actual fact of
forbidden elopement, this theft has symbolic significance in terms
of Middleton's tragic vision. Though Leantio knows that "To
have a being . . . is a fearful living, and a poor one," he has
presumed to ask a greater blessing of life than he, or any man,
is entitled to. But with all of Leantio's considerable and profound
thought on the subjects of life and love, he is still essentially an
innocent who, while fearing such happiness may be a blessing
beyond man's portion, still hopes that simply by means of a proper
mutual devotion it can be achieved.

Bianca expresses a devotion equal to her husband's, but
she is aware of a more ominous contingency:

> Kind mother, there is nothing can be wanting
> To her that does enjoy all her desires:
> Heaven send a quiet peace with this man's love,
> And I'm as rich as virtue can be poor,
> Which were enough after the rate of mind
> To erect temples for content plac'd here.
> I have forsook friends, fortunes, and my country,
> And hourly I rejoice in't. Here's my friends,
> And few is the good number. (I, i, 125–33)

Bianca "forsook friends, fortunes, and my country" in quest
of a dream of love, and she realizes that in forsaking the protection of her family she has exposed herself to a situation
which may have unforeseeable dangers beyond the simple power
of her will. If, unlike Leantio, she has no fear either of her

own or her husband's willful infidelity, she does fear that the realization of their hopes may not depend wholly upon their own efforts. She prays that "Heaven send a quiet peace with this man's love" because she knows that in such a peace she would "enjoy all her desires," but she is not as sure of Heaven's will as of her own. The ideal of these young hopefuls is as fine and earnest as their will to realize it; but for all their intellectual awareness of the possible dangers to their stolen love, theirs are still "innocent loves," as yet untried by life. When life finally does confront their love, it is in the terms feared by Bianca not by Leantio.

Their peace is all too soon invaded by the Duke's eye which, spying the "beauty, able to content a conqueror" (I, i, 26), will not remain unsatisfied. When, through the gullibility of her mother-in-law, Bianca finds herself alone with him, she learns that her "virtue" is indeed "poor" beside his might. Seeing that the Duke will have her by force if not persuasion, her first impulse is to "bold with death and deeds of ruin" (II, ii, 356); but she finally takes the rational course which is the corollary of Leantio's own teaching. It was this which had motivated Leantio to take a business trip the day after the wedding, although admitting "I would well wish myself where you would have me;/ But love that's wanton must be rul'd awile/ By that that's careful, or all goes to ruin" (I, iii, 40–2). This same subjugation of emotional preference to the dictates of reason was the subject of his mother's counsel to Bianca upon his departure: "'tis an old custom/ To weep for love" (I, iii, 71–2). The "old custom" of passionate love has been changed for one that affirms the preservation and enjoyment of life: "cannot love/ Be as well express'd in a good look" (I, iii, 67–8). Contrary emotional preferences must be suppressed and a good face put on even that which is most displeasing. When Bianca next sees Leantio, she tells him:

> 'Tis time to leave off dalliance; 'tis a doctrine
> Of your own teaching, if you be remember'd;
> And I was bound to obey it. (III, i, 169–71)

She had originally accepted Leantio's teaching with innocent faith, but events forced her to make a distasteful application of the basic tenet of their love.

She realizes that whether or not she accepts the Duke, his power to force her will has destroyed all her innocent hopes for "a quiet peace" with Leantio's love. Her alternatives, therefore, are either to destroy herself with the ruin of her love or to put a good face on her disaster and accept the less attractive but more viable love offered her by the Duke:

> But I give better in exchange,—wealth, honour. . . .
> Come, play the wise wench, and provide for ever;
> Let storms come when they list, they find thee shelter'd.
> Should any doubt arise, let nothing trouble thee;
> Put trust in our love for the managing
> Of all to thy heart's peace; . . . (II, ii, 375, 387–91)

The Duke seems to be echoing Leantio's earlier assurance:

> But let storms spend their furies; now we've got
> A shelter o'er our quiet innocent loves,
> We are contended: . . . (I, i, 51–3)

But if the shelter Leantio had promised her had collapsed under the Duke's greater power, the shelter the Duke offers her seems built of sturdier stuff. She is not seduced by the Duke's offer of wealth, since she truly desired a "quiet peace" with Leantio. But when, through no fault of their own, this peace is destroyed, she realizes that her only remaining chance for "heart's peace" lies in accepting the Duke's powerful protection. She sees that wisdom lies not in being true to an unrealizable ideal but in adapting herself to her true predicament, however flawed. Her first true experience of life teaches her that the ideal love for which she "forsook friends, fortune, and my country" was the projection of innocence, and she now finds herself responsible for the results of this innocent act. In leaving the protection of her friends, she had exposed herself to the Duke's power; she bargained for Leantio but got the Duke instead. Her position is identical with that of Beatrice who, in leaving Piracquo for Alsemero, found that she had unwittingly placed herself in the power of De Flores. But, unlike Beatrice, who could never fully accept her true position, Bianca does settle herself in what the act has made her. She is later to comment:

> How strangely woman's fortune comes about! . . .
> To meet it here, so far off from my birth-place,
> My friends, or kindred! (IV, i, 23, 28–30)

She little expected such a strange fortune to result from her innocent elopement with Leantio, but, if the "theft" of love be "sin" (I, i, 35), as Leantio admitted, she must accept its unhallowed rewards:

> Yet since mine honour's leprous, why should I
> Preserve that fair that caus'd the leprosy?
> Come, poison all at once. (II, ii, 429–31)

However innocent she may have been, both in the nature of the hopes that spurred her elopement and in her encounter with the Duke, she has somehow, in the process of these events, lost her native innocence. Beatrice had tried to maintain the outward appearance of respectability while living a vicious secret life, and this eventually split her personality in two; but Bianca invokes the total transformation of her personality which her new position requires: "Come, poison all at once." Though she has been "made bold" (II, ii, 444), by treacherous circumstances beyond both her desire and control, she adapts herself to her fate with a minimum of regret and a strong purpose to find what good there may be in this unwanted evil.

As she begins to find good in this new evil, so does she begin to find evil in her former good. Now that her love for Leantio has been soiled, she can no longer find an innocent contentment in the secluded poverty of her husband's home.

She greets her husband with a cynical abandon that destroys his faith in marriage as surely as the Duke, in similar manner, had destroyed hers: "What a peace/ Has he that never marries! (III, i, 280–1). His idealism collapses immediately under the first brutal blow of experience though he accepts its loss with less grace than Bianca, or than Alsemero did under similar circumstances. But, like Bianca, he sees that this betrayal of their faith was the result of his own sinful "theft" of a goodness beyond his right: "I see then 'tis my theft; we're both betray'd" (III, i, 300). The "theft" that had appeared noble in its first flush of idealism is now revealed in its true aspect, and Leantio accepts the justice of this strange fortune as fully as did Bianca. Also, like Bianca, after a momentary qualm and in much pain, he adapts himself to his new position:

> I cannot love her now, but I must like
> Her sin and my own shame too, and be guilty
> Of law's breach with her, and mine own abusing;
> All which were monstrous: then my safest course,
> For health of mind and body, is to turn
> My heart and hate her, most extremely hate her; (III, ii, 334–9)

Offered not only the captainship of the fort by the Duke but the bounteous Livia's love –"more goodness yet?" (III, ii, 67)— he accepts the rational alternative, just as Bianca did before him, feeling that the "health of mind and body" are more important than the indulgence of his grief. If the conclusions of reason, that he "must like/ Her sin and my own shame too" are "monstrous," it is because the world is not as ideal as, in his innocence, love had made him believe. But the immediacy with which both Bianca and Leantio drop all pretensions to fidelity and accept the less perfect order of the world argues that their first love was largely a construct of their reason, which only their innocence had allowed them to pursue. If this is the finest example of False Romantic Love that we have encountered, it is, for all its projection of an ideal of Worldly Love, no more

than this and follows the pattern of all False Romantic Love up
to this point: they unlawfully left their first condition for one
which they thought better only to find it far worse. At this
point, however, the pattern changes; for they accept their present
state and no longer desire a return to that former good which
is now barred to them. Bianca's history, in particular, from this
point on assumes the true pattern of Worldly Love tragedy.

After a brief interlude of discomfort in her relationships
with both the Duke and Leantio, she emerges as a fully matured
woman who disdains her earlier idealism with ironic good
humor. When she next meets the Duke at Livia's party, her
relaxed state of mind witnesses to her wholehearted acceptance
of the Duke's love:

> *Duke.* Come, Bianca,
> Of purpose sent into the world to show
> Perfection once in woman; I'll believe
> Henceforward they have every one a soul too. . . .
> Here's a health now, gallants,
> To the best beauty at this day in Florence.
>   *Bian.* Who'er she be, she shall not go unpledg'd, sir.
>   *Duke.* Nay, you're excus'd for this. . . .
> You are not bound to pledge your own health, lady.
>   *Bian.* That's a good way, my lord, to keep me dry.
>   *Duke.* . . . Here's to thyself, Bianca.
>   *Bian.* Nothing comes
> More welcome to that name than your grace.
>   (III, ii, 22–5, 77–80, 82–3, 86–8)

Though first attracted by her beauty, it is her spiritual qualities
that fully engage his heart: "A kiss *[kisses her]*; that wit deserves to be made much on" (III, ii, 235). But if he loves her
for her wit even more than for her beauty, it is he who has
released this side of her nature. This wit is the other face of
a worldly wisdom which has enabled her to accept with such
good will the imperfect love thrust upon her. When she sees
Isabella forced to parade her attractions before the fool to whom
she is betrothed, she says:

'Las, poor gentlewoman!
She's ill-bested, unless sh'as dealt the wiselier,
And laid in more provision for her youth;
Fools will not keep in summer. (III, ii, 119–22)

As she continues in this vein, Leantio adds in an aside, "True,
and damnation has taught you that wisdom" (III, ii, 134).
She has, indeed, been taught this wisdom by her experience
with the evil of an imperfect world which renders ideal marriage impossible. She has accepted this truth so fully that she is
sorry for Isabella if she harbors any idealism with regards to
her coming marriage and hopes that Isabella has made as fine
a compromise with imperfection as she has made. Her instinct,
in fact, leads her to suspect an affinity; and she is not wrong.

When Isabella learned that she must marry a fool, her
maidenly idealism about marriage revolted against it:

Marry a fool! . . .
The best condition is but bad enough;
When women have their choices, commonly
They do but buy their thraldoms. . . .
Yet honesty and love makes all this happy,
And, next to angels', the most bless'd estate. . . .
O, but this marriage! (I, ii, 163, 171–3, 180–1, 186)

Though realizing that marriage even under "the best condition
is but bad enough," she does envision the possibility of an ideal
marriage similar to that for which Bianca and Leantio had
eloped, a marriage in which "honesty and love makes all this
happy," and can produce "the most bless'd estate" in life. Bianca
and Leantio, while similarly aware that "the best condition"
might prove "bad enough," had nevertheless tried to realize
this ideal of marriage, only to find that in spite of their good
intentions their wost fears were justified. Isabella is deprived
even of this possibility. For a world in which ideal marriages
are impossible, the "marriage-goddess" (IV, ii, 217), she who
makes the state of marriage endurable, is fittingly portrayed by

a bawd. Livia is a brilliant court lady who assumes this role with inspired relish; as she contrived the meeting between Bianca and the Duke, so does she arrange a lover[15] for Isabella before the wedding takes place.

The first act sets up the ideal of marriage, which Bianca and Leantio attempt and Isabella despairs of realizing. In the second act, which takes place completely under Livia's roof, this ideal is viciously defeated and more realistic arrangements are made, which are then joyously celebrated at Livia's third act party. Bianca and the Duke openly celebrate their union while Isabella and Hippolito do so covertly, and a crowning finish is given to these rational arrangements when Leantio accepts the wealthy Livia's love: "Troth, then, I'll love enough, and take enough" (III, ii, 376). When Leantio, "because has got/ Fair clothes by foul means, comes to rail and show 'em" (IV, i, 111–2), Bianca says: "Sure I think, sir,/ We both thrive best asunder" (IV, i, 63–4). The innocent hopefuls who first appeared like Romeo and Juliet have now become Gigolo and Gigolette! It is, indeed, "a witty age" (II, ii, 401) which can applaud such a transformation, though Leantio adapts himself less perfectly to it than Bianca:

> *Duke.* Prithee, who's that?
> *Bian.* The former thing, my lord, to whom you gave
> The captainship; he eats his meat with grudging still.
> *Duke.* Still? (IV, i, 113–6)

Incredulous as the Duke is that Leantio should "still" resent the brutal defeat of all his hopes, Leantio is not fully appeased by his new finery and mistress, and comes threatening a bloody revenge upon Bianca and the Duke. When he leaves, Bianca says of the plague he threatened: "Get you gone first, and then I fear no greater;/ Nor thee will I fear long" (IV, i, 106–7). And the Duke quickly echoes her unspoken intent:

> *Bian.* And his threats . . . were as spiteful
> As ever malice utter'd, and as dangerous,

Should his hand follow the copy.
   Duke. But that must not:
Do not you vex your mind; prithee, to bed, go;
All shall be well and quiet.
   Bian. I love peace, sir.
   Duke. And so do all that love; take you no care for't,
It shall be still provided to your hand. (IV, i, 122–30)

Now that Bianca has completely accepted her forced relationship with the Duke she finds that her false romantic attachment to Leantio bars the way to the full fruition of this new love. When her peace with Leantio was invaded by the Duke, she exchanged it for the Duke's better protection; now that her new peace seems in danger of invasion, she lays claim to this protection. But it is a debaunched morality that can "love peace" at the price of murder, and Leantio was right when he said to her: "Why, here's sin made, and ne'er a conscience put to't" (IV, i, 93). The "peace" that Bianca and the Duke claim as the rightful property of "all that love" is as corrupt an ideal as her former peace with Leantio was pure, but it gains strength to endure from its very corruption. However corrupt this love may be, Bianca commits herself to it completely and is willing to murder and die for it. If her first love was virtuous, it was but a weak shadow to this strong commitment. She has emerged as a true worldly lover. But the murder of Leantio, which the Duke easily accomplishes by inciting Hippolito against his sister Livia's lover, does not ensure their peace even though its effects are played out entirely among the characters in the subplot.

   In the usual third pattern of Worldly Love, which *Women Beware Women* partly exemplifies, the murder of the husband causes society, either legally or through the family of the deceased, to revenge itself directly on the lovers. In *Women Beware Women*, however, the voice of society raised by the Cardinal is not directly related to the murder of Leantio, which remains untraced to the Duke. Having set the wheels in motion for the murder of Leantio just before the Cardinal starts berating him for his adultery, the Duke thinks he can easily satisfy his brother's

objections by legitimizing his relationship to Bianca. But the
Cardinal is not appeased by the Duke's conversion:

> Cease, cease! religious honours done to sin
> Disparage virtue's reverence, and will pull
> Heaven's thunder upon Florence: . . .
> Is not sin sure enough to wretched man,
> But he must bind himself in chains to't! worse;
> Must marriage, that immaculate robe of honour,
> That renders virtue glorious, fair, and fruitful
> To her great master, be now made the garment
> Of leprosy and foulness? (IV, iii, 1–3, 12–7)

He voices again that ideal of marriage which it has been the
business of the play to prove incapable of realization, rejecting
any compromise with the "sin" which is "sure enough to wretched
man." Against such an inflexible morality, however, Bianca raises
an opposing set of values which she has been taught by life:

> Sir, I have read you over all this while
> In silence, and I find great knowledge in you
> And severe learning; yet 'mongst all your virtues
> I see not charity written, which some call
> The first-born of religion. . . .
> Pray, whether is religion better serv'd,
> When lives that are licentious are made honest,
> Than when they still run though a sinful blood?
> 'Tis nothing virtue's temples to deface;
> But build the ruins, there's a work of grace!
>
> (IV, iii, 47–51, 65–9)

The ideal offered by the Cardinal, as by Leantio, is the result
of "severe learning" completely divorced from experience. Bianca's experience has taught her, however, the ease and speed
with which such innocent virtue can be defaced. Since the virtue
sprung from innocence is doomed, Bianca has learned that true
goodness is only possible for those who "build the ruins," that

the only good that can survive evil is that which is born from it. It was this insight that caused her to accept her defiler with the hope that with him she might still achieve some goodness out of the ruins of her innocence. And she has built well, converting the Duke's unholy lust into a love that desires the sanctity of marriage. Convinced that the goodness she has achieved is more valuable than that which she lost, she feels herself deserving of "charity." She feels that her desire to work out her own salvation even if outside the bounds of prescribed morality should be furthered by the tolerance of those who have been more fortunately sheltered from the evil she had to endure. All she asks of the world that shattered her innocent "temples of content" is to be allowed to "build the ruins" in "peace," and it is because the world does not allow her this minimal charity, that she is forced to resort to murder. As she is later to say: "envy and slander/ Are things soon rais'd against two faithful lovers;/ But comfort it, they're not long unrewarded" (V, i, 86–8). Had Leantio not come, spewing "envy and slander," to threaten revenge, she would have wished him well; but she could not allow him to jeopardize her new found peace. The Duke, under different circumstances, had said that he "never pitied any,—they deserve none,—/ That will not pity me," and as Bianca had earlier accepted Leantio's "teaching" of rational self-preservation, so does she now accept the Duke's harsher lesson. Like Vittoria, she asks for a charity to which she feels herself genuinely entitled; but if this is not forthcoming, she feels that her ungenerous adversaries "deserve none" from her.

As she concludes her appeal for charity, she confronts the opposing factors of the Cardinal's silent animosity and the Duke's inspired love:

> *Duke.* I kiss thee for that spirit; thou'st prais'd thy wit
> A modest way.—On, on, there!
>   *[Hautboys. Exeunt all except the Cardinal.]*
>   *Car.* Lust is bold,
> And will have vengeance speak ere't be controll'd (IV, iii,
>   70–3)

This testimony convinces her that her only hope lies in preserving the Duke's love at all costs. Though Bianca asks charity for their love from others, the love she has inspired in the Duke produces a more generous feeling in him:

> *Duke.* Now, our fair duchess, your delight shall witness
> How you're belov'd and honour'd; all the glories
> Bestow'd upon the gladness of this night
> Are done for your bright sake. . . .
> How perfect my desires were, might I witness
> But a fair noble peace 'twixt your two spirits!
> The reconcilement would be more sweet to me
> Than longer life to him that fears to die.—
> Good sir—
> > *Car.* I profess peace, and am content. . . .
> > *Bian.* But I've made surer work; this shall not blind me;
> He that begins so early to reprove,
> Quickly rid him, or look for little love: (V, i, 41–4, 50–, 57–9)

In the fruition of his love for Bianca, the Duke experiences a growth in compassion similar to that which Brachiano also felt on his wedding night. His joy overflows in a desire to "delight" his beloved Duchess and, still further, in his desire for a general "reconcilement." In this impulse toward reconcilement, the Duke's love comes close to that most noble form of Worldly Love manifested by the Duchess of Malfi and her Antonio. Indeed, Middleton follows Webster's lead in depicting the worldly lover's non-compassionate appeal for charity as well as the nobler fruition of this love in compassion. But this nobler fruition of Worldly Love is not achieved by Bianca. The quick succession of "envy and slander," to which her still young love had been exposed, has robbed her of the security on which a greater generosity of spirit might have developed. All she knows is that the peace promised her by her second love is again in danger and that its loss would leave her totally unsheltered against the evil storm that would be unleashed upon her.

But in the desperation of her struggle for life, she fatally miscalculates and it is the Duke who drinks the poisoned wine:

Accursed error!
Give me thy last breath, thou infected bosom,
And wrap two spirits in one poison'd vapour!
Thus, thus, reward thy murderer, and turn death
    [Kisses the dead body of the Duke.]
Into a parting kiss! . . .
Thou hast prevail'd in something, cursed poison!
Though thy chief force was spent in my lord's bosom;
But my deformity in spirit's more foul,
A blemish'd face best fits a leprous soul.
What make I here? these are all strangers to me,
Not known but by their malice now thou'rt gone,
Nor do I seek their pities. [Drinks from the poisoned cup.]
                    (V, i, 234–8, 244–50)

In searching for love's companionship, it has been her strange
fortune to stray further and further into isolation. Forsaking
her own family and friends for Leantio's circle—"Here's my
friends,/ And few is the good number"—she was forced to give
up even this small circle of friendship for the sole protection
of the Duke. At court she had always felt herself a stranger and
had withdrawn from its idle frivolities:

    Bian. So now I thank you, ladies; I desire
    Awhile to be alone. . . .
        First Lady. Faith, my desire and hers will ne'er be sisters.
                    (IV, i, 19–20, 22)

Her desire had always been for a peaceful love, though the defeat
of her first love had led her to believe that this could only be
achieved by an increase in power. The more uncertain her peace
became, the more fiercely did she desire it until she was willing
to embrace any evil that might further its realization, murdering with an abandon that reflected the desperate depravity of
her spirit. In embracing the love of the man who had caused
her fall, she had taken the first drink of poisonous evil: "Come
poison all at once." But the poison that had emboldened her
to destroy in the name of love inevitably infected the love it was

to preserve. Now she again embraces the "infected bosom" of the man whose love had become her whole world. Recognizing that his love had led her to an increasing "deformity in spirit," she accepts this too as the price of the love that has made her one with him, though it be the union of "two spirits in one poison'd vapour!" However infected their love may be, it is all she has to cling to, and her commitment to it becomes all the more firm as, in his death, she realizes her complete isolation: "What make I here? these are all strangers to me."

As she drinks the last of the poison she had once invoked, she has a momentary qualm:

> Leantio, now I feel the breach of marriage
> At my heart-breaking. O, the deadly snares
> That women set for women, without pity
> Either to soul or honour! (V, i, 252-5)

She wonders whether it might not have been better if she had tried to preserve her truth to Leantio. But she immediately realizes that she was not responsible for "the breach of marriage," that it was "the deadly snares" set for her which caused an irreparable breach against her will. Hers is not to be a tragedy of False Romantic Love for she does not reject her "deformity in spirit," as did Beatrice, but, at the last, affirms the love that caused it. Raising the empty cup in final tribute to this love, she proudly says:

> Pride, greatness, honours, beauty, youth, ambition,
> You must all down together, there's no help for't:
> Yet this my gladness is, that I remove
> Tasting the same death in a cup of love. *[Dies.]* (V, i, 260-3)

It is no matter that her worldly spirit must suffer the same defeat as her love since its only meaning for her was its apparent ability to further that love which, even at the cost of her life, it was her sole "gladness" to have experienced.

However poisoned the cup of Worldly Love may be, it is the

only form of love which, for Middleton, can be a tragic value; and this because it is capable of achieving the only possible form of earthly value, that which is built upon an acceptance of the world's evil. But Middleton is so thoroughly aware of the persistance with which the naive idealist refuses to face the actual facts of his condition that his primary concern is with the loss of innocence, a loss not only inevitable but necessary for a more meaningful affirmation of value. This is the reason why Middleton approaches the tragedy of Worldly Love through the avenue of False Romantic Love tragedy. Middleton, however, is the only tragedian of False Romantic Love to move beyond the establishment of a norm of truer love to the production of a full tragedy of this love.

Like the two great tragedians of Worldly Love who preceded him, Middleton needed to write a preliminary tragedy in which certain problems of Worldly Love were confronted before he could present its full fruition. For Shakespeare the major problem was that of personal sovereignty; for Webster, that of despair. For Middleton, the obstacle to the full affirmation of Worldly Love lay not simply in the character of the worldly lover but in a false romantic innocence which prevents his acceptance of this love in the first place. He begins, then, at a stage prior to that at which the other tragedians start. This may be why the point at which he arrives in his second tragedy is no further than that which Webster reached in his first.

Middleton does finally arrive at a healthier manifestation of Worldly Love in The Spanish Gipsy,[16] but by that time he had moved beyond his culminating moment of tragic awareness and returned to the comic vein, albeit grimmer, which he had mined during the major portion of his career. Not that there is any essential difference between the world of Middleton's comedies and the tragedies which succeed them;[17] both spheres are essentially corrupt and demand a cynical acceptance of this fact, and in both true goodness can be achieved only through evil. The major difference lies in the greater price that must be paid for this achievement in the tragedies. As the personal value of anything is related to the price which has been paid for it, Middleton affirms the profundity of the values that underlie

his comedies by putting them to the tragic test. The dispassionate cynicism which made possible his early and final comic acceptance of life also contained a perception of values sufficiently
powerful to compel a tragic affirmation, an affirmation all the
more powerful because it was a conclusion culminating from
rather than in contradiction to his cynicism. After the somber-
ness of Webster's vision, Middleton's cynical appraisal of reality
seems to flood his tragic world with a glaring brightness. Though,
in the critical light of reason, the longer shadows of infinity
have disappeared, the bright glare it throws upon the vicious
frivolity of life also reveals the tragic triumph that can be
achieved through a profounder acceptance of this limited reality.
In the scintillating light of the court, Bianca stands forth in
special radiance, her "cup of love" the last tragic tribute raised
to the ideal of Worldly Love.

Conclusion

13

Conclusions on
Elizabethan Love Tragedy

The discussion of the modes of love in the Introduction may have helped to explain the various manifestations of love in the Elizabethan drama, but it hardly prepared us for the unusual transformations in romantic idealization that were encountered. These transformations took two major, though related, forms: the proliferation of dramatic patterning, which enabled all three modes of love tragedy to articulate more perfectly the variety of spiritual attitudes within the changing sensibility of the age, and the broader historical shift in idealization from Courtly to Worldly Love. This conclusion will consider these two major factors in separate sections. To facilitate the historical analysis of the second section, a full chart of the plays has been inserted there.

Dramatic Patterns and Tragic Modes

Although there is no external evidence of a stockpile of dramatic structures, the fact that playwrights were able to produce quickly and on order such a vast amount of plays, that they could collaborate so freely, and that they so readily adapted each other's innovations in plotting, does seem to argue an awareness of the dramatic patterns available for different subjects and a mutual susceptibility to the modifications that these conventions in patterning were constantly undergoing. But as Robert Ornstein has argued: "we know the dramatic tradition more completely and scientifically than any Jacobean could have. Thus it is possible that we can discover conventions of plot and character which even the dramatists did not know existed." [1] In the preceding analyses I have tried to isolate the various developing patterns of dramatic action which the different groups of plays seem to exhibit. Whether or not they correspond to patterns consciously accepted by the playwrights there is no way of knowing. But as we have no certain knowledge of the way in which they actually structured their works, it is hoped these definitions of dramatic action will serve to illuminate and order the rich store of plays that make up the genre of Elizabethan love tragedy.

In gathering together the reflections on structure scattered throughout this work, it will now be possible to see deeper relationships which the patterns of the different modes of love bear to each other. Common to all the modes of love tragedy are distinct but analogous patterns for coping with the obstruction to true love, and it is the pattern's approach to this problem which largely determines its redemptive capacity. The force obstructing the union of the lovers, whether it be the husband, family, society or their combination, provides the apex of the eternal triangle of love which, with varying emphases and modifications, is shared by all the patterns.

In the Elizabethan non-adulterous tragedies of Courtly Love, the traditional role of the husband is taken either by the father of the beloved or a tyrant lover, both of whom personify the power and values of society. The important differences in the patterning of Courtly Love tragedy develop from the different emphases placed upon the three major characters of the thematic triangle: lover, beloved and personification of society.

The classic pattern of Courtly Love tragedy places its emphasis upon the relationship of the lovers, which develops in a condition of obstruction whose validity they never question;

and the actual source of the obstruction is not as highly lighted. The whole impetus of such a tragedy is toward the mutual, transfigured deaths of the lovers, deaths which prove redemptive not only for the lovers but also for the individuals and society whose hostility had led to the lovers' destruction. This pattern, first exemplified by *Tancred and Gismund* (1591), reaches mature form in *Romeo and Juliet* (1595).

In the second—or conflict—pattern of Courtly Love tragedy, the chief emphasis is not upon the lovers but upon the relationship of the lady to the obstructing force. In thematic terms, it is the conflict between the power of love and of society. Although such a pattern might develop into an internal struggle within the heart of the lady—in the form of the love-honor conflict it dominates the classic French tragedies of Courtly Love—it does not so develop in the Elizabethan tragedies of this love and for the probable reason that these courtly lovers are not adulterous. The fatal conflict they exemplify is that between the lady's defiant commitment to Courtly Love (a love reformulated in Stoic terms in the specifically Jacobean tragedies) and the external forces of oppression personifed by the tyrannic would-be lover, who may also bring to the conflict the differing concept of Worldly Love. This conflict resolves itself in the transcendent death of the courtly lover and the discomfiture, though not redemption, of the tyrannical love supported by the power of society, Courtly Love tragically triumphing over the worldly. This is the central emphasis in *Soliman and Perseda* (1590), *Sophonisba* (1605), and *The Second Maiden's Tragedy* (1611).

To the classic and conflict patterns of Courtly Love tragedy a third pattern might be added, although such a pattern moves beyond the confines of the genre of love tragedy. This pattern places its emphasis on the relationship of the lover to the personifications of society. To understand the connection of this pattern to the previous two, it might help to construct a hypothetical "basic plot" of Courtly Love tragedy. Such a plot would begin with the lovers subjected to severe pressure from the forces of society, this pressure leading either to the murder or suicide of one of the lovers. The surviving lover now has two courses open to him: the more noble course of suicide, or the less noble

course of revenging the beloved's death. To continue life without
the justification of revenge, as in the case of Massinissa (in
Sophonisba), brings the lover to shame. The mode of revenge
tragedy, when it is motivated by the defeat of love, may, then
be considered a third pattern of Courtly Love tragedy. As it is
dependent upon the lover's having chosen revenge rather than
suicide in response to his beloved's death, this pattern can only
properly begin after her death. The pattern of *Antonio's Revenge*
(1600) switches from the first to the third line of action after the
death of Mellida, that of *The Second Maiden's Tragedy* from
the second to the third line after the death of the Lady. In such
pure tragedies of revenge for love as that of Bel-imperia in *The
Spanish Tragedy* (1587) and, most importantly, *The Revenger's
Tragedy* (1606), the action is exclusively occupied with this third
line of action. As vengeance replaces the impulse to the love-
death, however, the purity of the lover's spirit becomes corrupted
and the possibility of redemption retreats from him.

The logical development through the three patterns would
seem to indicate that in the *mystique* of Courtly Love the redemptive power of love arises from a passive assent to the necessity
of the obstructing force, which is then transcended in a self-
sacrificial love-death, such a sacrifice redeeming the living as well.
To the extent that the necessity for the obstructing force is openly
contested, the circle of redemption dwindles to embrace only
the suicides. With the final movement from open defiance to
the active attempt to destroy the constituted authority, which
also involves a renunciaion of the love-death, the possibility of
redemption disappears. The impulse to revenge a defeated love
would seem, then, to be a perversion of the natural movement
of Courtly Love toward the love-death, the result of this perversion being to vitiate its redemptive power.

The logical progression of these patterns also shows a partial
correspondence to their historical manifestations. Although all
the patterns appear fairly close to the beginning of the period,
the classic first pattern displays the greatest power in the Elizabethan period proper, and it does not survive this earliest period.
The second and third patterns continue into the Jacobean period,
but as the revenge pattern now completely divorces the action

from its undramatized inspirational source in defeated love, it is the Stoic reformulation of the second pattern that perpetuates the courtly ideal most adequately within the genre of love tragedy. The progression of the genuine patterns of Courtly Love from an inspired mysticism to an embattled Stoicism is, then, both logical and historical, reflecting the changing spirit of the age.[2]

The eternal triangle of love tragedy is treated differently in the tragedies of False Romantic Love. Here the true love is not the lover but the husband and the dramatic movement traces an infidelity and attempted return to the original relationship, this movement defining a tragic initiation from innocence into experience. In this mode of love tragedy, it is not the opposing values and power of society that obstruct the fulfillment of true love but the adultery resulting from the lover's initial inadequacy of commitment. In his innocence of the deep spiritual investment demanded by love, the lover has contracted a relationship with a shallow complacency that bars its highest fulfillment and renders it vulnerable to the temptation of infidelity. Though he enters this infidelity with a continuing lack of moral seriousness, he is suddenly awakened from his innocence to discover that he has embraced evil. Finally recognizing the goodness of the original relationship that he had so casually betrayed, he sees it forever barred to him and, in remorse for his sin, turns to death as the only adequate penace. He is saved from despair by the loving forgiveness of the one he has wronged, but the higher marriage which would now be possible between them is deprived of earthly continuity by the tragic effects of his former infidelity. The three patterns of False Romantic Love tragedy are no more than successive elaborations of this basic structure.

In the classic pattern, exemplified by *A Woman Killed With Kindness* (1603), the wife thoughtlessly falls into a temptation that bars her return to a former happiness whose goodness has been fully dramatized. The strength of her moral rebound, heightened and directed by her husband's loving kindness, effects both her spiritual redemption and a tragic reconciliation with her wronged husband, tragic because it is predicated on her acceptance of penitent death.

The second pattern, best represented by *The Maid's Tragedy* (1610), eliminates the first stage of what is essentially a three-stage pattern, the action beginning with the fact of infidelity and then moving to the barred return. This return is barred not only by the simple moral lapse of infidelity, as in the first pattern, but also by the lover's accidental murder of the one he had betrayed. The loving forgiveness of the wronged party again redeems the faithless lover but, unlike the classic pattern, he accepts death not as penance for his sin but for the eternal fulfillment of his love. As the good of the earlier relationship has not been dramatized, however, the attempt to return to it has a nostalgic quality. This pattern is also reflected in *Cupid's Revenge* (1608) and *The Double Marriage* (1620).

The third pattern, represented most importantly by *The Changeling* (1622), is the most complex elaboration of the basic dramatic structure, effecting a synthesis of the two preceding patterns. The three stages of the classic pattern are restored—the contracting of a love relationship, the infidelity, and the barred return—but with the difference that the dramatized first relationship is itself, as in the second pattern, an act of infidelity to an original, undramatized pre-contract. Where infidelity repented led to suicide in the first two patterns, the need to stabilize the first infidelity through the elimination of the original pre-contract, leads, in this final pattern, to willful murder. It is the effects of this murder, accomplished through a second infidelity, that provide the tragic initiation. But the repentence that follows from this recognition of personal evil, no longer guided by the loving forgiveness of the wronged, is unredemptive and leads only to a thorough repudiation of self. This third pattern is also represented, with slight modifications, in *The Insatiate Countess* (1610) and *The Witch of Edmonton* (1621). *The English Traveller* (1625) differs only in the absence of murder.

The successive elaborations of the classic pattern of False Romantic Love reveal a decline in redemptive vision similar to that of the three patterns of Courtly Love. In the form given to the classic pattern of Courtly Love by *Romeo and Juliet*, the transcendent love-death is further associated with the Christian analogue of vicarious atonement, although such atonement is not a traditional factor in the redemptive model of Courtly Love. The classic pattern of False Romantic Love also reveals a type of vicarious atonement, the wronged party redeeming the one who had wronged him. As this pattern originates in the broader form of domestic tragedy, which is structured on the model of Christian redemption, the type of vicarious atonement it exemplifies seems more intrinsic to its nature than it does to the classic pattern of Courtly Love. Although the atonement through actual sacrificial victim in the second pattern of False Romantic Love allies it even more closely to the Christian model, its redemptive quality is not as convincing as that in the first pattern of False Romantic Love and so may also be compared to the loss of redemptive quality reflected in the second pattern of Courtly Love. The third patterns of these loves may be similarly compared. In both the willful destructiveness of the lovers prohibits any possibility of redemption.

Although both modes exhibit a similar decline in the spiritual capacity to affirm a redemptive faith, the difficulties encountered in such an affirmation differ significantly between the two modes. For Courtly Love the primary difficulty is the passive assent to the validity of the obstructing force, which, in the *mystique* of this love, is required for a proper spiritual transcendence. The conflict pattern shows increasing difficulty in making a passive assent to an obstruction it has declared to be invalid; and this difficulty becomes overwhelming in the revenge pattern, which finally renounces passive assent to destroy the obstruction. In False Romantic Love the obstruction to true love is the internal barrior to full commitment posed by an initial complacency, and it is conceded no legitimacy. The redemption from such false romanticism is accomplished through a tragic initiation that develops the lover's capacity for faith in proportion to his recognition of the value of the love he has forsworn. The successive elaborations of patterning reflect the increasing difficulty in achieving effective moral rebound to this forsworn faith. They are also a beautiful instance of formal adaptation to meet a changing spiritual context. For in this mode the logical progression of the patterns has an almost perfect correspondence to their historical manifestations, each pattern emerging at a successively later date and reflecting the historical shift of sensibility.

The three patterns of Worldly Love show a similar range of redemptive capacity which allies them with corresponding patterns of the other modes. But unlike the steady decline that the patterns of the other modes describe, the logical progression of these patterns may be graphed as a curve of the worldly lover's spiritual development. The worldly lover is defined by his strong sense of sovereign identity, and the three patterns of this mode describe a spiritual progression from complacency to despair with regard to the independent satisfactions of sovereignty divorced from love.

In the first pattern, the lover begins with a complacent assurance of his own worth and tries to accommodate his love to an otherwise sovereign life that claims his deepest commitment. His wife's attempts to actualize a higher vision of conjugal love, one that respects both individuals in a mutually supportive interdependence, are therefore perceived by him as an intolerable threat to his sovereign assertion. When she refuses to conform to his image of her as a simple adjunct to his own well-being, he is easily tempted into the belief that her independent assertion of will represents a betrayal of their marriage that justifies his murder of her. But it is he who has been unfaithful to her in his exclusive regard for himself. His painful recognition of this fault leads to a thorough repudiation of his independent worth for whose preservation he had murdered her. But the final compassion of his wife redeems him at the last from his destructive narcissism. Saved by the vision of love her death has finally granted him, but barred by that death from realizing the higher marriage that he now most desires, he accepts death as penace for his sin. This pattern is structured as a dialectic which, after conflict, brings the best and worst forms of Worldly Love into a final redemptive reconciliation. *Othello* (1604) and *The Duke of Milan* (1621) represent the fully developed first pattern, *Dido* (1587) an earlier effort in this direction, and *Mariam* (1604) a minor entry.

The first pattern of Worldly Love has strong associations with the essential pattern of False Romantic Love. Both seem to develop from a similar inadequacy of commitment and to bring the lover, through a tragic initiation, to a final perception of a higher mode of loving. *Othello* and *The Duke of Milan* even involve a kind of infidelity in that both the title characters are tempted by outside forces to forswear their love. The introduction of the tempter, in fact, completes the eternal triangle, which is otherwise missing from this category. But the infidelity of the worldly lover is not in terms of another love relationship, similar but seemingly better in this same kind; it is an infidelity to love caused by fidelity to self. The initial complacency of the worldly lover rests on the proven worth of this self, and this also differs from the shallow complacency of the false romantic lover which embraces an unearned happiness as its due. Though it is the complacency of both types of lovers which leads to the initial inadequacy of their commitment to love, the worldly lover's commitment, reflecting his stronger sense of personal value, is unlike that of the false romantic lover in being a commitment to the death. Fully committed to the wisdom if not the person of his choice, he cannot break their relationship without also destroying his image of himself. When the relationship makes unexpected demands upon him which threaten his sense of sovereignty, the only way he can free himself from it without destroying his pride is to find her guilty enough to justify murder. In the enormous emotional build-up and self-justification required for the murder he differs even more strikingly from the false romantic lover of the third pattern, who also willfully murders to free himself from a relationship. The temptation of sexual jealousy which consciously motivates the worldly lover to murder of the beloved is, however, structurally parallel to the classic false romantic's sexual infidelity, and its effect is the same: to bar the possibility of return to the violated relationship whose true value has been recognized too late. In both cases, moreover, the imperfect love which undergoes this tragic initiation is contrasted with a dramatically portrayed norm of truer love by which it is finally redeemed. Like the classic false romantic lover, this worldly lover accepts death as penance for his sin. But his sin is closer to that of the second type of false romantic lover in that it involves actual murder of the beloved, and his method of redemption is also parallel. Both are further allied to the classic pattern of Courtly Love in their similar vision of the redemptive capacity of a sacrificial victim to inspire in the hostile force which had defeated it a final saving commitment to its value.

But the very similarity of the first pattern of Worldly Love to the basic structure of False Romantic Love, as it is reflected in all three of its patterns, precludes it from consideration as the classic pattern of Worldly Love. For like Courtly Love, Worldly Love, is a mode of total romantic commitment, and it must pass beyond the internal inhibitions of the first pattern to achieve that highest spiritual health which can stand as its classic manifestation. This is the achievement of the second pattern, Worldly Love being the only mode of love tragedy which does not exhibit a progressive spiritual decline through the logical order of its patterns.

The second pattern of Worldly Love, first exemplified in *Cleopatra* (1593) and fully realized in *Antony and Cleopatra* (1607) and *The Duchess of Malfi* (1614), marks a stage of initial commitment beyond that of the first pattern and represents the noblest earthly realization of this ideal. Here the lovers begin by recognizing that the independent satisfactions of sovereignty have ceased to fulfill their spiritual needs. They turn to the communion with another individual that can give meaning to their personal survival and attempt to build a private life. The love to which they are so totally committed is, however, threatened both from within the relationship and from without. It is threatened from within, particularly in *Antony and Cleopatra,* by the discord which is possible between two independent wills; but its ability to transcend the internal betrayals of love is the measure of its saving grace. It is threatened from without by a society which will not so easily allow the lovers to forget the responsibilities of sovereignty and demands a final accounting. Although the claims of sovereignty have weakened the power of love to sustain both internal and external attack, the lovers affirm to the end their sovereign quality, which retains its value even after the defeat of their love. If they are victims of an uncharitable society aroused to wrath by their reckless surrender to love, the radiant fulfillment their love has given them enables them to accept the final defeat of their sovereign natures with a grace equal to that they had bestowed on life. But their deaths are not redemptive to the society that had denied them this minimal right to personal happiness and it remains the poorer for having sacrificed them to their higher vision of love.

This pattern has many associations with the second pattern of Courtly Love. In both patterns the lovers contest the uninspired or vicious values of society and attempt to create a personal *modus vivendi*. In its Jacobean reformulation, Courtly Love becomes fully assimilated to a Stoicism which enables it to become more a mode of life than of death. Though death is still a release of the soul from the imprisonment of the body, it is no longer, as it was to Romeo, "amorous," the object of a headlong flight to annihilating union. Where the Stoicism of such courtly lovers enables them to walk with a pure spirit through the world's evil, accomplishing an inner retreat from the prison of the world, the worldly lovers seem to exemplify an equally noble Epicureanism which retreats to the garden of personal relations while still remaining in and enjoying the good of the world. In both patterns, moreover, the lovers who commit suicide do not do so until there is no further escape with honor, though the honor that the courtly lovers would preserve—and this tragic type is composed wholly and significantly of women—is their sexual purity, while that of the worldly lovers is their sovereign dignity. In both, finally, the saving value of love cannot redeem the society whose hostility had destroyed the lovers.

The tragic liabilities of Worldly Love revealed in its classic second pattern are enormously increased in the third pattern by the desperation with which these lovers approach their love. Unable to endure the loneliness of their isolating sovereignty, they embrace love as their last salvation and are willing to destroy any obstruction that stands in their path. Where the worldly lovers of the second pattern are prepared to risk all that is truly theirs for disregarding the power of societal censure, the lovers

of the third pattern have moved beyond good and evil, becoming
the joint murderers of the marital partners to whom society has
bound them and for whom society will demand vengeance. The
desperation which will countenance murder for the fulfillment
of love also enters into the fabric of their relationship, giving
rise to fights and recriminations; but they transcend this with a
growth of charity within the relationship that stands in paradoxical
relief against the total lack of charity they show to the external
obstructions to their love. And when their uncharity is tragically
brought home to them, they still claim the blessedness of their
love, though it shall save them in no Christian universe. The
third pattren, first exemplified in the domestic tragedies *Arden
of Feversham* (1591) and *A Warning for Fair Women* (1599),
reaches mature form in *The White Devil* (1612) and *Women
Beware Women* (1623).[3]

The third pattern of Worldly Love has important similarities
with the third patterns produced by the other two modes of love
tragedy. In the third patterns of Courtly and Worldly Love a
destructiveness, as ruthless as it is guiltless, is the concomitant
of the lover's despair. The courtly lover's despair proceeds from
a loss of faith in the redemptive power of love. Unable either
to live or die for love, he can only justify his commitment after
the beloved's death by an unredemptive revenge against the
former, and now meaningless, obstruction to their love. It is the
worldly lover's despair, however, that has led him to a faith in
love's saving power that renders all other considerations irrelevant, and he destroys the obstruction in order to achieve the
earthly fulfillment of his love. The false romantic lover, neither
disillusioned with his love nor despairing in its absence, is urged
to murder by the same moral shallowness that defines his inadequate romantic commitment. Like the worldly lover, his
destructiveness is caused by a desire to stabilize an infidelity
through the elimination of a prior contract which obstructs its
fulfillment. But where the false romantic lover, coming to repent
of his infidelity, ends in a state of despair, the worldly lover,
glorying in his new love, transcends the despair with which he
began and achieves an existential redemption which defies the
moral categories of good and evil.

The similar range in redemptive capacity reflected in the patterns of all three modes is the product of the analogous difficulties faced by each mode in affirming a redemptive faith. If the primary difficulty of Courtly Love lies in the proper achievement of passive assent to the obstructing force, and that of False Romantic Love in the achievement of effective moral rebound to a forsworn faith, the difficulty that a full and productive commitment to Worldly Love encounters is a result of the legitimate preservation of sovereignty within the love relationship that defines this mode of love. The internal and external difficulties faced by a preserved sovereignty attend even the classic manifestation of this love in its second pattern, but they are enormously increased on both sides of this meridian by the complacency or despair with which the love is initially approached.

The logical progression through the three patterns of Worldly Love has a curious correspondence to the historical progression, for both describe not a downward line but a curve. The beginning and the end of the historical period are equally marked by the absence of any significant example of the most noble second pattern. Both progressions, then, seem to indicate a similar difficulty in achieving an adequate affirmation of this mode of love and both also show the ease with which such a fully affirmed love can suffer corruption. The nobler realization achieved in the classic pattern and period of Worldly Love coincides with the broader shift to worldly values that takes place at the height of the Jacobean period.

Though this study of Elizabethan love tragedy has been concerned with tracing the specific differences in dramatic patterning which the three modes of love afford, the similarities that have been noted between the patterns of different modes would also seem to indicate certain broad thematic structures which are equally subsumed by all the modes. These broader forms appear to depend upon the redemptive capacity of the ideal envisioned. The primary redemptive form involves some kind of vicarious atonement leading to a mutually redemptive final reconciliation. In the first pattern of Courtly Love, the obstruction to true love is a feuding society which is reconciled by the redemptive power of the lovers' mutual self-sacrifice. In the first two patterns of False Romantic Love, as well as the first pattern of Worldly Love, the source of the obstruction is a faithlessness within the love relationship, the loving kindness of the injured inspiring a repentence that redeems the faithless partner in a tragic reconciliation. The second redemptive form, exemplified by the second patterns of Courtly and Worldly Love, involves a disregard or open defiance of the values of society in an attempt to build a more meaningful personal life. But the redemption achieved by those who have sacrificed all for their private vision is limited in its power to heal the hostility of society by the very explicitness of their denial of social values. The final redemptive form, exemplified by the third patterns of all three modes of love tragedy, involves a destructiveness in the attainment of desired ends, which either begins with or leads to despair, and which largely vitiates the possibility of redemption. Though the differences in dramatic patterning for the three modes of love constantly assert themselves, they all take their place in the diminishing circle of redemption which, from Romeo to Bianca Capello, is contained in the tragic "cup of love."

In the Elizabethan love tragedies that have been considered, the decreasing scope of redemptive power also seems to reflect a shift in the model of redemption: the first redemptive form is specifically Christian in value or analogue, the second more animated by the pagan ethical systems of Stoicism or Epicureanism, and the third by a type of non-systematized Renaissance existentialism. For the Elizabethan tragedians, these spiritual orientations would seem to have corresponded to their sense of contracting redemptive possibility. One could go further and suggest that it was this range in the tragedians' spiritual attitude toward the possibility of redemption, whether this was the product of their personal developments or the changing sensibility of the age, that necessitated a fracturing of the discrete modes of love tragedy into the various and analogous dramatic patterns of tragic redemption.

The proliferation of analogous patterns was a complex product of the meeting of historical influence with the peculiar difficulties faced by each mode in affirming a redemptive faith. But the fact that the *degree* of redemptive possibility may be similarly indicated by the dramatic patterns of different modes of love tragedy does not obviate the more important distinction as to the *type* of redemption envisioned. It is this that the tragic modes define, and this is what makes the tragedies of the same mode more like each other, whatever their pattern, than they are like the corresponding patterns of the other modes. The dramatic patterns are secondary indicators, the tragic modes primary. For whether true love is represented as capable of redeeming the hostile force that has defeated it, of redeeming only itself, or of effecting no redemption through the perversion of love into an opposing hostility, is not as important in determining its essential tragic shape as the ideal to which it is committed and the adequacy of this commitment.

For each of the modes of love tragedy, this essential form is best represented by its classic pattern. Courtly and False Romantic Love are classically exemplified by their first patterns, the succeeding patterns representing a progressive decline in redemptive vision. For Worldly Love it is the second pattern that represents the meridian of productive fulfillment on a redemptive curve ranging from complacency to despair. The greatest similarity between the three classic patterns is that in them love's power is inspirational enough to meet the tragic testing of its faith without the lovers' resort to murder. The absence of murder cannot, however, be considered an absolute test of classic pattern since there are minor tragedies of other patterns in which none of the lovers murder, e.g., *Dido, Sophonisba,* and *The English Traveller.* But the non-classical patterns, however interesting in themselves and in their progressions, all betray degrees of spiritual failure which, with or without murder, corrupt the pure vision of love's saving power. In speaking generically of the three modes of love tragedy, then, it is to the classic patterns that reference is most specifically intended.

The three modes of love tragedy would seem, finally, to represent sharply distinguished types of tragic action. As the analysis of tragic form has tended to avoid the kind of division into tragic modes that I have been suggesting throughout this study, it would help to review Aristotle's theory of tragedy before arriving at any conclusions as to the theoretical importance of this differentiation.

An adequate understanding of the nature of tragedy has been hampered by the almost universal attempt of critics to force all modes of tragic action onto the Procrustean bed of Aristotle's "perfect plot." [4] The tragic hero required by this plot is "a man not preeminently virtuous and just, whose misfortune, however, is brought upon him not by vice and depravity but by some error of judgment . . . e.g. Oedipus." [5] The action issuing from this error of judgement or *hamartia* will be complex, involving a reversal of fortune from happiness to misery, *peripeteia,* and a recognition, *anagnoresis,* which corrects the condition of ignorance upon which the initial error of judgment was based: "The finest form of Discovery is one attended by Peripeties, like that which goes with the Discovery in *Oedipus.* . . . This [Discovery], with a Peripety, will arouse either pity or fear . . ." [6]

Aristotle's preference for the complex plot with a hero of intermediate moral character does not imply, however, that this is the only type of tragedy he recognized. On the contrary, he admits the existence of the simple plot, that in which "the change in the hero's fortune takes place without Peripety or Discovery," [7] even while arguing that "for the finest form of Tragedy, the Plot must be not simple but complex." [8] What would seem to determine whether the plot will be simple or complex is the manner in which the tragic deed is committed, "either knowingly or unknowingly." [9] Aristotle shows that this deed "may be done by the doer knowingly and consciously, as in the old poets, and in Medea's murder of her children in Euripides. Or he may do it, but in ignorance of his relationship, and discover that afterwards, as does the Oedipus in Sophocles." [10] If the hero commits himself to a course of behavior with full consciousness of its character, that is, without *hamartia,* a later discovery of his initial error of judgment is thereby prohibited and the plot will necessarily be simple. But while recognizing that the old poets, presumably including Aeschylus, and Euripides, had made extensive use of the simple plot, Aristotle characteristically concludes that the example of Oedipus is "best of all." [11]

From this preference for the complex plot, "It follows, therefore, that there are three forms of Plot to be avoided. (1) A good man must not be seen passing from happiness to misery, or (2) a bad man from misery to happiness. . . . The second is the most untragic that can be; it has no one of the requisites of Tragedy. . . . Nor, on the other hand, should (3) an extremely bad man be seen falling from happiness to misery." [12] Of the three possible forms of the simple plot, the second, that in which a bad man ends happily, is clearly to be rejected from any consideration of tragic action. But the first and third forms are not denied all of the requisites of tragedy even by Aristotle. Although inferior to the plot of *Oedipus* in his view, Aristotle does admit the existence of two other modes of tragedy based on the simple plot, those in which either a good man or a bad man passes from happiness to misery.

While Aristotle has provided our primarly illumination of the nature of tragedy by analyzing the sources of pity and fear in the plot of *Oedipus,* he has also done great disservice to our proper appreciation of such other monuments of Greek tragedy as *Antigone* and *Agamemnon.* These works clearly seem to conform to the two tragic modes of the simple plot, those involving the fall into misery of a good and bad personage, respectively, due to the hero's knowing commission of a deed. There are, then, on Aristotle's own analysis, not one but three possible forms of tragic action, and however much his admiration for the complex plot of *Oedipus* may have blinded him to the merits of the two simple plots, they have been recognized by tragedians from his day to ours, to the confusion of many an Aristotelian critic.

This reconsideration of Aristotle's theory of tragedy is relevant to the present study because the three modes of love tragedy which I have isolated in the Elizabethan drama seem to conform to the main outlines of Aristotle's three categories. I would, however, extend the implications of his three modes of tragic action by viewing the good hero's conscious commitment to his act as expressing the affirmation of an infinte ideal, the bad hero's conscious commitment the affirmation of a finite ideal, and the intermediate hero's error of judgment the absence of positive idealization.

The tragedies of "true love" are based upon the affirmation of an ideal, Courtly Love being the idealization of the infinite, Worldly Love of the finite. In either case, however, tragedy subsists in the inadequacy of the inspirational ideal. The inadequacy of the first is its other-worldly purity, of the second its worldly impurity. The tragic hero who embraces the infinite ideal, be he lover or not, is self-sacrificing and seeks union with the ideal at the expense of his finite nature. The tragic hero who embraces the finite ideal, again whether he is a lover or not, is self-centered and seeks realization of the full potentialities of his finite self. The first is passive, and is sacrificed to an ideal too pure for life to permit; the second is active, and is destroyed by the corruption of an ideal too flawed to sustain him. The first is in love with a divinizing death, the second too much in love with the unstable, if sometimes glorious, values of life. The mode of tragedy that includes Courtly Love is also the tragedy of the saint, of *Antigone, Prometheus,* and Eliot's *Murder in the Cathedral.* The mode of tragedy that includes Worldly Love is also the tragedy of the Elizabethan aspiring man, *Tamburlaine, Bussy D'Ambois,* and *Macbeth,* and of Greek *hubris, Agamemnon.* The mode of tragedy to which False Romantic Love belongs is antithetical to the tragedy of ideals, this type going back to the *Oedipus* commended by Aristotle. Here the hero is not informed by an ideal but by a smug assurance of his own happiness. In his moral innocence, he commits an error of judgment based upon ignorance, by means of which he is initiated into the nature of good and evil.

There would seem to be, then, not only three types of love tragedy but three general modes of tragedy to which the romantic patterns conform.[13] If the tragedies of the ideal affirmed reveal the inadequacy of the inspirational ideal, the tragic spirit nevertheless admits of no escape from the tragic human predicament through a denial of idealism. A retreat from active idealization is a retreat from a full spiritual commitment to life, and its result is to make one more vulnerable to the unstable condition of human happiness because more innocent of its true nature and therefore less able to cope with that which would undermine it. To be capable of true commitment one must be, to some degree, already an initiate into the nature of good and evil, must know his own powers and the nature of the ideal, or else he would break his commitment at the first sign of adversity. This being so, he is able to transcend his natural vulnerability by accepting it as a primary condition of his involvement. If he be committed to an infinite idea, he is prepared to forego his finite nature; if to a finite ideal, to accept its possible corruption. He is able, there-fore, to internalize his fate and make a tragic affirmation in his destruction. The morally innocent is incapable of true commit-ment and, therefore, cannot accept responsibility for acts he com-mitted in his innocence. When his unwitting acts turn on him for justice, he then learns through a painful initiation that he is, in Middleton's words, "the deed's creature." His first reaction to this new image of himself will be self-hate, but he may undergo a complete purgation and reach that higher level of awareness which enables him to accept and therefore internalize and trans-cend his fate, as Oedipus and Lear finally do. Tragedy, then, affirms the spirit's victory in defeat, a victory accomplished through commitment to that commingling of good and evil which is the essence of mortal life. The tragic victory accomplished through final commitment to that commingling of good and evil attendant upon the embrace of love has been the subject of this study.

A History of the Genre

The essential distinctions between the three modes of love tragedy might be expected to express themselves in differing rela-tionships to the changing spirit of the age since the questions with which they were concerned—commitment to earthly or abso-lute values and the capacity for faith in the redemptive power of either inspirational ideal—were also confronted by the age as a whole. One way in which the modes reflected the shifting nuances of historical values was through the proliferation and progression of their dramatic patterns, but the modes reflected this changing sensibility even more surely in their relative strengths during the successive stages of the period. As history shapes literary form, so a study of these forms and of their relative power to command the best creative efforts of their time may provide additional illumination of the nature of the age that produced them.

A chart of the tragedies considered in this study will help to clarify the significant historical relationships between them. This chart may also serve to define the extant corpus of love tragedy written during the period 1587–1625. This larger period will be broken down, for reasons that will be later explained, into three smaller phases: 1587–1600, 1601–1611, 1612–1625. To the listing of author, title, and date, I have also added, in roman numerals, the dramatic pattern of the mode of love to which the play conforms.

The historical phases into which the development of Elizabethan love tragedy seems naturally to fall bear a striking resemblance to the phases of the Elizabethan drama that Ellis-Fermor has distinguished: "I regard these phases as covering roughly the periods from the beginning of the Elizabethan drama to about 1598, from about 1598 to 1610 or 1611, and from about 1610 or 1611 to near the end of the reign of James I." [14] Although Henry H. Wells [15] does not distinguish between the first two phases, he, too, sees that there was an important watershed at 1611, the date of Shakespeare's retirement from the stage.

In the first period, Courtly and Worldly Love show equal strength as far as the production of love tragedies is concerned. A study of these tragedies, however, shows Courtly Love to be a dying ideal, Worldly Love an ideal struggling to be born. Courtly Love enters the first phase of the drama with the literary confidence bred of hundreds of years of literary tradition. In *Tancred and Gismund* this literary tradition is able to produce a perfect love tragedy almost unaided by individual talent. Through Shakespeare's genius this literary tradition is shaped into one of the supreme tragic masterpieces of Courtly Love, *Romeo and Juliet*. But, Courtly Love is a Medieval ideal and its inadequacy to express or counter the dominant sensibility of the Renaissance is already felt in this first phase of the drama. Kyd and Marston protest this dominant spirit but are unable to counter it with the full vitality of an opposing faith. In their hands Courtly Love becomes

Chart of Elizabethan Love Tragedies

Courtly Love	False Romantic Love	Worldly Love
Kyd?, *Soliman and Perseda*, 1590 (c. 1589–92), II. Wilmot, *Tancred and Gismund*, 1591, I. Shakespeare, *Romeo and Juliet*, 1595 (1591–97), I. (Marston, *Antonio and Mellida*, I and II, 1599, 1600, III.)		Marlowe, *Dido*, 1587 (c. 1587–93), I. Anonymous, *Arden of Feversham*, 1591 (1585–93), III. Daniel, *Cleopatra*, 1593, II. Anonymous, *A Warning for Fair Women*, 1599 (c. 1598–99), III.
Marston, Sophonisba, 1605 (1605–6), II. Chapman?, *Second Maiden's Tragedy*, 1611, II.	Heywood, *A Woman Killed With Kindness*, 1603, I. Beaumont and Fletcher, *Cupid's Revenge*, 1608 (c. 1607–12), II. Beaumont and Fletcher, *Maid's Tragedy*, 1610 (c. 1608–11), II. Marston, *Insatiate Countess*, 1610 (c. 1610–13), III.	Carey, *Mariam*, 1604 (1602–5), I. Shakespeare, *Othello*, 1604 (c. 1603–4), I. Shakespeare, *Antony and Cleopatra*, 1607 (c. 1606–8), II.
	Fletcher and Massinger, *Double Marriage*, 1620 (1619–23), II. Dekker, Ford and Rowley, *Witch of Edmonton* (subplot), 1621, III. Middleton and Rowley, *Changeling*, 1622, III. Heywood, *English Traveller*, 1625 (1621–33), III.	Webster, *White Devil*, 1612 (1609–12), III. Webster, *Duchess of Malfi*, 1614 (1612–14), II. Massinger, *Duke of Milan*, 1621 (1621–23), I. Middleton, *Women Beware Women*, 1623 (c. 1620–27), III.

diverted from its true end in the love-death to act as an instrument of revenge. This diversion of Courtly Love away from love tragedy proper and into the genre of revenge tragedy continues to be an important aspect of this genre, as can be seen in Tourneur's (?) *The Revenger's Tragedy* (1606) and Chapman's *The Revenge of Bussy D'Ambois* (1610). If *Antonio's Revenge* anticipates one of the tragic forms of Courtly Love in the second phase of the drama, *Soliman and Perseda* does another. This play reveals a rudimentary form of the conflict between Courtly and Worldly Love which is given greater expression in *The Second Maiden's Tragedy*. In one way or another the early plays of Kyd and Marston betray both a sense of conflict with the dominant mood of their age and also the enfeeblement of the ideal they would affirm resulting from this sense of conflict. It is only in the first phase of the drama that a pure Courtly Love is given powerful expression, and already in its classic phase the inadequacy of this ideal is felt.

In the tragedies of Worldly Love there is an almost opposite phenomenon. The problem here is the lack of a literary tradition of Worldly Love which might help to define the pattern of its love tragedy. The reason for this lack is that Worldly Love was not a literary ideal but an ideal embraced by actual historical figures of the Renaissance. It is primarily to history, then, that the writers who would express this new ideal turned. Recent English history provided the source of two anonymous tragedies, *Arden of Feversham* and *A Warning for Fair Women,* but these writers were unable to give clear expression to this new ideal because they adapted the alien form of domestic tragedy to a subject that defied this form. More scholarly writers turned to the great worldly lovers of ancient history: Antony and Cleopatra, Herod and Mariamne. I include Lady Carey's slightly later *Mariam* in this discussion of the first period because it seems to represent a survival of the concerns of this first period. The closet dramas of Daniel, Lady Carey, and the Countess of Pembroke, who translated Garnier's *Marco-Antoine* as *Antonius* (1590), are, however, coterie products related to the development of the living theatre only in having first given treatment to materials that Shakespeare and Massinger were later to use. In *Dido* Marlowe turns not to ancient history but to ancient literature for his model, and although he completely changes Vergil's concept of Dido's love, he is bound by a source that did not depict Worldly Love and therefore could not provide him with an adequate dramatic pattern of this love. Although the plays in this first period do manage to define patterns of Worldly Love tragedy which are to be given a better realization in the later development of the drama, their own expression of these patterns is clouded by the alien dramatic forms which, in lieu of a literary tradition, they tried to adapt to these new purposes. But the struggling vitality of these earliest Worldly Love tragedies points to the future ascendancy of their ideal.

The second phase of the drama witnesses the first appearance of False Romantic Love tragedy in its classic form, a mode that is to continue throughout the second and third phases. This mode of love tragedy is significant for an analysis of the conflict between courtly and worldly commitment precisely because it shows an inability to make a full commitment to either. Though unable to dramatize such full commitment, it can provide a critique of the excesses of such affirmation in terms of the higher norm it envisions. In the second phase of the drama, the norms of False Romantic Love tragedy are equally split between Worldly and Courtly Love: Heywood envisioning a norm of Worldly Love beyond that which had thus far been exhibited in the tragedies of this love, and Beaumont and Fletcher a purer norm of Courtly Love than that to which the Courtly Love tragedies of this second phase could give expression.

The true conflict between Courtly and Worldly Love in the second phase is, however, not that between the purer norms envisioned in the tragedies of False Romantic Love, but between the significant Jacobean reformulations of these ideals exhibited in the tragedies of these loves. The tragedies of Courtly Love no longer retain the ecstatic enthusiasm of the earlier period nor even the nostalgic remembrance of such vaulting idealism that can be seen in the Beaumont and Fletcher tragedies of False Romantic Love. The traditional courtly mysticism has been completely reformulated into Stoic terms, terms more acceptable to an age lacking an enthusiastic faith in spiritual purity.

In the Stoic tragedies of *Sophonisba* and *The Second Maiden's Tragedy,* the affirmation of Courtly Love is not only more restrained, as becomes their chastened ideal, but seriously qualified by the portrayal of perverted or ignoble adherents to the ideal so nobly championed by their tragic heroines. These plays are, in fact, more concerned with the qualifications of the ideal than with its affirmation.

In contrast to these expressions of a dying ideal, the second phase is distinguished by the great Shakespearean tragedies of Worldly Love. Shakespeare's shift of allegiance at this time from Courtly to Worldly Love is perhaps the most significant event in the whole history of Elizabethan love tragedy; and it further evidences his extreme sensitivity to the changing spirit of his age. The ideal of Courtly Love inspired him while it still retained the vitality of preceding ages; but with its decline, he breathed the fresher air of a new ideal struggling to find expression and gave it immortal form. He begins, in *Othello* by envisioning a higher norm of Worldly Love while studying the problems of this love which obstruct a full commitment. But with *Antony and Cleopatra,* he fully affirms this love, not in the form of its higher ideal, but in the form that the Jacobean period demanded, a triumphant Epicureanism. In the Jacobean period, then, the conflict between Courtly and Worldly Love has become translated into a conflict between Stoicism and Epicureanism, and it is in this form that Worldly Love achieves its full ascendancy.

One measure of the relative strengths of these two ideals in the first and second phases can be seen in the differentiation between the sexes with regard to the affirmation of these ideals, the full vitality of an ideal of love being indicated by its ability to inspire men as well as women to a tragic affirmation. In the first phase, Courtly Love is fully affirmed by both sexes, Guiszhard and Romeo being as able to embrace a triumphant love-death as their femine counterparts. In the second phase, only women are capable of the love-death, Massinissa and Govianus (in *Sophonisba* and *The Second Maiden's Tragedy,* respectively) accepting, in fact, the sacrifices of their ladies for their own future welfare. The situation is completely reversed in the case of Worldly Love. In the first phase, it is only women who can fully affirm the ideal of Worldly Love. Both Aeneas and Mosbie are inspired by worldly ambition rather than love, using the love of Dido and Alice Arden for ulterior purposes and rejecting them at the first opportunity. In the second phase, however, it is Worldly Love which, in *Antony and Cleopatra,* is gloriously affirmed by both sexes, and this double affirmation continues throughout the third phase.

There is another measure by which to gauge the shift of idealization that took place. If the classic periods of the three modes of love tragedy are considered, it will be seen that it was toward the final ideal of Worldly Love that the whole genre was moving. The classic period of Courtly Love occurred earliest, in the 1590's, and most brilliantly in *Romeo and Juliet.* The classic period for the tragedy of False Romantic Love followed hard upon the lingering death which the ideal of Courtly Love suffered in the two parts of *Antonio and Mellida,* occurring in the early 1600's with *A Woman Killed with Kindness.* Heywood's classic tragedy of False Romantic Love may be said to mark a transition from Courtly to Worldly Love; it begins with a romanticism without *mystique* and ends by projecting an exalted vision of Worldly Love. Shakespeare carried on this transitional phase in *Othello,* finally to produce the classic tragedy of Worldly Love, *Antony and Cleopatra.* If Courtly Love thrived best in the Elizabethan period, Worldly Love is essentially a Jacobean phenomenon. The classic period of Worldly Love tragedy comes at the end of the second phase of the drama and heralds its full ascendancy in the third.

In contrast to Ellis-Fermor, Wells indicated only one important watershed which demarcated the essential phases of the drama, and this second division is, indeed, more significant than the first. Although the first two phases produced a great many love tragedies, love was still but one of several tragic ideals. In a sense, the subordination of love to ambition, made by Marlowe's Aeneas at the very dawn of this great dramatic period, may stand as a symbol for the relative evaluations of these ideals in the first two phases. Although both Marlowe and Shakespeare wrote love tragedies, their major energies were not devoted to this genre.

The tragedy of aspiration, which began with *Tamburlaine* and ended with *Macbeth*, defined these first two phases more adequately than the tragedy of love. If the tragedians of Courtly Love were not as concerned with aspiration as the tragedians of Worldly Love, they still found more adequate expression, even for love, in a purely masculine revenge. Revenge and aspiration are the non-romantic ideals which correspond to Courtly and Worldly Love. In these first two phases, they were at least if not more significant than the idealization of love.

In the third phase of the drama, however, love emerges as the only tragic ideal. The history of the Elizabethan tragic drama shows a marked similarity in this to the history of Greek tragedy. The three Greek tragedians themselves represent three phases of the drama, and in the last phase Euripedes turns from the more universal concerns of his predecessors to an emphasis upon love tragedy and the psychology of women. But the love tragedies that dominate the third phase of the Elizabethan drama are significantly different from those of Euripedes in that they are no longer manifestations of Eros. In this last phase, the rival concept of Courtly Love has been completely silenced by an all-powerful Worldly Love. It is, then, not simply love but Worldly Love that is the final tragic ideal of the Elizabethan drama.

After 1611 the masterpieces of the tragic drama are all Worldly Love tragedies. Massinger's tragic masterpiece, *The Duke of Milan,* offers the clearest proof of the dominance of the Worldly ideal. Although his other works show a preference for the courtly ideal and are pervaded by the Stoic's love of purity, his talent for tragedy only approaches greatness in treating the dominant ideal of this period. But the true spirit of this last phase is epitomized in the tragedies of Webster and Middleton, all of which affirm the ideal of Worldly Love.

Alongside the four tragedies of Worldly Love written between 1612 and 1625 are two significant tragedies of False Romantic Love. It was earlier said that False Romantic Love tragedy provides a critique of the full affirmation of love by showing the inability of its characters to affirm such an ideal. What is significant about *The Witch of Edmonton* and *The Changeling*, however, is that the only viable ideal they envision is that of Worldly

Love. The tragedies of Worldly Love affirm this ideal; the tragedies of False Romantic Love qualify it but can envision no other norm. In *The Changeling,* Middleton pits the Stoic Courtly Love of Alsemero against the frankly Hedonistic Worldly Love of De Flores and reveals the greater vitality of the Worldly ideal. With this proof, he then goes on to write a tragedy of Worldly Love. Although all tragedians of False Romantic Love present a norm of love that their characters are tragically unable to affirm, Middleton is the only one who was sufficiently convinced by the value of his norm to be able to move beyond such envisionment to a tragic dramatization of this love. The ideal of Worldly Love had such vitality in this period that it inspired Webster's profoundly tragic view of life, was able to pull the imperfect sympathies of Massinger within its orbit, and to overcome Middleton's constitutional detachment.

The greatest tragedians of this last phase, Webster and Middleton, affirm Worldly Love as the only tragic ideal, the form in which this ideal is manifested being that which Shakespeare had given it in *Antony and Cleopatra,* a radiant Epicureanism. Whereas Marston's Sophonisba had stoically rejected love's pleasures in the belief that "Happiness makes us base," the Epicurean tragedies of Worldly Love affirm that "The nobleness of life is to do thus." It is the universal affirmation of this personal ideal that characterizes the last phase of this dramatic movement. The inspiration to build or wreck empires, which characterized the earlier phases, has completely vanished in a general indifference to the fate of Rome. It is another form of the Epicurean retreat to the garden, the desire for personal happiness.

The ideal of Worldly Love, first enunciated by Marlowe, raised to its greatest personal heights by Shakespeare, and universalized by Webster, gains its full ascendency in the last phase of the Elizabethan drama; but by that time this dramatic movement is already in its decline, and its decadence is reflected in the last of the Worldly Love tragedies. The worldly lovers of Webster and Middleton are disquieted and world-weary, striving for a happiness that they think love, no matter the cost, can bring them. They turn to love, in a manner more or less desperate, to salvage some meaning for their lives; but they are lives for which aspiration, duty, and even morality have lost their meaning and love is the only sustaining prop. In being pressed too hard for meaning, this prop ultimately becomes corrupted; but it had, while it maintained the lovers, that genuine inspirational power they still affirm in their defeat. Worldly Love is, however, the last tragic ideal that can be gloriously affirmed and, with it, the continuity of dramatic development, which had lasted through the Elizabethan and Jacobean periods, comes to its end.

When Middleton's Bianca Capello raises the "cup of love" to her lips, she not only closes the last significant phase of this dramatic movement but speaks as well the epitaph to Worldly Love tragedy. In the following Caroline period, the ideal of Worldly Love is completely extinguished and Courtly Love makes a triumphal, though decadent, return with Ford. His three Courtly Love tragedies, written sometime between 1629 and 1633 combine the English tradition of Marston and of Beaumont and Fletcher with the French form of Platonized Courtly Love imported with Queen Henrietta Maria. It is significant that it is only now, in *Love's Sacrifice,* that a glorified Courtly Love is presented in its proper, if chaste, form of adultery. But Ford's more brilliant tragedies, *The Broken Heart* and *'Tis Pity She's a Whore,* reveal a curious and highly original synthesis of the pattern of courtly revenge with that of False Romantic Love, both of which forms mark an equal inspirational failure of the courtly ideal.[16]

The conditions that bring about this return to Courtly Love, however, are no longer related to the genuine spirit of the age but to the last gasps of a dying aristocracy. The split between an increasingly Puritan populace and an inflexible aristocracy, which had been slowly developing during the reign of James I, becomes pronouced in the early years of Charles I's rule. As Caroline playwrights become increasingly identified with aristocratic values, so do they become alienated from the aroused Puritan populace which finally closes the theatre. But, as Patrick Cruttwell has shown:

> The Puritans had won their real war against it long before
> the actual theatres were closed; this, it seems likely, was the

real reason—one important reason, at any rate—for the remarkably swift degeneration of the drama after about 1620; the Puritans had been so successful in discrediting it, even among those who were not themselves Puritans, that the best minds and the finest spirits were no longer willing to write for it.[17]

The early 1620's represent the close of what Cruttwell has called "The Shakespearean Moment."

Thereafter, Courtly Love regains the dominant position in love tragedy which it had held before that great moment. From Ford to Hardy, Tolstoy to Lorca, and the even more significant operatic composers, Verdi and Wagner, Courtly Love is the only ideal of love tragedy. The novel, together with opera, becomes the principal medium of love tragedy. The love tragedies of the past few hundred years are almost exclusively tragedies of Courtly Love, although there have been such great tragic novels of False Romantic Love as Stendhal's *The Red and the Black* and Flaubert's *Madame Bovary*. But to the best of my knowledge there has been no tragedy of Worldly Love written since the time of Middleton. This is not to say that Worldly Love has been entirely absent from great literature. It is, in fact, the ideal with which *War and Peace* finally closes. But, though Tolstoy affirms as the highest earthly good the Worldly Love of Pierre and Natasha, when he turns to love tragedy it is the Courtly Love of Vronsky and Anna Karenina that inspires him. Modern literature may concede that Worldly Love is a better love to live with, if one is enamoured of life, but its love tragedies celebrate the imortal beauty of the *liebestod*.

In the whole history of Western sensibility, it is only in the Shakespearean moment that Worldly Love has been affirmed as a tragic ideal. But if Courtly Love has been the ideal of love tragedy in all other ages, it was not the dominant ideal of that age which produced the greatest expressions of the tragic spirit in modern Western history. The great Worldly Love tragedies of Marlowe, Shakespeare, Webster, and Middleton form a unique contribution to Western culture and, possibly, the most significant contribution of the Elizabethan drama.

Notes

Notes

Notes for Chapter 1

1. I extend the meaning of the term "Elizabethan" to include the Jacobean period, which immediately follows the Elizabethan period proper and continues the development of its mood. Since the drama loses its popular base in the Caroline period and becomes more of a coterie theatre, I have chosen to end this study before this break in the continuity of the dramatic development, though this involves the regrettable omission of Ford (but see p. 366 and extended note on Ford). This study of "Elizabethan" love tragedy, then, covers the period 1587-1625.
2. See Denis de Rougemont, *Love in the Western World*, trans. Montgomery Belgion (1st ed., New York, 1940), p. 78. The revised edition (New York: Doubleday Anchor Books, 1957) will be used for all future references.
3. See C. S. Lewis, *The Allegory of Love* (London, 1938), p. 2.
4. For an excellent review of this subject, see Theodore Silverstein, "Andreas, Plato and the Arabs: Remarks on Some Recent Accounts of Courtly Love," *MP*, XLVII (1949–50), p. 124 *et passim*.
5. Peter Dronke, *Medieval Latin and the Rise of European Love-Lyric* (Oxford, 1965), I, 93–4.
6. Andreas Capellanus, *The Art of Courtly Love*, trans. John Jay Parry (New York, 1941), p. 100.
7. *Ibid.*, p. 153.
8. Alexander J. Denomy, C. S. B., "Courtly Love and Courtliness," *Speculum*, XXVIII (1953), 44. For further expression of his views, see also "An Inquiry into the Origins of Courtly Love," *Medieval Studies*, VI (1944), 175–260; "Fin'amors, The Pure Love of the Troubadours," *Medieval Studies*, VII (1945), 139–207; and *The Heresy of Courtly Love* (New York, 1947).

9. De Rougemont, p. 26.
10. Andreas, pp. 106–7.
11. See Lewis, pp. 40–1.
12. Andreas, p. 171.
13. *Ibid.*, p. 28.
14. Maurice Valency, *In Praise of Love* (New York, 1958), p. 160.
15. Dronke, I, 7.
16. De Rougemont, p. 9.
17. *Ibid.*, p. 36.
18. *Ibid.*, p. 32.
19. Silverstein, p. 117.
20. In support of this attribution to Chapman, see my article "Authorship of *The Second Maiden's Tragedy:* A Reconsideration of the Manuscript Attribution to Chapman," *SP,* LXIII, 1 (Jan., 1966), 51–77.
21. See Vernon Lee, *Euphorion* (London, 1899), pp. 427–9.
22. See Gaston Paris, "Lancelot du Lac," *Romania,* XII (1883), 578.
23. Chrétien de Troyes, "Le Chevalier de la Charrette," in *Arthurian Romances,* trans. W. W. Comfort (London: Everyman's Library, 1955), p. 270.
24. See Lewis Freeman Mott, *The System of Courtly Love* (Boston, 1896), p. 97.
25. Chrétien, *Yvain,* pp. 212–3.
26. *Ibid.*, p. 213.
27. *Ibid.*, p. 216.
28. *Ibid.*, p. 240.
29. *Ibid.*
30. *Ibid.*, p. 265.
31. *Ibid.*, p. 269.
32. Tom Peete Cross and William Albert Nitze, *Lancelot and Guenevere: A Study of the Origins of Courtly Love* (Chicago, 1930), p. 69.
33. Andreas, p. 100.
34. *Ibid.*
35. Baldassare Castiglione, *The Courtier,* trans. Thomas Hoby, ed. Rossiter Johnson (New York, 1907), pp. 277–9.
36. Dronke, I, 3.
37. *Ibid.*, 1–46.
38. Lewis, p. 16.
39. Aristotle, "Nicomachean Ethics," in *The Basic Works of Aristotle,* ed. Richard Mckeon (New York, 1941), IX: 10, p. 1091.
40. *Ibid.*, IX: 4, pp. 1081–2.
41. *Ibid.*, VIII: 7, p. 1066.
42. Plato, "Symposium," in *The Dialogues of Plato,* trans. B. Jowett (New York, 1937), I, 334–5.
43. Plato, *Phaedo,* I, 447.
44. Aristotle, IX: 12, p. 1093.
45. *Ibid.*, VIII: 5, p. 1064.
46. *Ibid.*, IX: 5, p. 1083.
47. *Ibid.*, VIII: 4, p. 1062.
48. *Ibid.*, IX: 12, p. 1093.
49. *Ibid.*, VIII: 1, p. 1058.

50. The most important of these are Kierkegaard in *Stages on Life's Way*, De Rougemont in *Love in the Western World,* and Erich Fromm in *The Art of Loving*.
51. For a full discussion of the Elizabethan coterie theatre, see Alfred Harbage, *Shakespeare and the Rival Traditions* (New York, 1952).
52. Clifford Leech, *John Webster: A Critical Study* (London, 1951).
53. Madeleine Doran, *Endeavors of Art: A Study of Form in Elizabethan Drama* (Madison, 1954), p. 140.
54. I use this term in its more current Freudian rather than traditional Ovidian sense. See Sigmund Freud, "On Narcissism: An Introduction," *Collected Papers* (London: Hogarth Press, 1956), IV, 40–59.
55. Aristotle, IX: 8, p. 1086.
56. *Ibid.*, IX: 4, p. 1083.
57. *Ibid.*, VIII: 13, p. 1073.
58. *Ibid.*, VIII: 13, p. 1074.
59. *Ibid.*, IX: 1, p. 1076.
60. *Ibid.*, IX: 1, p. 1077.
61. St. Thomas Aquinas, *Summa Theologica,* trans. The English Dominican Fathers (London, 1921), II, I, 28, 5.
62. *Ibid.*, II, I, 26, 1.
63. *Ibid.*, II, I, 28, 1.
64. *Ibid.*, II, I, 26, 2.
65. *Ibid.*
66. *Ibid.*, II, I, 28, 4.
67. *Ibid.*
68. *Ibid.*, II, I, 28, 3.
69. *Ibid.*, II, I, 26, 3.
70. *Ibid.*, II, I, 28, 1.
71. *Ibid.*, II, II, 154, 8.
72. *Ibid.*, III, Supplement, 49, 5.
73. *Ibid.*, III, Supplement, 47, 3.
74. *Ibid.*
75. William and Malleville Haller, "The Puritan Art of Love," *HLQ*, V (1942), 238, 265–6.
76. See, for instance, Jacob Burckhardt, *The Civilization of the Renaissance in Italy,* trans. S. G. C. Middlemore (New York: Modern Library Edition, 1954), p. 332, and David Lloyd Stevenson, *The Love-Game Comedy* (New York, 1946), pp. 103–7.
77. Burckhardt, p. 340.
78. Lewis, p. 13.
79. See Harbage, pp. 224–5.
80. *Ibid.*, p. 228.
81. See Stevenson, pp. 100–4.
82. *Ibid.*, p. 215.
83. *Ibid.*, p. 73.
84. *Ibid.*, p. 105.
85. *Ibid.*, p. 107.
86. Harbage, p. 226.
87. *Ibid.*, p. 224.
88. For an insight into her strength of character and wily cunning, see

Reginald Pole's venemous description of Anne Boleyn in a letter written to Henry VIII and dated 1536, as quoted in Philip Hughes' *The Reformation in England* (London, 1950), I, 159.

89. Burckhardt, p. 17.

90. Henry C. Lea, in *The History of Sacerdotal Celibacy in the Christian Church* (New York, 1957), pp. 355–61, specifies some of these actual cases of clerical love tragedy in his treatment of the early movement toward sacerdotal marriage.

91. F. L. Lucas, ed., *The Complete Works of John Webster* (London, 1927), II, 16–7.

92. Harbage, pp. 237–8.

93. *Ibid.*, p. 249.

94. Geoffrey Chaucer, "Troilus and Criseyde," in *The Poetical Works of Chaucer*, ed. F. N. Robinson (Boston, 1933), p. 564.

95. This derivation was personally suggested to me by the late Professor Una Ellis-Fermor with whom I had the privilege of working at an early stage in the development of this book.

96. Henry H. Adams, *English Domestic Tragedy* (New York, 1943), p. 189.

Notes for Chapter 2

1. The following are the modern editions of these two plays: R. W. and others, *Gismund of Salerne*, ed. John S. Farmer, Student's Facsimile Texts (Amersham, Eng., 1914?), a photo-facsimile of the B. M. Hargrave MS. 205, f. 9; Robert Wilmot, *The Tragedy of Tancred and Gismund*, ed. W. W. Greg, Malone Society Reprints (Oxford, 1914). From my collation of these two versions, I have found that, though the revision involves much rewriting, it is mostly in the form of minute verbal polishing with the main lines of treatment remaining unchanged. Lines are added and subtracted freely, but this is less true for whole speeches and not at all true for scenes. Wilmot's only important structural change comes in the rewriting of his own original fifth act, which he greatly expands. Still, the revision makes the play, as far as possible, the product of one man's brain, the few lines he inserts from time to time elevating the tone of the whole. *Gismund of Salerne* is the only surviving love tragedy in the English drama to have been written before the date at which this study properly commences, 1587, so that this brief footnote may be said to extend the scope of this study to the beginnings of the English drama. Although I am resting my consideration of this play in this footnote, I should like simply to note that it is surprising that the work of five students, each writing an act, should have been as good as it is. In the following analysis, all quotations are from Greg's edition of *Tancred and Gismund*. Here and throughout the remainder of this study, I have not, when using original spelling texts, indicated the italicization of proper nouns, while I have uniformly italicized all of the stage directions.

2. In the Elizabethan tragedies of Courtly Love, Gismund and Guiszhard

are the only glorified courtly lovers who, though they desire marriage, fulfill their physical desires illicitly.

3. It is presumably from the comments of the chorus that Irving Ribner arrives at his conclusion: "Gismunda is characterized throughout as a lustful woman committing a mortal sin, one whose fate may serve as a warning to good women everywhere." See his "Then I Denie You Starres: A Reading of Romeo and Juliet," in *Studies in The English Renaissance Drama: In Memory of Karl Julius Holzknecht,* ed. Josephine W. Bennett, *et al.* (New York, 1959), p. 273. See also Annette T. Rottenberg, "The Early Love Drama," *College English,* XXIII (1962), 581–3, for a similar if less certain verdict. But Gismund is in good company, for Juliet and the Duchess of Malfi have been subjected to similar critical attempts to show that the expressions of their love would be understood by their original audiences as proof of their sins.

4. The outer limits of composition may be set as 1591–7. Here and throughout this study, I have, in the interest of uniformity, adopted the dating given in the *Annals of English Drama: 975–1700,* by Alfred Harbage, rev. S. Schoenbaum (Philadelphia, 1964). In the few cases where I have preferred another dating, I have indicated my reasons in notes.

5. Shakespeare, *Romeo and Juliet,* in *Works,* ed. George Lyman Kittredge (Boston, 1936), Prologue, 1. 9. All further references are to this edition.

6. Elmer Edgar Stoll, *Shakespeare's Young Lovers* (New York, 1937), p. 8.

7. See Harley Granville-Barker, *Prefaces to Shakespeare: Second Series* (London, 1946), pp. 52–4 and *passim.*

8. Franklin M. Dickey, *Not Wisely But Too Well: Shakespeare's Love Tragedies* (San Marino, California, 1957), p. 94.

9. See Paul N. Siegel, "Christianity and the Religion of Love in *Romeo and Juliet,*" SQ, XII (1963), 371-92.

10. For a similar interpretation of this speech, see Granville-Barker, pp. 52–3.

11. Caroline Spurgeon, in *Shakespeare's Imagery* (Cambridge, Eng., 1958), traces the same pattern of "light" imagery, seeing it, however, as primarily "building up a definite picture and atmosphere of brilliance swiftly quenched" (pp. 315–6).

Notes for Chapter 3

1. Arthur Freeman, in "Shakespeare and 'Solyman and Perseda,'" *MLR,* LVIII (1963), argues convincingly for the 1591–2 date (p. 485) and for authorship by the author of the *Spanish Tragedy* (p. 487). E. K. Chambers dates it c. 1589–92 in *The Elizabethan Stage* (Oxford, 1923), IV, 46 (see also his discussion of the authorship question); Samuel Schoenbaum, in the revision of Alfred Harbage's *Annals of English Drama: 975–1700* (Philadelphia, 1964), lists the play under the 1590 date; and F. S. Boas gives 1592 as its earliest date in *The Works of Thomas Kyd* (Oxford, 1955). All quotations are from the Boas edition of Kyd.

2. Una Ellis-Fermor, *The Jacobean Drama*, 3rd ed. (London, 1953), p. 2.
3. John Marston, *Antonio and Mellida: The First Part*, ed. G. K. Hunter (Lincoln, Neb., 1965). All further references are to this edition.
4. John Marston, *Antonio's Revenge: The Second Part of Antonio and Mellida*, ed. G. K. Hunter (Lincoln, Neb., 1965). All further references are to this edition.
5. *The Spanish Tragedy* is introduced by the ghost of Andrea, accompanied by Revenge, who demands that Andrea's beloved, Bel-imperia, revenge his death in battle at the hands of Don Balthazar. Although agreeing to the revenge, Bel-imperia soon accepts another lover, Horatio, rationalizing this change of heart by the feint of employing her second love to further her revenge. As Balthazar now courts her love, she will not only disdain his suit but throw her preference for Horatio in his face, content that this will satisfy the demands of vengeance. But when her brother, to further Balthazar's marital designs upon her, kills Horatio, she does vow bloody revenge against Balthazar, the murderer of her two loves. Thus she informs Hieronimo of the murderers' identity, rebukes him for delaying the revenge of a kindred and informs him of her own unusual resolve: "My selfe, a stranger in respect of thee,/ So loued his life, as still I wish their deathes./ Nor shall his death be vnreuengd by me" (IV, i, 21–3). Joining Hieronimo in revenge, she kills Balthazar and then herself, for "loue of him, whom they did hate too much" (IV, iv, 144–5). Her infidelity to the memory of Andrea going uncensured in the play, she finally proves her title as a courtly lover by dying for love of Horatio.
6. See Fredson Thayer Bowers' *Elizabethan Revenge Tragedy: 1587–1642* (Princeton, 1940) for a discussion of this traditional revenge motive. As Bowers is concerned to establish a genre of revenge tragedy in which revenge is seen to be the cause of the final catastrophe, he makes nothing of the distinction he notes between the filial and romantic motivation of revenge in Elizabethan tragedy.
7. Erich Auerbach, *Mimesis*, trans. Willard Trask (New York: Doubleday Anchor Books, 1957), p. 122.
8. *The Plays of John Marston*, 3 vols., ed. H. Harvey Wood (London, 1934), II, 63. All further references are to this edition. As Wood gives no line references, his page numbers have been substituted.
9. Andre Malraux, *Man's Fate*, trans. Haakon M. Chevalier, Modern Library Edition (New York, 1934), p. 245.
10. *The Insatiate Countess* deserves some comment as another instance of Marston's remarkable insight into the vagaries of passion. Isabella brings herself and others into shame because she does not properly understand the mechanism of Courtly Love which utilizes obstruction for the intensification of desire. She makes the repeated mistake, therefore, of trying to overcome the obstruction though aware that her desire only persists until it is satisfied. When on her wedding night all obstruction to her desire for Roberto has been removed, she loses even the wish for its consummation and her desire becomes fixed on one as yet unobtainable, Massino. But Isabella does not even know how to maintain adulterous desire. Rather than remaining in her husband's house, she establishes herself so comfortably in open residence with her lover

that her desire for this lover also fades before its consummation and fastens upon another, Gniaca. This time, however, she finally does achieve the conditions that can maintain her desire until its consummation, having arranged a secret tryst with one lover within the house she openly shares with another. Beginning to be satiated with the very mechanism of her own tormenting desire, she finally awaits its consummation for this very reason: "Desire, thou quenchlesse flame that burn'st our soules,/ Cease to torment me;/ The dew of pleasure shall put out thy fire" (III, i). But with this consummation, her desire takes a new form. When Massino revenges himself against her by writing scandalous ballads on her behavior, she vows herself to revenge, saying: "Revenge to me is sweeter now then lust" (IV, i). And when Gniaca, who champions her cause against Massino, is reconciled with him, she takes another lover, Don Sago, to be revenged against them both. Again we see a degenerate Courtly Love turning to revenge as the only activity that can fully inspire enthusiasm. Having unflinchingly portrayed the depravity to which the essential impulse of Courtly Love can lead when it ceases to use obstruction as a spiritual discipline preparatory to transfigured death, Marston now yields to the traditional remorse of the tragic false romantic lover. For Isabella, in attempting to experience the ecstasy of courtly desire without any initiation into its *mystique*, follows a pattern of behavior that is essentially false romantic. Sentenced to death for having instigated the murder of Massino, she undergoes a sudden conversion with the reappearance of her husband. When Roberto, who upon his disillusionment with Isabella had become a friar, ascends the scaffold to bring her to repentance, she suddenly sees herself as a loathed creature whose infidelities have only barred the way to her true happiness. With this new insight—like Mrs. Frankford—she now craves only his pardon. Unlike Mrs. Frankford, however, her former behavior still has a certain nostalgia for her: "O these golden nets,/ That have insnar'd so many wanton youthes,/ . . . Now to the block" (V, i). Isabella is the only tragic false romantic lover who has such nostalgia, this but the final indication of her unparalleled depravity in this type of Elizabethan tragedy. Like all of Marston's plays, this little-known work is memorable for the subtle originality of its characterization and also for one consummate poetic line: "Death is but empty Aire, the Fates have twisted" (IV, i).

11. For recent critical treatment of the play, see Samuel Schoenbaum, *Middleton's Tragedies* (New York, 1955); Richard Hindry Barker, *Thomas Middleton* (New York, 1958); and Richard Levin, "The Double Plot of *The Second Maiden's Tragedy*," SEL, III (Spring, 1963), 219–231.

12. In the dozen attempts at attribution made since 1829, attention has been devoted almost exclusively to the rival claims of Massinger, Tourneur, and Middleton, for none of whom there is any external evidence. For discussion of these authorship attributions, see Schoenbaum, p. 185, and my article on the subject cited in n. 14 below.

13. Algernon Charles Swinburne, "Introduction," *The Works of George Chapman: Poems and Minor Translations* (London: Chatto and Windus, 1875), p. xxxiv. The inclusion of *The Second Maiden's*

Tragedy in this edition is the last claim that has been made for Chapman's authorship of this play prior to my own.

14. See my article "Authorship of *The Second Maiden's Tragedy*: A Reconsideration of the Manuscript Attribution to Chapman," *SP*, LXIII (January, 1966), 51–77.

15. *The Second Maiden's Tragedy*, ed. W. W. Greg, The Malone Society Reprints (Oxford, 1919). All further references are to this edition.

16. For a fuller treatment of the way in which the subplot serves as a foil to the main action, see Richard Levin's article cited above in n. 9.

17. See Andreas Capellanus, *The Art of Courtly Love*, trans. John Jay Parry (New York, 1941), p. 153. Andreas here says that love may be increased after it has been consummated "if the lovers see each other rarely and with difficulty. . . . Love increases, likewise, if one of the lovers feels real jealousy."

18. In a sense Chapman(?) improves upon his already ironic source. The source of the subplot is the *novella* of "The Curious Impertinent" which Cervantes embedded in his *Don Quixote*. In the source, the lovers escape with all the husband's money; and the husband, finally learning the truth, dies of the grief that his foolish curiosity had brought upon him. The playwright at first allows Anselmus the splendid irony of dying as he would have wished. But then he bethought himself and inserted a conclusion closer to that of his source. In the insertion, Anselmus lingers on long enough to learn the truth and finally dies not as the glorious image of his desires but as an embittered fool.

19. Greg emends the "he," which here appears in the text, to "she."

20. Chapman's *Bussy D'Ambois* provides another instance.

Notes for Chapter 4

1. See Ellis-Fermor, *The Jacobean Drama*, pp. 2–3.

2. See Arthur Melville Clark, *Thomas Heywood: Playwright and Miscellanist* (Oxford, 1931), p. 192.

3. See the discussion of William and Malleville Haller's "The Puritan Art of Love" in the Introduction, pp. 23–4.

4. Thomas Heywood, *A Woman Killed with Kindness*," ed. by R. W. Van Fossen, The Revels Plays (Cambridge, Mass., 1961). All further references are to this edition which divides the play only into scenes, rather than the usual Act/Scene divisions.

5. I prefer this popular Q2 variant to the Q1 reading "play against" adopted by Van Fossen in this edition.

6. This would seem to have been the husband's response in Heywood's source, if Waldo F. McNeir is right in his derivation of the plot from a Yorkshire incident as transmitted first by George Gascoigne in a story interpolated in "The Adventures of Master F. J." (1573) and then reformulated by Robert Greene in "The Conversion of an English Courtesan" (1592). His persuasive argument appears in "Heywood's Sources for the Main Plot of *A Woman Killed With Kindness*," *Studies in the English Renaissance Drama*, ed. Josephine W. Bennett *et al.* (New York, 1959), 189–211.

7. Although inferior to the main plot in psychological realism and depth, the subplot universalizes the moral condition of Mrs. Frankford in its touching portrayal of Sir Charles Mountford, whose attempts to maintain his aristocratic honor are ever thwarted by the moral weakness which makes him a prey to the greater ignobility of society. When the mercenary Sir Francis Acton reneges on payment of the extravagant sporting wager that Sir Charles had proposed and won, and then not only insults his hawk and dogs but strikes him, Sir Charles is stirred by this abuse of his honor to a rage which results in his killing of two of Sir Francis' men. His remorse is so strong that he refuses to flee. But to secure his pardon from a corrupt court he must spend all his patrimony except for one small house upon his ancestral lands which still entitles him to the name of gentleman. Broken in spirit by his bankruptcy, he wishes he were in Heaven where his unthrifty nature could no longer dishonor him, and well he might; for when Shafton, in the hope of gaining his remaining land, offers him money he has no way of repaying, he accepts it. His sense of honor is again shocked by Shafton's speedy execution of the bond that had been seemingly offered as a charitable gesture, but he has no defense against the law and once more is jailed, this time without any means to buy his release. His sister Susan's efforts to raise the money from their relatives are met with selfish and self-righteous scorn. When he is released, it is through a "kindness" which his honor cannot tolerate. Sir Francis Acton, pursuing his revenge against Sir Charles through an attempted seduction of Susan and meeting only with a repulse which heightens his admiration and desire for her, had repayed Sir Charles' debts and secured his pardon in the hope of placing Susan under an obligation to him that would win her consent. Although Susan is horrified at the thought, she finally yields to the twisted sense of honor of her brother who, to escape such an unendurable obligation to an enemy, is willing to dishonor both his sister and his family name to redeem the honor his own moral weakness had forfeited. As such a redemption of honor would only further stain his name, he can see no escape from his moral dilemma but the resolve not to survive her shame. Susan is equally ready to take her own life if Sir Francis should accept the offer, but tragedy is averted by Sir Francis' final rise to true kindness as love, heightened by appreciation of her extreme virtue, causes him to accept her as his wife and to be reconciled to her brother. This sentimental conclusion does not, however, obviate the social commentary of the subplot, which is starker than the main plot in its general picture of moral corruption, a corruption that defeats any attempt to maintain honor by demanding an excessive payment for such innocent lapses of discretion as righteous rage and misplaced trust. These lapses, which are the product of a generous, aristocratic spirit, lead to unthrifty practises which are fastened upon by a mercenary society intent on the ruin of an honor it can neither understand nor countenance. In such a penalizing social context, the very attempt to maintain honor becomes self-corrupting, and the finer spirit can escape the paradoxes of experience only through suicide. The subplot compliments the main plot, then, not so much through the superficial victory of "kindness" with

which it ends but through its earlier exploration of the disastrous effects of such "kindness" upon a tortured creature whose yearning for honor can only overcome the impediment of moral weakness in a redemptive suicide. For other analyses of the structural importance of the sub-plot, see Freda L. Townsend, "The Artistry of Heywood's Double Plots," *PQ*, XXV (1946), 97-119; Peter Ure, "Marriage and the Domestic Drama in Heywood and Ford," *English Studies*, XXXII (1951), 200-16; and Irving Ribner, *Jacobean Tragedy* (New York, 1962), pp. 53-8.
8. Thomas Heywood, *Edward IV*, in *Dramatic Works*, Six Vols., ed. by R. H. Shepherd for J. Pearson (London, 1874), I, 182.

Notes for Chapter 5

1. Although *Theirry and Theodoret* cannot be considered a full love tragedy, the figure who motivates and dominates the action being the lustful Queen-Mother Brunhalt, it does illustrate Fletcher's lack of true belief in the ideal of Courtly Love. Theirry and Ordella glory in an obstructed love and embrace the possibility of suicide in its name, but Fletcher does not permit them to seize the opportunities presented to them for an exalted death and, all obstructions overcome, has them finally die from sheer exhaustion, a typical Massinger collaboration.
2. Lawrence B. Wallis, *Fletcher, Beaumont & Company* (New York, 1947), pp. vii–viii. See also Arthur Mizener, "The High Design of *A King and No King*," *MP*, XXXVIII (1940–41), 133–54; Eugene M. Waith, *The Pattern of Tragicomedy in Beaumont and Fletcher* (New Haven, 1952); and W. W. Appleton, *Beaumont and Fletcher* (London, 1956).
3. Francis Beaumont and John Fletcher, *Works*, ed. A. R. Waller, 10 Vols. (Cambridge, 1905–10). Quotations from this edition will be referred to by citing act, scene, and page, respectively, and, in first references, the volume of this edition.
4. Here and throughout this chapter, I base my discussion of scene authorship upon the work of Cyrus Hoy, "The Shares of Fletcher and his Collaborators in the Beaumont and Fletcher Canon (III)," *Studies in Bibliography*, XI (1958), 85–106. The authorship distribution for *Cupid's Revenge* is on pp. 90–91, for *The Maid's Tragedy* on p. 94. Hoy's attributions are remarkably close to the earlier effort of E. H. C. Oliphant, in *The Plays of Beaumont and Fletcher: An Attempt to Determine their Respective Shares and the Shares of Others* (New Haven, 1927), see particularly pp. 182, 351. In the Leucippus' scenes of *Cupid's Revenge*, Hoy differs from Oliphant's earlier attributions only in awarding Beaumont the two scenes that Oliphant had given to Field; I, i, and IV, v. In *The Maid's Tragedy* they differ only in that Hoy gives to Fletcher the few lines of conversation between court gentlemen at the end of V, i, which Oliphant had assigned to Beaumont.
5. If Hoy is correct in attributing this scene (IV, v, in his reckoning) to Beaumont. In Oliphant's earlier distribution, Beaumont had concluded his handling of Leucippus with that character's sentencing and self-

condemnation so that the shift in characterization had seemed to reflect a more basic difference of approach between our two authors, Beaumont emphasizing the character's guilt and Fletcher his innocence. Although this distinction is still largely true, it is somewhat blurred by the attribution of this scene to Beaumont.

6. John F. Danby, *Poets on Fortune's Hill: Studies in Sidney, Shakespeare and Beaumont and Fletcher* (London, 1952), pp. 201–2.

7. In discussing Evadne and Aspatia, Robert Ornstein has also noted Beaumont's "acute perception of the pathological sublimation of sexual desire in sadistic (or masochistic) acts . . ." See his *The Moral Vision of Jacobean Tragedy* (Madison, 1960), p. 176. As narcissism seems to have a peculiar association with Worldly Love, particularly in its less healthy form, so sado-masochism seems intimately related with some aspects of Courtly Love. The association at its most profound level may be clarified by reference to Theodore Reik's penetrating study, *Masochism in Modern Man* (New York, 1941). Reik shows that, contrary to the common opinion, the masochist does not love suffering. It is, rather, his excessive anxiety and fear that cause him to attempt to triumph over their source through what Reik calls "the flight forward" (pp. 115–24 *passim*).

Notes for Chapter 6

1. *The Changeling* is the joint production of Middleton and Rowley. As G. E. Bentley has noted: "It is usual to assign the comic scenes to Rowley and most of the scenes of the main plot to Middleton." [*The Jacobean and Caroline Stage* (Oxford, 1956), IV, 863.] I shall not be concerned with Rowley's share in the play but devote my attention to the main tragic action, which has been generally awarded to Middleton. For good analyses of the relations between these two plots, however, see William Empson, *English Pastoral Poetry* (New York, 1938), pp. 48–52, and M. C. Bradbrook, *Themes and Conventions of Elizabethan Tragedy* (Cambridge, 1935), p. 239 *et passim*.

2. For my discussion of the dating of *Women Beware Women*, see Note 14 (Par. 2) to Chapter 12.

3. T. S. Eliot, "Thomas Middleton," in *Selected Essays: 1917–1932* (New York, 1932), p. 141.

4. Bradbrook, p. 224.

5. Ellis-Fermor, *The Jacobean Drama*, p. 148. See also Bradbrook, pp. 225, 228; and Eliot, p. 142.

6. See Gamaliel Bradford, "The Women of Middleton and Webster," *Sewanee Review*, XXIX (1921), pp. 17, 21; and Ellis-Fermor, p. 143.

7. Samuel Schoenbaum, *Middleton's Tragedies* (New York, 1955), p. 150.

8. Richard Hindrey Barker, *Thomas Middleton* (New York, 1958), p. 152.

9. *Ibid.*, p. 151. This analysis by Barker is the basis of Schoenbaum's study.

10. N. W. Bawcutt, in the Introduction to his Revels Plays edition of *The Changeling* (London, 1958), has noted this use of the Adam and Eve

story in passing (p. lvi), but he makes little of it and his interpretation of its function differs from mine.

11. Thomas Middleton, *The Changeling,* in *Works,* ed. A. H. Bullen, 8 vols. (London, 1895), VI. All further references are to this edition.

12. For my discussion of the authorship question, as well as a much fuller critical analysis of the play than is given here, see my article "The Domestic Tragedy of Frank Thorney in *The Witch of Edmonton,*" SEL, VII (Spring, 1967), 311–328.

13. An additional line of influence may be suggested in Robert Ornstein's insistence that "the indebtedness of *The Changeling* to *The Maid's Tragedy* is specific enough, I think, to indicate that Middleton fulfilled his genius in tragedy as much through collaboration with Beaumont as with Rowley" (*The Moral Vision of Jacobean Tragedy,* p. 179). Although my analyses of these two plays differ importantly from his, if Ornstein is right in arguing for direct influence, then Middleton may very well have learned the essential pattern of False Romantic Love tragedy directly from this previous masterpiece in the form and then modified it in the more decadent direction that Ford and Dekker had given it in *The Witch of Edmonton,* as transmitted to Middleton by Rowley. Although I have tried to avoid the suggestion that the playwrights were as consciously aware of the developing patterns of tragic action as the modern critic may become through a total exploration of the drama, this may actually be a case where a tragic pattern was transmitted and reworked consciously from playwright to playwright. Nor is there any reason why such an instance might not be more, rather than less, typical of general dramatic practice.

14. Two further examples of this form of tragedy are to appear in 1625, the year with which this study closes. The first, *The English Traveller* by Heywood, has already been discussed in connection with Heywood's earlier masterpiece. The second, *The Vow Breaker, or The Fair Maid of Clifton* by William Sampson, is not truly a tragedy of False Romantic Love and is hardly worth even this mention. This thoroughly provincial product was, according to the title page, "acted divers times in Nottinghamshire" and recounts a local legend of infidelity punished by haunting. Anne Boote's public engagement to Young Bateman is barred by her father's late preference for a rich, old suitor. Anne vows eternal fidelity to Young Bateman but, hardly has he gone off to the wars to await the softening of her father's opposition, when she voluntarily accepts her father's choice of a rich husband, wisely, she feels, preferring wealth to love. Prompted by nightmares to return home, Bateman arrives immediately after her wedding. But Anne's only response to her heartbroken lover is the advice: "If you will be wise, and live one yeere a batchelour tis ten to one, thats odds, I bury my husband" (II, ii, 103–4). She does feel some momentary remorse as she goes to her wedding night —"I now/ Could weepe a Sea, to wash out my pollutions" (II, ii, 198–9) —but her only reaction to his suicide is scornful relief: "I never look'd for better end of him, he had a malevolent aspect in his lookes, ha, ha, ha!" (II, iv, 86–7). Her coldblooded hold on life is broken only by his continual haunting of her. Crazed by fear more than remorse, she finally yields to his direction and ends her life. Although the tragic action bears

some superficial similarity to the classsic pattern of False Romantic Love tragedy, Anne's infidelity is not prompted by even the delusion of love and she never returns to her earlier immature love for Bateman. While the plot shows none of the decadent sophistication of the other late examples of the type, the characterization of Anne does show some affinity to its contemporaries in her inability to achieve effective emotional rebound to the good of her lost love and in the sense of spiritual loss revealed by her final words: "Good Angels guard me! I goe, but cannot tell,/ Whether my journey be, to Heaven or hell" (IV, ii, 210–11). All quotations are from Hans Wallrath's edition in *Materialen zur Kunde des alteren Englischen Dramas* (Louvain, 1914).

15. Rowley, Dekker and Ford, *The Witch of Edmonton,* in Thomas Dekker, *Dramatic Works,* in 3 vols., ed. Fredson Bowers (Cambridge, Eng., 1958), III. All further references are to this edition.
16. The only good criticism that this excellent play has yet received is Edward Sackville West's "The Significance of *The Witch of Edmonton,*" *Criterion,* XVII (1937), 23–32. See especially pp. 26–8 for a similar distinction between Frank's two wives and his psychological responses to them.

Notes for Chapter 7

1. *A Warning for Fair Women,* ed. A. F. Hopkinson (London, 1893), p. 98, Act V, Scene, v. All further references are to this edition.
2. *Ibid.*
3. For a brief discussion of this similarity of dramatic patterning, see Note 11 to Chapter 12; for a full discussion of the play, see Note 12 of the present chapter.
4. A full list of the tragedies of Worldly Love with notation of the dramatic patterns they follow is given in the chart of Elizabethan love tragedy which appears in the Conclusion, p. 359.
5. The homosexual love of Edward and Gaveston is the most important Elizabethan example of the second pattern. I have excluded Marlowe's great history play from this study, however, because it cannot be considered exclusively as a love tragedy. For a full analysis of this play, viewed from this special perspective as a love tragedy, and a comprehensive discussion of Marlowe's handling of love in all his works, both of which concerns should provide additional illumination of the subject of this chapter, see my article *"Edward II:* Marlowe's Culminating Treatment of Love," *ELH,* XXXI (June, 1964), 139–155.
6. *The Aeneid of Vergil,* trans. Kevin Guinagh, Rinehart Editions (New York: 1954), p. 83.
7. *Ibid.,* p. 88.
8. *Ibid.,* pp. 97, 103.
9. Christopher Marlowe, *Dido Queen of Carthage,* edited together with *The Massacre at Paris* by H. J. Oliver for the Revels Plays (Cambridge, Mass., 1968). All further references are to this edition.

10. Without any textual justification, Oliver inserts a stage direction at this point indicating that the phrase "Do as I bid thee" is directed "[*To Anna*]." This editorial tampering, which violates the sense of the Quarto text, seems motivated by the editor's critical view of Dido as beyond reproach, but it gives us a much thinner Dido than Marlowe created. The reading of C. F. Tucker Brooke, in *The Works of Christopher Marlowe* (Oxford, 1910), is to be preferred here.

11. *Arden of Feversham*, ed. Hugh Macdonald, The Malone Society Reprints (Oxford, 1947). All further references are to this edition.

12. *A Warning for Fair Women* is a much more primitive play than *Arden of Feversham*, being content to portray most of the action through dumb shows, yet through it all we may glimpse the same pattern of action manifested by its more brilliant counterpart. The true nature of George Browne's love is early indicated when he says: "Then stand close, George, and with a lucky arm/ Sluice out his life, the hinderer of thy love" (II, i, p. 33). Though Anne had spurred him on to the murder of her husband, she turns against him in remorse for their crime. But neither Anne's rejection nor his arrest for murder can dampen his love for her. With the law at his heels, he still can say: "Commend me to my mistress, if you can" (III, vi, p. 63). Even at the end, his love is still more precious to him than the salvation of his soul and he refuses to confess her part in the murder: "Shall it be said Brown proved/ A recreant? And yet I have a soul—/ Well, God the rest reveal" (V, ii, p. 87). Gallant to the last, he leaps from the scaffold to his death. Anne's love, unfortunately, is not dramatized. She repents of a love that she had never dramatically affirmed, though it has changed her nature. A chaste and modest matron at the start, she is first induced to change by the new vistas that the bawd Nan Drury so brilliantly opens to her naive imagination. Drury had told her that Browne was "one for whom/ You were created in your birth a wife" (I, iv, p. 28), but after the murder she recognizes the bitter side of this truth, "that I was born to be so vile" (III, iii, p. 56). Her remorse does not prevent her, however, from attempting the most shabby shifts that may preserve her life and she fights her conviction to the end. Though her behavior shows similarity to the pattern of False Romantic Love, her revulsion at the murder does not bring with it a desire to return to an earlier happiness and her character remains essentially worldly.

13. Edward II's effeminacy only reinforces the distinction between the sexes.

Notes for Chapter 8

1. Samuel Taylor Coleridge, *Lectures on Shakespeare, etc.*, Everyman's Library No. 162 (London, 1951), p. 176.

2. A. C. Bradley, *Shakespearean Tragedy* (London, 1905), see especially pp. 191–4, 205.

3. Bernard Spivack, *Shakespeare and the Allegory of Evil* (New York, 1958).

4. Franklin M. Dickey, *Not Wisely But Too Well: Shakespeare's Love Tragedies* (San Marino, Calif., 1957).

5. D. A. Traversi, *An Approach to Shakespeare*, 2nd ed., Anchor Books (New York, 1956), p. 131.

6. *Ibid.*, p. 134.

7. *Ibid.*, p. 135.

8. *Ibid.*, pp. 141, 145.

9. See G. R. Elliott, *Flaming Minister: A Study of Othello as Tragedy of Love and Hate* (Durham, N. C., 1953), p. xxxiv, and Robert B. Heilman, *Magic in the Web: Action and Language in Othello* (Lexington, Ky., 1956), p. 3.

10. See Elliott, p. xxxi *et passim*.

11. See Heilman, pp. 138–51.

12. As will be apparent, my discussion of these scenes is deeply indebted to Elliott's analysis.

13. See Elliott, p. 36 *et passim*.

14. *Ibid.*, p. 111.

15. *Ibid.*, p. 223.

16. Robert Speaight, *Nature in Shakespearian Tragedy* (London, 1955), p. 74.

17. Richard Flatter, *The Moor of Venice* (London, 1950), pp. 102–7. See also G. B. Harrison, *Shakespeare's Tragedies* (London, 1951), pp. 137–43, for a similar view of Desdemona.

18. David S. Berkeley, "A Vulgarization of Desdemona," *SEL*, III (1963), 238.

19. M. L. Renald, "The Indiscretions of Desdemona," *SQ*, XIV (1963), 139.

20. Shakespeare, "Othello," in *Works*, ed. George Lyman Kittredge (Boston, 1936). All further references are to this edition.

Notes for Chapter 9

1. G. Wilson Knight, *The Imperial Theme* (London, 1951), pp. 200, 249, 251.

2. *Ibid.*, p. 263.

3. *Ibid.*, see pp. 265, 274, 292.

4. Samuel Taylor Coleridge, *Lectures on Shakespeare*, p. 97.

5. Knight, p. 318.

6. Willard Farnham, *Shakespeare's Tragic Frontier* (Berkeley, 1950), pp. 164, 196.

7. *Ibid.*, p. 194.

8. *Ibid.*, pp. 201–2.

9. Whereas Dickey had shown the love in *Romeo and Juliet* to be what the moralists and physicians attacked as "love melancholy," he shows the love in *Antony and Cleopatra* to be similar to the symptoms of what they attacked as "lust." But however interesting the distinction, he can in neither explain the glory that attends the two very different sets of lovers.

10. Harold S. Wilson, *On the Design of Shakespearian Tragedy* (Toronto, 1957), pp. 176–7.

11. While not denying the importance of this conflict and of the Roman characters, both in themselves and in their changing reactions to the lovers, my concern with this very complex play shall be, as it is throughout this work, focused upon the love theme.

12. Shakespeare, *Antony and Cleopatra,* in *Works,* ed. George Lyman Kittredge (Boston, 1936). All further references are to this edition.

Notes for Chapter 10

1. *The Complete Works of John Webster,* ed. F. L. Lucas, 4 vols. (London, 1927), I. All further references are to this edition.

2. It is only because Travis Bogard, like most critics of Webster, does not recognize the central importance of love in Webster's tragic vision that he can say: "what his satire revealed of the true nature of life is fused with the outcome of his tragic story." See his study *The Tragic Satire of John Webster* (Berkeley, 1955), p. 147. Ellis-Fermor, in *The Jacobean Drama,* comes closer to the matter when she says: "It is as though with the admission of . . . 'Compassion' there was released also [in Flamineo] an underlying clarity of thought and nobility in endurance . . . the quality of compassion, that touched Flamineo in a moment's bewilderment, is allowed to develop in Bosola, first to the wreaking of his policy, then to the freeing of his understanding" (pp. 178–9). But if Ellis-Fermor is finally forced, like Flamineo, to admit compassion, she does not go so far as to admit love as an effective ideal in Webster's tragic vision, and so it is finally not through love but resolution that she brings Vittoria and the Duchess together and vitiates the distinction she had been drawing between the two kinds of knowledge.

3. Clifford Leech, for instance, judges Vittoria on the basis of Flamineo's degrading comments, in *John Webster: A Critical Study* (London, 1951), p. 41 *et passim.*

4. In transferring the corpulence of Brachiano to Francisco and turning Vittoria's husband from an attractive and trusting youth to an impotent and pedantic dolt, he has made her historically verified love more dramatically probable. Conversely, by turning the historical wickedness of Brachiano's wife and Vittoria's mother into dramatic representations of ineffectual goodness, he has been able to define more perfectly the amoral grandeur of the love he wished to portray. Most important, in postdating Isabella's murder after Brachiano's meeting with Vittoria and making it the result of his love for Vittoria rather than Isabella's infidelity, he has both exercised dramatic economy and exposed this love to a harsher tragic light. Unfortunately, it was impossible for Webster to develop the tragic irony resulting from the fact that Vittoria's attractive husband would have become sole heir of the pope, and thus have raised her to a position above Brachiano, whereas his murder brought the power of the pope against her, frustrating her love and finally defeating her life. While the historical Vittoria's devotion to Brachiano, despite this ironic twist in her fortunes, is all the more touching, Webster wished

to present a world in which Vittoria's only chance for worldly fruition, however corrupt, was through Brachiano.

5. Delio's closing statement in *The Duchess of Malfi* on "integrity of life" has been viewed by most critics as the primary tragic value of Webster's plays. But as Irving Ribner (in *Jacobean Tragedy*) has observed: "The moral statement of *The Duchess of Malfi* is not implicit in the stock apothegms of such virtuous characters as Delio and Pescara which . . . sometimes bear but slight relation to the action" (p. 109). Nevertheless, Ribner sees Vittoria's "preservation even in evil of her 'integrity of life' " as the "one certain value" of *The White Devil* (p. 98). This value is further expanded to signify "a force of life, sketched faintly in Vittoria and more surely in the Duchess of Malfi" (pp. 106–7); but the love of the Duchess is viewed as only a minor reflection of this broader force "for harmony, life and generation" (p. 117), while that of Vittoria is shown to lead "instead into desecration and death" (p. 106).

6. As Stoicism has hitherto been association in this study only with Courtly Love, Webster's pervasive Stoicism calls for some comment. Despite Webster's commonplace book quotations from Stoic sources, his portrayal of Stoicism in action is similar to that of Shakespeare in *Antony and Cleopatra*. Antony may have been impelled to his death by considerations of Stoic honor, but he lived as an Epicurean and viewed his death as a tribute to rather than a rejection of the values by which he had lived. So, too, with Webster's characters. Webster's Stoic lovers, and these are Vittoria and Antonio, do not feel contempt for both pleasure and pain, as do the Stoic courtly lovers, but only for pain. Vittoria not only searches for happiness but feels it not ignoble to weep at its loss. It is only towards external oppression whether prison or death, that she shows a Stoic's contempt. Though Antonio shows less of an eagerness to pursue happiness, he still does allow it to influence his spirit, his Stoicism only disobeying the Duchess' desires in his refusal to fly his fate. In contrast to these occasional Stoics, Brachiano and the Duchess of Malfi may be considered full Epicureans, concerned primarily with the pursuit of happiness, this difference being most apparent in the way they meet death: Brachiano's spirit is totally undermined by the approach of death; the Duchess does manage to preserve her sanity, under even worse conditions of mental torture, but it is not through Stoicism but through her sustaining vision of love. Perhaps the most significant aspect of these marriages is the witness they bear to Webster's personal reconciliation of Stoicism and Epicureanism, one concerned with the "integrity of *life*" rather than an otherworldly purity and dedicated to gaining and preserving a worldly fulfillment. If Vittoria and Antonio meet death with a Stoic's contempt, an Epicurean vision of "the nobleness of life" informs these plays as surely as it does *Antony and Cleopatra*.

7. In this scene (V, vi, 1–166), Flamineo tries Vittoria's love for him by insisting, upon pain of death, that she join him in a suicide pact. Allowing her to shoot him first, he plays a death scene, with all the terror of death and anguish of betrayal, only to rise and inform both Vittoria and the audience that "The pistols held no bullets: 'twas a plot/ To prove your kindnesse to me" (V, vi, 151–2). This scene, with its surprise re-

versal and dramatically convincing tone preceding it, shows how heavily Webster was influenced by the "worthy composures of the both worthily excellent Maister Beaumont, & Maister Fletcher" (from "To the Reader," Webster's preface to *The White Devil*). The extent of this influence upon Webster's first independent production is further indicated by the formal patterning of the scene with Isabella (II, i, 1–279) and the scene between Francisco and Monticelso (IV, i). Indeed, in the plotting and execution of these scenes, Webster is not far inferior to his masters in this kind. Webster follows Beaumont and Fletcher more generally in focusing his attention upon the construction of individual scenes rather than upon a careful development of the total action, achieving his final consistency, as they do, through tone and character. The presence of this influence is not to be wondered at when one considers the fact that by 1612, the year in which *The White Devil* was probably composed, Beaumont and Fletcher were the most popular dramatists on the English stage.

Notes for Chapter 11

1. *The Complete Works of John Webster*, ed. F. L. Lucas, 4 vols. (London, 1927), II. All further references are to this edition.
2. Leech, *John Webster*, p. 77. For the contrary view, see Lucas, II, 19, and Ellis-Fermor, *The Jacobean Drama*, p. 177.
3. Leech has noted "evidences of Webster's impatience with law and custom, of a recurrent longing for a 'compassionate,' undisciplined Nature" (p. 81, see also pp. 79–89 *passim*). Gunnar Boklund, in *The Duchess of Malfi: Sources, Themes, Characters* (Cambridge, Mass., 1962), reduces the love action to an expression of "this 'nature theme' " (p. 165). This reduction of the significance of the Duchess' love, so characteristic of critics of Webster, is elsewhere shown when he says: "The silent part played by the children in *The Duchess of Malfi* turns what was merely a tragic love story into a family tragedy, with all the additional pathos and increased scope that this implies" (p. 96).

Notes for Chapter 12

1. In *The Tragedies of Herod and Mariamne* (New York, 1940), Maurice Valency has studied the more than forty dramatizations of the historical record in Josephus in various European countries from the Renaissance to the present. Although he does not give sufficient credit to the Jacobean dramatizations, his account of the tradition is definitive and penetrating. Valency summarizes the basic story as follows: "From the story in Josephus, we should expect a Mariamne play to involve three elements—a man loves a woman excessively; he does or has done some-

thing which causes her to turn cold toward him; this coldness he is incapable of separating in his mind from the suspicion of infidelity, every circumstance works upon this suspicion, and he is driven to kill the woman he loves. . . . the Mariamne situation is seen to be no distant relative of that in *Othello*. Both situations are based upon groundless jealousy and supposedly outraged honor; both end in the murder of the beloved and the agony of the lover; both involve the machinations of a malevolent third person" (pp. 15–7) . See also pp. 278–89 for a psychological analysis of the Herod character which comes very close to my analysis of Othello and the Duke of Milan.

2. As the plotting and characterization of Lady Carey's *Mariam* are almost identical with that of Massinger's far greater fictionalized version of the story, it will not require separate analysis here. But it should be noted that, however inferior her poetic and dramatic talents may be, Lady Carey's treatment of Herod does show a remarkable perception of one of the most complex of psychological types.

3. *Herod and Antipater* is not a love tragedy, the saint-like Mariam dying in the second act. In the Markham and Sampson tragedy, the love story is subordinated to the bloody chronicle of Herod's cruelty and Antipater's ambition. The form of the play is closer, indeed, to the Elizabethan chronicle history with its four dumb shows which manage to pack in even more of the varied incidents of Herod's long life.

4. Arthur Cyril Dunstan, *Examination of Two English Dramas: "The Tragedy of Mariam" by Elizabeth Carew; and "The true Tragedy of Herod and Antipater: with the Death of faire Marriam," by Gervase Markham and William Sampson* (Konigsberg, 1908), p. 96. This is the only available edition of these two plays.

5. Philip Massinger, *The Duke of Milan*, ed. Thomas Whitfield Baldwin (Lancaster, Pa., 1918). All further references are to this edition.

6. T. S. Eliot, "Philip Massinger," in *Selected Essays: 1917–1932* (New York, 1932), p. 191.

7. Baldwin, p. 47.

8. Eliot, p. 188.

9. See Valency, p. 179, and Eliot, p. 187.

10. Both *The Unnatural Combat* (1626) and *The Roman Actor* (1626) center about the conflict of lust and chastity, the former in association with Christian piety, the latter with Stoic honor. The values which Massinger had associated with chastity in these independent tragedies are the primary values of other collaborated efforts. In *The Fatal Dowry* (1619), written with Nathaniel Field, the tragic hero, Charalois, meets with firm constancy the death which has resulted from his Stoic honor, while in *The Virgin-Martyr* (1620), written with Dekker, the tragic heroine, Dorothea, meets with joy the death resulting from her Christian piety.

11. The same explanation would seem to account for Massinger's greatest dramatic achievement, the characterization of Sir Giles Overreach in his comic masterpiece *A New Way to Pay Old Debts,* which is also dated in 1621. Although the normative values of the play reject this aspiring usurer as an overreacher for disdaining the restraints imposed not only by religion but by class, Massinger invests Overreach's passionate energy

to overcome the injustices of social exclusion with a complexity, depth and human validity that reveals the deepest sympathies of Massinger's talent and has made Overreach an enduring favorite of tragic actors to the end of the nineteenth century. A narcissist like Sforza—"Why, is not the whole world/ Included in myself, (V, i, 355-6)—he "would be worldly wise" (II, i, 23) in directing a rare "spirit to dare and power to do" (II, ii, 17) toward the amoral enlarging of his position that manifests his superior worth: "I must have all men sellers,/ And I the only purchaser" (II, i, 32-3). Overreach is a direct descendent of Marlowe's Barabas and this not only in his aspiring vision of power through usury, and in the use of his daughter and subordinates as extensions of his own will, but in that depth of motivation arising out of the condition of his birth, a condition which dooms him to being a social outsider and which frustrates all his power and cunning until it finally confounds him. Excluded by his city origin from the society to which Wellborn naturally belongs despite his dubious morality, a society whose blood exclusiveness is smugly upheld by Lady Allworth and Lord Lovell, Overreach is passionately driven by the desire to buy his way into society through his daughter, even while recognizing the "strange antipathy,/ Between us and true gentry" (II, i, 88-9). But his daughter, who has internalized the values of the society that excludes them, thwarts his purpose by marrying for love. Like Barbaras and, still more significantly, like Sforza, Overreach's response to the independent assertion of the one being he had loved is the attempt to murder her, an attempt which is the prelude to the insane frenzy from which he will never recover because it is only this state which still permits him to believe in himself: "Shall I then fall/ Ingloriously, and yield? No; spite of Fate,/ I will be forc'd to hell like to myself" (V, i, 369-71). [All quotations are from *Elizabethan Plays,* ed. by Hazelton Spencer (Boston, 1933).] Massinger's sincere intellectual commitment to an increasingly Patrician form of stoic Christian morality not only frustrated his best creative powers in the majority of his works but caused his overt rejection of the only personality type with which he felt an imaginative sympathy, a worldly narcissism that reflected the true spirit of the age. It is perhaps because Massinger felt so antagonistic to this spirit that he was never able to go beyond the immature worldliness that invests both Sforza and Overreach with such powerful dramatic life.

12. My argument for a 1623 dating of *Women Beware Women* is given in Note 16, Par. 2, below.

13. In this regard Middleton's structure is remarkably similar to that of *A Warning for Fair Women* (1599). The striking similarity of title might even lead one to wonder whether Middleton could have modelled *Women Beware Women* upon this early domestic tragedy. The happily married Anne Sanders is drawn into adultery by the bawd Nan Drury, whose consummate manipulation of Anne rivals that of Middleton's Livia. Nan Drury's argument "Yet better's better" (I, iv) epitomizes the motive of all false romantic infidelity. But it is out of such an initial false romantic temptation that Anne's Worldly Love, like that of Bianca, will grow to murderous intensity.

14. Thomas Middleton, *Women Beware Women,* in *Works,* ed. A. H.

Bullen, 8 Vols. (London, 1885), VI. All further references are to this edition.

15. This lover is Isabella's uncle, Hippolito. Because of sisterly affection for Hippolito, Livia abuses her niece into believing that she and Hippolito are not blood relations, thus overcoming Isabella's horror of incest. When Hippolito's sense of "honor" leads him to murder his sister's lover, however, Livia's rage at such false morality causes her to tell the truth of his incestuous relations with Isabella. And Isabella, who had happily engaged in adultery without a moral qualm, is suddenly horri- fied to find her "honor" tainted. Both Hippolito and Isabella are, in a sense, false romantics who maintain a superficial idealism while engaging in relations of questionable morality. When they learn the truth of their actual situation, therefore, they undergo a personal revulsion which, in Isabella's case, leads her to vow revenge against Livia. This is but one of the several cross revenges which result in the general slaughter of all the characters in the subplot.

The significance of the subplot lies in the contrast it points between the love of Isabella and Hippolito and that of Bianca and the Duke. Whereas Isabella murders to revenge herself against the imperfection of her love, Bianca murders to defend even such a love. Unlike both Isa- bella and Beatrice, Bianca has settled herself so well in what the act has made her that she can even accept the corruption of her nature in virtue of it and strive at all costs to defend her imperfect love. Though both Isabella and Bianca die through the backfiring of their plots, it is only Bianca who dies with "gladness." Isabella dies without a word, but Hippolito's death speech speaks for both: "Lust and forgetfulness has been amongst us,/ And we are brought to nothing" (V, i, 187–8).

Between Hippolito's negation of the value of his love and Bianca's affirmation of hers there is a world of difference, the world of Middle- ton's tragic vision. It is because critics have refused to see Middleton's positive affirmation of Worldly Love that they have consistently misin- terpreted his tragic vision. Perhaps the best example of this is M. C. Bradbrook's comment on their deaths: " 'Measure for measure' is recog- nized by Hippolito and Bianca, and it is she who speaks the real epilogue: 'Pride, greatness, honours, beauty, youth, ambition,/ You must all down together, there's no help for't' " (Themes and Conventions of Elizabethan Tragedy, p. 233). What Bradbrook has left out, of course, are the last two lines of Bianca's death speech: "Yet this my gladness is, that I remove/ Tasting the same death in a cup of love." Such a willful omission can only lead to a total falsification of the meaning of Middle- ton's tragedies. And what is true here is true, to greater or lesser extent, of the criticism of all the Worldly Love tragedies, the last two lines, figuratively speaking, being generally overlooked.

16. The Spanish Gipsy begins with a scene of rape, which is a step beyond the Duke's enforced seduction of Bianca. In the hands of any other dramatist such an opening would lead inevitably to tragedy: for Middle- ton, it becomes the source of good. The virtuous Clara's first reaction to her dishonor is, like Bianca's, the desire for death; but this is quickly followed by her wish to have her defiler make proper reparations through marriage, a desire which Roderigo rejects. Though sorrowing

for her fall, she continues to exhibit the same basic practicality which
she showed after her disgrace. Rejecting all other suitors in the belief
that she will ultimately be able to marry the only man she honestly can,
a happy chance finally brings her to the remembered chamber of her
disgrace. Discovering at last the identity of the man who raped her, she
rationally appeals to his father for satisfaction and is rewarded. In the
interim, however, Roderigo has become so changed by repentance that
it is not now her physical but spiritual qualities that attract him. When,
after the marriage, he learns that his wife is the woman he had wronged
and that he has been able to make her proper reparations, he is overjoyed. But the final happiness of the pair would have been impossible
to both of them had the rape not occurred. Clara would have been
forced to marry her parent's foolish ward, and Roderigo would have
continued to live the meaningless life of a rake. The remorse which set
in immediately after the rape, when Roderigo realized what a noble
character he had wronged, had made of him a sensitive human being
with whom a fine marriage can be envisioned, and Clara's practical dedication to the task of bringing good out of that evil act bodes as well.
Where Beatrice was unable to settle herself in what the act had made
her and so came to a pathetic defeat, Bianca found a tragic happiness in
so doing and Clara was finally able to achieve a permanent happiness.

    The Spanish Gipsy was licensed on July 9, 1623, fourteen months
after *The Changeling*. Though the absence of any contemporary references to *Women Beware Women* makes any certain dating of this play
impossible, critical considerations would seem to indicate a dating for
Women Beware Women between the performance dates of *The Changeling* and *The Spanish Gipsy*, i.e. early in 1623. G. E. Bentley, basing his
argument primarily upon the dramatic maturity of the play, suggests a
late dating between 1624-27 (*The Jacobean and Caroline Stage*, IV,
906–7). This conclusion is seconded by Irving Ribner: "I would agree
with Bentley that *Women Beware Women* is the later play [later than
The Changeling], written some time shortly before Middleton's death
in 1627 (*Jacobean Tragedy*, p. 124). For the purpose of this study the
Bentley and Ribner chronology of Middleton's two tragedies is of primary importance. But while critical analysis indicates that *Women
Beware Women* was written after *The Changeling*, its development of
themes contained in Middleton's first tragedy might as well argue for its
being dated very soon afterwards and before *The Spanish Gipsy*, which
seems to conclude this thematic development. The Schoenbaum-Harbage
dating of 1621, offered as always in the *Annals* without argument, seems
to me unacceptable.

17. See Ellis–Fermor, pp. 139–40, and Barker, p. 151 *et passim*.

Notes for Chapter 13

1. Robert Ornstein, *The Moral Vision of Jacobean Tragedy*, p. 20.
2. But see Note 16 to this chapter which shows the final emergence of a
true third pattern of Courtly Love in Ford's Caroline love tragedies *The*

Broken Heart and *'Tis Pity She's a Whore*. From this extended historical perspective, the three patterns of Courtly Love tragedy show an almost perfect correspondence between their logical and historical progressions.

3. The dating of the plays throughout this study is that of the Alfred Harbage *Annals of English Drama*, rev. S. Schoenbaum (Philadelphia, 1964). This dating is also the basis of the chart of the extant genre of Elizabethan love tragedy that appears in the second section of this Conclusion. In the single case of *Women Beware Women*, both here and in the chart, I have substituted my own dating for that of the *Annals* for reasons given in Note 14 (Par. 2) to Chapter 12.

4. Aristotle, "Poetics," in *The Basic Works of Aristotle,* ed. Richard McKeon (New York, 1941), Ch. 13, p. 1467.

5. *Ibid.*

6. *Ibid.,* Ch. 11, p. 1465.

7. *Ibid.,* Ch. 10, p. 1465.

8. *Ibid.,* Ch. 13, p. 1466.

9. *Ibid.,* Ch. 14, p. 1468.

10. *Ibid.*

11. *Ibid.,* Ch. 14, p. 1469.

12. *Ibid.,* Ch. 13, pp. 1466–7.

13. There is an interesting association between the three types of tragedy I have defined and what Karen Horney, in *Neurosis and Human Growth* (New York, 1950), has defined as the three basic neurotic solutions to anxiety, the moves "toward, against, or away from others" (p. 19). The direction "toward" is further defined, in the words of the title to Chapter IX, as "The Self-Effacing Solution: The Appeal of Love," and her analysis of this type offers many suggestive parallels to the courtly-saintly type of tragic hero. The direction "against" is further defined in Chapter VIII as "The Expansive Solutions: The Appeal of Mastery," and again her analysis suggests parallels to the worldly-aspiring type. The direction "away from" is defined in Chapter XI as "Resignation: The Appeal of Freedom," the form of this solution categorized by her as "shallow living" (p. 281) having particular suggestiveness with regard to the false romantic-intermediate Aristotelian type. Whether this clear parallel of tragic and neurotic types implies that tragedy is an artistic sublimation of basic neurotic solutions to the problem of anxiety or that neurosis results from the inability to achieve the profound existential catharsis of anxiety that tragic insight accomplishes, I leave to the reader to ponder. The fact of the parallel remains and suggests that the three types of tragedy which I have deduced from Aristotle's analysis of tragedy and expanded in view of the three forms of love tragedy I isolated in the Elizabethan drama have more profound roots in the patterns of human psychology.

14. Una Ellis-Fermor, *The Jacobean Drama*, p. 1.

15. Henry H. Wells, *Elizabethan and Jacobean Playwrights* (New York, 1939), pp. 250–1.

16. In Ford's major tragedies, Courtly Love appears primarily in the decadent forms which Marston and which Beaumont and Fletcher had earlier given it, the vainglorious disenchantment of the courtly revenger and the final nostalgia of the false romantic for the courtly ideal. But

between these two forms he effects a unique synthesis which manifests the final corruption of Courtly Love tragedy. Following Middleton, Ford sees false romanticism as the primary obstruction to the fulfillment of a higher love. For Ford, however, False Romantic Love is an external obstruction which finally becomes the object of courtly revenge.

In *The Broken Heart* Ithocles begins, like the false romantic Leucippus of Beaumont and Fletcher's *Cupid's Revenge,* by denying the significance of love as he breaks the engagement of the true courtly lovers, Orgilus and Penthea. When his love for Calantha causes him to recognize his tragic error, it is too late, for his previous sin against the inviolability of a love contract subjects him, after the death of Penthea, to the revenge of Orgilus. Calantha, a Stoic representative of the second pattern of Courtly Love, soon follows him; but this positive, if shadowy, reflection of Stoic fortitude and devotion is eclipsed by the failure of Stoicism, whether to meet the imperfections of life or to transcend them in the mystic flowering of death, which is portrayed in the more brilliantly developed character of Penthea. The attempt to conform to an absolute standard of honor places Penthea in an insoluble conflict of honorable obligations to her abusive husband and her demanding lover that destroys both her mind and her life. It is neither through Calantha's broken heart nor Penthea's broken mind that the vitality of the courtly ideal finds expression, but through the vengeful passion of Orgilus. In this latter day descendent of Marston's Antonio, the sufferings of frustrated love so animate his purposes that his final movement into revenge does not carry him beyond the genre of love tragedy but seems to represent a genuine instance of the third pattern of Courtly Love tragedy, a "pattern" which has served heretofore to define a special category within the genre of revenge tragedy.

Ford's masterpiece *'Tis Pity She's a Whore* also manifests this third pattern, but the false romanticism which Giovanni revenges himself against is primarily the infidelity of his own beloved sister, Annabella. Like Penthea, Annabella accepts the marriage that circumstances have forced upon her and, though continuing to love her former lover, is finally willing to prove a true wife to her husband. Neither lady has that transcendent vision of love that guided Juliet, in a similar situation, to affirm her fidelity in a glorious love-death. When Annabella's religious conversion causes her repudiation of their relationship, Giovanni revenges the disappointment of his faith directly against his imperfect and unwilling beloved. This murder of the beloved is only the final symptom of his complete inversion of Courtly Love, which his incestuous involvement with the ultimate object of forbidden desire had otherwise revealed. A unique and masterful characterization of the criminal savant, Giovanni chooses the sensual ecstasy of forbidden love as the proper arena for his analysis and conquest of life. Exalted by his sister's sympathetic acquiescence to a sense of god-like power, he cannot endure the compromises which the imperfections of life demand of him and turns against her betrayal of his faith in himself with fatal vindictiveness.

His revenge against Annabella's infidelity is a prelude to his revenge against her husband Soranzo, the play's prime manifestation of the sin of False Romantic Love. Soranzo's marriage to Annabella represents an infidelity to his earlier adulterous attachment to Hippolita, and this not only exposes him to the evil of his wife's impurity but to the separate attempts of Hippolita and her husband Richardetto, among others, to revenge themselves against him. When three plots against Soranzo's life meet with cross purposes, Richardetto concludes that this manifests the working of Heaven, which will bring about Soranzo's destruction in its own manner. In this dramatic context, Giovanni's successful revenge against Soranzo raises him to the status of Providential agent. Like Job, Giovanni is divinely exalted by his refusal to accept conventional answers to the moral problems of existence. If his exploration of the mysteries of experience has led him to the most extreme transgressions of the moral law, it also transforms the final judgement which works both against and through him into a merciful fulfillment. Orgilus' revenge against Ithocles' false romantic sin also performs a Providential role in helping to fulfill the obscure prophecy of the oracle.

For Ford the commitment to Courtly Love is the highest human value but the false romantic obstruction to this commitment, posed by the shallow complacency of the individuals and society which would restrict the lovers' freedom, proves so great that the attempt to maintain fidelity can lead the feminine soul only to despairing death and the masculine spirit only to a revenge whose triumphant fulfillment reflects the Heavens' judgement against the prime human sin of false romanticism. The tragic vision that animates Ford's great love tragedies required his development of a unique form which finally manifests the genuine third pattern of Courtly Love tragedy.

The partial extension of this study to include Ford permits a more accurate historical analysis of the three patterns of Courtly Love tragedy. Seen from the Caroline perspective, this mode exhibits a full correspondence between the logical and historical progression of its patterns. Although all three patterns made at least a rudimentary appearance in the Elizabethan period, this period was distinguished by the greater brilliance of the classic pattern, which did not survive beyond it. In the Jacobean period, Courtly Love tragedy is adequately represented only by the Stoic reformulation of the second pattern. Finally in the Caroline period, Ford's two major tragedies exemplify the third pattern, a pattern in which the revenge motive is completely divorced from filial obligation and fully animated by the injury inflicted upon a dramatized love relationship. It is only with Ford that the third pattern of Courtly Love becomes a true category of the genre of love tragedy, but this epilogue to the continuity of dramatic development within the Elizabethan-Jacobean period revives the tragedy of Courtly Love only to define the final decadence of its form.

17. Patrick Cruttwell, *The Shakespearean Moment* (London, 1954), p. 160.